W9-BLL-099

Intelligence

From Secrets to Policy

Third Edition

Mark M. Lowenthal

CQ PRESS

A Division of Congressional Quarterly Inc.
Washington, DC

CQ Press
1255 22nd Street, NW, Suite 400
Washington, DC 20037

Phone: (202) 729-1900; toll-free, 1-866-427-7737 (1-866-4CQ-PRESS)

Web: www.cqpress.com

Photo credits: Space Imaging, Inc., 82–83; Central Intelligence Agency, 87.

Cover Design: Jeffrey Hall

♾ The paper used in this publication exceeds the requirements of the American National Standard for Information Sciences—Permanence of Paper for Printed Library Materials, ANSI Z39.48-1992.

Printed and bound in the United States of America

09 08 07 06   2 3 4 5

Library of Congress Cataloging-in-Publication Data

Lowenthal, Mark M.
    Intelligence : from secrets to policy / Mark M. Lowenthal.—3rd ed.
        p. cm.
    Includes bibliographical references and indexes.
    ISBN 1-933116-02-1 (alk. paper)
1. Intelligence service—United States.   2. Intelligence service.   I. Title.

JK468.I6L65 2006
327.1273—dc22   2005022674

For
Michael S. Freeman
1946–1999
Historian, Librarian, Friend

Contents

Tables, Figures, and Boxes   ix
Preface   xi
Acronyms   xiv

Chapter 1   WHAT IS "INTELLIGENCE"?   1

Why Have Intelligence Agencies?   2
What Is Intelligence About?   5
Key Terms   9
Further Readings   9

Chapter 2   THE DEVELOPMENT OF U.S. INTELLIGENCE   11

Major Themes   12
Major Historical Developments   19
Key Terms   28
Further Readings   29

Chapter 3   THE U.S. INTELLIGENCE COMMUNITY   30

Alternative Ways of Looking at the Intelligence Community   33
The Many Different Intelligence Communities   34
Intelligence Community Relationships That Matter   38
The Intelligence Budget Process   48
Key Terms   52
Further Readings   52

Chapter 4   THE INTELLIGENCE PROCESS—A MACRO LOOK:
WHO DOES WHAT FOR WHOM?   54

Requirements   55
Collection   59
Processing and Exploitation   60
Analysis and Production   61
Dissemination and Consumption   62
Feedback   64
Thinking about the Intelligence Process   65
Key Terms   67
Further Readings   67

Chapter 5   COLLECTION AND THE COLLECTION
DISCIPLINES   68

Overarching Themes   68
Strengths and Weaknesses   79
Conclusion   104
Key Terms   106
Further Readings   106

Chapter 6   ANALYSIS   109

Major Themes   110
Analytical Issues   124
Intelligence Analysis: An Assessment   139
Key Terms   142
Further Readings   142

Chapter 7   COUNTERINTELLIGENCE   145

Internal Safeguards   146
External Indicators and Counterespionage   149
Problems in Counterintelligence   150
Key Terms   155
Further Readings   155

Chapter 8   COVERT ACTION   157

The Decision-making Process   158
The Range of Covert Actions   162

Issues in Covert Action   165
Assessing Covert Action   171
Key Terms   172
Further Readings   172

Chapter 9   THE ROLE OF THE POLICY MAKER   174

The U.S. National Security Policy Process   174
Who Wants What?   177
The Intelligence Process: Policy and Intelligence   180
Further Readings   189

Chapter 10   OVERSIGHT AND ACCOUNTABILITY   191

Executive Oversight Issues   191
Congressional Oversight   195
Issues in Congressional Oversight   203
Internal Dynamics of Congressional Oversight   210
Conclusion   217
Key Terms   218
Further Readings   218

Chapter 11   THE LEGACY OF THE COLD WAR   220

The Primacy of the Soviet Issue   220
The Emphasis on Soviet Military Capabilities   222
The Emphasis on Statistical Intelligence   225
Collapse of the Soviet Union   226
Intelligence and the Soviet Problem   228
Key Terms   230
Further Readings   230

Chapter 12   THE NEW INTELLIGENCE AGENDA   232

U.S. National Security Policy after the Cold War   232
Intelligence and the New Priorities   236
Conclusion   252
Key Terms   253
Further Readings   253

Chapter 13   ETHICAL AND MORAL ISSUES IN
               INTELLIGENCE   255

General Moral Questions   255
Issues Related to Collection and Covert Action   260
Analysis-Related Issues   266
Oversight-Related Issues   270
The Media   272
Conclusion   273
Further Readings   273

Chapter 14   INTELLIGENCE REFORM   274

The Purpose of Reform   274
Issues in Intelligence Reform   276
Conclusion   287
Further Readings   288

Chapter 15   FOREIGN INTELLIGENCE SERVICES   290

Britain   290
China   294
France   296
Israel   298
Russia   300
Conclusion   303
Further Readings   304

Appendix 1   ADDITIONAL BIBLIOGRAPHIC CITATIONS
               AND WEB SITES   306

Appendix 2   MAJOR INTELLIGENCE REVIEWS
               OR PROPOSALS   310

Author Index   314
Subject Index   316

Tables, Figures, and Boxes

TABLES

5-1 A Comparison of the Collection Disciplines   105

FIGURES

3-1 The Intelligence Community: An Organizational View   32
3-2 Alternative Ways of Looking at the Intelligence Community:
     A Functional Flow View   34
3-3 Alternative Ways of Looking at the Intelligence Community:
     A Functional View   35
3-4 Alternative Ways of Looking at the Intelligence Community:
     A Budgetary View   50
3-5 The Intelligence Budget: Four Phases over Three Years   51
4-1 Intelligence Requirements: Importance versus Likelihood   58
4-2 The Intelligence Process: A Central Intelligence Agency View   65
4-3 The Intelligence Process: A Schematic   66
4-4 The Intelligence Process: Multilayered   67
8-1 The Covert Action Ladder   163

BOXES

The Terrorist Attacks on September 11, 2001: Another Pearl Harbor?   3
Policy versus Intelligence: The Great Divide   5
"And ye shall know the truth...."   7
Intelligence—A Working Concept   9
The Simplicity of Intelligence   35
Eight Simultaneous Budgets   52
Why Classify?   74
The Need for Photo Interpreters   86

SIGINT versus IMINT   91
Some Intelligence Humor   102
Metaphors for Thinking about Analysis   127
Who Spies on Whom?   146
Why Spy?   148
Assassination: The Hitler Argument   170
The Assassination Ban: A Modern Interpretation   171
Policy Makers and Intelligence Collection   182
Intelligence Uncertainties and Policy   184
Setting the Right Expectations   185
A Linguistic Aside: The Two Meanings of Oversight   192
Congressional Humor: Authorizers versus Appropriators   197
Intelligence Budget Disclosure: Top or Bottom?   206
Iraq's Nuclear Program—A Cautionary Tale   242
Analysts' Options: A Cultural Difference   269

Preface

In years past, when academics who taught courses on intelligence got together, one of the first questions they asked one another was "What are you using for readings?" They asked because there was no standard text on intelligence. Available books were either general histories that did not suffice as course texts or academic discussions written largely for practitioners and aficionados, not for undergraduate or graduate students. Like many of my colleagues, I had long felt the need for an introductory text. I wrote this book to fill this gap in intelligence literature.

Intelligence: From Secrets to Policy will not turn readers into competent spies or even better analysts. Rather, it is designed to give readers a firm understanding of the role that intelligence plays in making national security policy and insight into its strengths and weaknesses. The main theme of the book is that intelligence serves and is subservient to policy and that it works best—analytically and operationally—when tied to clearly understood policy goals.

The book has a U.S.-centric bias. I am most familiar with the U.S. intelligence establishment, and it is the largest, richest, and most multifaceted intelligence enterprise in the world. At the same time, readers with interests beyond the United States should derive from this book a better understanding of many basic issues in intelligence collection, analysis, and covert action and of the relationship of intelligence to policy.

This volume begins with a discussion of the definition of intelligence and a brief history and overview of the U.S. intelligence community. The core of the book is organized along the lines of the intelligence process as practiced by most intelligence enterprises: requirements, collection, analysis, dissemination, and policy. Each aspect is discussed in detail in terms of its role, strengths, and problems. The book's structure allows the reader to understand the overall intelligence process and the specific issues encountered in each step of the process. The book examines covert action and counterintelligence in a similar vein. Three chapters explore the performance of U.S. intelligence during and after the cold war and the moral and ethical issues that arise in intelligence. The book also covers intelligence reform and foreign intelligence services.

Intelligence has grown out of two courses that I have taught for many years: The Role of Intelligence in U.S. Foreign Policy, at the School for International and Public Affairs, Columbia University, and The History of U.S. Intelligence, at the Elliott School for International Affairs, George Washington University. As I tell my students, I provide neither a polemic against intelligence nor an apology for it. This volume takes the view that intelligence is a normal function of government: Sometimes it works well; sometimes it does not. Any intelligence service, including that of the United States, can rightly be the recipient of both praise and criticism. My goal is to raise important issues and to illuminate the debate over them, as well as to provide context for the debate. I leave it to professors and students to come to their own conclusions. As an introduction to the subject of intelligence, the book, I believe, takes the correct approach in not asking readers to agree with the author's views.

As an introductory text, the book is not meant to be the last word on the subject. It is intended instead as a starting point for a serious academic exploration of the issues inherent in intelligence. Each chapter concludes with a list of readings recommended for a deeper examination of relevant issues. Additional bibliographic citations and Web sites are provided in Appendix 1. Appendix 2 lists some of the most important reviews and proposals for change in the intelligence community since 1945.

The third edition of *Intelligence* was written during a period of remarkable flux and change for U.S. intelligence. The combination of the al Qaeda attacks of September 11, 2001, and the onset of military operations against Iraq in 2003—along with the failure to find expected weapons of mass destruction programs, contrary to the prewar intelligence—led to major structural changes. The implementation of the changes—provided for in a 2004 intelligence reform law—was only beginning as this edition was completed. The reforms undoubtedly have not played themselves out completely.

Given the dynamic nature of intelligence, any textbook on the subject runs the risk of containing dated information. This may be an even greater problem here, given the fluid situation created by implementation of the new intelligence reform law, thus replicating the intelligence analyst's dilemma of needing to produce finished intelligence during changing circumstances. The risk cannot be avoided. However, I am confident that most aspects of intelligence—and certainly the main issues discussed here—are more general, more long-standing, and less susceptible to being outdated rapidly than the ever-changing character of intelligence might suggest.

All statements of fact, opinion, or analysis expressed are those of the author and do not reflect the official positions or views of the Central Intelligence Agency (CIA) or any other U.S. government agency. Nothing in the contents should be construed as asserting or implying U.S. Government authentication of information or CIA endorsement of the author's views. This material has been reviewed by the CIA to prevent the disclosure of classified information.

Several words of thanks are in order: first, to my wife, Cynthia, and our children—Sarah and Adam—who have supported my part-time academic career despite the missed dinners it means. Cynthia also reviewed the text incisively and provided me with much help and support throughout the production. Next, thanks go to three friends and colleagues—the late Sam Halpern, Loch Johnson, and Jennifer Sims—who reviewed early drafts and made substantial improvements. The following scholars also provided extremely helpful comments for the previous editions: William Green, California State University at San Bernadino; Patrick Morgan, University of California at Irvine; Donald Snow, University of Alabama; James D. Calder, University of Texas at San Antonio; Robert Pringle, University of Kentucky; and L. Larry Boothe, Utah State University. Richard Best of the Congressional Research Service helped me keep the bibliographic entries up to date. None of these individuals is responsible for any remaining flaws or any of the views expressed. I would also like to thank the reviewers for the third edition: Kevin Hula of Loyola College in Maryland, Anna K. Nelson of American University, and Robert L. Wendzel of the Air War College, United States Air Force. Moreover, I have been most fortunate to collaborate with the following editors at CQ Press: Charisse Kiino, Colleen Ganey, and Anna Schardt on this edition, and Jerry Orvedahl and Elizabeth Jones on previous editions. Working with them has been most enjoyable. Thanks to the CIA for providing the "Star of David" photograph and to Space Imaging for supplying the series of overhead images of San Diego.

As I finished this third edition I also completed a three-year tour as the assistant director of central intelligence for analysis and production and as vice chairman for evaluation on the National Intelligence Council. I thank all of my colleagues across the intelligence community for all they have taught me and for their dedication to their work. Finally, thanks to all of my students over the years, whose comments and discussions have greatly enriched my courses and this book. Again, I am solely responsible for any shortcomings in this volume.

Mark M. Lowenthal
Reston, Virginia

Acronyms

ABM	Antiballistic missile
AIDS	Acquired immune deficiency syndrome
Aman	Agaf ha-Modi'in (Military Intelligence) (Israel)
AOR	Area of responsibility
ASAT	Anti-satellite
BDA	Battle damage assessment
BW	Biological weapons
CBW	Chemical and biological weapons
CCP	Consolidated Cryptographic Program
CDA	Congressionally directed action
CEO	Chief executive officer
CI	Counterintelligence
CIA	Central Intelligence Agency
CIARDS	CIA Retirement and Disability System
CIG	Central Intelligence Group
CMA	Community Management Account
CNA	Computer network attack
CNE	Computer network exploitation
COI	Coordinator of information
COMINT	Communications intelligence
COO	Chief operating officer
COS	Chief of station
CRS	Congressional Research Service
CSRS	Counter Surveillance Reconnaissance System
CW	Chemical weapons
D&D	Denial and deception
DARP	Defense Airborne Reconnaissance Program
DBA	Dominant battlefield awareness
DC	Deputies Committee (NSC)
DCI	Director of central intelligence
DCIA	Director of the Central Intelligence Agency

DCP	Defense Cryptologic Program
DGIAP	Defense General Intelligence Applications Program
DGSE	Directoire Générale de la Sécurité Extérieure (General Directorate for External Security) (France)
DHS	Department of Homeland Security; Defense Humint Service
DI	Directorate of Intelligence
DIA	Defense Intelligence Agency
DIA/Humint	Defense Humint Service
DICP	Defense Intelligence Counterdrug Program
DIS	Defence Intelligence Staff (Britain)
DISTP	Defense Intelligence Special Technologies Program
DITP	Defense Intelligence Tactical Program
DMZ	Demilitarized zone
DNI	Director of national intelligence
DO	Directorate of Operations (CIA)
DOD	Department of Defense
DOE	Department of Energy
DPSD	Directoire de la Protection et de la Sécurité de la Défense (Directorate for Defense Protection and Security) (France)
DRM	Directoire du Renseignement Militaire (Directorate of Military Intelligence) (France)
DS&T	Directorate of Science and Technology (CIA)
DSRP	Defense Space Reconnaissance Program
DST	Directoire de Surveillance Territoire (Directorate of Territorial Surveillance) (France)
ELINT	Electronic intelligence
EO	Electro-optical Executive order
EU	European Union
FAPSI	Federalnoe Agenstvo Pravitelstvennoi Sviazi I Informatsii (Federal Agency for Government Communications and Information) (Russia)
FBI	Federal Bureau of Investigation
FBIS	Foreign Broadcast Information Service
FCIP	Foreign Counterintelligence Program (DOD)
FISA	Foreign Intelligence Surveillance Act
FSB	Federal'naya Sluzba Besnopasnoti (Federal Security Service) (Russia)
GCHQ	Government Communications Headquarters (Britain)
GDIP	General Defense Intelligence Program

GEOINT	Geospatial intelligence
GNP	Gross national product
GRU	Glavnoye Razvedyvatelnoye Upravlnie (Main Intelligence Administration) (Russia)
HSC	Homeland Security Council
HSI	Hyperspectral imagery
HUMINT	Human intelligence
IAEA	International Agency for Atomic Energy
I&W	Indications and warning
IMINT	Imagery (or photo) intelligence
INF	Intermediate nuclear forces
INR	Bureau of Intelligence and Research (State Department)
INTs	Collection disciplines (HUMINT, IMINT, MASINT, OSINT, SIGINT)
IR	Infrared imagery
IRA	Irish Republican Army
ISG	Iraq Survey Group
ISR	Intelligence, surveillance, and reconnaissance
IT	Information technology
JCS	Joint Chiefs of Staff
JIC	Joint Intelligence Committee (Britain)
JICC	Joint Intelligence Community Council
JMIP	Joint Military Intelligence Program
KGB	Komitet Gosudarstvennoi Bezopasnosti (Committee of State Security) (Russia)
KJs	Key Judgments
MAD	Mutual assured destruction
MASINT	Measurement and signatures intelligence
MID	Military Intelligence Digest
MI5	Security Service (Britain)
MI6	Secret Intelligence Service (Britain)
MON	Memorandum of notification
Mossad	Ha-Mossad Le-Modin Ule Tafkidim Meyuhadim (Institute for Intelligence and Special Tasks) (Israel)
MSI	Multispectral imagery
NATO	North Atlantic Treaty Organization
NCIX	National Counterintelligence Executive
NCPC	National Counterproliferation Center
NCTC	National Counterterrorism Center
NFIP	National Foreign Intelligence Program
NGA	National Geospatial-Intelligence Agency
NIC	National Intelligence Council

NIE	National intelligence estimate
NIMA	National Imagery and Mapping Agency
NIO	National intelligence officer
NIP	National Intelligence Program
NIPF	National Intelligence Priorities Framework
NOC	Nonofficial cover
NRO	National Reconnaissance Office
NRP	National Reconnaissance Program
NSA	National Security Agency
NSC	National Security Council
NSPD	National security policy directive
NTM	National technical means
ODNI	Office of the Director of National Intelligence
OMB	Office of Management and Budget
OSD	Office of the Secretary of Defense
OSINT	Open-source intelligence
OSS	Office of Strategic Services
P&E	Processing and exploitation
PC	Principals Committee (NSC)
PDB	President's daily brief
PFIAB	President's Foreign Intelligence Advisory Board
PHOTINT	Photo intelligence
PIOB	President's Intelligence Oversight Board
QFR	Question for the record
RMA	Revolution in Military Affairs
SALT	Strategic arms limitation talks
SAM	Surface-to-air missile
SARS	Severe acute respiratory syndrome
SAS	Special Air Service (Britain)
SBS	Special Boat Service (Britain)
SCIFs	Sensitive compartmented information facilities
SDI	Strategic Defense Initiative
SEIB	Senior Executive Intelligence Brief
SGAC	Senate Governmental Affairs Committee
Shin Bet	Sherut ha-Bitachon ha-Klali (General Security Service) (Israel)
SIGINT	Signals intelligence
SIS	Secret Intelligence Service (Britain)
SMO	Support to military operations
SMS	Secretary's Morning Summary
SNIE	Special national intelligence estimate
SOCOM	Special Operations Command

SPA	Special political action
START	Strategic Arms Reduction Treaty
SVR	Sluzhba Vneshnei Razvedki (External Intelligence Service) (Russia)
TECHINT	Technical intelligence
TELINT	Telemetry intelligence
TIARA	Tactical Intelligence and Related Activities
TOR	Terms of reference
TPEDs	Tasking, processing, exploitation, and dissemination
TTIC	Terrorism Threat Integration Center
TUAVs	Tactical unmanned aerial vehicles
UAVs	Unmanned aerial vehicles
UN	United Nations
UNSCOM	United Nations Special Commission
USDI	Undersecretary of defense for intelligence
VoIP	Voice-over-Internet-Protocol
WMD	Weapons of mass destruction

Chapter 1

What Is "Intelligence"?

What is **intelligence**? Why is its definition an issue? Virtually every book written on the subject of intelligence begins with a discussion of what "intelligence" means, or at least how the author intends to use the term. This editorial fact reveals much about the field of intelligence. If this were a text on any other government function—defense, housing, transportation, diplomacy, agriculture—there would be little or no confusion about, or need to explain, what was being discussed.

Intelligence is different from other government functions for at least two reasons. First, much of what goes on is secret. Intelligence exists because governments seek to hide some information from other governments, which, in turn, seek to discover hidden information by means that they wish to keep secret. All of this secrecy leads some authors to believe that issues exist about which they cannot write or may not have sufficient knowledge. Thus, they feel the need to describe the limits of their work. Although numerous aspects of intelligence are—and deserve to be—kept secret, this is not an impediment to describing basic roles, processes, functions, and issues.

Second, this same secrecy can be a source of consternation, especially in a democratic country such as the United States. The U.S. intelligence community is a relatively recent government phenomenon. Since its creation in 1947, the intelligence community has been the subject of much ambivalence. Some Americans are uncomfortable with the concept that intelligence is a secret entity within an ostensibly open government based on checks and balances. Moreover, the intelligence community engages in activities—spying, eavesdropping, covert action—that some people regard as antithetical to what they believe the United States should be as a nation and as a model for other nations. Some citizens have difficulty reconciling American ideals and goals with the realities of intelligence.

To many people, intelligence seems little different from information, except that it is probably secret. However, distinguishing between the two is important. Information is anything that can be known, regardless of how it is discovered. Intelligence refers to information that meets the stated or understood needs of policy makers and has been collected, processed, and narrowed to meet those needs. Intelligence is a subset of the broader category of information. Intelligence and the entire process by which it is identified, obtained, and analyzed respond to the needs of policy makers. All intelligence is information; not all information is intelligence.

WHY HAVE INTELLIGENCE AGENCIES?

The major theme of this book is that intelligence exists solely to support policy makers. Any other activity is either wasteful or illegal. The book's focus is firmly on the relationship between intelligence, in all of its aspects, and policy making. The policy maker is not a passive recipient of intelligence, but actively influences all aspects of intelligence.

Intelligence agencies exist for at least four major reasons: to avoid strategic surprise, to provide long-term expertise, to support the policy process, and to maintain the secrecy of information, needs, and methods.

TO AVOID STRATEGIC SURPRISE. The foremost goal of any intelligence community must be to keep track of threats, forces, events, and developments that are capable of endangering the nation's existence. This goal may sound grandiose and far-fetched, but several times over the past one hundred years nations have been subjected to direct military attacks for which they were, at best, inadequately prepared—Russia was surprised by Japan in 1904, both the Soviet Union (by Germany) and the United States (by Japan) in 1941, Israel (by Egypt and Syria) in 1973. The terrorist attacks of September 11, 2001, on the United States are another example of this pattern, albeit carried out on a much more limited scale. (*See box, "The Terrorist Attacks on September 11, 2001: Another Pearl Harbor?"*)

Strategic surprise should not be confused with tactical surprise, which is of a different magnitude and, as Professor Richard Betts of Columbia University pointed out in his article, "Analysis, War, and Decision: Why Intelligence Failures Are Inevitable," cannot be wholly avoided. Putting the difference between the two types of surprise in perspective, suppose, for example, that Mr. Smith and Mr. Jones are business partners. Every Friday, while Mr. Smith is lunching with a client, Mr. Jones helps himself to money from the petty cash. One afternoon Mr. Smith comes back from lunch earlier than expected, catching Mr. Jones red-handed. "I'm surprised!" they exclaim simultaneously. Mr. Jones's surprise is tactical: He knew what he was doing but did not expect to get caught. Mr. Smith's surprise is strategic: He had no idea the embezzlement was happening.

The Terrorist Attacks on September 11, 2001: Another Pearl Harbor?

Many people immediately described the September 11, 2001, terrorist attacks on the World Trade Center in New York City and the Pentagon as a "new Pearl Harbor." This is understandable on an emotional level, as both were surprise attacks. However, important differences exist.

First, Pearl Harbor was a strategic surprise. U.S. policy makers expected a move by Japan but not against the United States. The Soviet Union was seen as a possible target, but the greatest expectation and fear was a Japanese attack on European colonies in Southeast Asia.

The terrorist attacks were more of a tactical surprise. The enmity of Osama bin Laden and his willingness to attack U.S. targets had been amply demonstrated in earlier attacks on the East African embassies and on the USS *Cole*. Throughout the summer of 2001, U.S. intelligence officials had warned of the likelihood of another bin Laden attack. What was not known—or guessed—was the target and the means of attack.

Second, Japan and the Axis powers had the capability to defeat and destroy U.S. power and the U.S. way of life. The terrorists do not pose a threat on the same level.

Tactical surprise, when it happens, is not of sufficient magnitude and importance to threaten national existence. Repetitive tactical surprise, however, suggests some significant intelligence problems.

TO PROVIDE LONG-TERM EXPERTISE. Compared with the permanent bureaucracy, all senior policy makers are transients. The average time in office for a president of the United States is five years. Secretaries of state and defense serve for less time than that, and their senior subordinates—deputy, under, and assistant secretaries—often hold their positions for even shorter periods. Although these individuals usually enter their respective offices with an extensive background in their fields, it is virtually impossible for them to be well versed in all of the matters with which they will be dealing. Inevitably, they will have to call upon others whose knowledge and expertise on certain issues are greater. Much knowledge and expertise on national security issues resides in the intelligence community, where the analytical cadre is relatively stable. Stability tends to be greater in intelligence agencies, particularly in higher-level positions, than in foreign affairs and defense agencies. Also, intelligence agencies tend to have far fewer political appointees than the State and Defense Departments do. However, these two personnel differences (stability and nonpolitical) have diminished somewhat over the past decade.

To Support the Policy Process. Policy makers have a constant need for tailored (meaning written for their specific needs), timely intelligence that will provide background, context, information, warning, and an assessment of risks, benefits, and likely outcomes. Their needs are met by the intelligence community.

In the ethos of U.S. intelligence, a strict dividing line exists between intelligence and policy. The two are seen as separate functions. The government is run by the policy makers. Intelligence has a support role and may not cross over into the advocacy of policy choices. Intelligence officers who are dealing with policy makers are expected to maintain a certain objectivity and not push specific policies, choices, or outcomes. To do so is seen as threatening the objectivity of the analyses they present. If intelligence officers have a strong preference for a specific policy outcome, their intelligence analysis may display a similar bias. This is what is meant by **politicized intelligence**, one of the strongest expressions of opprobrium that can be leveled in the U.S. intelligence community.

Three important caveats should be added to the distinction between policy and intelligence. First, the idea that intelligence is distinct from policy does not mean that intelligence officers do not care about the outcome and do not influence it. One must differentiate between attempting to influence (that is, inform) the process by providing intelligence, which is acceptable, and trying to manipulate intelligence so that policy makers make a certain choice, which is not acceptable. Second, senior policy makers can and do ask senior intelligence officials for their opinions, which are given. Third, this separation works in only one direction, that of intelligence advice to policy. Nothing prevents policy makers from rejecting intelligence out of hand or offering their own intelligence inputs—an action that they will likely see as being different from imposing their views on the intelligence product per se. This also politicizes intelligence, which is an accusation policy makers as well as intelligence officials hope to avoid, because it calls into question the soundness of their policy and the basis on which they have made decisions. Having rejected intelligence was central to the 2005 debate over the nomination of John Bolton to be U.S. ambassador to the United Nations. Critics charged that Bolton, as undersecretary of state, had engaged in this type of action when intelligence did not provide the answers he preferred. *(See box, "Policy versus Intelligence: The Great Divide.")*

To Maintain the Secrecy of Information, Needs, and Methods. Secrecy does make intelligence unique. That others would keep important information from you, that you need certain types of information and wish to keep your needs secret, and that you have the means to

Policy versus Intelligence: The Great Divide

One way to envision the distinction between policy and intelligence is to see them as two spheres of government activity that are separated by a semipermeable membrane. The membrane is semipermeable because policy makers can and do cross over into the intelligence sphere, but intelligence officials cannot cross over into the policy sphere.

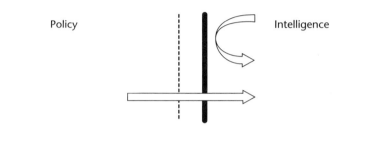

obtain information that you also wish to keep secret are major reasons for having intelligence agencies.

WHAT IS INTELLIGENCE ABOUT?

The word *intelligence* largely refers to issues related to national security—that is, defense and foreign policy and certain aspects of homeland security, which has been increasingly important since the terrorist attacks of 2001.

The actions, policies, and capabilities of other nations and of important nonstate groups (international organizations, terrorist organizations, and so on) are primary areas of concern. But policy makers and intelligence officers cannot restrict themselves to thinking only about enemies—those powers that are known to be hostile or whose policy goals are in some way inimical. They must also keep track of powers that are neutrals, friends, or even allies but are rivals in certain contexts. For example, the European Union is made up largely of nations that are U.S. allies. However, the United States competes with many of them for global resources and markets, so in that sense they are rivals. This is also true of Japan. Furthermore, circumstances may arise in which a country would need to keep track of the actions and intentions of friends. For example, an ally might be pursuing a course that could involve it in conflict with a third party.

Should this not be to a country's liking—or should it threaten to involve that country as well—it would be better to know early on what this ally was doing. Adolf Hitler, for example, might have been better served had he known in advance of Japan's plans to attack the U.S. fleet at Pearl Harbor in 1941. He had no interest in seeing the United States become an active combatant and might have argued against a direct attack by Japan (as opposed to a Japanese attack to the south against European colonies but avoiding U.S. territories). In the late twentieth and early twenty-first centuries it has become increasingly important for the United States to keep track of nonstate actors—terrorists, narcotics traffickers, and others.

Information is needed about these actors, their likely actions, and their capabilities in a variety of areas, including economic, military, and societal. The United States built its intelligence organizations in recognition of the fact that some of the information it would like to have is either inaccessible or being actively denied. In other words, the information is secret as far as the United States is concerned, and those who have the information would like to keep it that way.

The pursuit of secret information is the mainstay of intelligence activity. At the same time, reflecting the political transformation brought about by the end of the cold war, increasing amounts of once secret information are now accessible, especially in states that were satellites of or allied with the Soviet Union. The ratio of open to secret information has likely shifted dramatically. Still, foreign states and actors harbor secrets that the United States must pursue. And not all of this intelligence is in states that are hostile to the United States in the sense that they are enemies.

Most people tend to think of intelligence in terms of military information—troop movements, weapons capabilities, and plans for surprise attack. This is an important component of intelligence (in line with avoiding surprise attack, the first reason for having intelligence agencies), but it is not the only one. Many different kinds of intelligence (political, economic, social, environmental, health, and cultural) provide important inputs to analysts. Policy makers and intelligence officials must think beyond foreign intelligence. They must consider intelligence activities focused on threats to internal security, such as subversion, espionage, and terrorism.

Other than the internal security threats, domestic intelligence, at least in the United States and kindred democracies, is a law enforcement issue. This fact differentiates the practice of intelligence in Western democracies from that in totalitarian states. The Union of Soviet Socialist Republics' State Security Committee (*Komitet Gosudarstvennoi Bezopasnosti*, or KGB), for example, served a crucial internal secret police function that the Central Intelligence Agency (CIA) does not. Thus, in many respects, the two agencies were not comparable.

> ## *"And ye shall know the truth. . . ."*
>
> Upon entering the old entrance of the Central Intelligence Agency head-quarters, one will find the following inscription on the left-hand marble wall:
>
> "And ye shall know the truth, and the truth shall make you free."
>
> John VIII–XXXII
>
> It is a nice sentiment, but it overstates and misrepresents what is going on in that building or any other intelligence agency.

What is intelligence not about? Intelligence is not about truth. If something were known to be true, states would not need intelligence agencies to collect the information or analyze it. Truth is such an absolute term that it sets a standard that intelligence rarely would be able to achieve. It is better—and more accurate—to think of intelligence as proximate reality. Intelligence agencies face issues or questions and do their best to arrive at a firm understanding of what is going on. They can rarely be assured that even their best and most considered analysis is true. Their goals are intelligence products that are reliable, unbiased, and honest (that is, free from politicization). These are all laudable goals, yet they are still different from truth. (*See box, "And ye shall know the truth. . . ."*)

Is intelligence integral to the policy process? The question may seem rhetorical in a book about intelligence, but it is important to consider. At one level, the answer is yes. Intelligence should and can provide warning about imminent strategic threats, although several nations have been subjected to strategic surprise. Intelligence officials can also play a useful role as seasoned and experienced advisers. The information their agencies gather is also of value given that it might not be available if agencies did not undertake secret collection. Therein lies an irony: Intelligence agencies strive to be more than just collectors of information. They emphasize the value that their analysis adds to the secret information, although equally competent analysts can be found in policy agencies. The difference is in the nature of the work and the outcomes for which the two types of analysts are responsible—intelligence versus policy decisions.

At the same time, intelligence suffers from a number of potential weaknesses that tend to undercut its function in the eyes of policy makers. Not all of these weaknesses are present at all times, and sometimes none is present. They still represent potential pitfalls.

First, a certain amount of intelligence analysis may be no more sophisticated than current conventional wisdom on a given issue. Conventional wisdom is usually—and sometimes mistakenly—dismissed out of hand. But policy makers expect more than that, in part justifiably.

Second, analysis can become so dependent on data that it misses important intangibles. For example, a competent analysis of the likelihood that thirteen small and somewhat disunited colonies would be able to break away from British rule in the 1770s would have concluded that defeat was inevitable. After all, Britain was the largest industrial power; it already had trained troops stationed in the colonies; colonial opinion was not united (nor was Britain's); and Britain could use the Indians as an added force, among other reasons. A straightforward political-military analysis would have missed several factors—the strength of British divisiveness, the possibility of help from royalist France—that turned out to be of tremendous importance.

Third, **mirror imaging**, or assuming that other states or individuals will act just the way a particular country or person does, can undermine analysis. The basis of this problem is fairly understandable. Every day people make innumerable judgments—when driving, walking on a crowded street, or interacting with others at home and at the office—about how others will react and behave. They assume that their behavior and reactions are based on the golden rule. These judgments stem from societal norms and rules, etiquette, and experience. Analysts too easily extend this commonplace thinking to intelligence issues. However, in intelligence it becomes a trap. For example, no U.S. policy maker in 1941 could conceive of Japan's starting a war with the United States overtly (instead of continuing its advance while bypassing U.S. territories), given the great disparity in the strength of the two nations. In Tokyo, however, those same factors argued compellingly for the necessity of starting war sooner rather than later. The other problem with mirror imaging is that it assumes a certain level of shared rationality. It leaves no room for the irrational actor, an individual or nation whose rationality is based on something different or unfamiliar.

Fourth, and perhaps most important, policy makers are free to reject or to ignore the intelligence they are offered. They may suffer penalties down the road if their policy has bad outcomes, but policy makers cannot be forced to take heed of intelligence. Thus, they can dispense with intelligence at will, and intelligence officers cannot press their way (or their products) back into the process in such cases.

This host of weaknesses seems to overpower the positive aspects of intelligence. It certainly suggests and underscores the fragility of intelligence within the policy process. How, then, can it be determined whether intelligence matters? The best way, at least retrospectively, is to ask: Would policy makers have made different choices with or without a given piece of intelligence? If the answer is yes, or even maybe, then the intelligence mattered. (*See box, "Intelligence—A Working Concept."*)

Intelligence—A Working Concept

Intelligence is the process by which specific types of information important to national security are requested, collected, analyzed, and provided
to policy makers; the products of that process; the safeguarding of these
processes and this information by counterintelligence activities; and the
carrying out of operations as requested by lawful authorities.

What is intelligence? There are several ways to think about intelligence,
all of which will be used throughout this book, sometimes simultaneously.

- Intelligence as process: Intelligence can be thought of as the means
  by which certain types of information are required and requested,
  collected, analyzed, and disseminated, and as the way in which certain types of covert action are conceived and conducted.
- Intelligence as product: Intelligence can be thought of as the product of these processes, that is, as the analyses and intelligence
  operations themselves.
- Intelligence as organization: Intelligence can be thought of as the
  units that carry out its various functions.

KEY TERMS

intelligence
mirror imaging
politicized intelligence

FURTHER READINGS

Each of these readings grapples with the definition of intelligence, either by function or by role, in a different way. Some deal with intelligence on its own terms;
others attempt to relate it to the larger policy process.

Betts, Richard. "Analysis, War, and Decision: Why Intelligence Failures Are
    Inevitable." *World Politics* 31 (October 1978). Reprinted in *Power, Strategy, and
    Security*. Ed. Klaus Knorr. Princeton: Princeton University Press, 1983.
Hamilton, Lee. "The Role of Intelligence in the Foreign Policy Process." *Essays on
    Strategy and Diplomacy*. Claremont: Claremont College, Keck Center for Inter-
    national Strategic Studies, 1987.
Herman, Michael. *Intelligence Power in Peace and War*. New York: Cambridge Uni-
    versity Press, 1996.

Heymann, Hans. "Intelligence/Policy Relationships." In *Intelligence: Policy and Process*. Ed. Alfred C. Maurer and others. Boulder, Colo.: Westview Press, 1985.

Hilsman, Roger. *Strategic Intelligence and National Decisions*. Glencoe, Ill.: Free Press, 1958.

Kent, Sherman. *Strategic Intelligence for American Foreign Policy*. Princeton: Princeton University Press, 1949.

Laqueur, Walter. *A World of Secrets: The Uses and Limits of Intelligence*. New York: Basic Books, 1985.

Scott, Len, and Peter Jackson. "The Study of Intelligence in Theory and Practice." *Intelligence and National Security* 19 (summer 2004): 139–169.

Shulsky, Abram N., and Gary J. Schmitt. *Silent Warfare: Understanding the World of Intelligence*. 2d rev. ed. Washington, D.C.: Brassey's, 1993.

Shulsky, Abram N., and Jennifer Sims. *What Is Intelligence?* Washington, D.C.: Consortium for the Study of Intelligence, 1992.

Troy, Thomas F. "The 'Correct' Definition of Intelligence." *International Journal of Intelligence and Counterintelligence* 5 (winter 1991–1992): 433–454.

Chapter 2

The Development of
U.S. Intelligence

Each nation practices intelligence in ways that are specific—if not peculiar—to that nation alone. This is true even among countries that share a great deal of their intelligence, such as Australia, Britain, Canada, and the United States. A better understanding of how and why the United States practices intelligence is important because the U.S. intelligence system remains the largest and most influential in the world—as model, rival, or target. (The practices of several foreign intelligence services are discussed in chap. 15.) Such an understanding comes with knowledge of the major themes and historical events that shaped the development of U.S. intelligence and helped determine how it continues to function.

The phrase "intelligence community" is used throughout the book as well as in most other discussions of U.S. intelligence. The word "community" is particularly apt in describing U.S. intelligence. The community is made up of agencies and offices whose work is often related and sometimes combined, but they serve different clients and under various lines of authority and control. The intelligence community grew out of a set of evolving demands and without a master plan. It is highly functional and yet sometimes dysfunctional. One director of central intelligence (DCI), Richard Helms (1966–1973), testified before Congress that, despite all of the criticisms of the structure and functioning of the intelligence community, if one were to create it from scratch, much the same community would likely emerge. Helms's focus was not on the structure of the community, but on the services it provides, which are multiple, varied, and supervised by a number of individuals. This approach to intelligence is unique to the United States, although others have copied facets of it. The 2004 legislation that created a director of national intelligence (DNI) (see chap. 3) made changes in the superstructure of the intelligence community but not to the functions of the various agencies.

MAJOR THEMES

A number of major themes can be discerned in the development of the U.S. intelligence system.

THE NOVELTY OF U.S. INTELLIGENCE. Of the major powers of the twentieth and twenty-first centuries, the United States has the briefest history of significant intelligence beyond wartime emergencies. British intelligence dates from the reign of Elizabeth I (1558–1603), French intelligence from the sway of Cardinal Richelieu (1624–1642), and Russian intelligence from the reign of Ivan the Terrible (1533–1584). Even given that the United States did not come into being until 1776, its intelligence experience is brief. The first glimmer of a **national intelligence** enterprise did not appear until 1940. Although permanent and specific naval and military intelligence units date from the late nineteenth century, a broader U.S. national intelligence capability began to arise only with the creation of the Coordinator of Information (COI), the predecessor of the World War II–era Office of Strategic Services (OSS).

What explains this nearly 170-year absence of organized U.S. intelligence? For most of its history, the United States did not have strong foreign policy interests beyond its immediate borders. The success of the 1823 Monroe Doctrine (which stated that the United States would resist any European attempt to colonize in the Western Hemisphere), abetted by the acquiescence and tacit support of Britain, solved the basic security interests of the United States and its broader foreign policy interests. The need for better intelligence became apparent only after the United States achieved the status of a world power and became involved in wide-ranging international issues at the end of the nineteenth century.

Furthermore, the United States faced no threat to its security from its neighbors, from powers outside the Western Hemisphere, or—with the exception of the Civil War (1861–1865)—from large-scale internal dissent that was inimical to its form of government. This benign environment, so unlike that faced by all European states, undercut any perceived need for national intelligence.

Until the cold war with the Soviet Union commenced in 1945, the United States severely limited expenditures on defense and related activities during peacetime. Intelligence, already underappreciated, fell into this category. (Historians have noted, however, that intelligence absorbed a remarkable and anomalous 12 percent of the federal budget under President George Washington. This was the high-water mark of intelligence spending in the federal budget, a percentage that was never approached again. In 1999 intelligence accounted for roughly 1.6 percent of the federal budget, according to figures declassified by the director of central intelligence.)

Intelligence was a novelty in the 1940s. Policy makers in both the executive branch and Congress viewed intelligence as a newcomer to national security. Even within the Army and Navy, intelligence developed relatively late and was far from robust until well into the twentieth century. As a result, intelligence did not have long-established patrons in the government, but it did have many rivals among departments, particularly the military and the Federal Bureau of Investigation (FBI), which were not willing to share their sources of information. Furthermore, intelligence did not have well-established traditions or modes of operation and thus was forced to create these during two periods of extreme pressure: World War II and the cold war.

A THREAT-BASED FOREIGN POLICY. With the promulgation of the Monroe Doctrine, the United States assumed a vested interest in the international status quo. This interest became more pronounced after the Spanish-American War in 1898. With the acquisition of a small colonial empire, the United States achieved a satisfactory international position—largely self-sufficient and largely unthreatened. However, the twentieth century saw the repeated rise of powers whose foreign policies were direct threats to the status quo: Kaiserine Germany in World War I, the Axis in World War II, and then the Soviet Union.

Responding to these threats became the mainstay of U.S. national security policy. The threats also gave focus to much of the operational side of U.S. intelligence, from its initial experience in the OSS during World War II to its broader covert actions in the cold war. Intelligence operations were one way in which the United States countered these threats.

The terrorism threat in the late twentieth and early twenty-first centuries fits the same pattern of an opponent who rejects the international status quo and has emerged as an issue for U.S. national security. However, now the enemy is not a nation-state—even when terrorists have the support of nation-states—which makes it more difficult to deal with the problem. The refusal to accept the status quo could be more central to terrorists than it was to nation-states such as Nazi Germany and the Soviet Union, for whom the international status quo was also anathema. Such countries can, when necessary or convenient, forgo those policies and continue to function. Terrorists, however, cannot accept the status quo without giving up their raison d'etre.

THE INFLUENCE OF THE COLD WAR. Historians of intelligence often debate whether the United States would have had a large-scale intelligence capability had there been no cold war. The view here is that the answer is yes. The 1941 Japanese attack on Pearl Harbor, not the cold war, prompted the formation of the U.S. intelligence community.

Even so, the prosecution of the cold war became the major defining factor in the development of most basic forms and practices of the U.S. intelligence community. Until the collapse of the Soviet Union in 1991, the cold war was the predominant national security issue, taking up to half of the intelligence budget, according to former director of central intelligence Robert M. Gates (1991–1993). Moreover, the fact that the Soviet Union and its subject allies were largely closed targets had a major effect on U.S. intelligence, forcing it to resort to a variety of largely remote technical systems to collect needed information from a distance.

THE GLOBAL SCOPE OF INTELLIGENCE INTERESTS. The cold war quickly shifted from a struggle for predominance in postwar Europe to a global struggle in which virtually any nation or region could be a pawn between the two sides. Although some areas always remained more important than others, none could be written off entirely. Thus, U.S. intelligence began to collect and analyze information about and station intelligence personnel in every region.

A WITTINGLY REDUNDANT ANALYTICAL STRUCTURE. Intelligence can be divided into four broad activities: collection, analysis, covert action, and counterintelligence. The United States developed unique entities to handle the various types of collection (imagery, signals, espionage) and covert action; counterintelligence is a function that is found in virtually every intelligence agency. But, for analysis, U.S. policy makers purposely created three agencies whose functions appear to overlap: the Central Intelligence Agency (CIA) Directorate of Intelligence (DI), the State Department Bureau of Intelligence and Research, and the Defense Intelligence Agency. Each of these agencies is considered an all-source analytical agency; that is, they have access to the full range of collected intelligence, and all of them work on virtually the same issues.

Two major reasons explain this redundancy, and they are fundamental to how the United States conducts analysis. First, different consumers of intelligence—policy makers—have different intelligence needs. The president, the secretary of state, the secretary of defense, and the chairman of the Joint Chiefs of Staff do not have identical intelligence needs. Even when they are working on the same issue, each has different operational responsibilities. The United States developed analytical centers to serve each policy maker's specific and unique needs. Also, each policy agency wanted to be assured of a stream of intelligence dedicated to its needs.

Second, the United States developed the concept of **competitive analysis**. This is based on the belief that by having analysts in several agencies who have different backgrounds and perspectives work on an issue, parochial views more likely will be countered—if not weeded out—

and proximate reality is more likely to be achieved. Competitive analysis should, in theory, be an antidote to **groupthink** and forced consensus, although this is not always the case in practice. For example, during the assessment of Iraq's weapon of mass destruction (WMD) programs, divisions formed among agencies about the nature of some intelligence (such as aluminum tubes) and whether the totality of the intelligence indicated parts of a nuclear program or a more coherent program. Competitive analysis is not possible without multiple analytical agencies.

Competitive analysis entails a certain cost for the intelligence community in that it depends on this redundant structure. During the 1990s, as intelligence budgets contracted severely under the pressure of the post–cold war peace dividend and a lack of political support in either the executive or Congress, much of the capability to conduct competitive analysis was lost. There simply were not enough analysts to do it. According to DCI George J. Tenet (1997–2004), the entire intelligence community lost some twenty-three thousand positions during the 1990s, affecting all activities. One result was a tendency to do less competitive analysis and, instead, to allow agencies to focus on certain issues exclusively—a sort of analytical triage.

CONSUMER-PRODUCER RELATIONS. The distinct line that is drawn between policy and intelligence leads to questions about how intelligence producers and consumers should relate to each other. The nub of the issue is the degree of proximity that is desirable.

Two schools of thought have been evident in this debate in the United States. The distance school argued that the intelligence establishment should keep itself separate from the policy makers to avoid the risk of providing intelligence that lacks objectivity and favors or opposes one policy choice over others. Adherents of the distance school also feared that policy makers could interfere with intelligence to receive analysis that supported or opposed specific policies. This group believed that too close a relationship increased the risk of politicized intelligence.

The proximate group argued that too great a distance raised the risk that the intelligence community would be less aware of policy makers' needs and therefore produce less useful intelligence. This group maintained that proper training and internal reviews could avoid politicization of intelligence.

By the late 1950s to early 1960s the proximate school became the preferred model for U.S. intelligence. But the debate was significant in that it underscored the early and persistent fears about intelligence becoming politicized.

In the late 1990s some saw two subtle shifts in the policy–intelligence relationship. The first was a greatly increased emphasis on support to military operations, which some believed gave too much priority to this sector—at a time when threats to national security had decreased—at the expense of other intelligence consumers. The second was the feeling among some analysts that they were being torn between operational customers and analytical customers.

The apotheosis of the proximate relationship may have come under President George W. Bush (2001–) who, upon taking office, requested that he receive an intelligence briefing six days a week. DCIs George Tenet and Porter J. Goss (2004–2005) attended these daily briefings, which was unprecedented for a DCI. This greatly increased degree of proximity led some observers to question its possible effects on the DCI's ability to remain objective about the intelligence being offered.

THE RELATIONSHIP BETWEEN ANALYSIS AND COLLECTION AND COVERT ACTION. Parallel to the debate about producer-consumer relations, factions have waged a similar debate about the proper relationship between intelligence analysis, on the one hand, and intelligence collection and covert action, on the other.

The issue has centered largely on the structure of the CIA, which includes both analytical and operational components: the Directorate of Intelligence and the Directorate of Operations (DO). The latter is responsible for both espionage and covert action.

Again, distance and proximate schools of thought took form. The distance school argued that analysis and the two operational functions are largely distinct and that housing them together could be risky for the security of human sources and methods and for analysis. Adherents raised concerns about the ability of the DI to provide objective analysis when the DO is concurrently running a major covert action. Will pressure, either overt or subliminal, be brought to bear to have analysis support the covert action? This is not an abstract question. Such stresses existed between some analytical components of the intelligence community and supporters of the counterrevolutionaries (contras) who were fighting the Sandinista government in Nicaragua in the 1980s, for example. Some analysts questioned whether the contras would ever be victorious, which was seen as unsupportive by some advocates of the contras' cause.

The proximate school argued that separating the two functions deprives both analysis and operations of the benefits of a close relationship. Analysts gain a better appreciation of operational goals and realities, which can be factored into their work, as well as a better sense of the value of sources developed in espionage. Operators gain a better appreciation of the analyses they receive, which can be factored into their own planning.

Although critics of the current structure have repeatedly suggested separating the two functions, the proximate school has prevailed. In the mid-1990s the DI and DO entered a partnership, in which their front offices and various regional offices were located together.

THE DEBATE OVER COVERT ACTION. Covert action has always generated uneasiness in some quarters in the United States concerned about its propriety or acceptability as a facet of U.S. policy. Within that debate, another debate emerged, about the use of paramilitary operations—the training and equipping of large military units, such as the contras. Other than assassination, paramilitary operations have been among the most controversial aspects of covert action, and they have an uneven record. The vigor of the debate has varied widely over time. Little talk took place before the Bay of Pigs invasion (1961), and then little further discussion until the collapse of the bipartisan cold war consensus that had supported an array of measures to counter Soviet expansion and the revelations about intelligence community misdeeds in the mid-1970s. The debate revived during the contras' paramilitary campaign against Nicaragua's government in the mid-1980s. In the aftermath of the terrorist attacks in the United States in 2001, however, broad agreement emerged on a full range of covert actions.

THE CONTINUITY OF INTELLIGENCE POLICY. Throughout most of the cold war, no difference existed between Democratic and Republican intelligence policies. The cold war consensus on the need for a continuing policy of containment vis-à-vis the Soviet Union transcended politics until the Vietnam War, when a difference emerged between the two parties that was in many respects more rhetorical than real. For example, both Jimmy Carter and Ronald Reagan made intelligence policy an issue in their campaigns for the presidency. Carter, in 1976, lumped revelations about the CIA and other intelligence agencies' misconduct with Watergate and Vietnam; Reagan, in 1980, spoke of restoring the CIA, along with the rest of U.S. national security. Although the ways in which they supported and used intelligence differed greatly, it would be wrong to suggest that one was anti-intelligence and the other pro-intelligence. The report of the 9/11 Commission (formally called the National Commission on Terrorist Attacks Upon the United States) briefly became an issue in the 2004 election, as the Democratic presidential nominee, Sen. John Kerry of Massachusetts, endorsed all of the recommendations almost as soon as they were issued, but President Bush took a much more qualified stance.

A HEAVY RELIANCE ON TECHNOLOGY. Since the creation of the modern intelligence community in the 1940s, the United States has relied heavily on technology as the mainstay of its collection capabilities. A technological response to a problem is not unique to intelligence. It also describes how the United States has waged war, beginning as early as the Civil War in the 1860s. Furthermore, the closed nature of the major intelligence target, the Soviet Union, required remote technical means to collect information.

The reliance on technology is significant beyond the collection capabilities it engenders, because it has had a major effect on the structure of the intelligence community and how it has functioned. Some people maintain that the reliance on technology has resulted in an insufficient use of human intelligence collection (espionage). No empirical data are available supporting this view, but it has persisted since at least the 1970s. The main argument, which tends to arise when intelligence is perceived as having performed less than optimally, is that human intelligence can collect certain types of information (intentions and plans) that technical collection cannot. Little disagreement is heard about the strengths and weaknesses of the various types of collection, but such an assessment does not necessarily support the view that espionage always suffers as compared with technical collection. The persistence of the debate reflects an underlying concern about intelligence collection that has never been adequately addressed, that is, the proper balance—if one can be constructed—between technical and human collection. This debate has arisen again in the aftermath of the terrorist attacks in 2001. (See chap. 12 for a discussion of the types of intelligence collection required by the war on terrorism.)

SECRECY VERSUS OPENNESS. The openness that is an inherent part of a representative democratic government clashes with the secrecy required by intelligence operations. No democratic government with a significant intelligence community has spent more time debating and worrying about this problem than the United States. The issue cannot be settled with finality, but the United States has made an ongoing series of compromises between its values—as a government and as an international leader—and the requirements for some level of intelligence activity as it has continued to explore the boundaries of this issue.

THE ROLE OF OVERSIGHT. For the first twenty-eight years of its existence, the intelligence community operated with a minimal amount of oversight from Congress. One reason was the cold war consensus. Another was a willingness on the part of Congress to abdicate rigorous oversight. Secrecy was also a factor, which appeared to impose procedural difficulties in handling sensitive issues between the two branches. After 1975, congressional oversight changed suddenly and dramatically, increasing to the point where Congress became a full participant in the intelligence process and a major consumer of intelligence.

MAJOR HISTORICAL DEVELOPMENTS

In addition to the themes that have run through much of the history of the intelligence community, several specific events played pivotal roles in the shaping and functioning of U.S. intelligence.

THE CREATION OF COI AND OSS (1940–1941). Until 1940 the United States did not have anything approaching a national intelligence establishment. The important precedents were the Coordinator of Information and the Office of Strategic Services, both created by President Franklin D. Roosevelt. The COI and OSS were headed by William Donovan, who had advocated their creation after two trips to Britain before the United States entered World War II. Donovan was impressed by the more central British government organization and believed that the United States needed the same. As was typical with Roosevelt, he gave Donovan much of what he wanted but in such a way as to limit his authority, especially in his relationship to the military.

In addition to being the first steps toward the creation of a national intelligence capability, COI and OSS were important for three other reasons. First, both organizations were heavily influenced by British intelligence practices, particularly their emphasis on what is now called covert action—guerrillas, operations with resistance groups behind enemy lines, sabotage, and so on. For Britain this wartime emphasis on operations was the natural result of being one of the few ways the country could strike back at Nazi Germany in Europe until the Allied invasions of Italy and France. These covert actions, which had little effect on the outcome of the war, became the main historical legacy of the OSS.

Second, although OSS operations played only a small role in the Allied victory in World War II, they served as a training ground—both technically and in terms of esprit—for many people who helped establish the postwar intelligence community, particularly the CIA. However, as former DCI Richard Helms, himself an OSS veteran, points out in his memoirs, most of the OSS veterans had experience in espionage and counterintelligence and not in covert action.

Third, OSS had a difficult relationship with the U.S. military. The military leadership was suspicious of an intelligence organization operating beyond its control and perhaps competing with organic military intelligence components (that is, military intelligence units subordinated to commanders). The Joint Chiefs of Staff therefore insisted that OSS become part of its structure, refusing to accept the idea of an independent civilian intelligence organization. Therefore, Donovan and the OSS were made part of the Joint Chiefs structure. Tension between the military and nonmilitary intelligence components has continued, with varying degrees of severity or cooperation. It was evident as recently as 2004, when the Defense Department, and it supporters in Congress, successfully resisted efforts to expand the authority of the new director of national intelligence to agencies within Defense. (See chap. 3 for details.)

PEARL HARBOR (1941). Japan's surprise attack was a classic intelligence failure. The United States overlooked a variety of signals; U.S. processes and procedures were deeply flawed, with important pieces of intelligence not being shared across agencies or departments; mirror imaging blinded U.S. policy makers to a different assessment made in Tokyo. For U.S. intelligence, the attack on Pearl Harbor was most important as the purpose of the community that was established after World War II. Its fundamental mission was to prevent a recurrence of a strategic surprise of this magnitude, especially in an age of nuclear-armed missiles.

MAGIC AND ULTRA (1941–1945). One of the Allies' major advantages in World War II was their superior signals intelligence, that is, their ability to intercept and decode Axis communications. MAGIC refers to U.S. intercepts of Japanese communications; ULTRA, British, and later British–U.S., interceptions of German communications. This wartime experience demonstrated the tremendous importance of this type of intelligence, perhaps the most important type practiced during the war. Also, it helped solidify U.S.–British intelligence cooperation, which continued long after the war. Moreover, in the United States the military, not OSS, controlled MAGIC and ULTRA. This underscored the friction between the military and OSS. The military today continues to direct signals intelligence, in the National Security Agency (NSA). NSA is a Defense Department agency and is considered a combat support agency, a legal status that gives Defense primacy over intelligence support at certain times. However, both the secretary of defense and the DNI have responsibility for NSA.

THE NATIONAL SECURITY ACT (1947). The National Security Act gave a legal basis to the intelligence community, as well as to the position of director of central intelligence, and created a CIA under the director. The act signaled the new importance of intelligence in the nascent cold war and also made the intelligence function permanent, a step away from the previous U.S. practice of reducing the national security apparatus in peacetime. Implicitly, the act made the existence and functioning of the intelligence community a part of the cold war consensus.

Several aspects of the act are worth noting. Although the DCI could be a military officer, the CIA was not placed under military control. Nor was the CIA to have any domestic role or police powers. The legislation does not mention any of the activities that came to be most commonly associated with the CIA—espionage, covert action, even analysis. Its stated job, and President Harry S. Truman's main concern at the time, was to coordinate the intelligence being produced by various agencies.

Finally, the act created an overall structure (including a secretary of defense and the National Security Council) that was remarkably stable for fifty-seven years. Although minor adjustments of roles and functions have always been made, the 2004 intelligence legislation and the establishment of a director of national intelligence brought about a major revision of the structure created in the 1947 act.

KOREA (1950). The unexpected invasion of South Korea by North Korea, which triggered the Korean War, had two major effects on U.S. intelligence. First, the failure to predict the invasion led DCI Walter Bedell Smith (1950–1953) to make some dramatic changes, including putting increased emphasis on national intelligence estimates. Second, the Korean War made the cold war global. Having previously been confined to a struggle for dominance in Europe, the cold war spread to Asia and, implicitly, to the rest of the world. This broadened the scope and responsibilities of intelligence.

THE COUP IN IRAN (1953). In 1953 the United States staged a series of popular demonstrations in Iran that overthrew the nationalist government of Premier Mohammad Mossadegh and restored the rule of the shah, who was more friendly to Western interests. The success and ease of this operation made covert action an increasingly attractive tool for U.S. policy makers, especially during the tenure of DCI Allen Dulles (1953–1961).

THE GUATEMALA COUP (1954). In 1954 the United States overthrew the leftist government of Guatemalan president Jacobo Arbenz Guzmán because of concern that it might prove sympathetic to the Soviet Union. The United States provided a clandestine opposition radio station and air support for rebel officers. The Guatemala coup proved that the success in Iran was not unique, thus further elevating the appeal of this type of action for U.S. policy makers.

THE MISSILE GAP (1959–1961). In the late 1950s concern arose that the apparent Soviet lead in the "race for space" also indicated a Soviet lead in missile-based strategic weaponry. The main critics were Democratic aspirants for the 1960 presidential nomination, including Sens. John F. Kennedy of Massachusetts and Stuart Symington of Missouri. The Eisenhower administration knew, by virtue of the U.S. reconnaissance program, that the accusations were untrue, but it did not respond to the charges in an effort to safeguard the sources of the intelligence. When the Kennedy administration took office, it learned that the charges were indeed untrue, but the new secretary of defense, Robert S. McNamara, came to believe that intelligence had inflated the Soviet threat to safeguard the defense budget. This was an early example of intelligence becoming a political issue, raised primarily by the party out of power.

The way in which the missile gap is customarily portrayed in intelligence history is incorrect. According to legend, the intelligence community, perhaps for base and selfish motives, overestimated the number of Soviet strategic missiles. This is incorrect on several grounds. The overestimate came largely from political critics of the Eisenhower administration, not the intelligence agencies. In reality, critics overestimated the number of strategic-range Soviet missiles, and the intelligence community underestimated the number of medium- and intermediate-range missiles that the Soviets were building to cover their main theater of concern, Europe. McNamara's distrust of what he perceived as self-serving Air Force parochialism moved him to create the Defense Intelligence Agency.

This was one of the earliest instances of intelligence being used for political purposes. It also underscored the problem of secrecy, in that President Eisenhower did not believe he was able to reveal the true state of the strategic missile balance, which he knew. He did not want to be asked how he knew, which might have led to a discussion of the U-2 program, in which manned aircraft equipped with cameras penetrated deep into Soviet territory in violation of international law. U-2 flights over the Soviet Union ensued in May 1960, when Francis Gary Powers was shot down over Sverdlovsk. Powers survived and was put on trial. Eisenhower was afraid to admit responsibility for the overflights. (The Soviet Union knew about the U-2 flights and also knew the true state of the strategic balance, as the size of U.S. forces was not classified.)

THE BAY OF PIGS (1961). The Eisenhower administration began planning an operation in which Cuban exiles trained by the CIA would invade Cuba and force leader Fidel Castro from power. The operation was not launched until John Kennedy had assumed the presidency, and he took steps to limit overt U.S. involvement to preserve the fiction that the Bay of Pigs invasion was a Cubans-only exercise. The abysmal failure of the invasion showed the limits of large-scale paramilitary operations in terms of their effectiveness and of the United States' ability to mask its role in them. It was a severe setback for the Kennedy administration and for the CIA, several of whose top leaders—including DCI Allen Dulles—were retired as a result, as were all of the members of the Joint Chiefs of Staff.

THE CUBAN MISSILE CRISIS (1962). Although now widely seen as a success, the confrontation with the Soviet Union over its planned deployment of missiles in Cuba was initially a failure in terms of intelligence. All analysts, with the notable exception of DCI John McCone (1961–1965), had argued that Soviet premier Nikita Khrushchev would not be so bold or rash as to place missiles in Cuba. Analysts also assumed that no Soviet tactical nuclear missiles were in Cuba and that local Soviet commanders did not have authority to use nuclear weapons without first asking Moscow—both of which turned out to be false, although this was not known until 1992. The missile crisis was a success, in that U.S. intelligence discovered the missile sites before they were completed, giving President Kennedy sufficient time to deal with the situation without resorting to force. U.S. intelligence was also able to give Kennedy firm assessments of Soviet strategic and conventional force capabilities, which bolstered his ability to make difficult decisions. It was an excellent example of different types of collection working together to support one another and to provide tips to other potential collection opportunities. Finally, the intelligence community's performance went a long way toward rehabilitating its reputation after the Bay of Pigs.

THE VIETNAM WAR (1964–1975). The war in Vietnam had three important effects on U.S. intelligence. First, during the war concerns grew that frustrated policy makers were politicizing intelligence to be supportive of policy. The Tet offensive in 1968 is a case in point. U.S. intelligence picked up Viet Cong preparations for a large-scale offensive in South Vietnam. President Lyndon B. Johnson had two unpalatable choices. He could prepare the public for the event, but then face being asked how this large-scale enemy attack was possible if the United States was winning the war. Alternatively, he could attempt to ride out the attack, confident that it would be defeated. Johnson took the second choice. The Viet Cong were defeated militarily in Tet after some bitter and costly fighting, but the attack and the scale of military operations that the United States undertook to defeat them turned a successful intelligence warning and a military victory into a major political defeat. Many assumed that the attack was a surprise.

Often-heated debates on the progress of the war took place between military and nonmilitary intelligence analysts. This was seen most sharply in the order of battle debate, which centered on how many enemy units were in the field. Military leaders believed that intelligence analysis (primarily from the CIA) was not accurately reporting the progress being made on the battlefield. The argument on the enemy order of battle centered on CIA analysis that showed more enemy units than the military believed to be operating. Or, to put it conversely, if the United States was making the progress being reported by the military, how could the enemy have so many units in the field? Third, and more long-lasting and important, the war severely undercut the cold war consensus under which intelligence operated.

THE ABM TREATY AND SALT I ACCORD (1972). The Nixon administration negotiated limits on antiballistic missiles (ABMs) and strategic nuclear delivery systems (the missiles and aircraft, not the weapons on them) with the Soviet Union. These initial strategic arms control agreements—the ABM treaty and the strategic arms limitation talks (SALT I) accord—explicitly recognized and legitimized the use of **national technical means** or NTM (that is, a variety of satellites and other technical collectors) by both parties to collect needed intelligence, and they prohibited overt interference with national technical means. Furthermore, these agreements created the new issue of **verification**—the ability to ascertain whether treaty obligations were being met. (**Monitoring,** or keeping track of Soviet activities, had been under way since the inception of the intelligence community, even before arms control. Verification consists of judgments or evaluations based on monitoring.) U.S. intelligence was central to these activities, with new accusations by arms control advocates and opponents that intelligence was being politicized. Those concerned that the Soviets were cheating held that cheating was either being undetected or ignored. Arms control advocates argued that the Soviets were not cheating or, if they were, the cheating was minimal and therefore inconsequential, regardless of the terms of the agreements, and they maintained that some cheating was preferable to unchecked strategic competition. Either way, the intelligence community found itself to be a fundamental part of the debate.

INTELLIGENCE INVESTIGATIONS (1975–1976). In the wake of revelations late in 1974 that the CIA had violated its charter by spying on U.S. citizens, a series of investigations examined the entire intelligence community. A panel chaired by Vice President Nelson A. Rockefeller concluded that violations of law had occurred. Investigations by House and Senate special committees went deeper, discovering a much wider range of abuses.

Coming so soon after the Watergate scandal (which involved political sabotage and criminal cover-ups and culminated in the resignation of President Richard M. Nixon) and the loss of the Vietnam War, these intelligence hearings further undermined the public's faith in government institutions, in particular the intelligence community, which had been largely sacrosanct. Since these investigations, intelligence has never regained the latitude it once enjoyed and has had to learn to operate with much more openness and scrutiny. Also, Congress faced the fact of its own lax oversight. Both the Senate and the House created permanent intelligence oversight committees, which have taken on much more vigorous oversight of intelligence and are now major consumers of intelligence themselves.

IRAN (1979). In 1979, Ayatollah Ruhollah Khomeini's revolution forced the shah of Iran from his throne and into exile. U.S. intelligence, in part because of policy decisions made by several administrations that severely limited collection, was largely blind to the growing likelihood of this turn of events. Successive administrations had restricted contacts with opposition groups lest the shah would be offended. In addition to these limits placed on collection, some intelligence analysts failed to grasp the severity of the threat to the shah once public demonstrations began. The intelligence community took much of the blame for the result despite the restrictions within which it had been working. Some people even saw the shah's fall as the inevitable result of the 1953 coup that had restored him to power.

One ramification of the shah's fall was the closure of two intelligence collection sites in northern Iran that the United States used to monitor Soviet missile tests, thus impairing the ability to monitor the SALT I agreement and the SALT II agreement then under negotiation.

IRAN-CONTRA (1986–1987). The administration of Ronald Reagan used proceeds from missile sales to Iran (which not only contradicted the administration's own policy of not dealing with terrorists but also violated the law) to sustain the contras in Nicaragua fighting against the pro–Soviet Sandinista government—despite congressional restrictions on such aid. The Iran-contra affair provoked a constitutional crisis and congressional investigations. The affair highlighted a series of problems, including the limits of oversight in both the executive branch and Congress, the ability of executive officials to ignore Congress's intent, and the disaster that can result when two distinct and disparate covert actions become intertwined. The affair also undid much of President Reagan's efforts to rebuild and restore intelligence capabilities.

THE FALL OF THE SOVIET UNION (1989–1991). Beginning with the collapse of the Soviet satellite empire in 1989 and culminating in the dissolution of the Soviet Union itself in 1991, the United States witnessed the triumph of its long-held policy of containment, first postulated by George Kennan in 1946–1947 as a way to deal with the Soviet menace. The collapse was so swift and so stunning that few can be said to have anticipated it.

Critics of the intelligence community argued that the inability to see the fall coming was the ultimate intelligence failure, given the centrality of the Soviet Union as an intelligence community issue. Some people even felt that this failure justified radically reducing and altering the intelligence community. Defenders of U.S. intelligence argued that the community had made known much of the inner rot that led to the Soviet collapse.

This debate has not ended. Significant questions remain not only about U.S. intelligence capabilities but also about intelligence in general and what can reasonably be expected from it. (See chap. 11 for a detailed discussion.)

THE AMES SPY SCANDAL (1994) AND THE HANSSEN SPY CASE (2001). The arrest and conviction of Aldrich Ames, a CIA employee, on charges of spying for the Soviet Union and for post–Soviet Russia for almost ten years shook U.S. intelligence. Espionage scandals had broken before. For example, in the "year of the spy" (1985), several cases came to light—the Walker family sold Navy communications data to the Soviet Union, Ron Pelton compromised NSA programs to the Soviet Union, and Larry Wu-tai Chin turned out to be a sleeper agent put in place by China.

Ames's unsuspected treachery was, in many respects, more searing. Despite the end of the cold war, Russian espionage against the United States had continued. Ames's career revealed significant shortcomings in CIA personnel practices (he was a marginal officer with a well-known alcohol problem), in CIA counterespionage and counterintelligence, and in CIA–FBI liaison to deal with these issues. The spy scandal also revealed deficiencies in how the executive branch shared information bearing on intelligence matters with Congress.

The arrest in 2001 of FBI agent Robert Hanssen on charges of espionage underscored some of the concerns that first arose in the Ames case and added new ones. Hanssen and Ames apparently began their espionage activities at approximately the same time, but Hanssen went undetected for much longer. It was initially thought that Hanssen's expertise in counterintelligence gave him advantages in escaping detection but subsequent investigations revealed a great deal of laxness at the FBI that was crucial to Hanssen's activities. Hanssen, like Ames, spied for both the Soviet Union and post–Soviet Russia. Hanssen's espionage also meant that the damage assessment done after Ames was arrested would have to be revised, as both men had access to some of the same information. Finally, the Hanssen case was a severe black eye for the FBI, which had been so critical of the CIA's failure to detect Ames.

In addition to the internal problems that both scandals revealed, the two cases served notice that espionage among the great powers continued despite the end of the cold war. Some people found this offensive, in terms of either Russian or U.S. activity. Others accepted it as an unsurprising and normal state of affairs.

THE TERRORIST ATTACKS (2001). The terrorist attacks in the United States in September 2001 were important for several reasons. First, although al Qaeda leader Osama bin Laden's enmity and capabilities were known, the nature of these specific attacks had not been anticipated. Although some critics called for the resignation of DCI George Tenet, George W. Bush supported him. Congress, meanwhile, began a broad investigation into the performance of the intelligence community. Second, in the immediate aftermath of the attacks, widespread political support emerged for a range of intelligence actions to combat terrorism, including calls to lift the ban on assassinations and to increase the use of human intelligence. The first major legislative response to the attacks, the U.S.A. PATRIOT Act of 2001, allowed greater latitude in some domestic intelligence and law enforcement collection and took steps to improve coordination between these two areas. In 2004, in the aftermath of a second investigation (and prompted by the failure to find WMDs in Iraq that intelligence had argued were there), legislation passed to revamp the command structure of the intelligence community. (See chap. 3 for details.) Finally, in the first phase of combat operations against terrorism, dramatic new developments took place in intelligence collection capabilities, particularly the use of UAVs (unmanned aerial vehicles, or pilotless drones) and more real-time intelligence support for U.S. combat forces. (See chap. 5 for details.) The war on terrorism also resulted in an expansion of some CIA authorities, including its ability to capture suspected terrorists overseas and then **render** (deliver) them to a third country for incarceration and interrogation. This activity became controversial as some questioned the basis on which people were rendered and the conditions to which they were subjected in these third nations.

By 2004, two intensive investigations had taken place of U.S. intelligence performance prior to the 2001 terrorist attacks. Although both resulting reports noted a number of flaws, neither was able to point up the intelligence that could have led to a precise understanding of al Qaeda's plans. The tactical intelligence for such a conclusion (as opposed to strategic intelligence suggesting the nature and depth of al Qaeda's hostility) did not exist.

OPERATION IRAQI FREEDOM (2003–). The Bush administration was convinced, as was most of the international community, that Iraqi leader Saddam Hussein harbored weapons of mass destruction, despite his agreement at the end of the 1991 Persian Gulf War to dispose of them and to submit to international inspections. (The fall 2002 debate at the UN was over the best way to determine if he held these weapons and how best to get rid of them—not over whether or not Iraq had them.) However, more than two years after the onset of the ongoing military conflict, the WMDs had not been found. As a result, the two main issues that arose were how the intelligence could come to such an important conclusion that proved to be erroneous and how the intelligence was used by policy makers.

Coupled with the conclusions drawn from the two investigations of the 2001 terrorist attacks, intelligence performance in Iraq led to irresistible calls to restructure the intelligence community. The Senate Intelligence Committee found that groupthink was a major problem in the Iraq analysis, along with a failure to examine previously held premises. At the same time, the committee found no evidence that the intelligence had been politicized, that is, produced to support a specific policy outcome. The WMD Commission (formally the Commission on the Intelligence Capabilities of the United States Regarding Weapons of Mass Destruction), established by President George W. Bush, came to the same conclusion regarding politicization but was critical about how the intelligence community handled both collection and analysis on Iraqi WMD and on other issues.

As terrible as the 2001 terrorist attacks were, the Iraq situation points to much more fundamental questions for U.S. intelligence. The analytical failure in Iraq likely will be a burden for U.S. intelligence for many years to come.

INTELLIGENCE REORGANIZATION (2004–2005). Three impetuses contributed to the 2004 passage of legislation reorganizing the intelligence community: (1) reaction to the 2001 terrorist attack; (2) more specifically, the 2004 report of the 9/11 Commission; and (3) the absence of Iraqi WMDs, despite intelligence community estimates. Congress replaced the DCI with a director of national intelligence (DNI) who would oversee and coordinate intelligence, but would be divorced from a base in any intelligence agency. This was the first major restructuring of U.S. intelligence since the 1947 act. (See chap. 3 for details.) In March 2005, the Commission on the Intelligence Capabilities of the United States Regarding Weapons of Mass Destruction issued its report, recommending further changes in structure and in the management of analysis and collection.

KEY TERMS

competitive analysis
groupthink
monitoring
national intelligence

national technical means
render
verification

FURTHER READINGS

Most histories of U.S. intelligence tend to be CIA-centric, and these suggested readings are no exception. Nonetheless, they still offer some of the best discussions of the themes and events reviewed in this chapter.

Ambrose, Stephen E., with Richard H. Immerman. *Ike's Spies: Eisenhower and the Espionage Establishment.* Garden City, N.Y.: Doubleday, 1981.

Brugioni, Dino A. *Eyeball to Eyeball: The Inside Story of the Cuban Missile Crisis.* Ed. Robert F. McCort. New York: Random House, 1990.

Colby, William E., and Peter Forbath. *Honorable Men: My Life in the CIA.* New York: Simon and Schuster, 1978.

Draper, Theodore. *A Very Thin Line: The Iran-Contra Affair.* New York: Hill and Wang, 1991.

Gates, Robert M. *From the Shadows.* New York: Simon and Schuster, 1996.

Helms, Richard M. *A Look over My Shoulder: A Life in the Central Intelligence Agency.* New York: Random House, 2003.

Hersh, Seymour. "Huge CIA Operations Reported in U.S. against Anti-War Forces, Other Dissidents in Nixon Years." *New York Times,* December 22, 1974, 1.

Houston, Lawrence R. "The CIA's Legislative Base." *International Journal of Intelligence and Counterintelligence* 5 (winter 1991–1992): 411–415.

Jeffreys-Jones, Rhodri. *The CIA and American Democracy.* New Haven: Yale University Press, 1989.

Lowenthal, Mark M. *U.S. Intelligence: Evolution and Anatomy.* 2d ed. Westport, Conn.: Praeger, 1992.

Montague, Ludwell Lee. *General Walter Bedell Smith as Director of Central Intelligence: October 1950–February 1953.* University Park: Pennsylvania State University Press, 1992.

Moynihan, Daniel Patrick. *Secrecy: The American Experience.* New Haven: Yale University Press, 1998.

Persico, Joseph. *Casey: From the OSS to the CIA.* New York: Viking, 1990.

Powers, Thomas. *The Man Who Kept the Secrets: Richard Helms and the CIA.* New York: Knopf, 1979.

Prados, John. *Lost Crusader: The Secret Wars of CIA Director William Colby.* New York: Oxford University Press, 2003.

Ranelagh, John. *The Rise and Decline of the CIA.* New York: Touchstone, 1987.

Troy, Thomas F. *Donovan and the CIA: A History of the Establishment of the Central Intelligence Agency.* Frederick, Md.: University Publications of America, 1981.

U.S. Senate. Select Committee to Study Governmental Operations with Respect to Intelligence Activities [Church Committee]. *Final Report.* Book IV: *Supplementary Detailed Staff Reports on Foreign and Military Intelligence.* 94th Cong., 2d sess., 1976. (Also known as the Karalekas report, after its author, Anne Karalekas.)

Wohlstetter, Roberta. *Pearl Harbor: Warning and Decision.* Stanford: Stanford University Press, 1962.

Wyden, Peter. *Bay of Pigs: The Untold Story.* New York: Simon and Schuster, 1979.

Chapter 3

The U.S. Intelligence Community

Although various agencies had been added to the intelligence community over the years, the basic structure had been remarkably stable since its establishment in the National Security Act of 1947. This state of affairs changed in the aftermath of the September 11, 2001, terrorist attacks. The National Commission on Terrorist Attacks Upon the United States, more popularly known as the 9/11 Commission, made a series of recommendations in its 2004 report to restructure the intelligence community. Aided by a savvy public relations effort by the commission, its staff, and some of the September 11 families, many commission recommendations were enacted after a relatively brief debate and intense bargaining among members of Congress and the George W. Bush administration.

The major change made by the National Intelligence Security Reform Act of 2004 was the creation of a director of national intelligence (DNI), who supplanted the director of central intelligence (DCI) as the senior intelligence official, head of the intelligence community, and principal intelligence adviser to the president, the National Security Council (NSC), and the Homeland Security Council (HSC). The term "national intelligence" is defined to include those domestic issues that are part of homeland security, as opposed to the previous phrase "national foreign intelligence." Thus, the DNI has broader responsibilities than did the DCI for aspects of domestic intelligence. Much of the impetus behind the act was the concern that agencies did not share intelligence well. Therefore, the DNI is to have access to all intelligence and is responsible for ensuring that it is disseminated as needed across the intelligence community. The DNI also has legal responsibility for the protection of intelligence sources and methods.

Unlike the DCI, the DNI is not connected to any intelligence agency but oversees them all. The DNI does this through a large staff. The head of the Central Intelligence Agency (CIA) is now the director of the CIA or DCIA. In addition to his staff, the DNI controls the newly created National Counterterrorism Center (NCTC); a new National Counterproliferation Center; the National Intelligence Council (NIC); and the National Counterintelligence Executive (NCIX, see chap. 7 for details).

In short, the intelligence community has entered a new era, with major new offices and relationships. How well they work and whether they achieve the desired goals will not be entirely evident for several years. In February 2005, President Bush nominated the U.S. ambassador to Iraq, John Negroponte, to be the first DNI and Lt. Gen. Michael Hayden, director of the National Security Agency (NSA), to be his principal deputy.

The U.S. intelligence community is generally perceived as being hierarchical and bureaucratic, emphasizing vertical lines of authority. Figure 3-1 offers such a view but also categorizes agencies by intelligence budget sectors: National Intelligence Program (NIP, formerly the National Foreign Intelligence Program, renamed to recognize the inclusion of homeland security and domestic intelligence), Joint Military Intelligence Program (JMIP), and Tactical Intelligence and Related Activities (TIARA).

The National Security Council has authority over the director of national intelligence, who in turn oversees the CIA. The CIA, unlike the Bureau of Intelligence and Research (INR) at the Department of State or the Defense Intelligence Agency (DIA) at the Department of Defense (DOD), has no cabinet-level patron but reports to the DNI, although the DNI does not have operational control over the CIA. The CIA's main clients continue to be the president and the NSC. This relationship has both benefits and problems. The CIA has access to the ultimate decision maker, but it can no longer count on doing so through its own director given that much of his role now comes under the DNI. The DNI and the new DCIA could become rivals for access to the president. The CIA as a whole could find itself in a weaker position as compared with the other intelligence agencies. A disparity always had existed in that agencies other than the CIA had cabinet-level supporters. However, the DCI had authority across the intelligence community. With this lever gone, the CIA may find itself in a less enviable position. Signs were evident, both before and after passage of the new law, that other agencies sought to enlarge the areas in which they worked, usually at the expense of the CIA. The most prominent of these have been the Federal Bureau of Investigation (FBI) and the Defense Department.

The secretary of defense continues to control much more of the intelligence community on a day-to-day basis than does the DNI. The panoply of agencies that are part of the DOD—National Security Agency, Defense Intelligence Agency, National Geospatial-Intelligence Agency (NGA, formerly the National Imagery and Mapping Agency, NIMA), airborne reconnaissance programs, and the service intelligence units—vastly outnumbers the CIA and the components under the DNI, in terms of both people

FIGURE 3-1   The Intelligence Community: An Organizational View

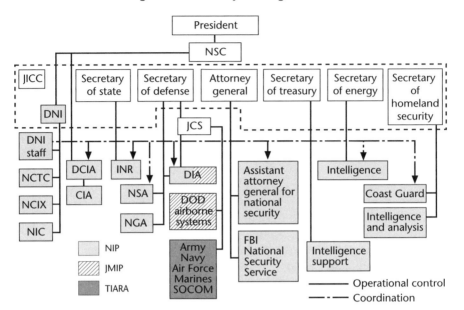

Note: CIA = Central Intelligence Agency; DCIA = director of the CIA; DIA = Defense Intelligence Agency; DNI = director of national intelligence; DOD = Department of Defense; FBI = Federal Bureau of Investigation; INR = Bureau of Intelligence and Research; JCS = Joint Chiefs of Staff; JICC = Joint Intelligence Community Council; JMIP = Joint Military Intelligence Program; NCIX = National Counterintelligence Executive; NCTC = National Counterterrorism Center; NIC = National Intelligence Center; NIP = National Intelligence Program; NGA = National Geospatial-Intelligence Agency; NSA = National Security Agency; NSC = National Security Council; SOCOM = Special Operations Command; TIARA = Technical Intelligence and Related Activities.

and dollars. At the same time, the secretary of defense is unlikely to have the same level of interest in intelligence as the DNI does. In fact, much of the responsibility for intelligence within DOD is delegated to the under-secretary of defense for intelligence (USDI), a relatively new office that was created in 2002.

Control of the intelligence budget was one of the most controversial parts of the debate over the new intelligence structure. Those who advocated less sweeping change had argued that giving the DCI budget execution authority over the NIP (that is, the ability to determine the actual spending of dollars) would have solved his authority problems across the community as well as significantly increased his leverage. However, such a minimalist solution was not politically palatable as it was not seen as sweeping enough. It also was opposed by the Defense Department and its supporters.

In the debate over the creation of the DNI, DOD and its supporters argued successfully that the department needed to maintain control over the budgets of some national intelligence components: the National Security Agency, the National Geospatial-Intelligence Agency, and the National Reconnaissance Office (NRO). This devolved into an odd and factually off-base debate about the military chain of command and control of specific reconnaissance assets. In a face-saving compromise, the law directs the president to write new regulations that preserve the current military chain of command and that "respect and do not abrogate" the position of intelligence in the chain of command. The real concern was the ability of military commanders to call upon intelligence support when they need it. This has been an area of growing controversy as the senior military commanders have increasingly come to treat national intelligence assets as their own.

The DNI "develops and determines" the NIP, based on the submissions made by the intelligence agencies. The DNI can provide the agencies with budget guidance. The DNI can transfer or reprogram up to $150 million or no more than 5 percent of any NIP funds for an agency. Certain criteria were set out for such transfers, such as a higher priority or emergent need. Such transfers cannot be used to terminate an acquisition program.

Figure 3-1 is somewhat deficient in that it does not describe the varied functions of the agencies, which are central to their relationships. Several different ways of looking at the U.S. intelligence community are needed to get a better appreciation of what it does and how it works.

ALTERNATIVE WAYS OF LOOKING AT
THE INTELLIGENCE COMMUNITY

Before examining further the structure of the intelligence community, it is useful to look at its basic functions.

The community has, in effect, two broad functional areas: management and execution. Within each of them are many specific tasks. Management covers requirements, resources, collection, and production. Execution covers the development of collection systems, the collection and production of intelligence, and the maintenance of the infrastructure support base. In Figure 3-2 a horizontal rule divides management and execution, but one function straddles the rule: evaluation. Evaluation is not one of the strongest functions of the intelligence community. Relating intelligence means (resources: budgets, people) to intelligence ends (outcomes: analyses, operations) is a difficult task and is not undertaken with great relish. However, it is an important task and one that could yield dividends to intelligence managers if done more systematically and broadly. Although all agencies make an effort to evaluate their performance, the

FIGURE 3-2   Alternative Ways of Looking at the Intelligence Community:
A Functional Flow View

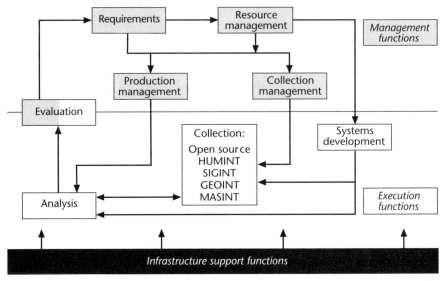

Source: U.S. House Permanent Select Committee on Intelligence, *IC21: The Intelligence Community in the 21st Century.* Staff study, 104th Cong., 2d sess., 1996.
Note: HUMINT = human intelligence; GEOINT = geospatial intelligence; MASINT = measurement and signatures intelligence; SIGINT = signals intelligence.

broadest evaluation activity in the intelligence community has been carried out by the assistant DCI for analysis and production, a job that no longer exists under the 2004 law but whose functions come under the office of the DNI.

The flow suggested by Figure 3-2 is idealized, but it gives a good idea of how the main managerial and execution concerns relate to one another. The flow is circular, going in endless loops. If one were to suggest starting at a particular point, it would be requirements. Without them, little that happens afterward makes sense. Given their proper role, requirements should drive everything else.

The various aspects of collection—systems development and collection itself—occupy much more of the figure than does analysis. This reflects the realities of the intelligence community, whether desirable or not.

THE MANY DIFFERENT INTELLIGENCE COMMUNITIES

Within the U.S. intelligence community are many different intelligence communities. (*See box, "The Simplicity of Intelligence."*) Figure 3-3 gives a

The Simplicity of Intelligence

In the baseball movie *Bull Durham,* a manager tries to explain to his hapless players the simplicity of the game they are supposed to be playing: "You throw the ball; you hit the ball; you catch the ball."

Intelligence has a similar deceptive simplicity: You ask a question; you collect information; you answer the question.

In both cases, many devils are in the details.

FIGURE 3-3   Alternative Ways of Looking at the Intelligence Community:
A Functional View

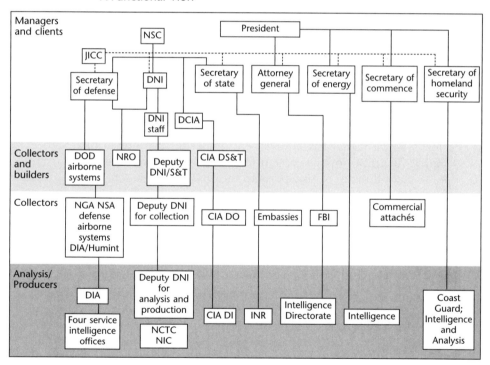

Note: CIA = Central Intelligence Agency; DCIA = director of the CIA; DIA = Defense Intelligence Agency; DIA/ Humint = Defense HUMINT Service; DI = Directorate of Intelligence; DIA = Defense Intelligence Agency; DNI = director of national intelligence; DO = Directorate of Operations; DOD = Department of Defense; DS&T = Directorate of Science and Technology; FBI = Federal Bureau of Investigation; HUMINT = human intelligence; INR = Bureau of Intelligence and Research; JICC = Joint Intelligence Community Council; NCTC = National Counterterrorism Center; NGA = National Geospatial-Intelligence Agency; NIC = National Intelligence Council; NRO = National Reconnaissance Office; NSC = National Security Council; S&T = science and technology.

better sense of what they are by showing what each agency or subagency component does, while preserving the sense of hierarchy. The vertical lines should be viewed as flowing from the topmost organizations through each of the agencies or components below.

At the top of the hierarchy are the entities that are major intelligence managers, major clients, or both. The president is the major client but is not an intelligence manager. The secretaries of defense, state, commerce, and energy and the attorney general are clients, and two of them—the secretaries of defense and state—control significant intelligence assets. State has INR; DOD has numerous defense intelligence organizations, which respond to a broad range of needs. DOD organizations participate in national-level intelligence processes and products, providing indications and warning of impending attack (see chap. 6) and intelligence support for military operations at all levels—from theater (broad regional commands) down to tactical (small units engaged in operations or combat). The Department of Homeland Security (DHS), created in 2002, has several components that are part of the intelligence community, such as the Coast Guard, which has its own intelligence unit, and the Office of Intelligence and Analysis. The attorney general has control over the FBI and now has an attorney general for national security in the Justice Department who oversees intelligence policy, counterintelligence, and counterespionage. Some see this as a move that could lead to an entity like Britain's MI5, which would constitute a major change for the United States, a country that has always kept domestic and foreign intelligence separate. The FBI now has a National Security Service, under an executive assistant director, who reports to the DNI. The new service combines the intelligence, counterintelligence, and counterterrorism elements of the FBI. The Department of Energy has a small intelligence office devoted to its specific concerns; and the Department of Commerce controls the commercial attachés, who are assigned to embassies and serve an overt intelligence function. The DCIA is manager of the CIA.

In overseeing the intelligence community, the DNI, in addition to his own staff, is assisted by a new Joint Intelligence Community Council (JICC). The JICC is made up of the DNI, who is chairman, and the secretaries of state, defense, commerce, and energy and the attorney general. Its purpose is to advise the DNI on intelligence requirements, help develop budgets, evaluate intelligence performance, and see to the execution of decisions made by the DNI.

At the next level down are the builders of technical collection systems. The main one is the National Reconnaissance Office, which is responsible for the design, building, and (via the Air Force or the National Aeronautics and Space Administration) the launch of satellite collection systems. DOD also has an airborne reconnaissance responsibility for "air breathing" systems such as unmanned aerial vehicles (UAVs) or drones, which are of increasing importance on the battlefield for tactical collection and, in the Afghanistan campaign and the war on terrorism, for air attack as well. Finally, the CIA Directorate of Science and Technology (DS&T) has a role in some technical collection programs.

A variety of offices is responsible for the collection (including processing and exploitation) of intelligence. Within DOD are the National Security Agency, which collects signals intelligence (SIGINT), the interception of various types of communication; the National Geospatial-Intelligence Agency, which processes and exploits what was known as imagery intelligence (IMINT)—that is, photos—and is now known as geospatial intelligence (GEOINT); the Defense Department airborne systems; and the Defense Humint Service (also called DHS; to avoid confusion, it will be referred to as DIA/Humint) of DIA, whose duties are reflected in its name. The CIA is responsible for espionage (human intelligence—HUMINT) collection via the Directorate of Operations (DO). (Types of intelligence are discussed in detail in chap. 5.) The State Department collects for itself and for others via its array of embassies and Foreign Service officers, although its activities are not "tasked intelligence"—that is, they are not undertaken in response to a specific requirement, as are the others. The Commerce Department collects via the commercial attachés. The FBI collects counterintelligence information through its National Security Division and has legal attachés posted in many U.S. embassies overseas. The DNI has authority to manage and task collection.

The most important of the producers of finished intelligence are the three agencies responsible for producing all-source intelligence: CIA's Directorate of Intelligence (DI), DIA's Directorate of Intelligence (DI), and State's INR. Within DOD, the four service intelligence offices also produce finished intelligence. FBI has a relatively new Intelligence Directorate, which is also codified in the 2004 legislation. DHS has the Directorate for Information Assurance; Energy has its intelligence office. The DNI controls the National Intelligence Council, which is made up of the national intelligence officers (NIOs) and is responsible for national intelligence estimates and some other analyses. He also has responsibility for the National Counterterrorism Center, which produces analysis on all terrorism and counterterrorism issues, except those that are purely domestic. Again, the DNI has authority to manage and task analysis.

The new law focuses much more on the analytic process. The DNI has three specific charges. First, he is to create a process to ensure the use of alternative analysis as appropriate. Second, he is to assign an official or office to be responsible for analytic integrity, which includes timeliness, objectivity, and the use of all appropriate sources and proper analytic tradecraft. Third, he is to appoint someone who will oversee and report on the objectivity of analysis and the quality of its associated tradecraft. These mandates reflect the unstated Iraq-related issues that shaped the legislation, not September 11, which was the ostensible basis for the changes.

Figure 3-3 does not delineate counterintelligence or counterespionage functions. Each agency has certain internal security responsibilities beyond the NCIX under the DNI. The FBI's National Security Division coordinates foreign counterintelligence activities in the United States. CIA DO has its own counterintelligence and counterespionage components. In addition, the director of NSA is also the director of the Central Security Service, with responsibility for safeguarding the communications of the United States from interception. The basic relationships, strengths, and weaknesses noted in Figure 3-1 are still evident, but discerning functions is easier in Figure 3-3.

INTELLIGENCE COMMUNITY RELATIONSHIPS THAT MATTER

All wiring diagrams, no matter how sophisticated, are deceptive. They portray where agencies sit in relation to one another, but they cannot portray how they interact and which relationships matter and why. Moreover, personalities do matter. However much people like to think of government as one of laws and institutions, the personalities and relationships of those filling important positions affect agency working relations.

THE DNI'S RELATIONSHIPS. The relationship between the DNI and the president is crucial for the institutional well-being of the intelligence community. The DNI is the embodiment of the intelligence community, and the president is the ultimate policy consumer. DCI Richard Helms (1966–1973) put it succinctly when he observed that the DCI's authority derived directly from the perception that he had access to the president. The same is now true for the DNI, although he will have even more rivals than did the DCI. If the DNI does not have access and is not included in meetings where intelligence should be a contributor, there are several ramifications. For the DNI, the problem is personal and professional; for the intelligence community, the problem is being left out of the process. The role of the DNI thus would be diminished in the perception of others who become aware of the situation. The cases of some past DCIs are instructive. DCI John McCone (1961–1965) enjoyed good access to President John F. Kennedy and, initially, to Lyndon B. Johnson, but Johnson began to exclude McCone when the DCI disagreed with his incremental approach to the Vietnam War. After a short period of frustration, McCone resigned. Similarly, DCI R. James Woolsey (1993–1995), after his resignation, made no secret of the fact that he had little access to President Bill Clinton.

How close should the relationship between the DNI and the president be? Some observers worry that if it is too close, the DNI may lose some of the intelligence objectivity that he should be bringing to the policy process. Policy makers must be able to rely upon the professionalism of the DNI. Still, if the intelligence community were forced to choose between the two extremes, an overly close relationship would probably be preferable to a very distant one. The relationship George J. Tenet (1997–2004) had with George W. Bush was probably the closest of any DCI to a president, but it was also controversial. The intelligence provided on the eve of the war with Iraq in 2003 concerning the presence of weapons of mass destruction (WMDs) is seen by some as an indicator of lost objectivity. However, a report issued by the Senate Intelligence Committee that was highly critical of intelligence analysis on Iraqi WMD also found that there was no evidence that intelligence had been politicized.

But the fact that the DNI has control over limited analytical components (NIC, NCTC, and the National Counterproliferation Center that was recommended in 2005 by the WMD Commission—the Commission on the Intelligence Capabilities of the United States Regarding Weapons of Mass Destruction) means that he, or his staff, will have to spend a great deal of time trying to keep track of analytic activities across the fifteen intelligence agencies. It also means that the DNI will have a relatively weak institutional base. Several of the heads of intelligence agencies will be rivals for the DNI as they will have greater insight into and control over activities that are of great concern to policy makers.

To make the appointment a more professional and less political one, suggestions were made in the past that the DCI, like the director of the FBI, be subject to a fixed term of office. (The FBI director serves for ten years. Politicization was always possible but did not become a reality until 1977, when incoming president Jimmy Carter asked for the resignation of DCI George Bush (1976–1977).) Another argument in favor of a fixed term was that it would allow DCIs to serve under presidents who had not appointed them, thus increasing the chances for objectivity. The main argument against it, and one that was voiced by several former DCIs, goes back to the personal nature of the relationship between the DCI and the president. The concern was that, under a fixed DCI term that overlaps the cycle of elections, the president would inherit a DCI not of his choosing and with whom there would be no rapport, thus increasing the likelihood that the DCI's access would diminish. Moreover, the DCI and the director of the FBI did not hold comparable positions. And today the DNI is responsible for the entire intelligence community, whereas the director of the FBI runs an agency within an executive department (Justice). The strained relations between FBI director Louis J. Freeh and both Attorney General Janet Reno and President Clinton during the latter part of the Clinton administration underscore the problems that can arise with a fixed term. The 2004 intelligence act did not set a fixed term for the DNI, who continues to serve at the pleasure of the president.

The relationship of the DNI with the CIA will be crucial, at least initially. The CIA has lost status within the intelligence community. However, it has retained several key roles, including all-source analysis, HUMINT, intelligence operations, and foreign liaison. Former DCIs William H. Webster (1987–1991) and Tenet argued that the DNI cannot be effective if he does not control these activities, but those in favor of the new law were adamant about keeping the DNI separate from any agency. Thus, tension likely will arise between the DNI and the DCIA as the DNI seeks insight into CIA activities for which he is ultimately responsible. To what degree will the DNI have insight into and oversight of covert actions, one of the most important and risky activities undertaken by intelligence agencies? Many observers wondered if the DNI would control the morning presidential briefing, which is central to the DNI's access to the president. The issue was settled when White House chief of staff Andrew Card announced that the DNI would be responsible for the president's daily brief (PDB). This still left open the question of who the DNI would rely upon to prepare the PDB. This was settled when the PDB was given over to the new deputy DNI for analysis. President Bush stated that the DCIA would be present at the morning briefings, which further confused the situation once again.

Similarly, senior CIA officers and analysts have usually provided the intelligence support for the **Principals Committee** (PC) and **Deputies Committee** (DC) of the NSC. The PC is the senior policy coordinating body of the NSC structure, consisting of the assistant to the president for national security affairs, sometimes the vice president, the secretaries of state and defense, the DNI, and the chairman of the Joint Chiefs of Staff. Other cabinet officials (secretaries of homeland security, energy, and so on) attend as necessary. The DC is made up of the deputies of the PC members and has a similar function, working on issues before the PC considers them. This intelligence function is important not only for its role in supporting policy but also for the insights it gives to intelligence officials as to the possible courses of policy being considered. Such support requires substantive knowledge of the issues being discussed. The DNI or the principal deputy DNI is the intelligence participant at PCs and DCs. They now rely primarily on national intelligence offices for analytic support. The NIOs are part of the NIC, which comes under the deputy DNI for analysis, who also serves as NIC chairman.

Much depends on how DNI Negroponte chooses to define his role. As Judge Richard Posner has pointed out (*Preventing Surprise Attacks: Intelligence Reform in the Wake of 9/11,* 2005), the DNI can function as the chief executive officer (CEO) or chief operating officer (COO) of the intelligence community. The CEO function will keep the DNI at a higher, community-level. The COO function will get the DNI more involved in details. The preliminary indicators are that the DNI is being forced into the chief operating function by virtue of such daily demands as the PDB, PCs, and DCs.

The DNI's relationship with the director of the NCTC is also important. The director of the NCTC has almost autonomous status. He is appointed by the president, confirmed by the Senate, and serves as the principal adviser to the DNI on analysis and operations related to terrorism and counterterrorism. Given the primacy of terrorism as a national security issue the DNI holds a powerful position. The director of NCTC is likely to enjoy a fair amount of access to senior officials, including the president, thus creating the potential for rivalry with the DNI. The 2004 law is specific in stating that the director of NCTC reports directly to the president on the planning and progress of joint counterterrorism operations.

The secretary of state is the chief foreign policy officer below the president; the DNI should be an arm of foreign policy. At least two issues are important in the relationship between the secretary of state and the DNI: coordinating proposed intelligence operations with foreign policy goals and using the State Department (that is, the Foreign Service) as cover for clandestine intelligence officers overseas. Inevitably, tension arises between the bureaucracies under these two officials. Using the State Department for cover could prove to be a source of concern between the secretary of state and the DCIA. Few DCIs and secretaries of state have the warm relationship that Allen Dulles (DCI, 1953–1961) and his brother John Foster Dulles (secretary of state, 1953–1959) enjoyed. More often, the relationship has a slight edge, if it is not outright competitive.

Overseas, a long tradition of tension has been evident between U.S. ambassadors and their senior CIA officers, usually called the chief of station (COS). The ambassador is in charge of the entire country team—all U.S. personnel assigned to the embassy, regardless of their parent organizations. (Larger country teams may have representatives from State, CIA, Defense, Justice, Treasury, Commerce, and Agriculture.) But chiefs of station have not always kept the ambassador—whether career Foreign Service or political appointee—apprised of their intelligence activities. Despite repeated efforts to address the problem, it still occurs. Several new issues have arisen. The first is who does the chief of station represent— the DNI, who oversees the community, or the DCIA, who oversees the agency that runs the station? Given the DCIA's continued responsibility for HUMINT, intelligence operations, and foreign liaison, it would seem logical that the stations are a key component of his activities. But tension between the DNI and the DCIA over control of HUMINT and covert action could make the stations even less willing to share information with ambassadors as yet another way of keeping it from the DNI.

On a day-to-day basis, the secretary of defense controls more of the intelligence community (NSA, DIA, NGA, and the service intelligence units) than does the DNI (CIA, NIC, NCTC, and other centers). The secretary of defense also represents the vast majority of the intelligence client base, because of the broad range of defense intelligence requirements. Moreover, the intelligence budget is hidden within the defense budget and, in many ways, is beholden to it. Therefore, the relationship between the secretary of defense and the DNI is vital. No matter how collegial the relationship may appear, it is not one of equals. The outcome of the debate over the intelligence budget in the 2004 intelligence act underscores the political clout of the secretary of defense in Congress. It is not clear if the DNI will be stronger or weaker than was the DCI in relationship to the secretary of defense. On the one hand, the DNI lacks the institutional base that the DCI could fall back on—the CIA. On the other hand, the DNI has a large staff and enough authority in law that, if exercised properly, could give the DNI a more equal relationship with Defense. Much will depend on how the first DNI chooses to exercise his authority.

Much of the secretary of defense's authority for intelligence usually devolves to the undersecretary of defense for intelligence, who becomes, in effect, the chief operating officer for defense intelligence. Prior to the 2004 intelligence act, many issues that arose between DOD and the DCI were worked out by the USDI and the deputy DCI for community management, a position that was eliminated by the new law. The DNI or senior members of his staff will now deal with the USDI. DOD tends to look at the intelligence community warily, worrying that the community managers might not be looking after DOD needs and that they might be assuming too much power over defense intelligence. The key to this relationship is the credibility of the DNI or his office with the Office of the Secretary of Defense (OSD); that is, the Office of the Director of National Intelligence (ODNI) should have a working knowledge of defense intelligence programs and needs and of the defense budget process. This helps explain why Lt. Gen. Mike Hayden was chosen to be the DNI's principal deputy, as he is both a career military officer and a career intelligence officer, most recently the director of NSA. The DNI and OSD have an unbalanced relationship, with OSD the stronger partner. If officials in OSD have the sense that the DNI is not paying adequate attention to DOD needs and privileges, they can stymie much that the DNI wants to do.

The relationship between the Department of Homeland Security and the intelligence community continues to evolve. Critics of the imbalance between Defense and intelligence sometimes refer to Defense as "the 800-pound gorilla." Some observers now recognize that DHS has the potential to be "the other 800-pound gorilla." In other words, the sheer size and complexity of DHS are likely to make it an increasingly important intelligence consumer. Therefore, the relationship of the DNI and the director of the NCTC with the secretary of DHS is important.

The relationship between the DNI and Congress has three key components. The first is the power of the purse. Congress not only funds the intelligence community (and the rest of the government) but also can, through its funding decisions, affect intelligence programs. Although it is generally believed that Congress reduces presidential budget requests, it has in many instances championed programs and funded them despite opposition from the executive.

The second is personal. Past DCIs have occasionally not gotten along with their overseers, to the ultimate detriment of the DCIs and the intelligence community. William J. Casey (1981–1987) was fairly contemptuous of the oversight process, which cost him support, even among his political allies. James Woolsey ended up in a constant public squabble with the chairman of the Senate Intelligence Committee, Dennis DeConcini, D-Ariz. John M. Deutch (1995–1997) had a difficult relationship with the House Intelligence Committee. The question of the rights and wrongs in each of these cases is irrelevant. Simply put, the DNI can only lose in the end. Also, having created the DNI to solve a set of perceived problems, Congress will be watching his performance closely in the initial period to see if he meets expectations.

The third is the public perception of intelligence and support for it. Because of the secrecy surrounding intelligence, citizens get a glimpse of it mainly through congressional activities. Even without knowing the details of hearings, the fact that a congressional committee is investigating an intelligence issue affects media and public perceptions. After all, if the intelligence community is doing its job, why have a hearing or investigation? And, as is usually the case, bad news tends to get reported more often than good news.

USDI AND THE DEFENSE INTELLIGENCE AGENCIES. USDI was created by Congress in 2002 at the behest of Secretary of Defense Donald H. Rumsfeld (2001–), who felt that he had too many people reporting to him on various aspects of defense intelligence and wanted the information funneled to one office. (This was similar to President Harry S. Truman's desire for one official—the DCI—to be responsible to him for all national intelligence issues.) The USDI is limited in law to a small staff (ninety-nine positions). It is entirely a management oversight function as it has no direct control over any line intelligence assets—collectors, operators, or analysts. Still, it is an extremely influential position in terms of defense intelligence policies, requirements, and budgets.

Tension has arisen between USDI and the heads of NSA and NGA, both of whom also had a responsibility to the DCI and now will have one to the DNI. Although they head combat support agencies and although their budgets will still come through Defense channels, the heads of these agencies struggle with their two masters within the executive branch—Defense and the DNI. During the congressional hearings about the 2004 intelligence legislation, the directors of NSA and NGA testified that they believed they should come under the new DNI, a view that was not pleasing to Defense officials. However, neither the DNI nor USDI can issue orders or directives to NSA or NGA without taking into account the sensibilities of the other office.

USDI AND ITS RELATIONSHIP WITH CONGRESS. USDI is one of two main conduits through which defense intelligence issues reach Congress, the other being DIA itself. But given the principle of civilian control of the military, USDI is more powerful and more important than DIA. USDI has jurisdiction over defense intelligence requirements, the various defense intelligence agencies (among them, NSA, DIA, and NGA), and some defense collection programs—the "air breathers." USDI deals with the House and Senate Armed Services Committees. Furthermore, the USDI staff functions as a guardian of the authority of the secretary of defense over defense intelligence, watching warily for any possible encroachments, such as from the DNI.

INR AND THE SECRETARY OF STATE. State's Bureau of Intelligence and Research is the smallest of the three all-source analytical components (compared with CIA and DIA) and is often thought of as the weakest. A great deal of INR's ability to get things done, both in its own department and as a player in the intelligence community, depends on the relationship between the INR assistant secretary and the secretary of state and one or two other senior State officials, who often are referred to collectively as "the seventh floor," where they are situated at the Department of State. In some respects, the relationship among these State officials parallels that between the DNI and the president. If INR has access to the seventh floor, then it plays a greater role and has greater bureaucratic support when needed. But it is a highly variable relationship, depending on the preferences of the secretary and key subordinates. For example, Secretary of State George P. Shultz (1982–1989) met with all of his assistant secretaries regularly; Secretary of State James A. Baker III (1989–1992) did not, preferring to meet with a few senior subordinates, who then dealt with the rest of the department. Thus, under Shultz, INR had more opportunities to gain access; under Baker, most of INR's clients were other bureaus, but less so the vaunted seventh floor.

In recent years INR has taken a number of steps to increase its visibility in the State Department and to involve other bureaus more actively in setting intelligence requirements. The goal has been to increase the bureaus' appreciation of the role of intelligence and of INR, thus making them potential sources of support. The degree to which these steps have improved INR's position in its department remains to be seen.

NEW AREAS OF RIVALRY. Increased rivalry has become evident among agencies both before and after the passage of the 2004 intelligence legislation. The war on terrorism has been a major impetus to this rivalry for at least two reasons. The first reason is that the war on terrorism has blurred distinctions between different types or fields of activity that were kept distinct, at least in U.S. practice. Most prominent are those between foreign and domestic intelligence issues and between intelligence and military operations. As became evident in 2001, terrorists could place themselves in the United States to plan and conduct attacks, creating what is both a foreign and domestic intelligence issue. The war against terrorism, particularly in places such as Afghanistan, called for greater intelligence-military cooperation but also blurred some of the distinctions between the areas in which both operated. For example, the initial liaison with and support of the Northern Alliance, which was fighting the Taliban, came via the CIA. The campaign against the Taliban had conventional and non-conventional (that is, special forces) aspects, as well as a large intelligence component. The second reason for increased rivalry has been the natural tendency of most organizations to increase activities, particularly during periods of crisis or war.

Rivalry has been an issue between the FBI and the CIA. The FBI, beginning before 2001, sought to increase its role both within the United States and overseas. In the mid-1990s, the FBI was aggressive about expanding the role of its legal attachés, who work out of U.S. embassies to foster greater cooperation with foreign law enforcement agencies. Press stories have alleged that the FBI has, on occasion, conducted overseas activities without informing the CIA. Within the United States, increased rivalry has emerged over the recruitment of foreigners who are in the United States and are then sent overseas to collect intelligence. Although the CIA cannot conduct intelligence within the United States or on U.S. citizens, this type of activity has been allowed as the recruited individuals are foreigners and their collection takes place outside of the country. The FBI has reportedly sought to take over this activity, arguing that it is domestic intelligence (as recruitment takes place in the United States), and has sought to be responsible for disseminating intelligence produced by foreigners in the United States. The CIA has resisted the FBI efforts. Some observers note that the FBI has little experience in this type of intelligence recruitment and that its own intelligence analytic effort just began in 2003 and is not ready to take over reporting of this type. Concern also arose that both agencies could end up controlling some portion of overseas collection, resulting either in duplication or in the two working at cross-purposes if they are not aware of the other's activities. The DNI has oversight over both sets of activities and may be asked to resolve the competing claims of the two agencies.

Rivalry also exists between the Defense Department and the CIA. This relationship has always been difficult because of the imbalance between the DCI's intelligence community responsibilities and the day-to-day control that the secretary of defense has exercised over some 80 percent of the intelligence community. Even though the new DCIA will be responsible for only one agency, areas of rivalry remain. The blurring of intelligence and military roles in the war on terrorism has been one source. There are both overt and covert military aspects to this war. The CIA can claim to have a stake only in the covert aspect, as in its work with the Northern Alliance against the Taliban in Afghanistan in 2001. But the military can claim to have responsibilities in both spheres and appears to want to expand its activities in the covert sphere. (See the discussion of paramilitary operations in chap. 8.)

A second source of CIA–Defense competition appears to be the desire of the Defense Department to gain greater control over any and all intelligence related to its missions. Several observers have noted that, once President George W. Bush decided to attack al Qaeda in its Afghan sanctuary, Secretary of Defense Rumsfeld was frustrated by the relative speed with which DCI Tenet was able to respond and begin inserting officers to link up with the Northern Alliance. Defense needed a much longer time span to plan and to deliver military combat units to Afghanistan. Rumsfeld was also reportedly displeased that the military had to depend largely on the CIA for human intelligence support.

In late 2004 and early 2005 a series of press reports indicated a unilateral expansion of Defense activities in intelligence. The fiscal year 2005 defense authorization bill included a provision allotting $25 million to the Special Operations Command to "support foreign forces, irregular forces, groups or individuals." Some believe this sounds like what the CIA has done and certainly did in Afghanistan. Some have questioned whether this puts the Defense Department into the business of covert actions without the attendant legal apparatus of presidential findings and reports to

Congress (for further discussion, see chap. 8). The consensus is that the situation also raised the possibility that some of these foreigners might double-dip, that is, solicit payments from both Defense and CIA. The WMD Commission had recommended that Defense be given greater authority for conducting covert action. However, according to press reports in June 2005, the Bush administration decided against the proposal. A new executive office will coordinate all overseas collection conducted by CIA, Defense, and the FBI.

More controversial were reports that DIA had created a Strategic Support Branch to augment its HUMINT capabilities. Again, this was seen as a way of minimizing Defense's need to rely on CIA for HUMINT. Some agreed that there could be unique Defense HUMINT requirements related to planned or ongoing operations that CIA might not be able or willing to fulfill if they competed with other priorities. But this activity raised questions about congressional oversight (including whether Congress had been informed about the creation of this new capability), the degree to which it overlapped with or encroached upon CIA's role, and whether sufficient coordination mechanisms were in place.

The new DNI could get involved in these types of issues, if only to assert his responsibilities for the entire intelligence community. The DNI will also have an interest in limiting Defense expansion in intelligence if only to try to maintain some balance with the secretary of defense.

CONGRESSIONAL RELATIONSHIPS. Also of great importance are the relationships of the two intelligence committees with each other and with the other House and Senate committees with which they must work. The oversight responsibilities of the House and Senate Intelligence Committees are not identical, which accounts for their differing sets of relationships. The Senate Intelligence Committee has sole jurisdiction over only the DNI, CIA, and the NIC. The Senate Armed Services Committee has always jealously guarded its oversight of all aspects of defense intelligence. The relationship between Senate Intelligence and Senate Armed Services has been standoffish at best and sometimes hostile. Antagonism has usually stemmed from the Senate Armed Services Committee's reactions to real or imagined efforts by Senate Intelligence to step beyond its carefully circumscribed turf. Senate Armed Services has usually responded with punitive actions of varying degrees (such as delaying action on the annual intelligence authorization bill).

Both committees also jealously and successfully guarded their oversight of intelligence against possible intrusions by the Senate Governmental Affairs Committee (SGAC). However, the legislation dealing with the reorganization of the intelligence community was referred to SGAC because of its role in government organization. This move was seen by some as a slap at the Senate Intelligence Committee, whose chairman, Pat Roberts, R-Kan., had offered a much more radical proposal for intelligence organization earlier in 2004.

The House Intelligence Committee has exclusive jurisdiction over the entire NIP—all programs that transcend the bounds of any one agency or are nondefense—as well as shared jurisdiction over the defense intelligence programs. This arrangement has fostered a better working relationship between House Intelligence and House Armed Services than exists between their Senate counterparts. This is not to suggest that moments of friction do not arise, but the overall relationship between the House committees has not approached the hostility exhibited in the Senate. However, the House Armed Services Committee was the strongest advocate for Defense Department interests in the debate over the 2004 legislation and in the 2005 intelligence authorization legislation.

Good relationships between the two intelligence committees and the House and Senate Defense Appropriations subcommittees are important for avoiding disjunctions between authorized programs and appropriated funds. Generally speaking, all appropriators tend to resent (and would sometimes like to ignore) all authorizers. Once again, the relationship between intelligence authorizers and appropriators has been smoother in the House than in the Senate.

The House Foreign Affairs and Senate Foreign Relations Committees oversee State Department activities, but the relationship with their respective Intelligence Committee tends to be less fractious than the relationship between the Intelligence and Appropriations Committees. Finally, the two Judiciary Committees oversee the FBI.

The two Intelligence Committees themselves have an important relationship. The House committee's jurisdiction is broader than the Senate's. However, the Senate Intelligence Committee has the exclusive and important authority to confirm the nominations of the DNI, his principal deputy, a few other subordinates, and the DCIA. The two committees often choose to work on different issues during the course of a session of Congress, apart from their work on the intelligence authorization bills. Despite differences of style and emphasis, hostility or rancor has rarely intruded, even in the face of divergent viewpoints.

THE INTELLIGENCE BUDGET PROCESS

The love of money is not only the root of all evil; money is also the root of all government. How much gets spent and who decides are fundamental powers. The intelligence budget is somewhat complex. It has three components: National Intelligence Program, Joint Military Intelligence Program, and Tactical Intelligence and Related Activities.

The NIP, as its name implies, consists of programs that either transcend the bounds of an agency or are nondefense in nature. The NIP receives over half of the intelligence budget.

Civilian Programs
   CIA
   CIA Retirement and Disability
      System (CIARDS)
   Counterintelligence (FBI)
   INR (State Department)
   Office of Intelligence Support
      (Treasury Department)
Defense Programs
   Consolidated Cryptographic
      Program (CCP)

DOD Foreign Counterintelligence Program (FCIP)
General Defense Intelligence
   Program (GDIP)
National Imagery and Mapping
   Program
National Reconnaissance Program (NRP)
Community-wide Program
Community Management
   Account (CMA)

JMIP is composed of programs within the Defense Department that are not confined to any one military service. As the titles of some JMIP programs indicate, many parallel NIP categories. The JMIP receives over a tenth of the intelligence budget.

Defense Airborne Reconnaissance Program (DARP)
Defense Cryptologic Program
   (DCP)
Defense General Intelligence
   Applications Program
   (DGIAP)
Defense Imagery and Mapping
   Program (DIMP)

Defense Intelligence Counterdrug Program (DICP)
Defense Intelligence Special
   Technologies Program
   (DISTP)
Defense Intelligence Tactical
   Program (DITP)
Defense Space Reconnaissance
   Program (DSRP)

TIARA is made up of the four service intelligence programs and intelligence for the Special Operations Command. TIARA receives about one-third of the intelligence budget.

Air Force intelligence
Army intelligence
Marine intelligence

Navy intelligence
Special Operations Command
   (SOCOM)

FIGURE 3-4   Alternative Ways of Looking at the Intelligence Community:
A Budgetary View

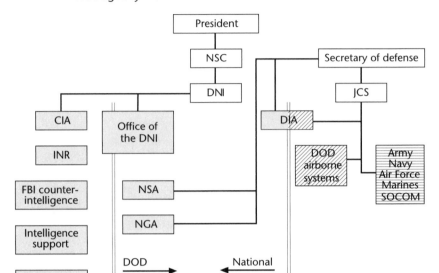

Note: CIA= Central Intelligence Agency; DCI = director of central intelligence; DIA = Defense Intelligence Agency; DOD = Department of Defense; DOE = Department of Energy; FBI = Federal Bureau of Investigation; INR = Bureau of Intelligence and Research; JCS = Joint Chiefs of Staff; JMIP = joint military intelligence program; NGA = National Geospatial-Intelligence Agency; NIP = national intelligence program; NSA = National Security Agency; NSC = National Security Council; SOCOM = Special Operations Command; TIARA = technical intelligence and related activities.

Figure 3-4 arranges the components of the intelligence community by budget sectors. Not all of the agencies within a budget sector are controlled by the same authority. The solid lines denote direct control. The two double vertical lines show which part of the budget and agencies are national and which are DOD. There is an overlap, as some agencies are both national and Defense, even if they fall into NIP or JMIP. DIA straddles the line, containing both NIP and several of the JMIP programs. Figure 3-4 also indicates the secretary of defense's preponderant control over intelligence community resources.

The intelligence budget is shaped by a process that is lengthy and complex (see Figure 3-5). The budget-building process within the executive branch takes more than a year, beginning around November when the DNI provides guidance to the intelligence program managers. The crosswalks between DNI and Defense—efforts to coordinate programs and to make difficult choices between programs—are major facets of the budget

FIGURE 3-5   The Intelligence Budget: Four Phases over Three Years

It takes about three years to develop a budget and then spend the money, beginning in March of any year and continuing until September two and a half years later. The figure shows the activity for each phase and the time during which it happens.

Year 1	March–September	October ⌐		
Year 2		↓ August	August ⌐	
Year 3			↓ September	October ⌐
Year 4				↓ September
Activity	**Planning**	**Programming**	**Budgeting**	**Execution**
	Guidance	Request and review	Build and submit	Obligate and spend
	Broad guidelines of planning, programming, and budgeting are established.	**Program resources are projected for future year requirements for dollar and manpower resources—a multiyear request.**	**Money or authority available to purchase goods and services or to hire people—for one or two years—is set.**	**Money on authorized programs is committed and spent.**

process. Crosswalks can take place at the program level or below and can go as high as the DNI and the secretary of defense. The budget process in the executive branch ends the following December, thirteen months after it began, with the DNI sending a completed intelligence budget to the president for final approval.

The following February the president's budget goes to Congress, where a new, eight-month process begins. It consists of hearings in the authorization and appropriations committees, committee markups of the bills, floor action, conference committee action between the House and Senate to work out differences (both houses must pass identical bills), and final passage, after which the bill goes to the president to be signed. By this time, the executive branch is already working on the next budget. A major difference between the president's budget and Congress's should be kept in mind. The president's budget is serious and detailed, but it is only a recommendation. Congress's budget allocates money. Or, as the old saying goes, "The president proposes and Congress disposes." Beyond this formal process is the increasing use of supplemental budget bills, which are appropriations above the amount approved by Congress in the regular budget process. **Supplementals** tend not to be favored by executive agencies as they may provide one-year money that is not sustained in the following years (see chap. 10 for more detail). For Congress, however, supplementals are a way to take care of agreed-upon needs without making long-term budget commitments.

This seemingly endless process points up another important aspect of the intelligence budget. At any time during the year, as many as eight

---

Eight Simultaneous Budgets

Over the course of a fiscal year (October 1 to September 30), eight con-current budgets are in some state of being. This shows the situation during fiscal 2005:

Fiscal 2003 and 2004: Past fiscal years; some funds still being spent
Fiscal 2005: Current fiscal year; funds being spent
Fiscal 2006: Budget for the next fiscal year being developed by executive branch and Congress
Fiscal 2007: Intelligence program nearing completion
Fiscal 2008: Budget in early development in executive branch
Fiscal 2009 and 2010: Budgets in long-range planning in executive branch

---

different fiscal year (October 1–September 30) budgets are in some form of use or development. *(See box, "Eight Simultaneous Budgets.")* Two past fiscal year budgets are still in use, in the form of funds that had been appropriated previously. Although funds for salaries and similar expenses are spent in a single fiscal year, other funds—such as those to build highly complex technical collection systems—are spent over the course of several years. Funds also are being spent for the current fiscal year.

The budget for the following fiscal year is going through the political processes. The budget for the year after that is being formulated by the executive branch and Congress. Finally, two future year budgets are in various states of planning. A great deal of influence accrues to those individuals in both branches of government who can master the process and the details of the budget.

KEY TERMS

Deputies Committee
Principals Committee
supplementals

FURTHER READINGS

The following readings provide background on the current organization and structure of the U.S. intelligence community. The list includes some studies of proposed changes that would enable the intelligence community to deal more effectively with the challenges it will face in the future.

Commission on the Intelligence Capabilities of the United States Regarding Weapons of Mass Destruction. Report to the president, March 31, 2005. (Available at www.wmd.gov.)

Elkins, Dan. *An Intelligence Resource Manager's Guide.* Washington, D.C.: Defense Intelligence Agency, Joint Military Intelligence Training Center, 1997.

Johnson, Loch K. *Secret Agencies: U.S. Intelligence in a Hostile World.* New Haven: Yale University Press, 1996.

Lowenthal, Mark M. *U.S. Intelligence: Evolution and Anatomy.* 2d ed. Westport, Conn.: Praeger, 1992.

National Commission on Terrorist Attacks Upon the United States [9/11 Commission]. *Final Report.* New York: W.W. Norton and Co., 2004.

Posner, Richard. "The 9/11 Report: A Dissent." *New York Times Book Review,* August 29, 2004, 1.

Richelson, Jeffrey T. *The U.S. Intelligence Community.* 4th ed. Boulder, Colo.: Westview Press, 1999.

U.S. Commission on the Roles and Responsibilities of the United States Intelligence Community. *Preparing for the 21st Century: An Appraisal of U.S. Intelligence.* Washington, D.C.: U.S. Government Printing Office, 1996.

U.S. House Permanent Select Committee on Intelligence. *IC21: The Intelligence Community in the 21st Century.* Staff study, 104th Cong., 2d sess., 1996.

Chapter 4

The Intelligence Process—
A Macro Look:
Who Does What for Whom?

The term *intelligence process* refers to the steps or stages in intelligence, from policy makers perceiving a need for information to the community's delivery of an analytical intelligence product to them. This chapter offers an overview of the entire intelligence process and introduces some of the key issues in each phase. Succeeding chapters deal in greater detail with the major phases. Intelligence, as practiced in the United States, is commonly thought of as having five steps, to which this book adds two. The seven phases of the intelligence process are identifying requirements, collection, processing and exploitation, analysis and production, dissemination, consumption, and feedback.

Identifying **requirements** means defining those policy issues or areas to which intelligence is expected to make a contribution, as well as decisions as to which of these issues has priority over the others. It may also mean specifying the collection of certain types of intelligence. The impulse is to say that all policy areas have intelligence requirements, which they do. However, intelligence capabilities are always limited, so priorities must be set, with some requirements getting more attention, some getting less, and some perhaps getting little or none at all. The key questions are: Who sets these requirements and priorities and then conveys them to the intelligence community? What happens, or should happen, if policy makers fail to set these requirements on their own?

Once requirements and priorities have been established, the necessary intelligence must be collected. Some requirements will be better met by specific types of collection; some may require the use of several types of collection. Making these decisions among always-constrained collection capabilities is a key issue, as is the question of how much can or should be collected to meet each requirement.

Collection produces information, not intelligence. That information must undergo **processing and exploitation** before it can be regarded as intelligence and given to analysts. In the United States, constant tension exists over the allocation of resources to collection and to processing and exploitation, with collection inevitably coming out the winner, to the point where much more is collected than can be processed or exploited.

Identifying requirements, conducting collection, and processing and exploitation are meaningless unless the intelligence is given to analysts who are experts in their respective fields and can turn the intelligence into reports that respond to the needs of the policy makers. The types of products chosen, the quality of the **analysis and production**, and the continuous tension between current intelligence products and longer-range products are major issues.

The issue of moving the analysis to the policy makers stems directly from the multitude of analytical vehicles available for disseminating intelligence. Decisions must be made as to how widely intelligence should be distributed and how urgently it should be passed or flagged for the policy maker's attention.

Most discussions of the intelligence process end here, with the intelligence having reached the policy makers whose requirements first set everything in motion. However, two important phases remain: **consumption** and **feedback**.

Policy makers are not blank slates or automatons who are impelled to action by intelligence. How they consume intelligence—whether in the form of written or oral briefings—and the degree to which the intelligence is used are important issues.

Although feedback does not occur nearly as often as the intelligence community might desire, a dialogue between intelligence consumers and producers should take place after the intelligence has been received. Policy makers should give the intelligence community some sense of how well their intelligence requirements are being met and discuss any adjustments that need to be made to any parts of the process. Ideally, this should happen while the issue or topic is still relevant, so that improvements and adjustments can be made. Failing that, even an ex post facto review can be tremendously helpful.

REQUIREMENTS

Each nation has a wide variety of national security and foreign policy interests. Some nations have more than others. Of these interests, the primacy of some is self-evident—those that deal with large and known threats, those that deal with neighboring or proximate states, and those that are more severe. But the international arena is dynamic and fluid, so occasional readjustments of priorities are likely even among the agreed-upon key interests. For example, the Soviet Union was the overwhelming top priority of U.S. intelligence from 1946 to 1991, after which the country, as it was, ceased to exist. The problems associated with its fifteen successor states have been very different. Also, terrorism has been a concern of U.S. national security policy since the 1970s, but the nature of the terrorism issue changed dramatically in 2001.

Given that intelligence should be an adjunct to policy and not a policy maker in its own right, intelligence priorities should reflect policy priorities. Policy makers should have well-considered and well-established views of their own priorities and convey these clearly to their intelligence apparatus. Some of the requirements may be obvious or so long-standing that no discussion is needed. The cold war concentration on the Soviet Union was one of these.

But what happens if the policy makers do not decide, find that they cannot decide, or fail to convey their priorities to the intelligence community? Who sets intelligence priorities then? These questions are neither frivolous nor hypothetical. Senior policy makers often assume that their needs are known by their intelligence providers. After all, the key issues are apparent. A former secretary of defense, when asked if he ever considered giving his intelligence officers a more precise definition of his needs, said, "No. I assumed they knew what I was working on." There is strong reason to believe that his view was not unique.

An obvious way to fill the requirements gap left by policy makers would be for the intelligence community to assume this task on its own. However, in a system such as that of the United States, where a strict line divides policy and intelligence, this solution may not be possible. Intelligence officials may feel that the limits on their role preclude making the decision; policy makers may view intelligence officials who seek to fill the void as a threat to their function and may even react with hostility.

The intelligence community thus faces two unpalatable choices. The first is to fill the requirements vacuum, running the risk of being wrong or accused of having overstepped into the realm of policy. The second is to overlook the absence of defined requirements and to continue collection and the phases that follow, based on the last-known priorities and the intelligence community's sense of priorities, knowing that it may be accused of failing to meet important priorities. In short, there is no good choice when such a vacuum occurs.

Some intelligence managers might take issue with this interpretation of their choices. They would note, correctly, that one function of intelligence is to look ahead, to identify issues that are not high priority at present but may be so in the future. But, as important as this function is, it is difficult to get policy makers to focus on issues that are far off or only possibly significant. They are hard-pressed to work on the issues demanding immediate attention. Thus, the requirements conundrum remains.

Conflicting or competing priorities are also an issue. Although some sense of order may be easily imposed on certain issues, others may end up claiming equal primacy. Again, policy makers should make the difficult choices. In reality, most governments are large enough to have various competing sectors of interest either between or within departments or ministries. The result is that, once again, the intelligence community may be left to its own devices. In an intelligence community such as that of the United States, parts of the community may reflect the preferences of the policy makers to whom they are most closely tied. In some cases, there may be no final adjudicating authority, leaving the intelligence community to do the best it can. In the U.S. system, the National Security Council (NSC) sets the policy and intelligence priorities. The director of national intelligence (DNI) should be the final adjudicator within the intelligence community, but the director's ability to impose priorities on a day-to-day basis across the entire intelligence community remains uncertain. All issues tend to get shorter shrift when too many are competing for attention.

One intellectual means of assessing requirements is to look at the likelihood of an event and its relative importance to national security concerns. Of great concern will be high likelihood and high importance events. It should be easier to assess importance (which should be based on known or stated national interests) than it is to assess likelihood (which is itself an intelligence judgment or estimate). (Likelihood, however, is not a prediction. See the discussion in chap. 6.) For example, during the cold war a Soviet nuclear attack would have been judged a high importance but low likelihood event. Italian government instability would have been judged a high likelihood but low importance event. Of the two, the Soviet issue would rank higher as a priority or intelligence concern because of its potential effect, even though an attack seemed possible in only a few instances and an Italian government fell several dozen times.

In both Panel A and Panel B of Figure 4-1, the issues that fall closer to the upper right reflect more important intelligence requirements. However, there may not be startling clarity as to likelihood or there may be a debate as to issues' relative importance.

The hidden factor that drives priorities is resources. It is impossible to cover everything. The United States, for example, has long had interests in every part of the globe, although some are more significant and more central than others. For decades, the U.S. intelligence community has used a variety of processes to set priorities. The most recent example is the National Intelligence Priorities Framework (NIPF), which supports a national security policy directive (NSPD) signed by President George W. Bush in February 2003.

FIGURE 4-1   Intelligence Requirements: Importance versus Likelihood

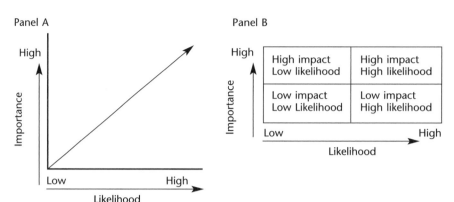

According to congressional testimony by director of central intelligence (DCI) George J. Tenet, the NIPF provides for semiannual reviews of intelligence priorities by the president and the NSC. Tenet described it as being more flexible and more precise than any previous intelligence priority system. The NIPF is connected directly to analytic and collection resources to ensure that the most urgent needs are being covered and that gaps can be identified quickly. The system is also used for planning in the five-year budget cycle. Other testimony revealed that each topic in the NIPF has an intelligence topic manager who helps determine collection requirements. The NIPF appears to be a more pervasive system in terms of overall intelligence community functions and a more flexible system than has been used in the past.

All priority systems must address the issue of **priority creep.** Issues can and do move up and down in a priority system. The problem is that issues cannot receive significant attention until after they have begun moving up to the higher-priority tiers, at which point they must compete with the issues already in that bracket. Priority creep can become a problem as analysts or policy makers seek higher priority for certain issues. Priority creep is further exacerbated by the difficulty encountered in returning issues to lower-priority status once they have become less urgent. Neither the intelligence analysts working on that issue nor the policy makers whom they support are eager to admit that the issue is no longer as important. After all, it is their issue. This underscores the problem with any intelligence requirements system. Such a system is, of necessity, static. Even if the requirements are reviewed and re-ranked periodically, such as the six-month review in the NIPF, they remain snapshots in time. Policy makers or intelligence officials must decide on the requirements and resources to be applied to them. However, the nature of international relations is such that unexpected issues inevitably crop up with little or no warning. These are sometimes referred to as **ad hocs**. When one of these arises, some policy makers and intelligence officers exert pressure to give the new issue a priority high enough to compete with other high-priority issues. Some resistance is felt, usually from those whose access to intelligence resources is threatened. Not every ad hoc merits higher priorities. (Some intelligence analysts speak of the **tyranny of the ad hocs**.) Moreover, a system that constantly responds to each ad hoc soon has little control over priorities. It quickly breaks down. Thus, the system that preserves a modicum of flexibility or a modest reserve capability is more responsive to the realities of intelligence requirements. Policy makers often have little time or inclination to conduct periodic reviews of intelligence priorities, even as often as annually. As a result, static, potentially outdated requirements and the necessity to make requirements decisions on its own can be problems for the intelligence community.

Moreover, if a requirement cannot be met with current collection systems, developing the technical systems or the human sources will take time. Thus, uncertainty about requirements or lower priorities for some of them will affect the development of collection capabilities.

COLLECTION

Collection derives directly from requirements. Not every issue requires the same types of collection support. The requirements depend on the nature of the issue and on the types of collection that are available. For example, concerns over possible threat from cyber attacks likely derive little useful intelligence from imagery as the locus of the threat cannot be captured in a photo. Much better intelligence might be derived from signals intelligence, which can reveal capabilities or intentions. Collection is also the first—and perhaps the most important—facet of intelligence where budgets and resources come into play in precise terms (as opposed to broader discussions when priorities are at issue). Technical collection is extremely expensive and, because different types of systems offer different benefits and capabilities, the administration and Congress must make difficult budget choices. Also, the needs of agencies vary, further complicating the choices.

How much information should be collected? Or, put another way, does more collection mean better intelligence? The answer to these questions is ambiguous. On the one hand, the more information that is collected, the more likely it will include the required intelligence. On the other hand, not everything that is collected is of equal value. Analysts must wade through the material—to process and exploit it—to find the intelligence that is really needed. This is often referred to as the "wheat versus chaff problem." In other words, increased collection also increases the task of finding the truly important intelligence.

An interesting phenomenon, found at least in the U.S. intelligence community, is that different analytical groups may prefer different types of intelligence. For example, the CIA may put greater store in clandestine human intelligence (espionage), in part because it is a product of CIA activities. Meanwhile, other all-source analysts may place greater emphasis on signals intelligence.

PROCESSING AND EXPLOITATION

Intelligence collected by technical means (imagery, signals, test data, and so on) does not arrive in ready-to-use form. It must be processed from complex digital signals into images or intercepts, and these must then be exploited—analyzed if they are images; perhaps decoded, and probably translated, if they are signals. Processing and exploitation are key steps in converting technically collected information into intelligence.

In the United States, collection outruns processing and exploitation. Much more is collected than can ever be processed and exploited. Furthermore, technical collection systems have found greater favor in the executive branch and Congress than the systems and personnel requirements for processing and exploitation. One reason for this appeal is emotional. A similar circumstance, for example, exists in formation of the defense budget. Les Aspin, chairman of the House Armed Services Committee (1985–1993) and later the secretary of defense (1993–1994), once observed that both Congress and the executive branch were more interested in procurement (buying new weapons) than operations and maintenance (keeping already purchased systems functioning). Buying new systems was more attractive to decision makers in both branches and, more important, to defense contractors. Operations and maintenance, although important, are less exciting and less glamorous. Collection is akin to procurement and is much more appealing than processing and exploitation.

Collection advocates argue, usually successfully, that collection is the bedrock of intelligence, that without it the entire enterprise has little meaning. Collection also has support from the companies (prime contractors and their numerous subcontractors) who build the technical collection systems and who lobby for follow-on systems. Processing and exploitation are in-house intelligence community activities. Although these **downstream activities** (the steps that follow collection) are also dependent on technology, the technology is not in the same league, in terms of contractor profit, as collection systems.

The large and still growing disparity between collection and processing and exploitation results in a great amount of collected material never being used. It simply dies on the cutting-room floor. Advocates of processing and exploitation therefore argue that the image or signal that is not processed and not exploited is identical to the one that is not collected—it has no effect at all.

No proper ratio exists between collection and processing and exploitation. In part, the ratio depends on the issue, available resources, and policy makers' demands. But many who are familiar with the U.S. intelligence community believe that the relationship between these two phases is badly out of balance. The congressional committees that oversee intelligence have increasingly expressed concern about this imbalance, urging the intelligence community to put more money into processing and exploitation. This is often referred to as the TPEDs (pronounced tee-peds) problem. TPEDs refers to tasking, processing, exploitation, and dissemination. Tasking is the assigning of collectors to specific tasks. Of the four parts of TPEDs, tasking and dissemination are the least problematic for the intelligence community or for Congress. The processing and exploitation gap is of highest concern to Congress.

ANALYSIS AND PRODUCTION

Major, often daily, tension is evident between current intelligence and long-term intelligence. Current intelligence focuses on issues that are at the forefront of the policy makers' agenda and are receiving their immediate attention. Long-term intelligence deals with trends and issues that may not be an immediate concern but are important and may come to the forefront, especially if they do not receive some current attention. The skills for preparing the two types of intelligence are not identical, and neither are the intelligence products that can or should be used to disseminate them to policy makers. But a subtle relationship exists between current and long-term intelligence. Like collection versus process and exploitation, a proper balance—not necessarily 50–50—should be the goal.

The U.S. system of competitive analysis—that is, having the same issue addressed by several different analytical groups—entails some analytical costs. Although the goal is to bring disparate points of view to bear on an issue, intelligence community products written within this system run the risk of succumbing to groupthink, with lowest common denominator language resulting from intellectual compromises. Alternatively, agencies can indulge in endless and—at least to the policy consumers—

meaningless **footnote wars**, whose only goal is to maintain a separate point of view regardless of the salience of the issue at stake.

Analysts should have a key role in helping determine collection priorities. Although the United States has instituted a series of offices and programs to improve the relationship between analysts and the collection systems on which they are dependent, the connection between the two has never been particularly strong or responsive. Improving this relationship has been one of the goals of the NIPF. The ideal state is one in which there is analytically driven collection, that is, collectors act in response to analytic needs and not more independently or opportunistically.

The training and the mind-sets of analysts are important. Analysts must often deal with intelligence that is contradictory, both internally and when viewed in light of their strongly held professional beliefs and perhaps their own past work. The way in which analysts deal with these contradictions depends on their training and the nature of the broader analytical system, including the review process.

Finally, analysts are not intellectual ciphers. They are likely to have ambitions and want their issues to receive a certain degree of high-level attention. This is not meant to suggest that they will resort to intellectually dishonest means to gain attention, but that possibility must be kept in mind by their superiors within the intelligence community and by policy makers.

DISSEMINATION AND CONSUMPTION

The process of **dissemination,** or moving the intelligence from the producers to the consumers, is largely standardized. The intelligence community has a set product line to cover the types of reports and customers with which it must deal. The product line ranges from bulletins on fast-breaking and important events to studies that may take a year or more to complete.

PRESIDENT'S DAILY BRIEF. The president's daily brief (PDB) is delivered every morning to the president and some of his most senior advisers by the PDB staff. This had been a CIA function but now comes under the DNI. The PDB is formatted to suit the preferences of each president.

SENIOR EXECUTIVE INTELLIGENCE BRIEF. The Senior Executive Intelligence Brief (SEIB)—for decades known as the National Intelligence Daily—is an early-morning intelligence newspaper prepared by the CIA, in coordination with the other intelligence producers, for several hundred senior officials in Washington, D.C. Copies are distributed throughout the executive branch, as well as to the intelligence oversight committees in Congress.

THE MILITARY INTELLIGENCE DIGEST (MID). Unlike the SEIB, which is theoretically a product of the entire intelligence community as all agencies have an opportunity to comment on articles, the Military Intelligence Digest (MID) is prepared by the Defense Intelligence Agency. Although it is produced primarily for Defense Department policy makers, the MID is also circulated elsewhere in the executive branch. Thus, in the sense of offering a different array of issues and perhaps different analyses, the MID is a counterpart to the SEIB. On any given day, the SEIB and MID cover some of the same issues, as well as issues that are of particular interest to their primary readers alone. The State Department Bureau of Intelligence and Research (INR) had long produced a similar morning report of its own, the Secretary's Morning Summary (SMS). In 2001, INR abandoned the SMS, relying on other vehicles to communicate with its major policy customers.

NATIONAL INTELLIGENCE ESTIMATES. National intelligence estimates (NIEs) are the responsibility of national intelligence officers (NIOs), who are members of the National Intelligence Council, which now comes under the DNI. NIEs represent the considered opinion of the entire intelligence community and, once completed and agreed to, are signed by the DNI for presentation to the president and other senior officials. The drafting of NIEs can take anywhere from a few months to a year or more. Special NIEs, or SNIEs (pronounced "sneeze"), are written on more urgent issues and on a fast-track basis.

The PDB, SEIB, and MID are all current intelligence products, focusing on events of the past day or two at most and on issues that are being dealt with at present or will be dealt with over the next few days. NIEs are long-term intelligence products that attempt to estimate (not predict) the likely direction an issue will take in the future. Ideally, NIEs should be anticipatory, focusing on issues that are likely to be important in the near future and for which sufficient time exists to arrive at a community-wide judgment. This ideal is not always met, and some NIEs are drafted on issues that are already on policy makers' agendas. If these same issues demand current analysis, it is distributed through other analytical vehicles or via a SNIE.

The following are questions the intelligence community must consider in the dissemination of information.

- Among the large mass of material being collected and analyzed each day, what is important enough to report?

- To which policy makers should it be reported—the most senior or lower-ranking ones? To many or just a few?
- How quickly should it be reported? Is it urgent enough to require immediate delivery, or can it wait for one of the reports that senior policy makers receive the next morning?
- How much detail should be reported to the various intelligence consumers? How long should the report be?
- What is the best vehicle for reporting it—one of the items in the product line, a memo, a briefing?

The intelligence community customarily makes these decisions. They entail a number of factors and occasional trade-offs between conflicting goals. Ideally, the community employs a layered approach, using a variety of intelligence products to convey the same intelligence (in different formats and degrees of detail) to a broad array of policy makers. Its decisions should also reflect an understanding of the needs and preferences of the policy makers and should be adjusted as administrations change.

Most discussions of the intelligence process do not include the consumption phase, given that the intelligence is complete and has been delivered. However, this approach ignores the key role played by the policy community throughout the entire intelligence process.

FEEDBACK

Communications between the policy community and the intelligence community are at best imperfect throughout the intelligence process. This is most noticeable after intelligence has been transmitted. Ideally, the policy makers would be giving continual feedback to their intelligence producers—what has been useful, what has not, which areas need continuing or increased emphasis, which can be reduced, and so on.

In reality, the community receives feedback less often than it desires, and it certainly does not receive feedback in any systematic manner, for several reasons. First, few people in the policy community have the time to think about or to convey their reactions. They work from issue to issue, with little time to reflect on what went right or wrong before pushing on to the next issue. Also, few policy makers think feedback is necessary. Even when the intelligence they are receiving is not exactly what they need, they usually do not bother to inform their intelligence producers. The failure to provide feedback is analogous to the policy makers' inability or refusal to help define requirements.

THINKING ABOUT THE INTELLIGENCE PROCESS

Given the importance of the intelligence process as both a concept and an organizing principle, it is worth thinking about how the process works and how best to conceptualize it.

Figure 4-2, published by the CIA in *A Consumer's Handbook to Intelligence,* presents the intelligence cycle (as the guide calls it) as a perfect circle. Beginning at the top, policy makers provide planning and direction, and the intelligence community collects intelligence, which is then processed and exploited, analyzed and produced, and disseminated to the policy makers.

FIGURE 4-2   The Intelligence Process: A Central Intelligence Agency View

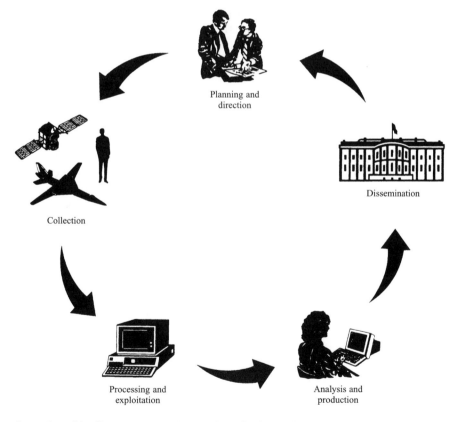

Planning and
direction

Dissemination

Collection

Processing and
exploitation

Analysis and
production

Source: Central Intelligence Agency, *A Consumer's Handbook to Intelligence* (Langley, Va.: Central Intelligence Agency; 1993).

Although meant to be little more than a quick schematic presentation, the CIA diagram misrepresents some aspects and misses many others. First, it is overly simple. Its end-to-end completeness misses many of the vagaries in the process. It is also oddly unidimensional. A policy maker asks questions and, after a few steps, gets an answer. There is no feedback, and the diagram does not convey that the process might not be completed in one cycle.

A more realistic diagram would show that at any stage in the process it is possible—and sometimes necessary—to go back to an earlier step. Initial collection may prove unsatisfactory and may lead policy makers to change the requirements; processing and exploitation or analysis may reveal gaps, resulting in new collection requirements; consumers may change their needs or ask for more intelligence. And, on occasion, intelligence officers may receive feedback.

This admittedly imperfect process can be portrayed as in Figure 4-3. This diagram, although better than the CIA's, remains somewhat unidimensional. A still better portrayal would capture the more than occasional need to go back to an earlier part of the process to meet unfulfilled or changing requirements, collection needs, and so on.

Figure 4-4 shows how in any one intelligence process issues likely arise (the need for more collection, uncertainties in processing, results of analysis, changing requirements) that cause a second or even third intelligence process to take place. Ultimately, one could repeat the process lines over and over to portray continuing changes in any of the various parts of the process and the fact that policy issues are rarely resolved in a single neat cycle. This diagram is a bit more complex, and it gives a much better sense of how the intelligence process operates in reality, being linear, circular, and open-ended all at the same time.

FIGURE 4-3   The Intelligence Process: A Schematic

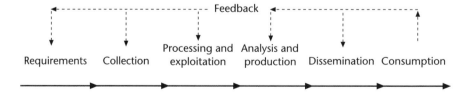

FIGURE 4-4   The Intelligence Process: Multilayered

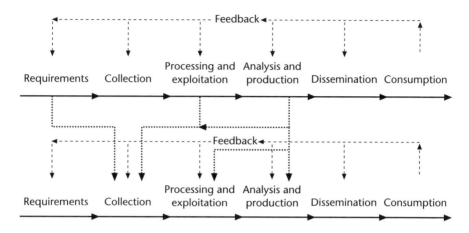

KEY TERMS

ad hocs
analysis and production
collection
consumption
dissemination
downstream activities

feedback
footnote wars
priority creep
processing and exploitation
requirements
tyranny of the ad hocs

FURTHER READINGS

The intelligence process in the United States has become so routinized in its basic steps and forms that it is not often written about analytically as an organic whole. These readings are among the few that attempt to examine the process on some broader basis.

Central Intelligence Agency. *A Consumer's Handbook to Intelligence.* Langley, Va.: CIA, 1993.

Johnson, Loch. "Decision Costs in the Intelligence Cycle." In *Intelligence: Policy and Process.* Ed. Alfred C. Maurer and others. Boulder, Colo.: Westview Press, 1985.

———. "Making the Intelligence 'Cycle' Work." *International Journal of Intelligence and Counterintelligence* 1 (winter 1986–1987).

Krizan, Liza. *Intelligence Essentials for Everyone.* Joint Military Intelligence College, Occasional Paper No. 6. Washington, D.C.: Government Printing Office, 1999.

Chapter 5

Collection and the Collection Disciplines

Collection is the bedrock of intelligence. Intelligence collection has been written about since the biblical references to spies in the Book of Joshua. Without collection, intelligence is little more than guesswork—perhaps educated guesswork, but guesswork nonetheless. The United States and several other nations use multiple means of collecting the intelligence they require. The means are driven by two factors: the nature of the intelligence being sought and the ability to acquire it in various ways. In the United States the means of collecting intelligence are sometimes referred to as **collection disciplines** or INTs. This chapter discusses the overarching themes that affect all means of collection, then addresses what the various INTs provide as well as their strengths and weaknesses.

Primarily in the military, collection is sometimes spoken of as ISR: intelligence, surveillance, and reconnaissance. The term covers three different types of activities.

1. Intelligence: a general term for collection
2. Surveillance: the systematic observation of a targeted area or group, usually for an extended period of time
3. Reconnaissance: a mission to acquire information about a target, sometimes meaning a one-time endeavor

OVERARCHING THEMES

Several themes or issues cut across the collection disciplines and tend to drive many of the debates and decisions on intelligence collection. These themes point out that collection involves more than the questions of "What can be collected?" or "Should that be collected?" Collection is a highly complex government activity that requires numerous decisions and has many stress points.

BUDGET. Technical collection systems, many of which are based on satellites, are very expensive. The systems and programs are a major expenditure within the U.S. intelligence budget. Thus, costs always constrain the ability to operate a large number of collection systems at the same time. Moreover, because different types of satellites are employed for different types of collection (imagery versus signals, for example), policy makers have to make difficult trade-offs. Significant costs are also associated with launching satellites. The larger the satellite, the larger the rocket required to put it into orbit. Finally, the costs of processing and exploitation (P&E), without which collection is meaningless, should be factored into the total expense. Builders of collection systems often ignore P&E as part of their estimates for collection.

During the cold war, cost issues for technical collection rarely surfaced. The sense of threat, coupled with the fact that no better way existed to collect intelligence on the Soviet Union, tended to support the high costs of the systems. Also, decision makers placed greater emphasis on collection systems than on the processing and exploitation needed to deal with the intelligence collected. In the immediate post–cold war period, given the absence of any large and potentially overwhelming threat, collection costs became more vulnerable politically. The terrorist attacks in 2001 raised further questions about the utility of these systems, as terrorist targets are less susceptible to collection via technical means and may require greater use of human intelligence.

The budget is also important because it is a major means by which Congress influences and even controls intelligence activities. Congress tended to be supportive of collection requirements throughout the cold war, but it was also inclined to support the disparity between collection and the less-favored processing and exploitation. Some changes began to appear in the mid-1990s. The House Intelligence Committee, for example, advocated the use of some smaller imagery satellites, both to have greater flexibility and to save on building and launching costs. This committee also tried to redress the collection and P&E balance, emphasizing the importance of TPEDs (tasking, processing, exploitation, and dissemination). However, the TPEDs problem remains and may grow worse as new collection systems are launched, as they will have increased collection capabilities.

LONG LEAD TIMES. All technical collection systems are extremely complex. They have to be able to collect the desired data, perhaps store it, and then send it to a remote location where it can be processed. All systems have to be rugged enough to endure difficult conditions, whether Earth-bound or space-based, although those in space face more austere challenges. No matter how satisfactory current collection capabilities are, there are several impetuses to build new systems: to improve collection capabilities, to take advantage of new technologies, and to respond to changing intelligence priorities.

The technological challenges alone are daunting and are a significant factor in the time required to build and launch a new system. From the point that a decision is made to the actual launch can be as much as ten to fifteen years. Reaching the decision to build a new system involves additional time (sometimes several years) as intelligence agencies and their policy customers debate which intelligence needs should take priority, which technologies should be pursued, and what trade-offs should be made among competing systems in an always constrained budget.

The net result of the lead times involved (not even counting for the decision time) is that, when a system is launched, its technology may be dated and a whole new set of intelligence priorities may have emerged that the system was not designed to address. There are no shortcuts in system development if a commitment has been made to improving capabilities on a regular basis, which remains the best choice.

COLLECTION SYNERGY. One of the major advantages of having multiple means of collection is that one system or discipline can provide tips or clues that can be further collected against by other systems. For major requirements, more than one type of collection is used; the collectors are designed to be cooperative when the system is working correctly. The goal of the U.S. intelligence community is to produce **all-source intelligence**, or fusion intelligence, that is, intelligence based on as many collection sources as possible to compensate for the shortcomings of each and to profit from their combined strength. The director of national intelligence (DNI) is responsible for ensuring that "finished intelligence [is] based upon all sources of available intelligence." This is a somewhat odd provision, akin to a DNI collection seal of approval. It is also ambiguous, as it can be interpreted to mean all sources that should be brought to bear on an issue or all the sources that are available, taking into account other priorities as well. All-source intelligence reflects collection in depth. At the same time, the diverse array allows collection managers to increase collection in breadth, that is, to increase the number of issues being covered, albeit with less depth for a particular issue.

An excellent example of collection synergy is the Cuban Missile Crisis of 1962. Although analysts were slow to understand that Soviet premier Nikita Khrushchev was willing to make such a risky move as deploying medium- and intermediate-range missiles in Cuba, the intelligence community brought a variety of collection means to bear. Anti–Fidel Castro Cubans still on the island provided some of the first reliable evidence that missiles were being deployed. A human source provided the data that targeted the U-2 flights over a trapezoid-shaped area bounded by four towns in western Cuba. Imagery then provided crucial intelligence about the status of the missile sites and the approximate time before completion, as did Soviet technical manuals turned over to the United States by Soviet colonel Oleg Penkovsky, a spy in the employ of the United States and Britain. Imagery and naval units gave the locations of Soviet ships bringing the missiles to the almost-completed sites. Finally, Penkovsky provided the United States with excellent authoritative information on the state of Soviet strategic forces, which indicated overwhelming U.S. superiority.

THE VACUUM CLEANER PROBLEM. Those familiar with U.S. technical collection systems often note that they are vacuum cleaners, not microscopes. Collectors sweep up a great deal of information, within which may be the intelligence being sought. This problem is sometimes referred to as **wheat versus chaff**. Roberta Wohlstetter, in her classic study *Pearl Harbor: Warning and Decision,* refers to the problem as **noise versus signals**, noting that the signals one wishes to receive and to know are often embedded in a great deal of surrounding noise.

No matter which metaphor one uses, the issue is the same: Technical collection is less than precise. The problem underscores the importance of processing and exploitation.

The issue then becomes how to extract the desired intelligence from the mountain of information. One answer would be to increase the number of analysts who deal with the incoming intelligence, but that raises further demands on the budget. Another possible response, even less palatable, would be to collect less. But, even then, there would be no assurance that the "wheat" remained in the smaller volume still being collected.

THE PROCESSING AND EXPLOITATION IMBALANCE. A large imbalance exists between the amount of images or signals that are collected and the amount that are processed and exploited. This reflects, in part, the sheer amount that is collected. It also reflects years of budget choices by the intelligence community and Congress that have favored new collection systems over improving P&E capabilities. According to the Defense Department, for example, the National Security Agency (NSA) records 650 million events daily, which results in ten thousand reports. Although methodologies are in place to ensure that the most important intelligence is processed and exploited, an important image or message could be overlooked. The Defense Department is considering posting all collected intelligence in a single repository and then processing those items selected by analysts. This would, in theory, ensure that only the intelligence that was needed would be processed and analyzed, but it would also increase the burden on analysts to find the intelligence they needed instead of having it sent to them. The Central Intelligence Agency (CIA) is evaluating technology that would automatically examine digital images or video clips to look for details (such as a car) that are the same as those stored in an imagery library. Neither of these suggestions gets at the central issue—that P&E requires more manpower and more funding if it is to have a better chance of getting the necessary intelligence out of the vast amount of information that is collected.

COMPETING COLLECTION PRIORITIES. Given that the number of collection platforms, or **spies**, is limited, policy makers must make choices among competing collection requirements. They use various systems to set priorities, but some issues inevitably get shorter shrift, or may be ignored altogether, in favor of those that are seen as more pressing.

Both policy makers and the intelligence officers acting on their behalf request increased collection on certain issues. However, their requests are made within a system that is inelastic in terms of both technical and human collectors. Every collection request that is fulfilled means another collection issue or request goes wanting; it is a zero-sum game. That is why a priority system is necessary in the first place. Moreover, the system has little or no surge capacity; few collection systems (airplanes, drones, and ship-based systems) or spies are waiting in reserve for an emergency. Even if additional satellites have already been built, launching them requires a ready rocket of the appropriate size, an available launch pad, and other resources. (The Soviet Union used a different collection model. Soviet satellites lacked the life spans of their U.S. counterparts. During crises, the Soviets supplemented current collection assets with additional, usually short-lived, satellites, which were kept on hand with launch vehicles ready.) Similarly, one does not simply tap a spy and send him off to a new assignment. Cover stories need to be created, along with the inevitable paraphernalia; training may be necessary; and a host of other preparations must be made. Inelasticity of resources makes the priorities system difficult at best.

The shifting—or nonshifting—of collection resources in the face of novel situations or emergencies is always subject to 20/20 hindsight. For example, in May 1998 the newly elected government of India resumed testing nuclear weapons, as it had promised in its election campaign. The U.S. intelligence community had not detected the test preparations. As a result, Director of Central Intelligence (DCI) George J. Tenet (1997–2004) asked retired admiral David Jeremiah to review the intelligence community's performance on this hard-target issue—preventing the proliferation of nuclear weapons.

Jeremiah reported several findings, including the fact that—given the Indian government's avowed intention to test, which required no clandestine collection to learn—intelligence performance could have been better. But he noted that collection assets that might have picked up indications of the impending test were focused on the Korean demilitarized zone (DMZ), at the request of the commander of U.S. forces in Korea. As an NSA director put it, the Korean DMZ was the only place in the world in the late 1990s where someone else could decide if the United States would go to war. Although the Korean DMZ remains a constant concern, for a brief period in 1998, Indian test activities perhaps should have been accorded a higher priority.

COLLECTION SWARM BALL. A major problem that has occurred in managing collection is the phenomenon known as collection **swarm ball**. It refers to the tendency of all collectors or collection agencies to collect on an issue that is deemed to be important, whether or not they brought anything useful to this issue or offered an appropriate type of collection. It is called "swarm ball" as it resembles the tactics of small children playing soccer, in which both teams converge on the ball en masse regardless of their assigned positions. Swarm ball has usually involved high-priority issues. For example, if a high-priority issue was the cyber attack capabilities of a hostile state, little value would be gained by imagery, although imagery collection managers might be tempted to contribute to the issue based solely on its priority. The impetus for swarm ball is clear: It allows collectors to show that they are working on high-value issues, regardless of their contribution, which will be important in the next round of budget allocations.

The solution to swarm ball is twofold. First, agreement must be reached on which INTs are responsible for collecting against specific issues or priorities. Second, the agreement must be rigorously enforced, and agencies must not be penalized for not collecting against issues not suited to them regardless of the issues' importance and must be recognized for concentrating on the issues about which they can collect needed intelligence.

PROTECTING SOURCES AND METHODS. The details of collection capabilities—and even the existence of some capabilities—are among the most highly classified secrets of any state. In U.S. parlance, classification is referred to as the protection of **sources and methods**. It is one of the primary concerns of the entire intelligence community and a task specifically assigned by law to the director of national intelligence.

Several levels of classification are in use, reflecting the sensitivity of the intelligence or intelligence means. *(See box, "Why Classify?")* The security classifications are driven by concerns that the disclosure of capabilities

Why Classify?

Numerous critics of the U.S. classification system have argued—not incorrectly—that classification is used too freely and sometimes for the sake of denying information to others who have a legitimate need for it.

However, a rationale and some sense are behind the way in which classification is intended to be used. Classification derives from the damage that would be done if the information were revealed. Thus, classification related to intelligence collection underscores both the importance of the information and the fragility of its source—something that would be difficult to replace if disclosed.

The most common classification is SECRET (CONFIDENTIAL is rarely used any longer), followed by TOP SECRET. Within TOP SECRET are numerous TOP SECRET/CODEWORD compartments—meaning specific bodies of intelligence based on their sources. Admission to any level of classification or compartment is driven by an individual's certified need to know that specific type of information.

Each classification level is defined; current definitions are found in Executive Order 13292 of March 25, 2003.

• CONFIDENTIAL: information whose unauthorized disclosure "could be expected to cause damage to the national security."

• SECRET: information whose unauthorized disclosure "could be expected to cause serious damage to the national security."

• TOP SECRET: information whose unauthorized disclosure "could be expected to cause exceptionally grave damage to the national security."

Higher levels of access are useful bureaucratic levers for those who have them in contrast to those who do not.

will allow those nations that are collection targets to take steps to prevent collection, thus effectively negating the collection systems. However, the levels of classification also impose costs, some of which are financial. The physical costs of security—guards, safes, and special means of transmitting intelligence—are high. Added to these is the expense of security checks for individuals who are to be entrusted with classified information (see chap. 7 for details).

Critics maintain that the classification system is sometimes used inappropriately and even promiscuously, classifying material too highly or, in some cases, classifying material that does not deserve to be. Critics are also concerned that the system can be abused to allow the intelligence community to hide mistakes, failures, or even crimes.

Beyond the costs of the classification system and its potential abuse, the need to conceal sources and methods limits the use of intelligence as a policy tool. For example, in the late 1950s Khrushchev broke a nuclear test moratorium and blustered about the Soviet Union's growing strategic nuclear forces. President Dwight D. Eisenhower, bolstered by the first images of the Soviet forces, knew that the United States enjoyed a strong strategic superiority. But, to protect sources and methods, Eisenhower did not reply to Khrushchev's false boasts. What might have been the results if the United States had released some imagery to counter the Soviet claims? Would the release have spurred the Soviets to greater weapons-building efforts? Would it have severely undercut Soviet foreign policy? Would it have affected U.S. intelligence capabilities, even though the Soviets already knew their country was being overflown by satellites and U-2s? These questions are not answerable, but they give a good feel for the nature of the problem.

More recently, the U.S. intelligence community has grown concerned about protecting intelligence sources and methods during post–cold war military operations that involve cooperation with nations that are not U.S. allies. Even among allies the United States employs gradations of intelligence sharing, having the deepest such relationship with Britain, followed closely by Australia and Canada. Intelligence relations with other North Atlantic Treaty Organization (NATO) allies are close, albeit less so than with the "Commonwealth cousins." But some recent operations, such as in Bosnia, have involved military operations with nations that are viewed with lingering suspicion, such as Russia and Ukraine. In these cases the need to protect intelligence sources and methods must be balanced against the need to share intelligence—not only for the sake of the operation but also to ensure that military partners in the operation are not put in a position where their actions or inactions prove to be dangerous to U.S. troops.

Another intelligence sharing issue arose in 2002–2003, in the months prior to Operation Iraqi Freedom. The United States and Britain said they would provide intelligence on Iraqi weapon of mass destruction (WMD) activities to United Nations (UN) inspectors but not necessarily all available intelligence. Some controversy arose after DCI Tenet said the United States was cooperating fully but the CIA later revealed that it had shared intelligence on 84 of 105 suspected priority weapons sites, which some members of Congress felt was not what they had understood to be the agreed level of intelligence sharing.

LIMITATIONS OF SATELLITES. All satellites are limited by the laws of physics. Most orbiting systems can spend only a limited time over any target. On each successive orbit the satellites shift to a slightly different coverage pattern. (Satellites correspond to the motion of the earth, as they are trapped within Earth's gravitational pull. Thus, satellites' orbits move from west to east with each pass.) Moreover, satellites travel in pre-dictable orbits. Potential targets of a satellite can derive the orbit from basic knowledge about its launch and initial orbit. For a variety of rea-sons, some individuals and organizations attempt to publicize this infor-mation. This enables nations to take steps to avoid collection—in part by engaging in activities they wish to keep secret only when satellites are not overhead.

Satellites that are in **geosynchronous orbit** stay over the same spot on Earth at all times. But to do this they must be twenty-two thousand miles above Earth. The great distance between the collectors and their tar-gets raises the problem of transmitting collected information back to Earth. Collection can be precise only up to a point, thus explaining the vacuum cleaner problem. Satellites can also be flown in **sun-synchronous orbits,** that is, moving in harmony with the earth's rotation so as to always remain where there is daylight, but this produces an easily tracked orbit. Sun-synchronous orbit is better for commercial satellites than for national imagery satellites.

THE STOVEPIPES PROBLEM. Intelligence practitioners often refer to col-lection "stovepipes." This term refers to two characteristics of intelligence collection. First, all of the technical collection disciplines—imagery (IMINT), signals intelligence (SIGINT), and measurement and signa-tures intelligence (MASINT)—and the nontechnical human intelligence (HUMINT), or **espionage,** have end-to-end processes, from collection through dissemination. (Open-source intelligence—OSINT—does not.) Thus, a pipeline forms from beginning to end. Second, the collection dis-ciplines are separate from one another and are often competitors. The INTs sometimes vie with one another to respond to requests for intelligence— largely as a means of assuring continuing funding levels—regardless of which INT is best suited to provide the required intelligence. Often, sev-eral INTs respond, regardless of their applicability to the problem, thus creating the swarm ball. Within the U.S. intelligence system, a variety of positions and fora has been designed to coordinate the INTs, but no single individual exercises ultimate control over all of them. During testimony about the 2004 intelligence legislation, some of the tension between the DCI and the Department of Defense over control of the National Geospatial-Intelligence Agency (NGA) and NSA was evident. These are, as the names indicate, national intelligence agencies and come under the DNI (or the DCI at the time of the hearings). But NGA and NSA are also Defense Department agencies and are designated as combat support agencies, thus indicating a degree of control by the secretary of defense as well. The leg-islation creating the DNI does not clarify this situation. The stovepipes are therefore complete but individual and separate processes.

Intelligence officers also sometimes talk about the "stovepipes within the stovepipes." Within specific collection disciplines, separate programs and processes likely work somewhat independently of one another and do not have insights into one another's operations, but they have an aggregate competitive effect that influences a particular INT. This is, in part, the natural result of the compartmentation of various programs for the sake of security, but it further exacerbates the stovepipes issue.

The stovepipes problem clearly runs counter to the desire to achieve high levels of synergy among the different INTs.

THE OPACITY OF INTELLIGENCE. One of the stated goals or ideals of the U.S. intelligence process is to have analysis-driven collection. This is a shorthand way of recognizing that collection priorities should reflect the intelligence needs of those crafting the analysis. It further reflects the expectation, occasionally misplaced, that analysts have received a sense of the priorities from policy makers. In reality, however, the collection and analytical communities do not operate as closely as this ideal would imply. One of the most striking aspects of this separation is the view held by many analysts, including veteran ones, that the collection system is a black box into which they have little insight. Analysts say that they have no real sense of how collection-tasking decisions are made, what gets collected for which reasons, or how they receive their intelligence. To many analysts, the collection process is something of a mystery. This could simply be dismissed as the failure of one professional group to understand the methods of another group. But the divide goes to the heart of collection, often leaving analysts believing that they have no influence on collection and that whatever sources they do get are somewhat random and fortuitous. This view is also significant in that the intelligence community spends a substantial amount of time educating analysts about collection, with little apparent return on the investment. This perceived opacity of collection also undercuts the goal of having analysis drive collection. It is difficult to know how to task a system that one does not fully understand.

DENIAL AND DECEPTION. In an obverse of the problem in which a target uses knowledge about the collection capabilities of an opponent to avoid collection (known as **denial**), the target can use the same knowledge to transmit information to a collector. This information can be either true or false (if the latter, it is called **deception**). For example, a nation can display an array of weapons as a means of deterring attack. Such a display may reveal actual capabilities or may be staged to present a false image of strength. A classic example was when the Soviet Union sent its limited number of strategic bombers in large loops around Moscow during parades so they could be repeatedly counted by U.S. personnel in

attendance, thus inflating Soviet air strength. The use of decoys or dummies to fool imagery, or false communications to fool SIGINT, also falls
into this category. In World War II, the Allies exploited these techniques
prior to D-Day to raise German concerns about an invasion in the Pas de
Calais instead of Normandy. The Allies created a nonexistent invasion
force, replete with inflatable dummy tanks and streams of false radio traffic, all under the supposed command of Gen. George S. Patton.

The intelligence community has devoted ever-increasing resources to
the issue of denial and deception, also known as D&D. Intelligence officials
seek to know which nations are practicing D&D, determine how they may
have obtained the intelligence that made D&D possible, and then seek to
design countermeasures to circumvent D&D. As more information about
U.S. intelligence sources and methods becomes publicly available, D&D is
an increasing constraint on collection.

However, D&D is also a complex analytical issue and must be
approached carefully. Assume, for example, that a potentially hostile state,
which has practiced D&D, is believed to be fielding a new weapons system. Collectors are tasked to find it, if possible, but they cannot. Why? Is
it a case of D&D or is there no system to find? One cannot simply assume
that failed collection is a result of D&D. The completely innocent state
and the state with very good D&D both look identical to the observer.
Thus, within D&D analysis lies the potential pitfall of self-deception.
(One intelligence community wag put it this way: "We have never discovered a successful deception activity.")

RECONNAISSANCE IN THE POST–COLD WAR WORLD. The U.S. collec-
tion array was largely built to respond to the difficulties of penetrating the
Soviet target, a closed society with a vast land mass, frequent bad weather,
and a long-standing tradition of secrecy and deception. At the same time,
the primary targets of interest—military capabilities—existed in extensive
and well-defined bases with a large supporting infrastructure and exercised with great regularity, thus alleviating the problem to some extent.

Does the United States require the same extensive array of collection
systems to deal with post–cold war intelligence issues? On the one hand,
the threat to the United States has lessened. On the other hand, intelligence targets are more diffuse and more geographically disparate than
before. Also, some of the leading intelligence issues—the so-called
transnational issues such as narcotics, terrorism, and crime—may be less
susceptible to the technical collection capabilities built to deal with the
Soviet Union or other classic political-military intelligence problems.
Many of the current collection targets are nonstate actors with no fixed
geographic location and no vast infrastructure that offers collection
opportunities. These transnational issues may require greater human

intelligence, albeit in geographic regions where the United States has fewer capabilities.

Overhead imagery capabilities have gone commercial. *IKONOS, LANDSAT, SPOT,* and other satellites have ended the U.S. and Russian monopoly on overhead imagery. Any nation—or transnational group—can order imagery from commercial vendors. They may even do so through false fronts to mask their identity. This commercial capability remains so new that its implications have not been completely thought out by those building the commercial systems and by intelligence agencies. On the positive side, commercial imagery offers opportunities, freeing classified collection systems for the truly hard targets. On the negative side, it may offer hostile states or terrorists access to useful imagery via false fronts—buyers who serve to mask the ultimate users of the imagery. **Shutter control** (that is, who controls what the satellites will photograph) is already an issue between those in the U.S. government who seek to limit photography of Israel and those who own the satellites. Dramatic changes occurred in the U.S. use of commercial imagery during the Afghanistan campaign (2001–), affecting each of these issues and perhaps suggesting a new relationship between the intelligence community and these commercial providers.

Finally, open-source information is growing rapidly. The collapse of a number of closed, Soviet-dominated societies drastically reduced the **denied targets** area. One intelligence veteran observed that during the cold war 80 percent of the information about the Soviet Union was secret and 20 percent was open, but in the post–cold war period the ratio had more than reversed for Russia. Theoretically, the greater availability of open-source intelligence should make the intelligence community's job easier. However, this community was created to collect secrets; collecting open-source information is not a wholly analogous activity. The intelligence community has had difficulties assimilating open-source information into its collection stream. Moreover, the intelligence community harbors some institutional prejudice against open-source intelligence, as it seems to run counter to the purposes for which the intelligence community was created. (The World War II Office of Strategic Services had an overt branch—Research and Analysis—but it had little influence on the operations of the postwar intelligence community.)

STRENGTHS AND WEAKNESSES

Each of the collection disciplines has strengths and weaknesses. But when evaluating them—especially the weaknesses—it is important to remember that the goal is to involve as many collection disciplines as possible on the major issues. This should allow the collectors to gain advantages from mutual reinforcement and from individual capabilities that can compensate for shortcomings in the others.

IMAGERY. IMINT, also referred to as PHOTINT (photo intelligence), is a direct descendant of the brief practice of sending soldiers up in balloons during the U.S. Civil War (1861–1865). In World War I (1914–1918) and World War II (1939–1945), both sides used airplanes to obtain photos. Airplanes are still employed, but several nations now utilize imagery satellites. In the United States, the National Reconnaissance Office (NRO) develops these satellites. The National Geospatial-Intelligence Agency (which was the National Imagery and Mapping Agency, NIMA, until 2003) is responsible for processing and exploiting imagery. Some imagery also comes via the Defense Department's airborne systems, such as unmanned aerial vehicles (UAVs), or drones.

NGA prefers the term *geospatial intelligence,* or GEOINT, to *imagery.* NGA defines GEOINT as "information about any object—natural or manmade—that can be observed or referenced to the Earth, and has national security implications." For example, an image of a city includes natural objects (rivers, lakes, and so on) and man-made objects (buildings, roads, bridges, and so on) and can have overlaid on it utility lines, transport lines, and so on. Thus, a more complete picture is drawn that may be of greater intelligence value.

The term *imagery* is somewhat misleading in that it is generally considered to be a picture produced by an optical system akin to a camera. Some imagery is produced by optical systems, usually referred to as electro-optical (EO) systems. Early satellites contained film that was jettisoned in capsules and subsequently recovered. Modern satellites transmit their images as signals, or data streams, that are received and reconstructed as images.

Infrared imagery (IR) produces an image based on the heat reflected by the surfaces being recorded. IR provides the ability to detect warm objects (for example, engines on tanks or planes inside hangars). Imagery can also be produced by radar, which has the ability to see through cloud cover. Some systems, referred to as multispectral or hyperspectral imagery (MSI and HSI, respectively), derive images from spectral analysis. These images are not photographic per se but are built by reflections from several bands across the spectrum of light, some visible, some invisible. They are usually referred to as measurement and signatures intelligence (MASINT).

The level of detail provided by imagery is called **resolution.** Resolution refers to the smallest object that can be distinguished in an image, expressed in size. Designers of imagery systems must make a trade-off between the resolution and the size of the scene being imaged. The better the resolution, the smaller the scene. The degree of resolution that analysts desire depends on the nature of the target and the type of intelligence that is being sought. For example, one-meter resolution allows fairly detailed analysis of man-made objects or subtle changes to terrain. Ten-meter resolution loses some detail but allows the identification of buildings by type or the surveillance of large installations and associated activity. Twenty- to thirty-meter resolution covers a much larger area but allows the identification of large complexes such as airports, factories, and bases. Thus, the degree of resolution has to be appropriate to the analyst's need. Sometimes high resolution is the correct choice; sometimes it is not.

During the cold war it was often popular to refer to the ability to "read the license plates in the Kremlin parking lot"—a wholly irrelevant parameter. Different collection needs have different resolution requirements. For example, keeping track of large-scale troop deployments requires much less detail than tracking the shipment of military weapons. The U.S. intelligence community developed the science of crateology, by which analysts were able to track Soviet arms shipments based on the size and shape of crates being loaded or unloaded from Soviet-bloc cargo vessels. (This analytical practice was subject to deception simply by purposely using misleadingly sized crates to mask the nature of the shipments.)

Several press accounts say that U.S. satellites now have resolutions of ten inches. Commercial imagery is available at a resolution of 0.5 meter (or just under twenty inches), meaning that an object half a meter in size can be distinguished in an image. (By agreement with the U.S. government, commercial vendors are subject to a twenty-four-hour delay from the time of collection before they can release any imagery with a resolution better than 0.82 meter, or just over thirty-two inches.)

Imagery offers a number of advantages over other collection means. First, it is sometimes graphic and compelling. When shown to policy makers, an easily interpreted image can be worth the proverbial thousand words. Second, imagery is easily understood much of the time by policy makers. Even though few of them, if any, are trained imagery analysts, all are accustomed to seeing and interpreting images. From family photos to newspapers, magazines, and news broadcasts, policy makers, like many people, spend a considerable part of their day not only looking at images but also interpreting them. Imagery is also easy to use with policy makers in that little or no interpretation is necessary as to how it was acquired. Although the method by which images are taken from space, transmitted to Earth, and processed is more complex than using a 35mm camera, policy clients are sufficiently informed to trust it and take it for granted.

These satellite photos of San Diego, California, illustrate differences in resolution. (Resolution numbers indicate the size of the smallest identifiable object.) They also show recent advances in commercial satellite imagery. The top photo has 25-meter (75 feet) resolution; major landforms—the hills and Mission Bay—are identifiable at lower center. Larger manmade objects—piers, highways, runways at North Island U.S. Naval Air Station—can be seen on the peninsula to the right.

At 5-meter (15 feet) resolution, clarity improves dramatically. North Island and San Diego International Airport are visible, as are rows of boats in the marinas and wakes of boats in the bay. Taller buildings in downtown San Diego can be seen at upper center. Shadows indicate this image was taken in mid- to late morning.

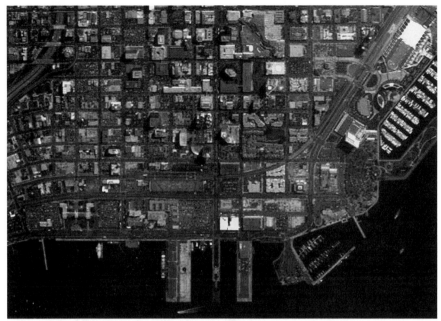

At 4-meter resolution (12 feet), individual buildings and streets can be seen, along with each boat in the marinas. At the bottom, a cruise ship is docked at the terminal. Individual cars can be seen in the parking lot above the piers.

At 1-meter (39 inch) resolution, each building stands out. Individual cars are seen in parking lots and streets. Railroad tracks are visible on a diagonal at the top right, as are paths and small groups of trees in the Embarcadero Marine Park, just below the marina at the upper right. Photos courtesy of Space Imaging, Inc.

Another advantage of imagery is that many of the targets make themselves available. Military exercises in most nations are conducted on regular cycles and at predictable locations, making them highly susceptible to IMINT. Finally, an image of a certain site often provides information not just about one activity but some ancillary ones as well. A distinction must be made, though, between these military targets, which are familiar to the intelligence community, and the challenges posed by terrorism. In brief, terrorism presents a smaller imagery target. Although training camps may have been set up, as was the case of al Qaeda in Afghanistan, terrorist cells or networks are far smaller, less elaborate, and have less visible infrastructure than do the traditional political-military targets.

Imagery also suffers from a number of problems. The graphic quality that is an advantage is also a disadvantage. An image can be too compelling, leading to hasty or ill-formed decisions or to the exclusion of other, more subtle intelligence that is contradictory. Also, the intelligence on an image may not be self-evident; it may require interpretation by trained photo interpreters who can see things that the untrained person cannot. At times, the policy makers must take on faith that the skilled analysts are correct. (*See box, "The Need for Photo Interpreters."*)

Another disadvantage of imagery is that it is only a snapshot, a picture of a particular place at a particular time. This is sometimes referred to as the "where and when" phenomenon. Imagery is a static piece of intelligence, revealing something about where and when it was taken but nothing about what happened before or after. Analysts perform a **negation search**, looking at past imagery to determine when an activity commenced. This can be done by computers comparing images, in a process called **automatic change extraction**. The site can be revisited to watch for further activity. But a single image does not reveal everything.

Because details about U.S. imagery capabilities have become better known, states can take steps to deceive collection—through the use of camouflage or dummies—or to preclude collection by conducting certain activities at times when they are unlikely or less likely to be observed.

The war against terrorism led to two major developments in the use of imagery. First, the government greatly expanded its use of commercial imagery. In October 2001, NGA (then known as NIMA) bought exclusive and perpetual rights to all imagery of Afghanistan taken by the *IKONOS* satellite, operated by the Space Imaging Company. This satellite has a resolution of 0.8 meter. The agency's actions expanded the overall collection capability of the United States and allowed it to reserve more sophisticated imagery capabilities for those areas where they were most needed, while *IKONOS* took up other collection tasks. The use of this commercial imagery also makes it easier for the United States to share imagery with other nations or the public without revealing classified capabilities. At the same time, foreign governments that may be hostile to the United States or may see the Afghanistan campaign as a means of gauging U.S. military capabilities were denied access to imagery. The purchase also denied the use of this commercial imagery to news media, which might be eager to use it as a means of reporting on and assessing the conduct and success of the war.

An ancillary effect of the purchase of commercial imagery was to circumvent the shutter control issue. The United States can impose shutter control over commercial satellites operated by U.S. companies for reasons of national security. Concerns arose that civil liberties groups or the news media would mount a legal challenge to an assertion of shutter control, the outcome of which was uncertain. By simply purchasing the imagery, NIMA avoided the entire issue. (The French Ministry of Defense banned the sale of *SPOT* images of the Afghan war zone. *SPOT* has a ten-meter resolution.)

Increased use of commercial imagery to support intelligence has become official U.S. intelligence policy. In June 2002, DCI George Tenet ordered that commercial imagery would be "the primary source of data for government mapping," with government satellites to be used for this purpose only in "exceptional circumstances." Tenet had two goals: to reserve higher resolution satellites for collection tasks more demanding than map making and to provide a base for a continuing U.S. commercial satellite capability. This policy was expanded in April 2003, when President George W. Bush signed a directive stating that the United States would rely on commercial imagery "to the maximum practical extent" for a wider range of requirements: "military, intelligence, foreign policy, homeland security and civil uses." Again, U.S. government systems are to be reserved for the more demanding collection tasks.

In addition to shutter control, the U.S. government reserves the right to limit collection and dissemination of commercial imagery. (The secretary of commerce regulates and licenses the U.S. commercial imagery industry. The secretaries of state and defense determine policy with regard to protecting national security and foreign policy concerns.) The new policy also allows the use of foreign commercial imagery. NGA's current contracts with commercial imagery firms call for 0.5 meter resolution (1.6 feet) by 2006. One U.S. company has applied to the Department of Commerce for a 0.25 meter (less than ten inches) resolution.

A second major imagery development has centered on unmanned aerial vehicles (UAVs). The use of pilotless drones for imagery is not new, but their role and capability have expanded greatly. UAVs offer two clear advantages over satellites and manned aircraft. First, unlike satellites, they can fly closer to areas of interest and loiter over them instead of making

The Need for Photo Interpreters

Two incidents underscore the difficulty of interpreting even not-so-subtle images.

A sign of planned Soviet missile deployments in Cuba in 1962 was an image of a peculiar road pattern called "the Star of David" because of its resemblance to that religious symbol. To the untrained eye it looked like an odd road interchange, but trained U.S. photo interpreters recognized it as a pattern they had seen before—in Soviet missile fields. Without explaining the image, and perhaps without showing photos of Soviet missile fields, interpreters could have faced ridicule from policy makers.

In the late 1970s and early 1980s, when Cuba was sending expeditionary forces to various parts of the Third World, newly constructed baseball fields indicated their arrival. To understand the significance of these fields, policy makers need to know that Cuban troops play baseball for recreation. Interpreters would have to supply supporting analysis, perhaps a note explaining how serious Cubans take baseball, to avoid being dismissed out of hand. New fields, in this case, could have meant large troop concentrations.

a high-altitude orbital pass. Second, unlike manned aircraft, UAVs do not put lives at risk, particularly from surface-to-air missiles (SAMs). Not only are UAVs unmanned, but operators also can be safely located great distances (even thousands of miles) from the area of operation, linked to the UAV by satellite. A third advantage is that the UAVs produce real-time images—they carry high-definition television and infrared cameras—that is, video images are immediately available for use instead of having to be processed and exploited first.

The United States currently relies on two UAVs, the Predator and the Global Hawk. Predator operates at up to twenty-five thousand feet, flying at the relatively slow speeds of 84 to 140 miles per hour. It can be based as far as 450 miles from a target and operate over the target for sixteen to twenty-four hours. Predator provides real-time imagery and has been mated with air-to-ground missiles, allowing immediate attacks on identified targets instead of having to relay the information to nearby air or ground units. In the war on terrorism, Predators have been armed with Hellfire missiles, which are guided to the target by a laser. Thus, once a target has been located and identified, no time is lost in calling in an airstrike. The Predator was used in this manner against al Qaeda terrorists in Yemen. Global Hawk operates at up to sixty-five thousand feet at a speed of up to four hundred miles per hour. It can be based three thousand miles from the target and can operate over the target for twenty-four

The famous "Star of David" photo of a Soviet air defense site in Cuba, 1962. The unique road pattern, previously seen only in the USSR, helped alert U.S. analysts to the pending Soviet missile deployment. Photo courtesy of the Central Intelligence Agency.

hours. Global Hawk is designed to conduct both broad area and continuous spot coverage.

In 2005 Secretary of Defense Donald H. Rumsfeld talked about building fifteen Predator squadrons (twelve UAVs per squadron) over the next five years, emphasizing both the intelligence collection and the hunter killer missions in which the UAVs carry missiles as well.

A growing number of much smaller UAVs (some weighing as little as two kg. or 4.5 lbs.) can be carried and launched by individuals. These UAVs (sometimes called TUAVs—tactical UAVs) have smaller operating ranges and shorter flight times but are useful for tactical intelligence collection. Some UAV advocates have shown interest in stealth UAVs that could begin collection close to a presumed enemy prior to hostilities without detection. Critics argue that overflights of territory by UAVs would be precluded prior to hostilities (an incursion violating international law) and that therefore stealth is unnecessary.

The Defense Department is also examining the utility of very small satellites, sometimes referred to as microsatellites (approximately twenty inches high and forty-one inches in diameter). *TacSat-1* (tactical satellite) could be launched as demands for collection increased. Tactical satellites would not have the multiyear orbital lives of the more traditional large satellites and would not carry as large a payload of sensors, but they would provide a more flexible collection array.

The third major imagery development related to the war on terrorism has been the use of NGA imagery platforms on potential terrorist targets within the United States. These have included the 2002 Olympics in Utah, the 2004 political conventions, and other public events that would attract large crowds or locations (such as nuclear power plants) that might be targets. Unlike CIA and NSA, NGA is not restricted in its activity within the United States, although the agency cannot be used for such purposes as supporting law enforcement. Still, various groups that are concerned about intrusive government activities have raised questions about this domestic imagery collection.

Finally, space-based imagery capabilities have proliferated. Once the exclusive preserve of the United States and the Soviet Union, this field has expanded rapidly. France and Israel have independent imagery satellites. India has a nascent capability; China is rapidly developing one and has announced that it is building a national engineering and research center to design small satellites, hoping to produce six to eight annually. China plans on launching more than one hundred satellites by 2020 for a variety of monitoring tasks within China itself—economic, ecological, and others. Germany has decided to create its own satellite capability. Furthermore, cooperation among current and would-be imagery satellite powers has increased. Israel is reported to have cooperative imagery relationships with India, Taiwan, and Turkey. Brazil and China are cooperating on satellites. Perhaps more significant, France is working with several European partners—Belgium, Italy, and Spain—on its next generation of imagery satellites. This independent capability within NATO could prove troublesome, as the United States may have to deal with allies having their own imagery and different interpretations of events. This apparently happened in 1996, when France refused to support a U.S. cruise missile attack on Iraq because the French maintained that their imagery did not show significant Iraqi troop movements into Kurdish areas. France, Germany, and Israel also have indigenous UAV programs. In 2004, Iran admitted supplying eight UAVs to the Hezbollah terrorist group, one of which penetrated Israeli airspace.

Imagery proliferation also has a commercial aspect. A British firm, Surrey Satellite Technology, has pioneered a range of imagery satellites, including nanosatellites and microsatellites weighing as little as 6.5 kilograms, or just over fourteen pounds. These satellites do not approach resolutions of the best national systems, but they are sufficient for many nations' needs. Among the firm's clients are Algeria, Britain, China, Nigeria, and Thailand. These satellites also have the ability to get close to other satellites and image them, which is of concern to the United States because of their potential to be used as anti-satellite (ASAT) weapons. Several nations, including Australia, Malaysia, and South Korea as well as some current Surrey customers, are looking at small satellite demonstration projects.

The proliferation of imagery capabilities could become a problem for the United States should it become engaged in hostilities with a state that has access to space-borne imagery satellites. Therefore, the Defense Department has begun considering countermeasures. One such system, Counter Surveillance Reconnaissance System (CSRS, pronounced "scissors"), would have blinded or dazzled imagery satellites with directed energy. However, Congress refused to fund the program.

SIGNALS INTELLIGENCE. SIGINT is a twentieth-century phenomenon. British intelligence pioneered the field during World War I, successfully intercepting German communications by tapping underwater cables. The most famous product of this work was the Zimmermann Telegram, a German offer to Mexico of an anti-U.S. alliance, which Britain made available to the United States without revealing how it was obtained. With the advent of radio communications, cable taps were augmented by the ability to pluck signals from the air. The United States also developed a successful signals intercept capability that survived World War I. Prior to World War II, the United States broke Japan's Purple code; Britain, via ULTRA, read German codes.

Today, signals intelligence can be gathered by Earth-based collectors—ships, planes, ground sites—or satellites. Again, U.S. SIGINT satellites are built by the NRO. The National Security Agency is responsible for both carrying out U.S. signals intelligence activities and protecting the United States against hostile SIGINT. UAVs, which have been primarily IMINT platforms, are being used for SIGINT as well. Global Hawk will be configured to carry ELINT and COMINT payloads. This enhances the utility of the UAV, as it allows collection synergy between IMINT and SIGINT on a single platform that can be targeted or retargeted during flight. A greatly increased cooperation between SIGINT and IMINT has been a recent development. NSA and NGA created a Geocell, which is jointly manned. This collaboration allows quick handoffs between the two INTs, which can be especially important when tracking fast-moving targets, such as suspected terrorist activities.

As with IMINT, the United States seeks ways to deny enemies their own SIGINT capabilities. Although the CSRS against imagery was not funded, the Defense Department has declared the Counter Communications

System operational. The system temporarily jams communications satellites with radio frequencies.

SIGINT consists of several different types of intercepts. The term is often used to refer to the interception of communications between two parties, which is also known as communications intelligence (COMINT). SIGINT can also refer to the pickup of data relayed by weapons during tests, which is sometimes called telemetry intelligence (TELINT). Finally, SIGINT can refer to the pickup of electronic emissions from modern weapons and tracking systems (military and civil), which are useful means of gauging their capabilities, such as range and frequencies on which systems operate. This is sometimes referred to as electronic intelligence (ELINT).

The ability to intercept communications is highly important, because it gives insight into what is being said, planned, and considered. It comes as close as one can, from a distance, to reading the other side's mind, a goal that cannot be achieved by imagery. Reading the messages and analyzing what they mean is called **content analysis**. Tracking communications also gives a good **indication and warning**. As with imagery, COMINT relies to some degree on the regular behavior of those being watched, especially among military units. Messages may be sent at regular hours or regular intervals, using known frequencies. Changes in those patterns—either increases or decreases—may be indicative of a larger change in activity. Monitoring changes in communications is known as **traffic analysis**, which has more to do with the volume and pattern of communications than it does with the content. (*See box, "SIGINT versus IMINT."*) One other important aspect of COMINT is that it provides both content (what is being said) and what might be called texture, meaning the tone, the choice of words, the accent (such as when distinguishing one type of French- or Spanish- or Arabic-speaker). Texture is like listening to the tone or watching the facial expression of a speaker. This can tell you as much—or sometimes more—as the words.

COMINT has some weaknesses. First and foremost, it depends on the presence of communications that can be intercepted. If the target goes silent or opts to communicate via secure landlines instead of through the air, then the ability to undertake COMINT ceases to exist. Perhaps the landlines can be tapped, but doing so is a more difficult task than remote interception from a ground site or satellite. The target also can begin to **encrypt**—or code—its communications. Within the offensive-defensive struggle over SIGINT is a second struggle, that between encoders and codebreakers, or **cryptographers**. Crypies, as they are known, like to boast that any code that can be constructed can also be solved. But the present-day is far removed from the Elizabethan age of relatively simple ciphers. Computers greatly increase the ability to construct complex, one-

SIGINT versus IMINT

A National Security Agency director once made a distinction between imagery intelligence (IMINT) and signals intelligence (SIGINT): "IMINT tells you what has happened; SIGINT tells you what will happen."

While an exaggeration—and said tongue in cheek—the statement captures an important difference between the two collection disciplines.

time-use codes. Meanwhile, computers also make it more possible to attack these codes. Finally, the target can use false transmissions as a means of creating less compromising patterns or of subsuming important communications amid a flood of meaningless ones—in effect, increasing the ratio of noise to signals.

Another issue is the vast quantity of communications now available: telephones of all sorts, faxes, e-mails, and so on. In 2002, for example, there were some 180 billion minutes of international phone conversations, from some 2.8 billion cellular phones and 1.2 billion fixed phones. Instant messaging, a relatively new medium, generates 530 billion messages daily. As communications switch to fiber optic cable, the available volume will increase. Also, more phone calls are going over the Internet using the Voice-over-Internet-Protocol (VoIP) technology.

Even a focused collection plan collects more COMINT than can be processed and exploited. One means of coping with this is the **key-word search**, in which the collected data are fed into computers that look out for specific words or phrases. The words are used as indicators of the likely value of an intercept. The system is not perfect, but it provides a necessary filter to deal with the flood of collected intelligence. TELINT and ELINT offer valuable information on weapons capabilities that would otherwise be unknown or would require far more risky human intelligence operations to obtain. However, as the United States learned from its efforts to monitor Soviet arms, the weapons tester can employ many techniques to maintain secrecy. Like communications, test data can be encrypted. It can also be encapsulated—that is, recorded within the weapon being tested and released in a self-contained capsule that will be recovered—so that the data are never transmitted as a signal that would be susceptible to interception. If the data are transmitted, they can be sent in a single burst instead of throughout the test, greatly increasing the difficulty of intercepting and reading the data. Or the data can be transmitted via a spread spectrum, that is, using a series of frequencies through which the data move at irregular intervals. The testing nation's receivers can be programmed to match the frequency changes, but such action greatly increases the difficulty of intercepting the full data stream.

One issue that arises in SIGINT, especially in COMINT, is **risk versus take**. This refers to the need to consider the value of the intelligence that is going to be collected (the take) against the risk of discovery—either in political terms or in the collection technology that may then be revealed to another nation.

The war against terrorism has underscored a growing concern for SIGINT. As with the other collection disciplines, SIGINT was developed to collect intelligence on the Soviet Union and other nations. Terrorist cells offer much smaller signatures, which may not be susceptible to interception by remote SIGINT sensors. Therefore, a growing view is that future SIGINT will have to rely on sensors that have been physically placed close to the target by humans. In effect, HUMINT will become the enabler for SIGINT. Signs also are evident that terrorist groups have increasing knowledge about U.S. SIGINT capabilities and therefore take steps to evade SIGINT detection by such means as using cell phones only once or avoiding cell phones and faxes.

Another SIGINT weakness is found within COMINT—foreign language capabilities. During the cold war, the United States emphasized the need for Russian speakers through a series of government-sponsored educational programs. Today, different languages are at issue: Arabic (which has many spoken varieties), Farsi, Pushto, Dari, Hindi, Urdu, and other languages common to the Middle East and South Asia. None of these languages has much academic support in the United States, and they all have the added difficulty of not being written in the Roman alphabet (which is also true of Russian, Chinese, and some six thousand other languages). It takes about three years (full time) to train someone to the desired capability in a non–Roman language. The United States suffers in its language capabilities because of the decline in language requirements in colleges and universities. According to the Modern Language Association, only 8 percent of schools have language requirements, down from 87 percent in the 1950s. The United States, being an immigrant nation, has among its citizens speakers of most languages. But they need to be recruited, cleared, and trained. In some cases, their native language skills are very good but their ability to translate into English, which is the required outcome, is poor. For the foreseeable future, language skills will be a major problem for COMINT and for all intelligence activities.

An important aspect of SIGINT operations for the United States in combating terrorism is the legal issues involved. If the SIGINT target is within the United States, the operation becomes the responsibility of the Federal Bureau of Investigation (FBI), not NSA. To undertake wiretaps in the United States, the FBI must get a court order. Foreign intelligence wiretaps (as opposed to criminal case wiretaps) come under the jurisdiction of the Foreign Intelligence Surveillance Act (FISA) Court, created by the FISA in 1978. This is not a major legal barrier, as the FISA court has reportedly approved 13,164 requests and denied four since its inception.

A controversy involving U.S. and British SIGINT operations arose in 2004. A Government Communications Headquarters employee alleged that NSA had conducted SIGINT at the UN, against Security Council members, during the debates prior to the war against Iraq. Both governments refused to confirm the allegations. The UN, by treaty, is deemed to be inviolate from such activity. At the same time, all nations know that the UN is an excellent intelligence collection target as virtually all nations of the world have missions and representatives there. (See chap. 13 for a fuller discussion.)

MEASUREMENT AND SIGNATURES INTELLIGENCE. TELINT and ELINT are both major contributors to a little-understood branch of intelligence known as measurement and signatures intelligence. MASINT refers to weapons capabilities and industrial activities. Multispectral and hyperspectral imagery also contribute to MASINT.

An arcane debate rages between those who see MASINT as a separate collection discipline and those who see it as simply a product, or even a by-product, of SIGINT and other collection capabilities. For our purposes here, it is sufficient to understand that MASINT exists and that, in a world increasingly concerned about such issues as proliferation of weapons of mass destruction, it is of growing importance. For example, MASINT can help identify the types of gases or waste leaving a factory, which can be important in chemical weapons identification. It can also help identify other specific characteristics (composition, material content) of weapons systems.

MASINT practitioners think of their INT as having six disciplines.

1. Electro-optical: the properties of emitted or reflected energy in the infrared to ultraviolet part of the spectrum, including lasers and various types of light—infrared, polarized, spectral, ultraviolet, and visible

2. Geophysical: the disturbance and anomalies of various physical fields at, or near, the surface of Earth, such as acoustic, gravity, magnetic, and seismic

3. Materials: the composition and identification of gases, liquids, or solids, including chemical-, biological-, and nuclear-related material samples

4. Nuclear radiation: the qualities of gamma rays, neutrons, and x-rays

5. Radar: the properties of radio waves reflected from a target or objects, including various types of radars such as line-of-sight and over-the-horizon and synthetic apertures
6. Radio frequency: the electromagnetic signals generated by an object, either narrow- or wide-band.

MASINT can be used against a wide array of intelligence issues, including WMD development and proliferation, arms control, environmental issues, narcotics, weapons developments, space activities, and denial and deception practices.

MASINT has suffered as a collection discipline because of its relative novelty and its dependence on the other technical INTs for its products. Often analysts or policy makers look at a MASINT product without knowing it. MASINT is a potentially important INT still struggling for recognition. It is also more arcane and requires analysts with more technical training to be able to use it fully. At present, policy makers are less familiar—and probably less comfortable—with it than they are with IMINT or SIGINT. Responsibility for MASINT is shared by the Defense Intelligence Agency (DIA) and NGA; it is not a separate agency. Some of its advocates believe that MASINT will never make a full contribution until it has more bureaucratic clout. Others, even some sympathetic to MASINT, do not believe this INT needs the panoply of a full agency.

HUMAN INTELLIGENCE. HUMINT is espionage—spying—and is sometimes referred to as the world's second-oldest profession. It is as old as the Bible. Joshua sent two spies into Canaan before leading the Jewish people across the Jordan River. Spying is what most people think about when they hear the word "intelligence," whether they conjure up famous spies from history such as Nathan Hale or Mata Hari (both failures) or the fictional spies such as James Bond. In the United States, HUMINT is largely the responsibility of the CIA, through its Directorate of Operations (DO). DIA also has a HUMINT capability with the Defense Humint Service, which it has sought to expand since the war in Afghanistan.

HUMINT largely involves sending agents to foreign countries, where they attempt to recruit foreign nationals to spy. The process of recruiting spies has several steps and a unique vocabulary. The process of managing spies is sometimes referred to as the **agent acquisition cycle**. The cycle has five steps.

1. Targeting or spotting: identifying individuals who have access to the information that the United States may desire
2. Assessing: gaining their confidence and assessing their weaknesses and susceptibility to be recruited; done via the **asset validation system**

3. Recruiting: making a **pitch** to them, suggesting a relationship; a **source** may accept a pitch for a variety of reasons: money, disaffection with their own government, blackmail, or thrills

4. Handling: managing of the asset

5. Termination: ending the relationship for any of several reasons—unreliability, a loss of access to needed intelligence, a change in intelligence requirements, and so on

Another HUMINT term of art is the **developmental,** a potential source who is being brought along—largely through repeated contacts and conversations to assess his value (validation) and susceptibilities—to the point where he can be pitched. Once the pitch has been accepted, the agent must meet with his sources regularly to receive information, holding meetings in a manner and in places that reduce the risk of being caught and then transmitting the information back home. The source may rely on sources of his own, known as **sub-sources,** to provide intelligence that he then conveys to the agent.

Diplomatic reporting is a type of HUMINT, although it tends to receive less credibility in some circles because of its overt nature. After all, the foreign government official knows, when speaking to a diplomat, that his remarks are going to be cabled to that diplomat's capital. An espionage source is likely to be thinking the same thing. Nonetheless, some people prefer more traditional HUMINT, even if the source's reliability remains uncertain, rather than diplomatic reporting.

HUMINT requires time to be developed. Agents need to learn a variety of skills (foreign languages, evasion techniques, recruiting skills and other aspects of HUMINT tradecraft, the ability to handle various types of communications equipment, weapons training, and so on). Like all other professions, it takes time to become adept. In the case of HUMINT agents, it takes up to seven years according to some accounts.

In addition to gaining the skills required for this activity, agents have to maintain their cover stories—the overt lives that give them a plausible reason for being in that foreign nation. There are two types of cover: official and nonofficial. Agents with **official cover** hold another government job, usually posted at the embassy. Official cover makes it easier for the agent to maintain contact with her superiors but raises the risk of being suspected as an agent. Nonofficial cover (NOC, pronounced "knock") avoids any overt connection between the agent and her government but can make it more difficult to keep in contact. NOCs need a full-time job that explains their presence; they cannot make contact with superiors or colleagues overtly. (This led to a bureaucratic problem for the CIA in that NOCs had to at least appear to be paid at a level commensurate with their cover job, which was sometimes higher than their government salary.

This then raised the issue of being liable for taxes higher than their actual salary. Congress authorized the CIA to pay NOCs "in a manner consistent with their cover.")

For the CIA, at least, some limits exist on the jobs that NOCs can hold. Clergy and Peace Corps volunteers are both off-limits. Journalism is an ideal cover for a NOC, as journalists have a plausible reason for being in a foreign country, for seeking out officials, and for asking questions. However, professional journalists have long protested any such use of cover, arguing that if one spy posing as a journalist were to be unmasked, then all journalists would be suspect and perhaps in danger. Proponents counter that journalism is a profession like any other and should be available for use. All told, the use of NOCs is more complex than is official cover for spies.

Some HUMINT sources volunteer. They are called **walk-ins**. Spies Oleg Penkovsky of the Soviet Union, Aldrich Ames of the CIA, and Robert Hanssen of the FBI were all walk-ins. Walk-ins raise a host of other issues: Why have they volunteered? Do they really have access to valuable intelligence? Are they real volunteers or a means of entrapment—called **dangles**? Dangles can be used for a number of purposes, including identifying hostile intelligence personnel or gaining insights into the intelligence requirements or methods of a hostile service. According to press accounts reporting on the investigation led by former FBI director and DCI (1987–1991) William H. Webster, the Soviet Union suspected that Hanssen was a dangle and protested to the United States. The United States denied the charge but did not follow up.

In addition to recruiting foreign nationals, HUMINT agents may undertake more direct spying, such as stealing documents or planting sensors. Some of their information may come through direct observation of activity. Thus, HUMINT involves more than just espionage.

An important adjunct to one's own country's HUMINT capabilities are those of allied or friendly services. Known as foreign liaison relationships, they offer several important advantages. First, the friendly service has greater familiarity with its own region. Second, its government may maintain a different pattern of relations with other states, more friendly in some cases or even having diplomatic relations where one's own government does not. These HUMINT-to-HUMINT relationships are somewhat formal in nature and tend to be symbiotic. They also entail risks, as one can never be entirely sure of the liaison partner's security procedures. Thus, there are different degrees of liaison, depending on past experience, shared needs, the sense of security engendered, the depth and value of the intelligence being shared, and so forth. Furthermore, some liaison relationships may be with intelligence services that do not have the same standards in terms of operational limits, acceptable activities, and other criteria. A choice therefore has to be made between the value of the information being sought or exchanged and the larger question of the propriety of a relationship with this service. Nevertheless, liaison is an important means of increasing the breadth and depth of available HUMINT.

Foreign intelligence liaison is carried out on an agency-by-agency basis instead of by the intelligence community as a whole. CIA, DIA, NGA, and NSA, for example, create and conduct their own liaison relationships, which does raise questions about the possible need for better coordination to avoid duplication. Thus, the stovepipes problem carries over into foreign liaison. This may prove to be a problem for the DNI who is charged with overseeing the coordination of these relationships.

In the war against terrorism, several nations have apparently offered intelligence support to the United States, including some whose services may be considered occasionally hostile. These types of liaison relationships call for extra caution regarding intelligence sharing, and questions may arise about the depth and detail of the intelligence received. However, exchanging useful intelligence is a good way for nations to build confidence in one another. For example, according to press accounts, Russian officers placed nuclear detection equipment in North Korea at the request of the United States to help track possible nuclear developments.

Espionage provides a small part of the intelligence that is collected. IMINT and SIGINT produce a greater volume of intelligence. But HUMINT, like SIGINT, has the major advantage of affording access to what is being said, planned, and thought. Moreover, clandestine human access to another government may offer opportunities to influence that government by feeding it false or deceptive information. For intelligence targets in which the technical infrastructure may be irrelevant as a fruitful target—such as terrorism, narcotics, or international crime, where the signature of activities is small—HUMINT may be the only available source.

HUMINT also has disadvantages. First, it cannot be done remotely, as is the case with various types of technical collection. It requires proximity and access and therefore must contend with the counterintelligence capabilities of the other side. It is also far riskier, as it jeopardizes individuals and, if they are caught, could have political ramifications that are less likely to occur with technical collectors.

HUMINT is far less expensive than the various technical collectors, although it still involves costs for training, special equipment, and the accoutrements spies need to build successful cover stories.

Like all the other collection INTs, HUMINT is susceptible to deception. Some critics argue that it is the most susceptible to deception. The bona fides of human sources are always subject to question initially and, in some cases, may never be wholly resolved. Many questions arise and linger. Why is this person offering to pass information—ideology, money, vengeance? She will claim to have good access to valuable information, but how good is it? Is it consistent, or is this a single event? How good is the information? Is this person a dangle, offered as a means of passing information that the other side wants to have passed—either because it is false or because it will have a specific effect? Is this person a double agent who is collecting information on your intelligence agency's HUMINT techniques and capabilities even as she passes information to you?

HUMINT agents must walk a fine line between prudent caution and the possibility that too much caution will lead them to deter or reject a promising source. For example, the United States initially rejected the services of Penkovsky, who then turned to the British, who accepted him. Only later did the United States take on this valuable spy. Deception is particularly difficult to deal with, because people naturally are reluctant to accept that they are being deceived. However, people might slip into a position where they trust no one, which can result in turning away sources who might have been valuable.

HUMINT's unique sources and methods raise another issue. These sources are considered to be extremely fragile, given that good human penetrations take so long to develop and risk the lives of the case officers, their sources, and perhaps even the sources' families. Therefore, the intelligence analysts who receive HUMINT reports may not be told the details of the source or sources. Analysts are not informed, for example, that "this report comes from a first secretary in the Fredonian Foreign Ministry." Instead, the report includes information on the access of the source, the past reliability of the source, or variations on this concept. Sometimes several sources may be blended together in a single report. Although the masking of HUMINT sources promotes their preservation, it may have the unintended effect of devaluing the reports for analysts, who may not fully appreciate the value of the source and the information. This became an issue in the aftermath of the Iraq WMD experience, when it was recognized that some sources had been of questionable reliability and that analysts were not always given as much information as would have been desirable about the nature of some of the HUMINT reporting. It also denies all-source analysts the ability to make an independent judgment of the HUMINT source when compared with the other sources to which they have access. (HUMINT reports come with captions provided by reports officers as to the nature of the source: a reliable source, an untested source, a source with proven access, a source with unknown access, and so on.)

Also, as DCI Richard Helms (1966–1973) observed, most HUMINT sources are recruited for a specific assignment or requirement, based on their access to the desired intelligence. They cannot be assigned from issue to issue as they are extremely unlikely to have access to other intelligence. Helms also believed that spies who no longer had the desired access should not be held in reserve but should be dropped. He said that a well-run station (the base from which agents operate overseas) "does not cling to spent spies." Thus, even successful HUMINT, although extremely valuable, is narrow in focus.

HUMINT also puts one in contact—and perhaps into relationships—with unsavory individuals such as terrorists and narco-traffickers. If one is going to penetrate such groups or develop other types of relationships with them, some may become recipients of money or other forms of payment. These types of relationships raise moral and ethical issues for some people (see chap. 13). In the aftermath of the September 2001 attacks, special attention was given to the so-called Deutch rules about HUMINT recruitment. In 1995, DCI John M. Deutch (1995–1997) ordered a scrub of all HUMINT assets, with a particular focus on persons who in the past had been involved in serious criminal activity or human rights violations. The scrub was the result of revelations that some past CIA assets in Guatemala had violated human rights, including those of some American residents in that country. New rules were promulgated, requiring headquarters approval of any such recruitments in the future. After the terrorist attacks, the rules were widely criticized, with many people asserting that they had limited the CIA's ability to penetrate terrorist groups. CIA officials maintained that no valuable relationship was ever turned down because of the Deutch rules. Critics countered, however, that the very existence of the rules bred timidity in the DO, as officers would be more cautious about whom they recruited, running the risk of losing useful sources, instead of having these recruitments be scrutinized on the basis of changing standards. By the end of 2001, the Deutch rules were no longer considered an operational factor as field stations were told they could be ignored. In July 2002 they were formally rescinded.

Writing in the aftermath of the September 2001 attacks, Deutch defended his rules, arguing that they allowed DO officers to recruit with clear guidelines and focused on acquiring high-quality agents.

In the United States, constant tension exists between HUMINT and the other collection disciplines. The dominance of technical collection periodically gives rise to calls for a greater emphasis on HUMINT. So-called intelligence failures, such as the fall of the shah of Iran in 1979, the unexpected Indian nuclear tests in 1998, and the 2001 terrorist attacks have led to demands for more HUMINT. There is something odd about this recurring call for more HUMINT in that successful HUMINT is not a question of the mass of agents being assigned to a target. Some targets, such as terrorist cells, or the inner sanctum of totalitarian regimes, will always be difficult to penetrate. There is no reason to believe that the twentieth agent who is sent will succeed when the first nineteen have not. It is not possible to swarm agents against a difficult HUMINT target in terms of the agents' availability and, more important, the risk. Such an effort would be more likely to alert the target to possible penetration attempts, further hampering HUMINT.

Again, no right balance can be struck between HUMINT and the other collection disciplines. Such an idea runs counter to the concept of an all-source intelligence process that seeks to apply as many collection disciplines as possible to a given intelligence need. But not every collection INT makes an equal or even similar contribution to every issue. Clearly, having a collection system that is strong and flexible and can be modulated to the intelligence requirement at hand is better than one that swings between apparently opposed fashions of technical and human collection.

As with all other INTs, it is difficult, if not impossible, to put an ultimate value on HUMINT. It is one of the two most democratic INTs (along with OSINT), as any nation or group can conduct HUMINT. Clearly, it would be preferable to have good HUMINT access for key issues. But cases such as Ames and Hanssen raise questions about HUMINT's value. These two spies provided the Soviet Union and post–Soviet Russia with invaluable information, largely about U.S. spy penetrations in that country but also, in the case of Hanssen, about technical collection operations and capabilities. When their activities are added to past espionage revelations—such as Kampiles (IMINT), the Walkers (SIGINT), and Pelton (SIGINT)—the Soviet Union and post–Soviet Russia gained substantial knowledge about U.S. collection capabilities. Yet the Soviet Union lost the cold war and ceased to exist as a state. One could argue, on the one hand, that all of this HUMINT ultimately proved to be of no value, thus raising questions about HUMINT's utility. On the other hand, one could argue that no amount of HUMINT—or any other INT—can save a state that has profound internal problems.

Critics of HUMINT argue that the most important spies (Penkovsky, Ames, Hanssen, and many others) have tended to be walk-ins rather than recruited spies, which raises a serious question about HUMINT capabilities. If one accepts the idea that collection is a synergistic activity, than even the recruitment of lower-level spies adds to one's overall knowledge. Also, even if the most productive spies are walk-ins, some sort of apparatus is needed to handle them, to get out the intelligence they provide, and so on.

One of the major concerns in HUMINT is the possibility that a spy will be caught and unmasked, with attendant personal risk for the spy and political embarrassment for the state that sent him. Even a successful long-term espionage penetration can prove costly. The case of Gunter

Guillaume is illustrative. Guillaume was an East German spy who was able to penetrate the West German government, rising to a senior position in the office of Chancellor Willy Brandt. When Guillaume's espionage was uncovered in 1974, Brandt was forced to resign. Many people believed that the political cost of the operation exceeded any gains in intelligence. Brandt's *Ostpolitik*—or favorable policy toward East Germany—was never resumed by his successors, at great cost to East Germany, perhaps even greater than any intelligence that Guillaume produced over the years. Similarly, the fate of Jonathan Pollard (see chap. 15 for more details), who passed classified intelligence to Israel, became a constant irritant in U.S.–Israeli relations, again outweighing the value of the intelligence that Pollard provided.

For the United States, at least, it remains important to view HUMINT as part of a larger collection strategy instead of as the single INT that meets the country's most important intelligence needs. To place that sort of expectation on any one INT is bound to set it up for disappointment at best and perhaps even failure.

OPEN-SOURCE INTELLIGENCE. To some, OSINT may seem like a contradiction in terms. How can information that is openly available be considered intelligence? This question reflects the misconception that intelligence must inevitably be about secrets. Much of it is, but not to the exclusion of openly available information. Even during the height of the cold war, according to one senior intelligence official, at least 20 percent of the intelligence about the Soviet Union came from open sources.

OSINT includes a wide variety of information and sources.

- Media: newspapers, magazines, radio, television, and computer-based information
- Public data: government reports, official data such as budgets and demographics, hearings, legislative debates, press conferences, and speeches
- Professional and academic: conferences, symposia, professional associations, academic papers, and experts.

In addition to these open sources, each of the classified INTs has an OSINT component. The most obvious is commercial imagery and IMINT. One can also conduct a variety of SIGINT–type activities on the Worldwide Web, such as traffic analysis (the number of people who visit a Web site) or changes in Web sites. Given that some aspects of MASINT are related to geophysical phenomena, there are open aspects of MASINT. Finally, there is open HUMINT—the use of overt experts for their own knowledge or as sources of elicitation. This list is by no means exhaustive, but it does give a feel of the range of OSINT within the other INTs. (*See box, "Some Intelligence Humor."*)

Some Intelligence Humor

In addition to IMINT (imagery intelligence), SIGINT (signals intelligence), HUMINT (human intelligence), OSINT (open space intelligence), and MASINT (measurement and signatures intelligence), intelligence officers, in their lighter moments, speak of other INTs (collection disciplines). One of the most famous is PIZZINT—pizza intelligence. This refers to the belief that Soviet officials based in Washington, D.C., would keep watch for large numbers of pizza delivery trucks going late in the evening to the Central Intelligence Agency, the Defense Department, the State Department, and the White House as an indication that a crisis was brewing somewhere. The notion was that, after seeing many trucks making deliveries, the officials would hurry back to the Soviet embassy to alert Moscow that something must be going on somewhere in the world.

Some other INTs that intelligence officers talk about are
LAVINT: lavatory intelligence, such as heard in the men's room,
RUMINT: rumor intelligence,
REVINT: revelation intelligence, and
DIVINT: divine intelligence.

One of the hallmarks of the post–cold war world is the increased availability of OSINT. The ratio of open source to classified intelligence on Russia has more than reversed from its 20:80 ratio during the cold war. The number of closed societies and **denied areas** has decreased dramatically. Some of the former Warsaw Pact states are now NATO allies. This does not mean that classified collection disciplines are no longer needed, but that the areas in which OSINT is available have expanded.

The major advantage of OSINT is its accessibility, although it still requires collection. OSINT needs less processing and exploitation than the technical INTs or HUMINT, but it still requires some P&E. Given the diversity of OSINT, it may be more difficult to manipulate for the purpose of deception than are other INTs. OSINT is also useful for helping put the secret information into a wider context, which can be extremely valuable.

The main disadvantage of OSINT is its volume. In many ways, it represents the worst wheat and chaff problem. Some argue that the so-called information revolution has made OSINT more difficult without a corresponding increase in usable intelligence. Computers have increased the ability to manipulate information; however, the amount of derived intelligence has not increased apace.

The OSINT phenomenon **echo** is the effect of a single media story being picked up and repeated by other media sources until the story takes on a much larger life of its own, appearing more important than it actually is. Echo is difficult to deal with unless one is aware of the original story and can therefore knowingly discount its effect.

Popular misconceptions about OSINT persist, even within the intelligence community. OSINT is not free. Buying print media costs the intelligence community money, as do various other services that are useful—if not essential—in helping analysts manage, sort, and sift large amounts of data more efficiently. Another misconception is that the Internet is the main fount of OSINT. Experienced intelligence practitioners have discovered that the Internet—meaning searches among various sites—yields no more than 3 to 5 percent of the total OSINT take.

Even though OSINT has always been used, it remains undervalued by significant segments of the intelligence community. This attitude derives from the fact that the intelligence community was created to discover secrets. If OSINT could largely meet the United States' national security needs, the intelligence community would look very different. Some intelligence professionals have mistakenly equated the degree of difficulty involved in obtaining information with its ultimate value to analysts and policy makers. Contributing to this pervasive bias is that OSINT has always been handled differently by the intelligence community. All of the other INTs have dedicated collectors, processors, and exploiters. With the exception of the Foreign Broadcast Information Service, (FBIS), which monitors foreign media broadcasts, OSINT does not have dedicated collectors, processors, and exploiters. Instead, analysts are largely expected to act as their own OSINT collectors, a concept that other INTs would consider ludicrous. This is unfortunate, because OSINT is the perfect place to start any intelligence collection. By first determining what material is available from open sources, intelligence managers could focus their clandestine collectors on those issues for which such means were needed. Properly used, OSINT could be a good intelligence collection resource manager. The 2004 intelligence law mandates that the DNI must decide how he wishes to deal with OSINT, either by creating a dedicated OSINT center or by some other means. The WMD Commission (the Commission on the Intelligence Capabilities of the United States Regarding Weapons of Mass Destruction) recommended that CIA create an Open Source Directorate. President George W. Bush endorsed this recommendation and left its implementation to the DNI.

The 1999 Kosovo air war produced a new OSINT stream. Individuals in Serbia who said they were opposed to the Slobodan Milosevic government sent e-mails to intelligence firms in the United States, giving reports on the relative success of NATO air strikes, the mood in Belgrade, and related matters. Dealing with such reports is problematic as no assured means exists of authenticating them. The most reliable reports would come from known and trusted sources, probably based on past reporting. Establishing an independent capability to accomplish this may not be possible during hostilities. Some sources may prove to be reliable over time. But one has to be on guard for the possibility, if not the likelihood, of at least some level of disinformation from the targeted regime. In the case of Kosovo, at least some of the sources proved to be reliable, thus establishing a new OSINT stream.

CONCLUSION

Each collection discipline offers unique advantages that are well suited to some types of intelligence requirements but brings with it certain disadvantages as well (see Table 5-1). By deploying a broad and varied array of collection techniques, the United States derives two advantages. First, it is able to exploit the advantages of each type of INT, which, ideally, will compensate for the shortcomings of the others. Second, it is able to apply more than one collection INT to an issue, which enhances the likelihood of meeting the collection requirements for that issue. However, the intelligence community cannot provide answers to every question that is asked, nor does it have the capability to meet all possible requirements at any given time. The collection system is simultaneously powerful and limited.

The cost of collection was rarely an issue during the cold war because of the broad political agreement on the need to stay informed about the Soviet threat. In the post–cold war world, prior to the September 2001 attacks, the absence of any overwhelming strategic threat made the cost of collection systems more difficult to justify. As a result, some people questioned whether a need existed for the level of collection capability that the United States maintained during the cold war. Prior to the terrorist attacks, the United States experienced greatly diminished threats to its national security but faced ongoing concerns that are more diverse and diffuse than was the largely unitary Soviet problem, raising new collection challenges. As horrific as the September 2001 attacks were, terrorism still does not pose the same potentially overwhelming threat to the existence of the United States as did a hostile nuclear-armed Soviet missile force. Ultimately, no yardstick can measure national security problems against a collection array to determine how much collection is enough. For the foreseeable future, collection requirements likely will continue to outrun collection capabilities.

TABLE 5-1   A Comparison of the Collection Disciplines

INT	Advantages	Disadvantages
IMINT	Graphic and compelling	Perhaps overly graphic and compelling
	Use seems familiar to policy-makers	Still requires interpretation
	Ready availability of some targets—particularly military exercises	Literally a snapshot of a moment; very static
	Can be done remotely	Subject to problems of weather, spoofing
		Expensive
SIGINT	Offers insights into plans, intentions	Signals may be encrypted or encoded—requiring them to be broken
	Voluminous material	Voluminous material
	Military targets tend to communicate in regular patterns	May encounter communications silence, use of secure lines, spoofing via phony traffic
	Can be done remotely	Expensive
HUMINT	Offers insights into plans, intentions	Riskier in terms of lives, political fallout
	Relatively inexpensive	Requires more time to acquire and validate sources
		Problems of dangles, false feeds, double agents
MASINT	Extremely useful for issues such as proliferation	Expensive
	Can be done remotely	Little understood by most users
		Requires a great deal of processing and exploitation
OSINT	More readily available	Voluminous
	Extremely useful as a place to start all collection	Less likely to offer insights available from clandestine INTs

Note: INT = collection discipline; IMINT = imagery (or photo) intelligence; SIGINT = signals intelligence; HUMINT = human intelligence; MASINT = measurement and signatures intelligence; and OSINT = open-source intelligence.

KEY TERMS

agent acquisition cycle
all-source intelligence
asset validation system
automatic change extraction
collection disciplines
content analysis
cryptographers
dangles
deception
denial
denied areas
denied targets
developmental
echo
encrypt
espionage
geosynchronous orbit
indication and warning

key-word search
negation search
noise versus signals
official cover
pitch
resolution
risk versus take
shutter control
source
sources and methods
spies
sub-sources
sun-synchronous orbits
swarm ball
traffic analysis
walk-ins
wheat versus chaff

FURTHER READINGS

For ease of use, these readings are grouped by activity. Although there are numerous books by spies and about spying, few of them have good discussions of the
craft of espionage and the role it plays, as opposed to its supposed derring-do
aspects.

General Sources on Collection

Best, Richard A., Jr. *Intelligence, Surveillance, and Reconnaissance (ISR) Programs:
    Issues for Congress.* Washington, D.C.: Congressional Research Service, updated
    August 24, 2004.
Burrows, William. *Deep Black: Space Espionage and National Security.* New York:
    Random House, 1986.
Wohlstetter, Roberta. *Pearl Harbor: Warning and Decision.* Stanford: Stanford Uni-
    versity Press, 1962.

Espionage

Burgstaller, Eugen F. "Human Collection Requirements in the 1980's." In *Intelli-
    gence Requirements for the 1980's: Clandestine Collection.* Ed. Roy F. Godson.
    Washington, D.C.: National Strategy Information Center, 1982.
Hitz, Frederick P. "The Future of American Espionage." *International Journal of
    Intelligence and Counterintelligence* 13 (spring 2000): 1–20.
———. *The Great Game: The Myth and Reality of Espionage.* New York: Alfred
    Knopf, 2004.
Hulnick, Arthur S. "Intelligence Cooperation in the Post–Cold War Era: A New
    Game Plan?" *International Journal of Intelligence and Counterintelligence* 5 (win-
    ter 1991–1992): 455–465.
Phillips, David Atlee. *Careers in Secret Operations: How to Be a Federal Intelligence
    Officer.* Frederick, Md.: Stone Trail Press, 1984.

Wirtz, James J. "Constraints on Intelligence Collaboration: The Domestic Dimension." *International Journal of Intelligence and Counterintelligence* 6 (spring 1993): 85–89.

Imagery

Baker, John C., Kevin O'Connell, and Ray A. Williamson, eds. *Commercial Observation Satellites: At the Leading Edge of Transparency.* Washington, D.C.: RAND Corporation, 2001.

Best, Richard A., Jr. *Airborne Intelligence, Surveillance, and Reconnaissance (ISR): The U-2 Aircraft and Global Hawk UAV Programs.* Washington, D.C.: Library of Congress, Congressional Research Service, 2000.

Brugioni, Dino A. "The Art and Science of Photo Reconnaissance." *Scientific American* (March 1996): 78–85.

———. *Eyeball to Eyeball: The Inside Story of the Cuban Missile Crisis.* Ed. Robert F. McCort. New York: Random House, 1990.

———. *From Balloons to Blackbirds: Reconnaissance, Surveillance, and Imagery Intelligence—How It Evolved.* McLean, Va.: Association of Former Intelligence Officers, 1993.

Central Intelligence Agency. *CORONA: America's First Satellite Program.* Ed. Kevin C. Ruffner. Washington, D.C.: Central Intelligence Agency, 1995.

Day, Dwayne A., and others, eds. *Eye in the Sky: The Story of the Corona Spy Satellites.* Washington, D.C.: Smithsonian Institution Press, 1998.

Lindgren, David T. *Imagery Analysis in the Cold War.* Annapolis: U.S. Naval Institute Press, 2000.

Peebles, Christopher. *The Corona Project: America's First Spy Satellite.* Annapolis: U.S. Naval Institute Press, 1997.

Richelson, Jeffrey T. *America's Secret Eyes in Space: The U.S. Keyhole Spy Satellite Program.* New York: Harper and Row, 1990.

———. "High Flyin' Spies." *Bulletin of the Atomic Scientists* 52 (September–October 1996): 48–54.

Shulman, Seth. "Code Name CORONA." *Technology Review* 99 (October 1996): 23–25, 28–32.

SPOT Image Corporation. "Satellite Imagery: An Objective Guide." Reston, Va.: SPOT Image Corporation, 1998.

Taubman, Philip. *Secret Empire: Eisenhower, the CIA, and the Hidden Story of America's Space Espionage.* New York: Simon and Schuster, 2003.

Open-Source Intelligence

Lowenthal, Mark M. "Open Source Intelligence: New Myths, New Realities." *Defense Daily News,* November 1998. (Available at www.defensedaily.com/reports; www.defensedaily.com/reports/osintmyths.htm.)

———. "OSINT: The State of the Art, the Artless State." *Studies in Intelligence* (fall 2001): 61–66.

Mercado, Stephen C. "Sailing the Sea of OSINT in the Information Age." *Studies in Intelligence* 48, no. 3 (2004). (Available at www.cia.gov.csi/studies.)

Satellites

Klass, Philip. *Secret Sentries in Space.* New York: Random House, 1971.

U.S. National Commission for the Review of the National Reconnaissance Office. *Report: The National Commission for the Review of the National Reconnaissance*

Office. Washington, D.C.: U.S. Government Printing Office, November 14, 2000. (Available at www.nrocommission.com.)

Secrecy
Moynihan, Daniel Patrick. *Secrecy: The American Experience.* New Haven: Yale University Press, 1998.
Secrecy. Report of the Commission on Protecting and Reducing Government Secrecy, Washington, D.C., 1997.

Signals Intelligence
Aid, Matthew M., and Cees Wiebes. *Secrets of Signals Intelligence during the Cold War and Beyond.* Portland, Ore: Frank Cass, 2001.
Bamford, James. *Body of Secret: Anatomy of the Ultra-Secret National Security Agency—From the Cold War through the Dawn of a New Century.* New York: Doubleday, 2001.
————. *The Puzzle Palace: A Report on America's Most Secret Agency.* Boston: Viking, 1982.
Brownell, George A. *The Origin and Development of the National Security Agency.* Laguna Hills, Calif.: Aegean Park Press, 1981.
Kahn, David. *The Codebreakers.* Rev. ed. New York: Scribner, 1996.
National Security Agency and Central Intelligence Agency. *VENONA: Soviet Espionage and the American Response, 1939–1957.* Ed. Robert Louis Benson and Michael Warner. Washington, D.C.: National Security Agency and Central Intelligence Agency, 1996.
Warner, Michael, and Robert Louis Benson. "Venona and Beyond: Thoughts on Work Undone." *Intelligence and National Security* 12 (July 1996): 1–13.

Denial and Deception
Godson, Roy, and James Wirtz, eds. *Strategic Denial and Deception.* New Brunswick, N.J.: Transaction Books, 2002.

Chapter 6

Analysis

> Casting aside the perceived—and I must admit the occasion-
> ally real—excitement of secret operations, the absolute essence
> of the intelligence profession rests in the production of current
> intelligence reports, memoranda and National Estimates on
> which sound policy decisions can be made.
>
> Richard Helms, *A Look Over My Shoulder*

As Director of Central Intelligence (DCI) Richard Helms (1966–1973) observed, despite all the attention lavished on the operational side of intelligence (collection and covert action), analysis is the mainstay of the process. Intelligence analysis provides civil and military policy makers with information directly related to the issues they face and the decisions they have to make. Intelligence products do not arrive once or twice a day, but in a steady stream throughout the day. Certain products, particularly the daily intelligence reports and briefings, are received first thing in the morning, but other intelligence reports can be delivered when they are ready or may be held for delivery at a specific time.

Although not all intelligence practitioners agree, the ongoing produc-tion and delivery of intelligence can have a numbing effect on policy mak-ers. Intelligence analysis can become part of the daily flood of information—intelligence products, commercially provided news, reports from policy offices, embassies, and military commands, and so on. One of the challenges for intelligence is to make itself stand out from this steady stream.

This goal can be achieved in two ways. One is to emphasize the unique nature of the intelligence sources. But this option is not the pre-ferred choice of intelligence officials, who believe that they are much more than just conduits for their sources. The other way for intelligence to achieve prominence is to produce analysis that stands out on its own mer-its by adding value. The value added includes the timeliness of intelli-gence products, the ability of the community to tailor products to specific policy makers' needs, and the objectivity of the analysis. One analyst who had been a presidential briefer put it this way: "My value was telling the president something he didn't already know about something he needed to know." But the fact that value-added intelligence is discussed as often as it is within the intelligence community suggests that it is not achieved as often as desired.

MAJOR THEMES

Prescribing how to produce value-added intelligence—or to measure the frequency with which it is produced—is difficult because intelligence officers and their policy clients do not agree on what adds value. For policy clients, value added is an idiosyncratic and personal attribute.

Analysis is much more than sitting down with the collected material, sifting and sorting it, and coming up with a brilliant piece of prose that makes sense of it all. Major decisions have to be made in the analytical process, and several areas of controversy have proved to be resilient or recurrent.

FORMAL REQUIREMENTS. In the ideal intelligence-process model, policy makers give some thought to their main requirements and then communicate them to the intelligence managers. Such a formal process has not appeared often in the history of the intelligence community, leaving managers to make educated guesses, many of which are either obvious or well grounded.

Some people argue that a less formal process is, in reality, much better than the ideal one, because most of the requirements are fairly well known and do not need to be defined. For example, most people, if asked to name the main U.S. intelligence priorities during the cold war, would mention a number of Soviet-related issues. Even in the less clear post–cold war period prior to the September 2001 attacks, a similar exercise would yield such answers as narcotics, terrorism, proliferation, Russia's reform and stability, and the regional trouble spots of the moment, such as the Balkans, the Middle East, and North Korea. The list parallels the U.S. intelligence priorities as stated in the Clinton administration's Presidential Decision Directive 35. After September 2001, terrorism became the primary, but not the sole, issue.

The real importance of the requirements process may lie in giving the intelligence community some sense of priority among the requirements, instead of defining the issues that need coverage. Formal discussions about priorities between senior policy makers and intelligence officers tend to revolve around relative degrees of importance instead of issues that have been added to the priorities list or overlooked. Assigning priorities is especially important and difficult in the absence of a single overwhelming issue, as was the case from roughly 1991 (the end of the Soviet Union) until 2001. The real problem is that, when several issues are considered to be of roughly equal importance, no single one of them has priority.

CURRENT VERSUS LONG-TERM INTELLIGENCE. The struggle between current and long-term intelligence is a perennial analytical issue. **Current intelligence**—reports and analysis on issues that may not extend more than a week or two into the future—is the mainstay of the intelligence community, the product most often requested and seen by policy makers. In many respects, current intelligence pays the rent for the intelligence community. Current intelligence always predominates over other types, but the degree of this predominance varies over time. During a crisis or war, current intelligence increases, as many of the decisions made during these periods are tactical in nature—even among senior policy makers—thus demanding current intelligence.

But many intelligence analysts are frustrated by the emphasis on current intelligence. Having developed expertise in an area and analytical skills, they wish to write longer-range analyses that look beyond current demands. However, few policy makers are likely to read papers with longer horizons—not owing to lack of interest but to lack of time and the inability to pull away, even briefly, from pressing matters. Thus, a conflict arises between what the policy makers need to read and what many analysts wish to produce. Current intelligence products also tend to be shorter by their nature and goals, further limiting the ability of analysts to add the depth or context that they deem valuable. A further concern is that if current intelligence represents the majority of what analysts produce, then a risk arises that they will largely become reporters of that day's collection instead of true analysts. Building true depth of expertise is difficult on a steady diet of current intelligence.

Some middle ground exists simply because the intelligence community does not make a stark choice between one type of analysis and another on any given day. A range of analysis is produced. But because of the limited number of analysts, managers have to decide where to put their resources and the fact remains that the current intelligence products predominate in terms of resources and the way policy makers perceive the intelligence community.

The current versus mid-term or **long-term intelligence** conundrum is not the only way to think about this issue, although it is the most common. Instead of thinking about intelligence as a matter of time, think about it as a depth versus breadth issue, or a tactical versus strategic issue. By its nature, most current intelligence tends to emphasize depth over breadth. However, one's analytical sights can be raised to create intelligence that is current as well strategic. Intelligence may be current in that it is focused on issues on the agenda right now or in the near future, but it also may attempt to give the policy maker a broader look at the issues involved, such as providing more context, more interconnection with other issues or possible solutions, and so on. A more strategic current intelligence is not produced often but it can be done without pushing the analysis into areas that policy makers are less likely to find useful.

BRIEFINGS. Briefings for policy makers are a form of current intelligence. Many are routine and take place first thing in the morning. Briefings are one of the main ways in which current intelligence is conveyed. Briefings raise a set of issues all their own. One of the main advantages of briefings is the intelligence officer's ability to interact directly with the policy maker, to get a better idea of the policy maker's preferences and reactions to the intelligence, thus overcoming the absence of a formal feedback mechanism. Risks also are involved, though. Briefings, as their name indicates, tend to be brief. Given policy makers' schedules, most briefings are limited by the time allotted for them. Moreover, the morning briefings usually must cover several topics. Thus, providing the necessary context and depth in a briefing can be difficult.

At their best, briefings can be a give-and-take between the policy maker and the intelligence officer. This sort of exchange can be stimulating, but it runs risks. The briefer must be sure of his information, some of which may not be in the material that was prepared for the briefing. Briefers have to be taught to say "I don't know" and offer to get the desired information later, not hazard guesses. Furthermore, an ephemeral quality exists to the briefing. The briefer may not be able to recapture all that was said after the fact.

Briefings raise issues associated with analysts' more proximate relationship with policy makers, particularly the ability to and necessity of keeping some distance from policy to maintain analytic objectivity. The regularly assigned briefers have a two-way role, conveying intelligence to the policy makers and conveying the policy makers' needs or reactions back to the intelligence community. The briefers must avoid slipping into a role of advocacy or support for the policy makers' policies, either writ large or in bureaucratic debates.

An area of controversy that arose in the aftermath of the terrorist attacks was the nature of the Central Intelligence Agency (CIA) briefing for the president and his senior officials. The briefing, which centers around the president's daily brief (PDB), was a CIA publication, conducted exclusively by the CIA. Although senior officials in the executive departments and in the intelligence community are privy to the PDB, this group is very small. Thus, other intelligence agencies do not necessarily know what the president is being told. This engenders a certain amount of jealousy and can lead to a situation in which analytic components of the intelligence community are working at cross-purposes.

In the aftermath of the passage of the 2004 intelligence legislation, control of the PDB shifted. The PDB staff became part of the Office of the Director of National Intelligence, coming under the deputy director of national intelligence for analysis. For the CIA, control over the PDB was one of its crown jewels, giving it an assured level of access. Responsibility for conducting the morning briefing has passed to the director of national intelligence (DNI).

Some believe that too much emphasis has been placed on the PDB, which has had a negative effect on overall analytic efforts. Spending time with the president on a regular basis and being able to put an intelligence product before him routinely are valuable assets. No intelligence manager would decline these opportunities. But decisions still have to be made about how much effort to put into preparing one discreet entity (the PDB) and how much goes into broader and perhaps deeper products. Analyses that go into the PDB or any other morning intelligence publication are nonurgent enough to wait until the next day. If the items reported on were crucial, they would be briefed to the president and other senior officials at once. Thus, the shift to the DNI may prove to be an opportune moment to rethink the PDB and its relationship to broader analytic activities.

CRISES VERSUS THE NORM. One way in which requirements are set is in response to crises. Crisis-driven requirements represent the ultimate victory of current over long-range intelligence needs.

Given the limited nature of collection and analytical resources, certain issues inevitably receive short shrift or even no attention at all. And just as inevitably, annual or semiannual requirements planning regularly fail to predict which of the seemingly less important issues will erupt into a crisis. Thus, the planning exercises are to some degree self-fulfilling—or self-denying—prophecies.

Analytical managers must find a way to create or preserve some minimal amount of expertise against the moment when a less important issue erupts and suddenly moves to the top of policy makers' concerns. The intelligence community has only a small collection reserve, no analytical reserve, and a limited capacity to move assets to previously uncovered but now important topics. Assets therefore move from hot topic to hot topic, with other matters receiving little or no coverage.

Despite the problem of defining requirements and the vagaries of international relations, the intelligence community is on the spot when it misses an issue; that is, fails to be alert to its eventuality or is unprepared to deal with it when it occurs. In part, the high expectations are deserved, given that one function of intelligence is strategic warning. But strategic warning is usually taken to mean advance notice on issues that would pose a threat to national security, not regional crises that might require some level of involvement. Such crises strain the image of the intelligence community as well as its resources, because policy makers in both branches and the media tend to be harsh—sometimes fairly, sometimes not—in their view of misses.

One aspect of dealing with crises that has arisen in recent years has been the demands of the combatant commanders (the four-star officers who command U.S. forces in Europe, the Pacific, and so on) for intelligence support from national intelligence collection assets. The issue is one of conflicting priorities. The combatant commanders are responsible for huge swaths of the globe and react to unrest in any of the countries in their area of responsibility (AOR). However, policy makers and intelligence officers in Washington, D.C., may not have the same sense of urgency about events in some of the smaller and less important states. Thus, there is a difference of perspective and perception. Efforts have been made to wean the combatant commanders off their desire to call upon national assets for any and all emergencies in their AOR and to rely more on their own, admittedly less capable, theater intelligence assets.

THE WHEAT VERSUS CHAFF PROBLEM. The wheat versus chaff problem, although part of collection, ultimately becomes an analytical issue. Although much that is collected does not get processed and exploited, the amount that does is still formidable. Even in the age of computers, few technical shortcuts have been found to help analysts deal with the problem. The intelligence community has adopted some analytical tools (that is, software programs to assist in parts of information management, such as text mining and data mining) and has examined many others, but no major breakthroughs have been made. Thus, to a large degree, the analysts' daily task of sifting through the incoming intelligence germane to their portfolio remains a grind, whether done electronically or on paper. Sifting is not just a matter of getting through the accumulated imagery, signals, open-source reporting, and other data. It is also the much more important matter of seeing this mass of material in its entirety, of being able to perceive patterns from day to day and reports that are anomalous. To repeat, there are no shortcuts. Sifting requires training and experience. Although some intelligence practitioners think of analysts as the human in the loop, the analysts' expertise should be an integral part of collection sorting as well.

ANALYST FUNGIBILITY. When requirements change or when crises break out, analysts must shift to areas of greater need. As with collection, they are participating in a zero-sum game. The analysts have to come from some other assignment, and not every analyst can work on every issue. Each analyst has strengths, weaknesses, and areas that he simply does not know. Even though analysts far outnumber collection systems, analysts are less fungible—that is, easily interchanged or replaced—than the technical collection systems. A signals intelligence satellite that has been collecting against a French-speaking target will not plead ignorance or inability if redirected against an Arabic-speaking target. Significant issues of targeting, access, frequencies, and so on come up, but no language barrier exists per se. Streams of digital communications data do not have indecipherable accents. However, not every analyst has the requisite language, regional, or topical skills to move to an area of greater need. Very real limits exist on **analyst fungibility**, which is a major management concern. This is also sometimes referred to as **analyst agility**, again meaning the need for analysts who have more than one (or two) areas of expertise and therefore can be shifted to higher priority accounts during times of need. Fungibility or agility relies on three factors: the talents and background of the analysts when they are recruited; their training and education within the intelligence community; and the management of their careers, which should give them sufficient opportunities to develop this expertise in a few areas.

U.S. intelligence managers often speak about **global coverage**, which can be a dangerous and misleading term. By *global coverage,* intelligence officers mean their acknowledged requirement to cover any and all issues. Members of the intelligence community cannot say to a policy maker, for example, that they do not have much capability to analyze the current crisis is Fiji, but they are very good on Finland. No bait and switch is allowed. If the situation in a country or region becomes a matter of concern, the intelligence community is expected to cover it. The pitfall in the term *global coverage* is the real possibility that it leaves the impression among policy makers of more depth and breadth than is available in the intelligence community. Intelligence managers understand the resource limitations within which they are working, but by using the term *global coverage* they may be misinterpreted as promising more than they can deliver.

Part of the problem stems from the limitations of the analyst hiring process. In the United States, recruiters go to colleges and universities looking for potential analysts. Other candidates simply apply on their own. But this is a seller's market. The intelligence agencies can hire only those people who evince an interest. Certain schools may have programs that tend to produce more analysts of a certain interest or skill, but this does not appreciably solve the problem. Congress has given the intelligence community a limited ability to offer scholarships for analysts with particular skills, in return for which the analysts must work for the intelligence community for a set number of years. Although a valuable change, such ability does not solve the recruitment problem.

Thus, the intelligence community has greater analytic capabilities in some areas than in others. The situation can be ameliorated to some extent by moving analysts around from issue to issue, but sacrificing depth for breadth can result. The point remains that all analysts have limitations that can curtail the ability of the intelligence community to respond as expected and as the community would prefer.

ANALYST TRAINING. Until recently, the intelligence community did not spend a significant amount of time on analyst training. Training is most useful in giving incoming analysts a sense of what is expected of them, how the larger community works, and its ethos and rules. No amount of training, however, can obviate the fact that much of what an analyst needs to know is learned on the job. Analysts arrive with certain skills garnered from their college or graduate school studies and then are assimilated into their specific intelligence agency or unit. They learn basic processes and requirements, the daily work schedule, and preferred means of expression, which vary from agency to agency. They become familiar with the types of intelligence with which they will be working.

The minimum skills for all analysts are knowledge of one or more specific fields, appropriate language skills, and a basic ability to express themselves in writing. A senior official used to ask his subordinates two questions about new analysts they wished to hire: Do they think interesting thoughts? Do they write well? This official believed that, with these two talents in hand, all else would follow with training and experience. (Napoleon, by contrast, reportedly asked new officers on his staff: Are you lucky? Napoleon understood that luck in battle was a useful attribute.)

The basic skills are a foundation upon which better skills must be built. Some of the new skills to be mastered are parochial. Each intelligence agency has its own corporate style that must be learned. More important, analysts must learn to cope with the wheat versus chaff problem and to write as succinctly as possible. These two skills reflect the demands of current intelligence and the fact that policy makers are busy and prefer economies of style. The bureaucratic truism remains that shorter papers will usually best longer papers in the competition for policy makers' attention.

Training analysts about collection systems appears to fall short of desired goals, given the ignorance expressed by even some senior analysts about this important topic. Furthermore, the U.S. intelligence community has no common training for analysts. Each agency trains its own analysts, in effect creating stovepipes at the outset of analysts' careers.

Another important skill that analysts must learn is objectivity. Although intelligence analysts can and often do have strong personal views about the issues they are covering, their opinions have no place in intelligence products. Analysts are listened to because of their accumulated expertise, not the forcefulness of their views. Presenting personal conclusions would cross the line between intelligence and policy. Still, analysts need training to learn how to filter out their views, especially when they run counter to the intelligence at hand or the policies being considered.

A more subtle and difficult skill to master is cultivating the intelligence consumer without politicizing the intelligence as a means of currying favor.

Finally, there is the question of how far training (or experience) can take a given analyst. Any reasonably intelligent individual with the right skills and education can be taught to be an effective analyst. But the truly gifted analyst—like the truly gifted athlete, musician, or scientist—is inherently better at his job by virtue of inborn talents. Being able to analyze and synthesize intuitively and quickly and having a good nose for the subtext of a situation are innate skills that are hard to acquire. In all fields, such individuals are rare. They must be nurtured. But the benefits they derive from training are different from those that accrue to less gifted analysts.

MANAGING ANALYSTS. Managing intelligence analysts presents a number of unique problems. A major concern is developing career tracks. Analysts need time to develop true expertise in their fields, but intellectual stagnation can set in if an analyst is left to cover the same issue for too long. Rotating analysts among assignments quickly helps them avoid becoming stale and allows them to learn more than one area. But this career pattern raises the possibility that analysts will never gain expertise in any one area, becoming instead generalists. Ideally, managers seek to create some middle ground—providing analysts with assignments that are long enough for them to gain expertise and substantive knowledge while also providing sufficient opportunities to shift assignments and maintain intellectual freshness. Nor is there any specific time frame for assignments; the length depends on the individual analyst, the relative intensity of the current assignment, and the demands generated by intelligence requirements at the time. More intense jobs tend to argue for somewhat shorter tours to avoid burnout. But hot issues also tend to have higher priority, demanding greater expertise and consistency of staffing. Thus, there are again competing needs.

The criteria for promotion are another management issue. As government employees, intelligence analysts are generally assured of promotions up to a level that can be described as high-middle. The criteria for promotion through the grades are not overly rigorous. Promotions should come as a result of merit, not time served. But what criteria should a manager consider in evaluating an intelligence analyst for merit promotion: accuracy of analysis over the past year, writing skills, increased competence in foreign languages and foreign area knowledge, participation in a specific number of major studies? And how should a manager weigh the various criteria?

The competition is stronger for more senior assignments than for those at the lower level, and the criteria for selection are different. The qualities that first merit promotion—keen analytical abilities—are the ticket to management positions, where responsibilities and pay are greater. Ironically, or perhaps sadly, analytical skills have little to do with, and are little indication of, the ability to carry out managerial duties. But, with few exceptions, management positions have been the only route to senior promotion. The CIA has created a Senior Analytical Service, which allows analysts to reach senior ranks solely on the basis of their analytical capabilities.

ANALYSTS' MIND-SET. Analysts, as a group, exhibit a set of behaviors that can affect their work. Not all analysts exhibit each of these characteristics all of the time, and some analysts may never display any of them. Still, many of these traits are common among this population.

One of the most frequent flaws of analysts is **mirror imaging**, which assumes that other leaders, states, and groups share motivations or goals similar to those most familiar to the analyst. "They're just like us" is the quintessential expression of this view. The prevalence of mirror imaging is not difficult to understand. People learn, from an early age, to expect certain behavior of others. The golden rule is based on the concept of reciprocal motives and behavior. Unfortunately, as an analytical tool, mirror imaging fails to take into account such matters as differences of motivation, perception, or action based on national differences, subtle differences of circumstance, different rationales, and the absence of any rationale.

A classic example of mirror imaging was the U.S. analysis of Japan's likely actions in 1941. Although many U.S. analysts and policy makers expected Japan to attack somewhere, they ruled out a direct attack on the United States largely because, if put in a similar position, they would not have attacked a nation so much more powerful in terms of war-making potential. But in Tokyo the steady decline in the Japanese potential dictated a different answer—a direct attack on the most formidable foe. Simon Montefiore (*Stalin: The Court of the Red Tsar*) quotes Josef Stalin as saying: "When you're trying to make a decision, NEVER put yourself in the mind of the other person because if you do, you can make a terrible mistake." For example, during the cold war, some Kremlinologists and Sovietologists talked about Soviet hawks and doves and tried to assess which Soviet leaders belonged to which group. No empirical evidence existed to suggest that there were Soviet hawks and doves. Instead, the fact that the U.S. political spectrum included hawks and doves led to the facile assumption that the Soviet system must have them as well. Also, during the late 1980s, some analysts working on Iran spoke of Iranian extremists and moderates. When pressed by skeptical peers as to their evidence for the existence of moderates, the analysts argued: If there are extremists, there must be moderates. Again, they were reflecting other political systems they knew, as well as making a faulty assumption. Some of their colleagues argued that Iranian politics might include extremists and ultra-extremists.

To avoid mirror imaging, managers must train analysts to recognize it when it intrudes in their work and must establish a higher-level review process that is alert to this tendency.

Clientism is a flaw that occurs when analysts become so immersed in their subjects—usually after working on an issue for too long—that they lose their ability to view issues with the necessary criticality. (In the State Department this phenomenon is called "clientitis," which can be defined as "an inflammation of the client," although the term is used when referring to someone who has "gone native" in his thinking.) Analysts can spend time apologizing for the actions of the nations they cover instead of analyzing them. The same safeguards that analysts and their managers put in place to avoid mirror imaging are required to avoid clientism.

An issue that has arisen more recently, largely as a result of the Iraq weapons of mass destruction (WMDs) experience, is **layering.** Layering refers to the use of judgments made in one analysis as the basis for judgments in another analysis without also carrying over the uncertainties that may be involved. This can be especially dangerous if the earlier judgments were based on meager collection sources. Layering tends to give these earlier judgments greater certainty and can mislead analysts and, more important, policy makers. Both the Senate Intelligence Committee and the WMD Commission (Commission on the Intelligence Capabilities of the United States Regarding Weapons of Mass Destruction) accused intelligence analysts of layering when they analyzed Iraq's alleged possession of WMDs.

ON THE GROUND KNOWLEDGE.   Analysts have varying degrees of direct knowledge about the nations on which they write. During the cold war, U.S. analysts had difficulty spending significant amounts of time in the Soviet Union or its satellites, and they were unable to travel widely in those nations. Similarly, intelligence analysts may have less contact with the senior foreign officials about whom they write than do the U.S. policy makers who must deal with these foreigners. Analysts' distance from the subjects being analyzed can occasionally be costly in terms of how their policy consumers view the intelligence they receive. Some policy clients also may have more in-country experience than do the intelligence analysts.

This problem can be compounded when dealing with terrorists, with whom few opportunities arise for direct or prolonged contact and perhaps little shared basis of rationality by which to gauge their motives or likely next actions.

Analysts, like everyone else, are proud of their accomplishments. Once they have mastered a body of knowledge, they may look for opportunities— no matter how inappropriate—to display that knowledge in detail. Analysts can have difficulty limiting their writing to those facts and analyses that may be necessary for a specific consumer need. Analysts may want the consumer to have a greater appreciation for where the issues being discussed fit in some wider pattern. Unfortunately—and perhaps too frequently—the policy client wants to know "only about the miracles, and not the lives of all the saints who made them happen." Analysts require training, maturity, and supervision to cure this behavior. Some analysts get the message sooner than others; some never get it and produce analysis that requires greater editing to get to the essential message, which can cause resentment. Furthermore, the intelligence provider may lose the attention of the policy client if he gives too much material, large portions of which do not seem relevant to the policy maker's immediate needs.

Just as analysts want to show the depth of their knowledge, so, too, they want to be perceived as experienced—perhaps far beyond what is true. Again, this is a common human failing. Professionals in almost any field, when surrounded by peers and facing a situation that is new to them but not to others, are tempted to assert their familiarity, whether genuine or not. Given the choice between appearing jaded ("been there, done that") and naïve ("Wow! I've never seen that before!"), analysts usually choose the former. The risk of being caught seems small enough, and it is preferable to being put down by someone else who displays greater experience ("The same thing happened in Bessarabia in 1958. I thought you knew that.").

Sometimes, however, large consequences are at stake. For example, in April 1986 the operators of the Chernobyl nuclear reactor in the Soviet Union, while running an unauthorized experiment, caused an explosion. The next afternoon, Sweden reported higher than normal radioactive traces in its air monitors, which had been placed in many cities. In the United States an intelligence manager asked a senior analyst what he made of the Swedish complaints. The analyst played them down, saying the Swedes were always concerned about their air and often made such complaints for the smallest amounts of radiation. Upon learning the truth, analysts spent the following day frantically trying to catch up with the facts about Chernobyl. The jaded approach precluded the analysts from making the simplest inquiries such as into the types of radiation Sweden detected. The answer would have identified the source as a reactor and not a weapon. And the prevailing winds over Sweden could have been surveyed to identify the source. (Some years later the intelligence manager met with some of his Swedish counterparts. They initially concluded, based upon analysis of the radiation and wind conditions, that a reactor at nearby Ignalina, across the Baltic Sea in Soviet territory, was leaking. Although they misidentified the source, which was a reactor much farther away, they were much closer to the truth than were U.S. intelligence officials.)

The costs of the jaded approach are threefold. First, this approach represents intellectual dishonesty, something all analysts should avoid. Second, it proceeds from the false assumption that each incident is much like others, which may be true at some superficial level but may be false at fundamental levels. Third, it closes the analyst's thinking, regardless of his level of experience, to the possibility that an incident or issue is entirely new, requiring wholly new types of analysis.

Credibility is one of the most highly prized possessions of analysts. Although they recognize that no one can be correct all of the time, they are concerned that policy makers are holding them accountable to an impossible standard. Their concern about credibility—which is largely faith and trust in the integrity of the intelligence process and in the ability of the analysts whose product is at hand—can lead them to play down or perhaps mask sudden shifts in analyses or conclusions. For example, suppose intelligence analysis has long estimated a production rate of fifteen missiles a year in a hostile state. One year, because of improved collection and new methodologies, the estimated production rate (which is still just an estimate) goes to forty-five missiles per year. Policy makers may view this increase—on the order of 300 percent—with alarm. Instead of presenting the new number with an explanation as to how it was derived, an analyst might be tempted to soften the blow. Perhaps a brief memo is issued, suggesting changes in production. Then a second memo, saying that the rate is more likely twenty to twenty-five missiles per year, and so on, until the policy maker sees a more acceptable analytical progression to the new number and not a sudden spike upward. Playing out such a scenario takes time, and it is intellectually dishonest.

Intelligence products that are written on a recurring basis—such as certain types of national intelligence estimates—may be more susceptible than other products to this type of behavior. They establish benchmarks that can be reviewed more easily than, say, a memo that is not likely to be remembered unless the issue is extremely important and the shift is dramatic.

Although policy makers have taken retribution on analysts for sudden changes in estimates, more often than not the fear in the minds of analysts is greater than the likelihood of a loss of credibility. Much depends on the prior nature of the relationship between the analyst and the policy maker, the latter's appreciation for the nature of the intelligence problem, and the intelligence community's past record. If several revisions have been made in the recent past, there is reason to suspect a problem.

If revision is an isolated phenomenon, it is less problematic. The nature of the issue, and its importance to the policy maker and the nation, also matters.

For example, the level of Soviet defense spending—then usually expressed as a percentage of gross national product (GNP)—was a key intelligence issue during the cold war. At the end of the Ford administration (1974–1977), intelligence estimates of Soviet GNP going to defense rose from a range of 6–7 percent to 13–14 percent, largely because of new data, new modeling techniques, and other factors unrelated to Soviet output. The revision was discomforting to the incoming Carter administration. In his inaugural address, Jimmy Carter signaled that he did not want to be constantly concerned with the Soviet issue, that he had other foreign policy issues to pursue. A more heavily armed Soviet Union was not good news. Carter prided himself on his analytical capabilities. When faced with the revised estimates, he reportedly chided the intelligence community, noting that it had just admitted to a 100 percent error in past estimates. That being the case, why should he believe the analyses now?

Few intelligence products are written by just one analyst and then sent along to the policy client. Most have peer reviews and managerial reviews and probably the input of analysts from other offices or agencies. This is especially true for the intelligence products (analytical reports) that agencies call **estimates** in the United States or **assessments** in Australia and Britain. Participation of other analysts and agencies adds a further dimension to the analytical process—bureaucratics—which brings various types of behaviors and strategies.

More likely than not, several agencies have strongly held and diametrically opposed views on key issues within an estimate. How should these be dealt with? The U.S. system in both intelligence and policy making is consensual. No votes are taken; no lone wolves are cast out or beaten to the ground. Everyone must find some way to agree. But if intellectual arguments fail, consensus can be reached in many other ways, few of which have anything to do with analysis.

- Backscratching and logrolling. Although usually thought of in legislative terms, these two behaviors can come into play in intelligence analysis. Basically, they involve a trade-off: "You accept my view on p. 15 and I'll accept yours on p. 38." Substance is not a major concern.
- False hostages. Agency A is opposed to a position being taken by Agency B but is afraid its own views will not prevail. Agency A can stake out a false position on another issue that it defends strongly, not for the sake of the issue itself, but so that it has something to trade in the backscratching and logrolling.

- Lowest-common-denominator language. One agency believes that the chance of something happening is high; another thinks it is low. Unless these views are strongly held, the agencies may compromise—a moderate chance—as a means of resolving the issue. This example is a bit extreme, but it captures the essence of the behavior—an attempt to paper over differences with words that everyone can accept, that is, the **lowest-common-denominator language.**
- Footnote wars. Sometimes none of the other techniques works. In the U.S. estimative process, an agency can always add a footnote in which it expresses alternative views. Or more than one agency might add a footnote, or agencies may take sides on an issue. This can lead to vigorous debates as to whose view appears in the main text and whose in the footnote.

In U.S. practice, an estimate may refer to "a majority of agencies" or a "minority." This is an odd formulation. First, it is vague. How many agencies hold one view or the other? Is it a substantial majority (say, eleven of the fifteen agencies) or a bare one? Second, the formulation strongly implies that the view held by the majority of agencies is more likely the correct one, although no formal or informal votes are taken in the NIE process. The British practice is different. In Britain, if all agencies participating in an assessment cannot agree, then the views of each are simply laid out. This may be more frustrating for the policy maker reading the assessment, but it avoids false impressions about consensus or correct views based on the vague intellectual notion of a majority.

One critique of the intelligence community's analysis of Iraqi WMD was the absence of different views and the problem of **groupthink.** The Senate Intelligence Committee held that the analysts did not examine their assumptions rigorously enough and thus lapsed too easily into agreement. The case highlights a conundrum for managers and analysts, particularly those involved in estimates. As a rule, policy makers prefer consensus views, which save them from having to go through numerous shades of opinion on their own. After all, isn't that what the intelligence community is supposed to be doing? Thus, there has always been some impetus to arrive at a consensus if possible. In the aftermath of Iraq, however, most consensus views—even if arrived at out of genuine agreement—could be viewed with suspicion. How does one determine, when reading intelligence analysis, the basis upon which a consensus has been achieved?

ANALYTICAL STOVEPIPES. Collection stovepipes emerge because the separate collection disciplines are managed independently and often are rivals to one another. **Analytical stovepipes** also appear in the U.S.

all-source community. The three all-source analytical groups—the CIA Directorate of Intelligence, Defense Intelligence Agency Directorate of Intelligence, and the State Department Bureau of Intelligence and Research (INR)—exist to serve specific policy makers. They also come together on a variety of community analyses, most often the national intelligence estimates (NIEs). Efforts to manage or, even more minimally, to oversee and coordinate their activities reveal a stovepipe mentality not unlike that exhibited by the collection agencies. The three all-source agencies tend to have a wary view of efforts by officials with community-wide responsibilities to deal with them as linked parts of a greater analytical whole. The analytical agencies manifest this behavior less overtly than do the collectors, so it is more difficult to recognize. It thus may be surprising to some people, perhaps more so than when collectors exhibit this behavior. After all, each of the collectors operates in a unique field, with a series of methodologies that are also unique. The analytical agencies, however, are all in the same line of work, often concerned with the same issues. But bureaucratic imperatives and a clear preference for their responsibilities in direct support of their particular policy clients, as opposed to interagency projects, contribute to analytical stovepipes.

All of these behaviors can leave the impression that the estimative process—or any large-group analytical efforts—is false intellectually. That is not so. However, it is also not a purely academic exercise. Other behaviors intrude, and more than just analytical truths are at stake. The estimative process yields winners and losers, and careers may rise and fall as a result.

ANALYTICAL ISSUES

In addition to the mind-set and behavioral characteristics of analysts, several issues within analysis need to be addressed.

COMPETITIVE VERSUS COOPERATIVE ANALYSIS. As important as the concept of **competitive analysis** is to U.S. intelligence, a need has been seen to bring together analysts of agencies or disciplines to work on major ongoing issues, in addition to the collaborative process of NIEs. DCI Robert M. Gates (1991–1993) thus created centers, most of which focused on transnational issues—terrorism, nonproliferation, narcotics, and so on.

The intelligence community also formed task forces to deal with certain issues; among these was the Balkans task force, which has operated since the 1990s, monitoring the range of issues related to the breakup of Yugoslavia.

The 9/11 Commission (National Commission on Terrorist Attacks Upon the United States) recommended organizing all analysis around either regional or functional centers. The 2004 intelligence law mandated the establishment of the National Counterterrorism Center (NCTC), which was basically an expansion of the Terrorism Threat Integration Center that DCI George J. Tenet (1997–2004) had created. The law also requires that the DNI examine the utility of creating a National Counterproliferation Center and gives the DNI the authority to create other centers as necessary. The problem with the center approach for all analysis is that it becomes somewhat inflexible. Inevitably, some issues or some nations do not fit easily into the center construct. What happens to them? Also, although creating a center is easy, centers—like all other offices—do not like to share or lose resources. Centers therefore run counter to the desire for analytic workforce agility. To date, centers have been organized along functional lines and are staffed by analysts who tend to be more expert in the issue than in the national or regional context within which that issue has been raised. A functional center therefore runs the risk of providing technical analysis that is divorced from its political context. For example, analyzing the state of WMD development in a nation is not enough. One should also analyze the internal or regional political factors driving the program, as these will give important indicators as to its purpose and scope. Being housed in a center does not preclude a functional analyst from seeking out her regional counterparts. Analysts do this on a regular basis. But it requires some effort and can be dropped during the press of the day's work. The center concept can serve to make this collaboration more difficult.

Centers can become competitors for resources with offices in agencies. This appears to have been the case with the NCTC and CIA's Counterterrorism Center, according to the WMD Commission. As has been seen from the time that DCI Gates began creating centers in the early 1990s, the heads of agencies are not willing to siphon away scarce resources to an activity over which they will have no control (centers fell under the jurisdiction of the DCI and now are under the DNI) and from which they will receive no direct results. The WMD Commission recommended the creation of an additional center, the National Counterproliferation Center, which would have a managerial role in line with the commission's concept of mission managers to coordinate collection and analysis on specific issues or topics.

A bureaucratic debate has ensued on the nature of the centers. Although their goal is to bring the intelligence components into a single place, most centers have been located in and dominated by the CIA. Some people argue that the arrangement undercuts the centers' basic goal— to reach across agencies. Defenders of the system argue that housing the centers in the CIA gives them access to many resources not available elsewhere and also protects their budgets and staffing. A 1996 review by the House Intelligence Committee staff validated the concept of the centers but urged that they be less CIA-centric. Given the location of the centers, however, other agencies are sometimes loath to assign analysts to them, fearing that they will be essentially lost resources during their center service. (A similar problem used to occur on the Joint Staff, which supports the Joint Chiefs of Staff. The military services—Army, Navy, Air Force, Marines—naturally preferred to keep their best officers in duties directly related to their service. This ended when Congress passed the Goldwater-Nichols Act, in 1986, which mandated a joint service tour as a prerequisite for promotion to general or admiral.) Centers now are overseen by the DNI, which should serve to make the centers more community-based in terms of staffing. However, the setup raises new issues about how the DNI staffs the centers when he has no direct control over any analytic components comparable to the control that the DCI had over the CIA.

Another issue for the centers is their duration. In government—in all sectors—ostensibly temporary bodies have a way of becoming permanent, even when the reasons for their creation have long since ended. A certain bureaucratic inertia sets in. Some people wish to see the body continue, as it is a source of power; others fear that by being the first to suggest terminating it they will look like shirkers. The situation has a comic aspect to it, but also a serious one, as these temporary groups absorb substantial amounts of resources and energy.

Thus, the question for the centers—or any other groups—is, When are they no longer needed? Clearly, the transnational issues are all ongoing, but even they may change or diminish over time. One former deputy DCI suggested a five-year sunset provision for all centers, meaning that every five years each center would be subject to a hard-nosed review of its functions and the requirement for its continuation.

Finally, some critics question the focus of the centers, arguing that they are concentrating tactically on operational aspects of specific issues instead of on the longer-term trends. Center proponents note the presence of analysts and the working relationship between the centers and the national intelligence officers (NIOs), who can keep apprised of the centers' work, offer advice, and are responsible for the production of NIEs.

Ultimately, there is no best way to organize analysts. Each scheme has distinct advantages and disadvantages. And each scheme still revolves around either functional or regional analysts. The goal should be to ensure that the right analysts of both types are brought to bear on topics as needed—either on a permanent or temporary basis, depending on the issue and its importance. Flexibility and agility remain crucial. (*See box, "Metaphors for Thinking about Analysis."*)

Metaphors for Thinking about Analysis

Metaphors are often used to describe the intelligence analysis process.

Thomas Hughes, a former director of the Department of State Bureau of Intelligence and Research, wrote that intelligence analysts were either butchers or bakers. Butchers tend to cut up and dissect intelligence to determine what is happening. Bakers tend to blend analysis together to get the bigger picture. Analysts assume both roles at different times.

In the aftermath of the September 11 terrorist attacks, the phrase "connect the dots" became prevalent. Connecting the dots depends on all of the dots being present to draw the right picture. (The dots also come numbered sequentially, which helps considerably.) As a senior intelligence analyst pointed out, the intelligence community was accused of not connecting the dots in the run-up to September 11 but was accused of connecting too many dots regarding the alleged Iraqi weapons of mass destruction.

A more useful description is that intelligence analysis is similar to assembling a mosaic, but one in which the desired final picture may not be clear. Not all of the mosaic pieces are available. Further complicating matter, in the course of assembling the mosaic, new pieces appear and some old ones change size, shape, and color.

DEALING WITH LIMITED INFORMATION. Analysts rarely have the luxury of knowing everything they wish to know about a topic. In some cases, little may be known. How does an analyst deal with this problem?

One option is to flag the problem so that the policy client is aware of it. Often, informing policy consumers of what intelligence officials do not know is as important as communicating what they do know. Secretary of State Colin Powell (2001–2005) used the formulation: "Tell me what you know. Tell me what you don't know. Tell me what you think." Powell said he held intelligence officers responsible for the first two but that he was responsible if he took action based on the last one. But admitting ignorance may be unattractive, out of concern that it will be interpreted as a failing on the part of the intelligence apparatus. Alternatively, analysts can try to work around the problem, utilizing their own experience and skill to fill in the blanks as best they can. This may be more satisfying intellectually and professionally, but it runs the risk of giving the client a false sense of the basis of the analysis or of the analysis being wrong.

Another option is to arrange for more collection, time permitting. Yet another is to widen the circle of analysts working on the problem to get the benefit of their views and experience.

A reverse formulation of this same problem has arisen in recent years. To what degree should analysis be tied to available intelligence? Should intelligence analyze only what is known, or should analysts delve into issues or areas that may be currently active, but for which no intelligence is available? Proponents argue that the absence of intelligence does not mean that an activity is not happening, only that the intelligence about it is not available. Opponents argue that this sort of analysis puts intelligence out on a limb, where there is no support and the likely outcome is highly speculative worst-case analysis. On the one hand, intelligence analysis is not a legal process in which findings must be based on evidence. On the other hand, analysis written largely on supposition is not likely to be convincing to many and may be more susceptible to politicization.

The concerns about dealing with limited intelligence arose in the reviews of intelligence performance prior to the 2001 terrorist attacks and the intelligence prior to the Iraq war (2003–). The problems in each case were not identical. In the case of the September 11 attacks, some people criticized analysts for not putting together intelligence they did have to get a better sense of the al Qaeda threat and plans. Intelligence officials were also criticized for not being more strident in their warnings—a charge that intelligence officials rebutted—and policy makers were criticized for not being more attuned to the intelligence they were receiving. However, no one has been able to make the case that sufficient intelligence existed to forecast the time and place of the attacks. The admonition about strategic versus tactical surprise is apropos (see chap. 1). Stopping a terrorist attack requires tactical insights into the terrorists' plans.

In the case of Iraq, the critique is just the opposite, that is, that intelligence analysts made too many unsubstantiated connections among various pieces of collected intelligence and created a false picture of the state of Iraqi WMD programs. Implicit in this critique is the view, among some, that analysts should not analyze beyond the collected intelligence lest they draw the wrong conclusions. This would be a deviating and alarming practice from the norm, given the likelihood at all times of less than perfect collection. Analysts are trained to use their experience and their instinct to fill in the collection gaps as best they can. That is one of the value-added aspects of analysts.

If a lesson is to be drawn from these two analytical experiences it may be no more than that the analytical process is imperfect under any and all conditions. No Goldilocks formula has been devised as to the right amount of intelligence upon which analysis should be based. The quality of that intelligence matters a great deal, as does the nature of the issue being analyzed.

CONVEYING UNCERTAINTY. Just as everything may not be known, so, too, the likely outcome may not be clear. Conveying uncertainty can be difficult. Analysts shy away from the simple but stark "We don't know."

After all, they are being paid, in part, for making some intellectual leaps beyond what they know. Too often, analysts rely on weasel words to convey uncertainty: "on the one hand," "on the other hand," "maybe," "perhaps," and so on. (President Harry S. Truman was famous for saying he wanted to meet a one-handed economist so that he would not have to hear "on the one hand, on the other hand" economic forecasting.) These words may convey analytical pusillanimity, not uncertainty. (Conveying uncertainty seems to be a particular problem in English, which is a Germanic language and makes less use of the subjunctive than do the Romance languages.)

Some years ago a senior analytical manager crafted a system for suggesting potential outcomes by using both words and numbers—that is, a 1-in-10 chance, a 7-in-10 chance. Such numerical formulations may be more satisfying than words, but they run the risk of conveying to the policy client a degree of precision that does not exist. What is the difference between a 6-in-10 chance and a 7-in-10 chance, beyond greater conviction? In reality, the analyst is back to relying on gut feeling. (One chairman of the National Intelligence Council became incensed when he read an analysis that assessed "a small but significant chance" of something happening.)

One way to help convey uncertainty is to identify in the analysis the issues about which there is uncertainty or the intelligence that is essentially missing but which would, in the analyst's view, either resolve the unknowns or cause him to reexamine currently held views. This raises another issue: the known unknowns (that is, the things one knows that one does not know) versus the unknown unknowns (that is, the things one did not know that one did not know). By definition, the second group cannot be bounded or reduced as it is unknown. But one's analysis must constantly be examined to identify known unknowns and to give attention to resolving these issues if possible.

The use of language becomes important, not only here but in all analysis. Analysts tend to use a stock set of verbs to convey their views: "believe," "assess," "judge." For some analysts the words have distinct and separate meanings that convey the amount of intelligence supporting a particular view and their certainty about this view. However, the intelligence community has not reached a consensus as to what each verb means. Efforts have been made to create a dictionary, although analysts recognize that this would be of little use unless it was also shared with the policy makers. (The British experience on this issue appears to be the opposite, according to the Butler report on intelligence about Iraqi WMD. The Butler report states that British policy makers assumed the different words had different meanings, but British analysts said they just wrote naturally, using the terms interchangeably.)

INDICATIONS AND WARNINGS. Indications and warning, or I&W as it is known among intelligence professionals, is one of the most important roles of intelligence—giving policy makers advance warning of significant, usually military, events. The emphasis placed on I&W in the United States reflects the cold war legacy of a long-term military rivalry and the older roots of the U.S. intelligence community in Pearl Harbor, the classic I&W failure.

I&W is primarily a military intelligence function, with an emphasis on surprise attack. It relies, to a large extent, on the fact that all militaries operate according to certain regular schedules, forms, and behaviors, which provide a baseline against which to measure activity that may raise I&W concerns. In other words, analysts are looking for anything that is out of the ordinary, any new or unexpected activity that may presage an attack: calling up reserves, putting forces on a higher level of alert, dropping or increasing communications activity, imposing sudden communications silence, or sending more naval units to sea. But none of these can be viewed in isolation; they have to be seen within the wider context of overall behavior.

During the cold war, for example, U.S. and North Atlantic Treaty Organization (NATO) analysts worried about how much warning they would receive of a Warsaw Pact attack against Western Europe. Some analysts believed that they could provide policy makers, minimally, several days' warning, as stocks were positioned, additional units were brought forward, and so on. Others believed that the Warsaw Pact had sufficient forces and supplies in place to attack from a standing start. Fortunately, the issue was never put to the test.

For analysts, I&W can be a trap, not an opportunity. Their main fear is failing to pick up on indicators and give adequate warning, which in part reflects the harsh view of intelligence when it misses an important event. In reaction, analysts may lower the threshold and issue warnings about everything, in effect crying wolf. Although this may reduce the analyst's exposure to criticism, it has a lulling effect on the policy maker and can cheapen the function of I&W.

Terrorism presents an entirely new and more difficult I&W problem. Terrorists do not operate from elaborate infrastructures, and they do not need to mobilize large numbers of people for their operations. One attraction of terrorism as a political tool is the ability to have a large effect with minimal forces. Thus, an entirely new I&W concept is needed to fight terrorism, one more likely to catch the much smaller signs of impending activity. Terrorism also raises the **duty to warn** issue. If credible evidence indicates a potential attack, does the government have a responsibility to warn its citizens? A warning may tip off the terrorists to the fact that their plot has been penetrated, thus putting sources and methods at risk. Also, citizens may become inured—if not downright cynical—about recurring changes in the level of warning, especially if the attacks do not occur. Some may come to believe that the government, and especially the intelligence agencies, is trying to cover itself in case an attack does occur. This phenomenon has been seen in the United States since 2001 as alerts have been issued and then withdrawn after the threat subsided or failed to materialize.

OPPORTUNITY ANALYSIS. Indications and warning is not only one of the most important analytic functions, but it is also one that comes naturally to intelligence analysts. A primary reason to have intelligence agencies is to avoid strategic surprise (see chap. 1). I&W is a means to that end. But, I&W can become something of a trap, a theme that is reverted to too often lest something be missed.

Policy makers understand that I&W leaves them in the position of reacting to intelligence. But policy makers also want to be actors, to achieve goals and not just prevent bad things from happening. As more than one senior policy maker has said, "I want intelligence that helps me advance my agenda, that makes me the actor, not the reactor." This is often referred to as **opportunity analysis.**

Opportunity analysis is a sophisticated but difficult type of analysis to produce. First, it requires that the intelligence managers or analysts have a good sense of the goals that the policy maker seeks to achieve. Successful opportunity analysis may require some degree of specific and detailed knowledge of these goals. For example, knowing that a goal is arms control may not suggest many useful avenues of opportunity analysis beyond broad generalities. Knowing that the goals include certain types of weapons or restrictions would be more helpful. Thus, again, emphasis is placed on the importance of the intelligence analysts knowing the intended directions of policy. Second, opportunity analysis often seems more difficult or riskier as it requires positing how foreign statesmen or nations will react to policy initiatives. Positing a foreign action and then describing either the consequences or possible reactions often seems easier than the reverse process. After all, an analyst often feels more comfortable understanding how his nation or policy makers are likely to react even if he is an expert in the politics of another country. Finally, opportunity analysis brings the intelligence community close to the line separating intelligence from policy. Writing good opportunity analysis without appearing to be prescriptive can be difficult even if that is not the intended message or goal.

In general, opportunity analysis is not engaged in often and is easily misunderstood when it is produced.

ALTERNATIVE ANALYSIS. One critique of the intelligence community's performance on Iraqi WMD was the alleged failure to examine alternative analytical lines. Even if true, it remains difficult in the case of Iraq to come up with analytically and intellectually sensible arguments that, in 2003, Saddam Hussein had come clean and had no WMD and was telling the truth when he made this case. Still, looking beyond the Iraq WMD case, the issue of alternative analysis is an important one. The 2004 intelligence law requires that the DNI create a process to ensure the effective use of alternative analysis.

The main driver is the concern that analysts can fasten on to one line of analysis, especially for issues that are examined and reexamined over the years, and then will not be open to other possible hypothesis or alternatives. Should this happen, the analyst will then not be alert for changes, discontinuities, or surprises, even if they are not threatening. One way to attempt to avoid this potential intellectual trap is to create alternative analyses or red cells.

For several reasons, the intelligence community has not always embraced the concept. First, concerns arise that the process can be political in nature or can lead to politicization. The Team A and Team B example from the cold war (see chap. 11) remains a warning in this regard. The alternative analysis group (Team B) was made up of individuals who were more hawkish about dealing with the Soviet Union. Thus, it was no surprise that they found the NIEs on Soviet strategic goals wanting. The existence of an alternative analysis, especially on controversial issues, can lead policy makers to shop for the intelligence they want or cherry-pick analysis, which also results in politicization. Second, only so many analysts are available to deal with any issue or have the requisite expertise on any issue. Therefore, a decision has to be made as to which analysts are assigned to the mainstream and which to the alternative group. Their levels of expertise should be roughly equal. For analysts who have been on the losing side of issues in the area in the past, the chance to participate in alternative analysis may be an irresistible opportunity to reopen old arguments or settle scores. Finally, one of the prerequisites for alternative analysis is that it provide a fresh look at an issue. Therefore, as soon as this type of capacity is institutionalized and made a regular part of the process, it loses the originality and vitality that were sought in the first place.

Alternative analysis consists of more than simply asking a contrafactual question. As in the case of Iraq WMD, the contrafactual question (make the case that Saddam is telling the truth and has no WMDs) would likely not have yielded a better analytical result. The analyst or the analytical manager has to be alert to the nature of the issue under consideration and the type of contrafactual question that will probe the generally held premise. It may be necessary to try several such questions before coming up with one that truly challenges the prevailing wisdom.

The 2004 intelligence law puts great emphasis on alternative analysis, competitive analysis, and red teaming, which are all variants on the same theme—an effort to avoid groupthink. The DNI is responsible for institutionalizing processes for these other types of analysis.

ESTIMATES. The United States creates and uses analytical products called estimates (or assessments in Britain and Australia). These serve two major purposes: to see where a major issue or trend will go over the next several years and to present the considered view of the entire intelligence community, not just one agency. In the United States their community-wide origin is signified by the fact that the director of central intelligence signed (and now, presumably, the director of national intelligence will sign) completed estimates.

Estimates are not predictions of the future but rather considered judgments as to the likely course of events regarding an issue of importance to the nation. Sometimes, more than one possible outcome may be included in a single estimate. The difference between estimate and prediction is crucial but often misunderstood, especially by policy makers. Prediction foretells the future—or attempts to. Estimates are more vague, assessing the relative likelihood of one or more outcomes. If an event or outcome were predictable—that is, capable of being foretold—one would not need intelligence agencies to estimate its likelihood. It is the uncertainty or unknowability that is key. As American baseball icon Yogi Berra said: "It is very difficult to make predictions, especially about the future."

The bureaucratics of estimates are important to their outcome. In the United States, national intelligence officers are responsible for preparing estimates. They circulate the terms of reference (TOR) among colleagues and other agencies at the outset of an estimate. The TOR may be the subject of prolonged discussion and negotiation, as various agencies may believe that the basic questions or lines of analysis are not being framed properly. The drafting is not done by the NIOs, but by someone from the NIO's office, or the NIO may recruit a drafter from one of the intelligence agencies. Once drafted, the estimate is coordinated with other agencies, that is, the other agencies read it and give comments, not all of which are accepted, because they may be at variance with the drafter's views. Numerous meetings are held to resolve disputes, but the meetings may end with two or more views on some aspects that cannot be reconciled. The DNI chairs a final meeting, which is attended by senior officials from a number of agencies. After the DNI signs the estimate, signifying she is satisfied with it, the estimate becomes hers. DCIs were known to change the views expressed in estimates with which they disagreed. This usually displeased the drafter but was within the DCI's authority.

In addition to the bureaucratic game playing that may be involved in drafting estimates, issues of process influence outcomes. Not every issue is of interest to every intelligence agency. But each agency understands the necessity of taking part in the estimative process, not only for its intrinsic intelligence value but also as a means of keeping watch on the other agencies. Furthermore, not every intelligence agency brings the same level of expertise to an issue. For example, the State Department is much more concerned on a day-to-day basis about human rights violations than are other agencies, and INR reflects this in its work for its specific policy makers and in the expertise it chooses to develop on this issue. Or, the Defense Department is much more concerned about the infrastructure of a nation in which U.S. troops may be deployed. Rightly or wrongly, however, estimates are egalitarian experiences in that the views of all agencies are treated as having equal weight.

Some issues are the subjects of repeated estimates. For example, during the cold war, the intelligence community produced an annual estimate (in three volumes) on Soviet strategic forces, NIE 11-3-8. For issues of long-term importance, regular estimates are a useful way of keeping track of an issue, of watching it closely and looking for changes in perceived patterns. However, a regularly produced estimate can also be an intellectual trap, as it establishes several benchmarks that analysts do not want to tinker with in the event of possible changes. Having produced a long-standing record on certain key issues, the estimative community finds it difficult to admit that major changes are under way that, in effect, undercut its past analysis.

This issue may be less crass than preserving one's past record. Having come to a set of conclusions based on collection and analysis, what does it take for an analyst or a team of analysts working on an estimate to feel compelled to walk away from their past work and come to an opposite conclusion? One can create a scenario in which some new piece of intelligence completely reverses analysts' thinking. Such an occasion is extremely rare. Is it possible to start from scratch and ignore past work? If one tries to, what is the cutoff point for old collection that is no longer of use? Although the influence of past analysis can be a problem, it is less easily solved than is commonly thought. Intelligence analysis is an iterative process that lacks clear beginning and end points for either collection or analysis.

Some people question the utility of estimates. Both producers and consumers have had concerns about the length of estimates and their sometimes plodding style. Critics also have voiced concerns about timeliness, in that some estimates take more than a year to complete. One of the worst examples of poor timing came in 1979. An estimate on the future political stability of Iran was being written—including the observation that Iran was "not in a prerevolutionary state"—even as the shah's regime was unraveling daily. This incongruity led the House Intelligence Committee to observe that estimates "are not worth fighting over."

After the start of the Iraq war (2003–), the estimate process came under intense scrutiny and criticism. Among the concerns were the influence of past estimates, the groupthink issue, the use of language that seemed to suggest more certainty than existed in the sources, inconsistencies between summary paragraphs (called Key Judgments or KJs) and actual text, and the speed with which the estimate was written. This last criticism was interesting in that the estimate was written at the request of the Senate, to meet its three-week deadline before voting on the resolution granting the president authority to use force against Iraq. Frequent leaks of NIEs on a variety of Iraq-related topics led some to charge that the intelligence community was at war with the Bush administration.

COMPETITIVE ANALYSIS. The U.S. intelligence community believes in the concept of competitive analysis—having different agencies with different points of view work on the same issue. Because the United States has several intelligence agencies—including three major all-source analytical agencies (CIA, Defense Intelligence Agency, and State's Bureau of Intelligence and Research)—every relevant actor understands that the agencies have different analytical strengths and, likely, different points of view on a given issue. By having each of them—and other agencies as well on some issues—analyze an issue, the belief is that the analysis will be stronger and more likely to give policy makers accurate intelligence.

Beyond the day-to-day competition that takes place among the intelligence publications of each agency, the intelligence community fosters competition in other ways. Intelligence agencies occasionally form red teams, which take on the role of the analysts of another nation or group as a means of gaining insights into their thinking. A now-famous competitive exercise was the 1976 formation of Teams A and B to review intelligence on Soviet strategic forces and doctrine. Team A consisted of intelligence community analysts, and Team B consisted of outside experts, but with a decidedly hawkish viewpoint. The teams disagreed little on the strategic systems the Soviets had built; the key issue was Soviet nuclear doctrine and strategic intentions. Predictably, Team B believed that the intelligence supported a more threatening view of Soviet intentions. However, the lack of balance on Team B largely vitiated the exercise, which could have been useful not only for gaining insight into Soviet intentions but also for validating the utility of competitive intelligence exercises.

Dissent channels—bureaucratic mechanisms by which analysts can challenge the views of their superiors without risk to their careers—are helpful but not widely used. Such channels have long existed for Foreign Service officers in the State Department. Although less effective than competitive analysis for articulating alternative viewpoints, they offer a means by which alternative views can survive a bureaucratic process that tends to emphasize mutual consent.

A broader issue is the extent to which competitive intelligence can or should be institutionalized. To some degree, in the U.S. system it already is. But the competition among the three all-source agencies is not often pointed. They frequently work on the same issue, but with different perspectives that are well understood, thus muting some of the differences that may be seen.

Competitive analysis requires that enough analysts with similar areas of expertise are working in more than one agency. This was certainly true during the zenith of competitive analysis, in the 1980s. But the capability began to dwindle as the intelligence community faced severe budget cuts and personnel losses in the 1990s, after the end of the cold war. As analytic staffs got smaller, agencies began to concentrate more on those issues of greatest importance to their policy customers. Thus, the ability to conduct competitive analysis declined. To rebuild the capability requires two things: more analysts and the time for them to become expert in one or more areas.

Although the intelligence community believes in competitive analysis, not all policy makers are receptive to the idea. Some see no reason that agencies cannot agree on issues, perhaps assuming that each issue has a single answer that should be knowable. One main reason that President Truman created the Central Intelligence Group (CIG) and its successor, the CIA, was his annoyance over receiving intelligence reports that did not agree. He wanted an agency to coordinate the reports so that he could work his way through the contradictory views. Truman was smart enough to realize that agencies might not agree, but he was not comfortable receiving disparate reports without some coordination that attempted to make sense of the areas of disagreement. Other policy makers lack Truman's subtlety and cannot abide having agencies disagree, thus vitiating the concept of competitive analysis.

Finally, those who are not familiar with the idea of competitive analysis, and even some who are, may regard the planned redundancy as more wasteful than intellectually productive.

POLITICIZED INTELLIGENCE. The issue of politicized intelligence arises from the line separating policy and intelligence. This line is best thought of as a semipermeable membrane; policy makers are free to offer assessments that run counter to intelligence analyses, but intelligence officers are not allowed to make policy recommendations based on their intelligence. For example, in the State Department in the late 1980s, the assistant secretary responsible for the Western Hemisphere, Elliot Abrams, often disagreed with pessimistic INR assessments as to the likelihood that the contras would be victorious in Nicaragua. Abrams would often write more positive assessments on his own that he would forward to Secretary of State George P. Shultz.

Policy makers and intelligence officers have different institutional and personal investments in the issues on which they work. The policy makers are creating policy and hope to accrue other benefits (career advancement, reelection) from a successful policy. Intelligence officers are not responsible for creating policy or for its success, yet they understand that the outcomes may affect their own status, both institutional and personal.

The issue of politicization arises primarily from concerns that intelligence officers may intentionally alter intelligence, which is supposed to be objective, to support the options or outcomes preferred by policy makers. These actions may stem from a number of motives: a loss of objectivity regarding the issue at hand, a preference for specific options or outcomes, an effort to be more supportive, career interests, or outright pandering.

Intentionally altering intelligence is a subtle issue because it does not involve crossing the line from analysis to policy. Instead, the analyst is tampering with his own product so that it is received more favorably. The issue is also made more complex by the fact that, at the most senior levels of the intelligence community, the line separating intelligence from policy begins to blur. Policy makers ask senior intelligence officials for their personal views on an issue or policy, which they may give. It is difficult to conceive of a DCI (or, now, a DNI) always abstaining when the president or the secretary of state asks such a question.

The size or persistence of the politicization problem is difficult to determine. Some who raise accusations about **politicized intelligence** are losers in the bureaucratic battles—intelligence officers whose views have not prevailed or policy makers (in the executive branch or Congress, either loyal to the current administration or in opposition) who are dissatisfied with current policy directions. Thus, their accusations may be no more objective than the intelligence that concerns them. Those unfamiliar with the process are often surprised to hear intelligence practitioners talk about winners and losers. But these debates—within the policy or the intelligence community—are not abstract academic discussions. Their outcomes have real results that can be significant and even dangerous. And careers can rise and fall as well. Just as intelligence officers serve policy makers, career officers—both intelligence and policy—serve political appointees, who are less interested in the objectivity of analysis.

For example, in the late 1940s and early 1950s, many State Department experts on China (the "China hands") had their careers sidetracked or were forced from office over allegations that they had lost China to the communists. Numerous scholars and officials interpreted their treatment as a gross injustice. But, as Harvard University professor Ernest R. May pointed out, the U.S. public in the elections of the early 1950s largely repudiated the anti–Chiang Kai-shek views of the China hands by returning the pro–Chiang Republicans to power. So the China hands not only had ideological foes within the government, but they also had no political basis upon which to pursue their preferred policies. Similarly, the careers of many intelligence officers and Foreign Service officers involved in crafting and promoting the strategic arms limitation talks (SALT II) treaty during the Carter administration failed to prosper when Ronald Reagan, who opposed the treaty, took office. Again, their careers suffered only because of an electoral victory. One can argue that these punishments were not what the electorate had in mind, but they underscore the fact that the government and the underlying policy processes are essentially political in nature.

Politicization by intelligence officers may also be a question of perception. A consensus could probably be reached on what politicized intelligence looked like, but much less agreement would emerge on whether a specific analysis fit the definition.

Thus, politicized intelligence remains a concern, albeit a somewhat vague one, which may make it more difficult and important. Many issues surrounding politicized intelligence came up in the hearings on Robert Gates's second nomination as DCI, such as when several analysts charged that Gates had altered analyses on the Soviet Union to meet policy makers' preferences. (Gates asked President Reagan to withdraw his first nomination during the Iran-contra affair. He was subsequently renominated by President George Bush and confirmed in 1991.)

Politicization was also a concern in the Iraq WMD issue. In 2003 the press reported that Vice President Dick Cheney had been out to the CIA several times to receive briefings on Iraq. Critics saw the visits as an attempt to influence the analysts, even though intelligence officials and analysts maintained that they were not. Is there a proper number of times a senior official should be briefed on a highly sensitive topic, after which it appears to be politicization? The answer likely is no. What matters is the substance of the exchange. Also, such exchanges are a primary reason for intelligence agencies—to help officials make decisions. In Britain, charges of politicization on Iraq centered on accusations that Prime Minister Tony Blair or his office asked Defence Ministry officials to "sex up" their intelligence on Iraq WMD, which the government denied. Three external reviews of intelligence on Iraq, by the Senate Intelligence Committee and the WMD Commission in the United States and by Lord Butler in Britain, all concluded that the intelligence had not been politicized.

A fourth report, done for the Australian government, came to the same conclusion.

A second type of politicized intelligence is caused by policy makers who may react strongly to intelligence, depending on whether it confirms or refutes their preferences for policy outcomes. For example, according to press accounts in November 1998, Vice President Al Gore's staff rejected CIA reports about the personal corruption of Russian premier Viktor Chernomyrdin. Staff members argued that the administration had to deal with Chernomyrdin, corrupt or not, and that the intelligence was inconclusive. Analysts countered that the administration set the standard for proof so high that it was unlikely to be met by intelligence. The analysts found that they were censoring their reports to avoid further disputes with the White House. Both policy and intelligence officers denied the allegations.

Policy makers may also use intelligence issues for partisan purposes. Two examples in the United States were the missile gap (1959–1961) and the window of vulnerability (1979–1981). In both cases, the party that was out of power (the Democrats in the first case, the Republicans in the second) argued that the Soviet Union had gained a strategic nuclear advantage over the United States, which was being ignored or not reported. In both cases, the accusing party won the election (not because of its charges) and subsequently learned that the intelligence did not support the accusations—which it then simply claimed had been resolved.

INTELLIGENCE ANALYSIS: AN ASSESSMENT

Sherman Kent, an intellectual founder of the U.S. intelligence community and especially of its estimative process, once wrote that every intelligence analyst has three wishes: to know everything, to be believed, and to influence policy for the good (as he understands it). Kent's three wishes offer a yardstick by which to measure analysis. Clearly, an analyst can never know everything in a given field. If everything were known, the need for intelligence would not exist—nothing would be left to discover. But what Kent is getting at in his first wish is the desire of the analyst to know as much as possible about a given issue before being asked to write about it. The amount of intelligence available varies from issue to issue and from time to time. Analysts must therefore be trained to develop some inner, deeper knowledge that enable them to read between the lines, to make educated guesses or intuitive choices when the intelligence is insufficient.

Kent's second wish—to be believed—goes to the heart of the relationship between intelligence and policy. Policy makers pay no price for ignoring intelligence, barring highly infrequent strategic disasters such as

Josef Stalin's refusal to accept the signs of an imminent German attack in 1941. Intelligence officers see themselves as honest and objective messengers who add value to the process, who provide not just sources but also analysis. Their reward, at the end of the process, is to be listened to, which varies greatly from one policy maker to another.

Finally, and derived from his second wish, Kent notes that intelligence officers want to have a positive effect on policy, to help avert disaster and to help produce positive outcomes in the nation's interests. But analysts want to be more than a Cassandra, constantly warning of doom and disaster. Their wish to have a positive influence also indicates the desire to be kept informed about what policy makers are doing to enable the intelligence officers to play a meaningful role.

What, then, constitutes good intelligence? This is no small question, and one is reminded of Justice Byron White's response when he was asked to define pornography: "I can't define it, but I know it when I see it." Good intelligence has something of the same indistinct quality. At least four qualities come to mind. Good intelligence is

- Timely. Getting the intelligence to the policy maker on time is more important than waiting for every last shred of collection to come in or for the paper to be pristine, clean, and in the right format. The timeliness criterion runs counter to the first of Kent's three wishes: to know everything. And time can change the perspective on an occurrence. Napoleon died on St. Helena in May 1821; word of his death did not reach Paris until July. Charles Maurice de Talleyrand, once Napoleon's foreign minister and later one of his foes, was dining at a friend's house when they heard of Napoleon's passing. The hostess exclaimed, "What an event!" Talleyrand corrected her: "It is no longer an event, Madam, it is news."

- Tailored. Good intelligence focuses on the specific information needs of the policy maker, to whatever depth and breadth are required, but without extraneous material. This must be done in a way that does not result in losing objectivity or politicizing the intelligence. Tailored intelligence products (those responding to a specific need or request) are among the most highly prized by policy makers.

- Digestible. Good intelligence has to be in a form and of a length that allow policy makers to grasp what they need to know as easily as possible. The requirement tends to argue in favor of shorter intelligence products, but it is primarily meant to stress that the message be presented clearly so that it can be readily understood. This does not mean that the message cannot be complex, or even incomplete. But whatever the main message is, the policy maker must be able to understand it with a minimum of effort. Being succinct and clear is an important skill for analysts to learn. Writing a good two-page memo is much more difficult than writing a five-page memo on the same subject. As Samuel Clemens (Mark Twain) observed in a letter to a friend, "I am writing you a long letter because I don't have time to write a short one."

- Clear regarding the known and the unknown. Good intelligence must convey to the reader what is known, what is unknown, and what has been filled in by analysis, as well as the degree of confidence in the material. The degree of confidence is important because the policy maker must have some sense of the relative firmness of the intelligence. All intelligence involves risk by the very nature of the information being dealt with. The risk should not be assumed by the analysts alone but should be shared with their clients.

Objectivity was not one of the major factors defining good intelligence. Its omission was not an oversight. The need for objectivity is so great and so pervasive that it should be taken as a given. If the intelligence is not objective, then none of the other attributes—timeliness, digestibility, clarity—matters.

Accuracy also is not a criterion. Accuracy is a more difficult standard for assessing intelligence than might be imagined. Clearly, no one wants to be wrong, but everyone recognizes the impossibility of infallibility. Given these limits, what accuracy standard should be used? One hundred percent is too high and 0 percent is too low. Splitting the difference at 50 percent accuracy is still unsatisfactory. Thus, what is left is a numbers game—something more than 50 percent and less than 100 percent.

The issue of accuracy became more demanding in the aftermath of September 11 and the onset of the Iraq war. The political system seemed to have decreasing tolerance for the imperfection that is inherent in intelligence analysis. Even though all observers understand that perfection is not possible, each and every mistake seemed to incur a large political cost for the intelligence agencies. This can have a further cost in the analytic system if analysts become risk-averse because of the political costs of being wrong.

As unsatisfactory as this standard is, other metrics are not much better. For example, a batting average could be constructed over time—for an issue, for an office, for an agency, for a product line. Or the quality of intelligence could be assessed on the basis of the number of products produced—estimates, analyses, images. But these measures are inadequate, too. Furthermore, they are not meant to be as frivolous as they seem. They are meant to give a feel for the difficulty of assessing what is good intelligence.

However, producing good intelligence is not some sort of holy grail that is rarely achieved. Good intelligence is often achieved. But one must distinguish between the steady stream of intelligence that is produced on a daily basis and the small amount within that daily production that stands out for some reason—its timeliness, the quality of its writing, its effect on policy. The view here—and it is one that has been debated with the highest intelligence officials—is that effort is required to produce acceptable, useful intelligence on a daily basis, but that producing exceptional intelligence is much more difficult and less frequently achieved. A conflict arises between the goal of consistency and the desire to be exceptional. An entire intelligence community cannot be exceptional all the time, but it does hope to be consistently helpful to policy. Consistent intelligence and exceptional intelligence are not one and the same. (As a cynic once said: "Only the mediocre are at their best all the time.") Consistency is not a bad goal, but it allows analysis to fall into a pattern that lulls both the producer and the consumer. Thus, for all that is known about the distinctive characteristics of good intelligence, it remains somewhat elusive in reality, at least as a widely seen daily phenomenon. But, for analysts, that is one of the positive challenges of their profession.

KEY TERMS

analyst agility
analyst fungibility
analytical stovepipes
assessments
clientism
competitive analysis
current intelligence
duty to warn
estimates

global coverage
groupthink
layering
long-term intelligence
lowest-common-denominator
  language
mirror imaging
opportunity analysis
politicized intelligence

FURTHER READINGS

The literature on analysis is rich. These readings discuss both broad general issues and some specific areas of intelligence analysis that have been particularly important. The CIA has declassified many of its estimates on the Soviet Union and related issues (see chap. 11).

Adams, Sam. "Vietnam Cover-Up: Playing with Numbers; A CIA Conspiracy against Its Own Numbers." *Harper's* (May 1975).

Bell, J. Dwyer. "Toward a Theory of Deception." *International Journal of Intelligence and Counterintelligence* 16 (summer 2003): 244–279.

Berkowitz, Bruce. "The Big Difference between Intelligence and Evidence." *Washington Post.* February 2, 2003, B1.

Caldwell, George. *Policy Analysis for Intelligence.* Report by the Central Intelligence Agency, Center for the Study of Intelligence. Washington, D.C.: Central Intelligence Agency, 1992.

Clark, Robert M. *Intelligence Analysis: Estimation and Prediction.* Baltimore: American Literary Press, 1996.

Davis, Jack. *The Challenge of Opportunity Analysis.* Report by the Central Intelligence Agency, Center for the Study of Intelligence. Washington, D.C.: Central Intelligence Agency, 1992.

Ford, Harold P. *Estimative Intelligence.* McLean, Va.: Association of Former Intelligence Officers, 1993.

———. *Estimative Intelligence: The Purposes and Problems of National Intelligence Estimating.* Washington, D.C.: Defense Intelligence College, 1989.

Gates, Robert M. "The CIA and American Foreign Policy." *Foreign Affairs* 66 (winter 1987–1988).

Gazit, Shlomo. "Estimates and Fortune-Telling in Intelligence Work." *International Security* 4 (spring 1980): 36–56.

———. "Intelligence Estimates and the Decision-Maker." *International Security* 3 (July 1988): 261–287.

George, Roger Z. "Fixing the Problem of Analytical Mind-Sets: Alternative Analysis." *International Journal of Intelligence and Counterintelligence* 17 (fall 2004): 385–404.

Heuer, Richards J., Jr. *Psychology of Analysis.* Washington, D.C.: Central Intelligence Agency, History Staff, 1999.

Johnson, Loch K. "Analysis for a New Age." *Intelligence and National Security* 11 (October 1996): 657–671.

Lockwood, Jonathan S. "Sources of Error in Indications and Warning." *Defense Intelligence Journal* 3 (spring 1994): 75–88.

Lowenthal, Mark M. "The Burdensome Concept of Failure." In *Intelligence: Policy and Process.* Ed. Alfred C. Maurer and others. Boulder, Colo.: Westview Press, 1985.

MacEachin, Douglas J. *The Tradecraft of Analysis: Challenge and Change in the CIA.* Washington, D.C.: Consortium for the Study of Intelligence, 1994.

Nye, Joseph S. *Estimating the Future.* Washington, D.C.: Consortium for the Study of Intelligence, 1994.

Pipes, Richard. "Team B: The Reality Behind the Myth." *Commentary* 82 (October 1986).

Price, Victoria. *The DCI's Role in Producing Strategic Intelligence Estimates.* Newport: U.S. Naval War College, 1980.

Reich, Robert C. "Reexamining the Team A–Team B Exercise." *International Journal of Intelligence and Counterintelligence* 3 (fall 1989).

Rieber, Steven. "Intelligence Analysis and Judgmental Calibration." *International Journal of Intelligence and Counterintelligence* 17 (spring 2004): 97–112.

Stack, Kevin P. "A Negative View of Comparative Analysis." *International Journal of Intelligence and Counterintelligence* 10 (winter 1998): 456–464.

Steury, Donald P., ed. *Sherman Kent and the Board of National Estimates.* Washington, D.C.: Central Intelligence Agency, Center for the Study of Intelligence, History Staff, 1994.

Turner, Michael A. "Setting Analytical Priorities in U.S. Intelligence." *International Journal of Intelligence and Counterintelligence* 9 (fall 1996): 313–336.

U.S. House Permanent Select Committee on Intelligence. *Intelligence Support to Arms Control.* 100th Cong., 1st sess., 1987.

————. *Iran: Evaluation of U.S. Intelligence Performance Prior to November 1978.* 96th Cong., 1st sess., 1979.

U.S. Senate Select Committee on Intelligence. *The National Intelligence Estimates A–B Team Episode Concerning Soviet Strategic Capability and Objectives.* 95th Cong., 2d sess., 1978.

————. *Nomination of Robert M. Gates.* 3 vols. 102d Cong., 1st sess., 1991.

————. *Nomination of Robert M. Gates to Be Director of Central Intelligence.* 102d Cong., 1st sess., 1991.

————. *Report on the U.S. Intelligence Community's Prewar Intelligence Assessments on Iraq.* 108th Cong., 2d sess., 2004.

Wirtz, James J. "Miscalculation, Surprise, and American Intelligence after the Cold War." *International Journal of Intelligence and Counterintelligence* 5 (spring 1991): 1–16.

————. *The Tet Offensive: Intelligence Failure in War.* Ithaca: Cornell University Press, 1991.

Chapter 7

Counterintelligence

Counterintelligence (CI) refers to efforts taken to protect one's own intelligence operations from penetration and disruption by hostile nations or their intelligence services. It is both analytical and operational. Counterintelligence is not a separate step in the intelligence process but pervades the entire process. CI does not fit neatly with human intelligence, although CI is, in part, a collection issue. Nor does it fit with covert action. CI is one of the most difficult intelligence topics to discuss.

Most nations have intelligence enterprises of some sort. As a result, these agencies are valuable intelligence targets for other nations. Knowing what the other side knows, does not know, and how it goes about its work is always useful. Moveover, knowing if the other side is undertaking similar efforts is extremely helpful. *(See box, "Who Spies on Whom?")*

However, counterintelligence is more than a defensive activity. There are at least three types of CI.

- Collection: gaining information about an opponent's intelligence collection capabilities that may be aimed at one's own country
- Defensive: thwarting efforts by hostile intelligence services to penetrate one's service
- Offensive: having identified an opponent's efforts against one's own system, trying to manipulate these attacks either by turning the opponent's agents into **double agents** or by feeding them false information that they report home

The world of spy and counterspy is murky at best. Like espionage, counterintelligence is a staple of intelligence fiction. But, like all other aspects of intelligence, it has less glamour than it does grinding, painstaking work.

Who Spies on Whom?

Some people assume that friendly spy agencies do not spy on one another. But what constitutes "friendly"? The United States and its "Commonwealth cousins"—Australia, Britain, and Canada—enjoy a close intelligence partnership and do not spy on one another. Beyond that, all bets are off.

In the 1990s, the United States allegedly spied on France for economic intelligence. In the 1980s, Israel willingly used Jonathan Pollard, a U.S. Navy intelligence employee who passed sensitive U.S. intelligence that he believed Israel needed to know. Some people were surprised—if not outraged—that post–Soviet Russia would continue using Aldrich Ames to spy against the United States. (Subsequent revelations about the espionage of Robert Hanssen stirred less surprise—perhaps a sign of increased maturity gained through painful experience.) In the late 1990s, a House committee found that China stole nuclear secrets from the United States at a time when the two nations were strategic partners against the Soviet Union.

In the 1970s a "senior U.S. government official" (probably Secretary of State Henry A. Kissinger) observed, "There is no such thing as 'friendly' intelligence agencies. There are only the intelligence agencies of friendly powers."

INTERNAL SAFEGUARDS

All intelligence agencies establish a series of internal processes and checks, the main purposes of which are to weed out applicants who may be unsuitable and to identify current employees whose loyalty is questionable. The vetting process for applicants includes extensive background checks, interviews with the applicants and close associates, and, in the United States at least, the use of the polygraph at most agencies. The ideal candidate is not necessarily someone whose past record is spotless. Most applicants likely have engaged in some level of experimentation—either sexual or drugs, or both. Some may have committed minor criminal offenses. It is crucial, however, that applicants be forthcoming about their past and be able to prove that they are no longer exhibiting behaviors that are criminal, dangerous, or susceptible to blackmail.

The **polygraph**, sometimes mistakenly referred to as a lie detector, is a machine that monitors physical responses (such as pulse and breathing rate) to a series of questions. Changes in physical signs may indicate false-hoods or deceptions. The use of the polygraph by U.S. intelligence remains controversial, as it is imperfect and can be deceived. A 2002 study by the National Research Council found that polygraphs are more useful in criminal investigations, where specific questions can be asked, than for counterintelligence, where the questions are more general and therefore are more likely to yield false-positive responses.

At least two spies, Larry Wu-tai Chin and Aldrich Ames, passed polygraph tests while they were involved in espionage against the United States. Advocates of the polygraph argue that it does serve as a deterrent. They are also quick to assert that the machine is only a tool that can point to problem areas, some of which may be resolved without prejudice. However, an individual's inability or failure to resolve such issues can lead to termination. In addition to new employees, current employees are polygraphed at intervals of several years; contractors are subject to polygraphs; and the machines are used with defectors. Polygraphs are not used consistently throughout the national security structure, however. The Central Intelligence Agency (CIA), Defense Intelligence Agency (DIA), National Reconnaissance Office, and National Security Agency (NSA) all use polygraphs; the State Department and Congress do not. The Federal Bureau of Investigation (FBI) began using polygraphs in the aftermath of the 2001 Robert Hanssen espionage case, which revealed that polygraphs had not been in use at the FBI. This is not to suggest that some agencies are more rigorous or more lax than others. But it does underscore a range of standards in terms of personnel security.

Categorizing the different types of polygraph exams depends on the questions being asked and the information being sought. Thus, intelligence agencies have what they call the **lifestyle poly** (personal behavior) and the **counterintelligence poly** (foreign contacts, handling of classified information). In some instances, such as vetting a source, only a few pertinent questions are asked.

Beyond taking a polygraph (known as "being put on the box"), employees and prospective employees are evaluated for other possible indicators of disloyalty. Changes in personal behavior or lifestyle—marital problems, increased use of alcohol, suspected use of drugs, increased personal spending that seems to exceed known resources, running up large debts—may be signs that an individual is spying or susceptible to being recruited or volunteering to spy. Any of these personal difficulties may befall an individual who would never consider becoming a spy, but past espionage cases indicate some reason for concern. (*See box, "Why Spy?"*) The response of counterintelligence agents to the discovery of such problems would depend on the suspect's larger patterns of behavior, how long the problem persisted, and evidence of potentially hostile activity. In the aftermath of the Ames case—in which marginal performance, alcohol abuse, and a sudden increase in fairly ostentatious personal spending should have been taken as indicators of a problem—U.S. intelligence increased the amount of personal financial information that intelligence personnel must report on a regular basis. These financial-reporting forms

Why Spy?

U.S. counterintelligence emphasizes personal financial issues in assessing security risks. Many people involved in the worst espionage cases suffered by the United States—Aldrich Ames, Robert Hanssen, the Walker spy ring, Ronald Pelton—were motivated largely by greed, not ideology. Some exceptions were Julius Rosenberg, Alger Hiss, Larry Wu-tai Chin, and Ana Montes.

By contrast, many involved in the worst espionage cases in Britain—Kim Philby and his associates or George Blake, for example—spied because of ideological devotion to the Soviet Union.

Although espionage cases of either type (greed or ideology) can arise in either country, some observers have been struck by the difference. It can be explained, in part, by the fact that Britain has had (and still has) a class system that makes ideology a more likely reason for betrayal, although the most serious British spies have come from the upper class. In the United States, the main competition has always been based on economic status, not social class.

Spies may also be motivated by vengeance toward superiors or agencies, by blackmail against themselves or family members, by thrills, or by involvement with a foreign national. Still, most of the spies suffered by the United States have been motivated primarily by money.

assume, however, that ill-gotten gains show up in some way that is detectable with or without the cooperation of the recipient—cash, stocks, or new homes, cars, and so forth bought with cash received. However, as was learned from both the Ames and the Hanssen cases, the country supporting the espionage may be putting some or all of the money in escrow accounts that will not be detected—or even accessed—until years after the espionage is completed. Again, the cases of Ames and Hanssen are instructive. Ames's lifestyle clearly changed—new house, new car, better clothes, cosmetic dental work—but before the financial-reporting forms were required. Outwardly, Hanssen's life showed no signs of increased wealth.

Another internal means of thwarting espionage attacks is the classification system. In U.S. intelligence parlance, the system is **compartmented**. In other words, an employee being accorded the privilege of a clearance does not automatically get access to all of the intelligence information available. Admission to various compartments is based on a **need to know**. Thus, someone working on a new imagery system is likely to have different clearances than someone involved in running human intelligence (HUMINT). There are also compartments within compartments.

For example, a clearance involving HUMINT may include only specific cases or types of HUMINT—perhaps proliferation or narcotics.

The clearance system limits access and therefore reduces the damage that can be caused by any one source of leaks. The system is not without costs. It may become an obstacle to analysis, either wittingly or inadvertently, by excluding some analysts from a compartment crucial to their work. Administering such a system has direct costs: devising a system, tracking documents, running security checks on employees, and so forth. Indirect costs include safes, couriers, security officers to check officers' clearances, and color-coded or numerically tagged papers, to name a few. This list gives some sense of what is involved in a thorough classification scheme. And, if such a scheme is not thorough, it is nothing more than annoying and wasteful.

Other safeguards include the certified destruction of discarded material; the use of secure phones, which cannot be easily tapped, for classified conversations; and restricted access to buildings or to parts of buildings where sensitive material is used. These are called sensitive compartmented information facilities (SCIFs).

EXTERNAL INDICATORS AND COUNTERESPIONAGE

Besides internal measures taken to prevent or to identify problems, counterintelligence agents look for external indicators of problems. They may be more obvious, such as the sudden loss of a spy network overseas, a change in military exercise patterns that corresponds to satellite tracks, or a penetration of the other service's apparatus that reveals the possibility of one's own having been penetrated as well. (This apparently is how Robert Hanssen was detected.) The indicators may be more subtle—the odd botched operation or failed espionage meeting or a negotiation in which the other side seems to be anticipating one's bottom line. These are all murkier indicators of a leak or penetration—what some have described as a "wilderness of mirrors."

In 1995 the CIA and NSA published signal intelligence (SIGINT) intercepts (code-named VENONA) that had been used to detect Soviet espionage in the United States. From 1943 to 1957 VENONA products helped identify Alger Hiss, Julius Rosenberg, Klaus Fuchs, and others working for Soviet intelligence. As VENONA showed, SIGINT can offer indications of ongoing espionage, although the references to spying may be oblique and are unlikely to identify the spy outright. The VENONA intercepts used code names for the spies but often provided enough information to help narrow the search.

The serious problems resulting from having been penetrated by a hostile service also highlight the gains to be made by carrying out one's own successful penetration of the hostile service. Among the intelligence that may be gathered are

- An opponent's HUMINT capabilities and targets, strengths, and weaknesses;
- An opponent's main areas of intelligence interest and current shortfalls;
- Possible penetrations of one's own service or other services;
- Possible intelligence alliances (for example, the Soviet-era KGB used Polish émigrés in the United States for some defense industry espionage and Bulgarian operatives for "wet affairs"—assassinations); and
- Sudden changes in an opponent's HUMINT operations—new needs, new taskings, changed focuses, a recall of agents from a specific region—each of which can have a host of meanings.

Discovering the presence of foreign agents may not lead automatically to their arrest. The agents also present opportunities, as they are conduits to their own intelligence services. At a minimum, efforts could be made to curtail some of their access without their becoming aware of it and then false information could be fed to them to send home. Alternatively, counterintelligence officers may try a more aggressive approach, attempting to turn them into double agents who, although apparently continuing their activities, now provide information on their erstwhile employer and knowingly pass back erroneous information. But just as there are double agents, so there are triple agents—agents who have been turned once, discovered, and then turned again by their own side. The effect, again, is a wilderness of mirrors.

PROBLEMS IN COUNTERINTELLIGENCE

Several problems arise in assessing counterintelligence operations. First, by its very nature, any counterintelligence penetration is going to be covert. Counterintelligence officers are unlikely to come across initially compelling evidence about a successful hostile penetration.

Second, the basic tendency within any intelligence organization (or any organization, for that matter) is to trust its own people, who have been vetted and cleared. They work with one another every day. Familiarity can lead to lowering one's guard or being unwilling to believe that one's own people may have gone bad. This appears to have been a problem in uncovering the espionage of Ames; the CIA was slow to look inward for the cause of severe losses of assets in Moscow. It was originally thought that Hanssen escaped detection for more than twenty years because of his familiarity with U.S. counterintelligence policy and techniques. However, a 2003 report by the inspector general of the Justice Department (FBI is part of that department) found that internal laxity and poor oversight allowed Hanssen, who was portrayed as erratic and bumbling, to avoid detection. Most telling, the FBI first concentrated on a CIA officer when hunting for the spy who turned out to be one of their own—Hanssen. It is easier to believe that the problem lies in another agency.

But the alternative behavior—unwarranted suspicion—can be just as debilitating as having a spy in one's midst. James Angleton, who was in charge of the CIA's counterintelligence from 1954 to 1974, became convinced that a Soviet **mole**—a deeply hidden spy—had penetrated the CIA. Some believed that Angleton was reacting to the fact that a close British associate, Kim Philby, had turned out to be a Soviet agent. Angleton was unable to find the mole, and some believe that he tied the CIA in knots by placing virtually anyone under suspicion. Some suggested that Angleton himself was the mole and that he created a furor to divert attention. Angleton remains a controversial figure, but his activities give some indication of the intellectual issues that can be involved in spying and counterintelligence.

For many years counterintelligence was a major source of friction between the CIA and the FBI. Some of the friction was a legacy of long-time FBI director J. Edgar Hoover's resentment toward the CIA and that agency's reciprocation of Hoover's feelings. The friction also stemmed from differing views of the problem. A discovered spy is a problem as well as a **counterespionage** opportunity that the CIA may wish to exploit. Counterespionage can be thought of as a subset of the larger counterintelligence issue. CI seeks to thwart or exploit any and all attempts to undercut or penetrate intelligence activities. Counterespionage works against the HUMINT aspects (both offensive and defensive) of the CI problem. For the FBI, spying is a prelude to prosecution. As late as the Ames case of the early 1990s, the CIA and FBI were not coordinating their counterintelligence efforts, which probably prolonged Ames's activities. As a result of his arrest and the subsequent investigation, the CIA and FBI created a jointly staffed counterintelligence office to correct the mistakes of the past.

Like so much else in intelligence, suspicions of espionage may not always be proven. The case of Wen Ho Lee, the scientist at Los Alamos National Laboratory, is instructive but complex. In brief, Lee's case came up hard on the heels of a congressional report put out by the Cox Committee (U.S. House Select Committee on U.S. National Security and Military/Commercial Concerns with the People's Republic of China), which was headed by Rep. Christopher Cox, R-Calif., and investigated a series of allegations about Chinese spying that largely targeted high-end technology, including U.S. nuclear weapons designs. Given the issues involved, the Department of Energy (DOE) and the national laboratories were likely places to look. (A series of nasty arguments also played out in public between current and former DOE intelligence and counterintelligence officers, as well as between some of them and the FBI, over the issue of responsibility.) Lee, who was born in Taiwan, had been under investigation since 1994, but the investigation was fitful and inconclusive. He had downloaded some 400,000 pages of classified nuclear data unrelated to his work at Los Alamos. In 2000, Lee was arrested, charged with fifty-nine counts, and held in jail for more than nine months, mostly in solitary confinement. However, the government was unable to discover evidence of espionage, that is, passing the material to a foreign power. A Justice Department report castigated the FBI's handling of the investigation, concluding that if Lee was a spy, the FBI let him get away, and if he was not a spy, the bureau failed to consider other lines of investigation. Lee was eventually released and agreed to plead guilty to one felony count of illegally downloading sensitive nuclear data. The case remains, at best, inconclusive. It calls to mind Scottish law, which gives a jury the option to return a verdict of "not proven," instead of either guilty or not guilty.

In intermediate cases, officers come under suspicion for reasons other than espionage but still pose risks. A good example is Edward Howard, a CIA Directorate of Operations (DO) officer who was slated to be posted to Moscow in the 1980s. Howard was revealed to have ongoing drug and criminal problems that made the posting impossible. He was suspected of being a counterintelligence problem, but handling the situation was difficult. If sending him to Moscow was not an option, he would have to be reassigned or fired. If he were reassigned, he would still be in a position to see classified material even though he remained a security risk because of his personal behavior. Moreover, he would most likely feel aggrieved because of the cancellation of his overseas posting, further making him a risk. Alternatively, to fire him was risky, as he had thorough knowledge of DO tradecraft plus information about operations in Moscow. Once fired, it would be difficult, if not impossible, to keep watch on him. Ultimately, Howard was fired, but he was kept under FBI surveillance. He eluded surveillance and fled to Moscow, claiming that he had not been a spy but had been driven away by the CIA. David Wise, a veteran intelligence author and sometimes critic of U.S. intelligence, interviewed Howard in Moscow and came away convinced that Howard's disloyalty predated his flight. The Howard case illuminates yet another problem in dealing with counterintelligence cases.

Once a spy has been identified and arrested, the intelligence community conducts a **damage assessment**, to determine what intelligence has been compromised. Having the cooperation of the captured spy would be useful. In the United States, this cooperation often becomes a major negotiating point between government prosecutors and the spy's attorney: cooperation in exchange for a specific sentence or for consideration for the spy's family. As with everything else in counterintelligence, however, issues always linger. The most obvious is the degree to which the spy is being honest and forthcoming. Those conducting the damage assessment must avoid the temptation to use the fact of a discovered spy to explain intelligence losses that are unrelated to that person's espionage. The focus must stay firmly on the intelligence to which the spy had access. More than one spy may have been operating at the same time, with access to the same intelligence. This appears to have been the case with Ames and Hanssen, whose espionage was contemporaneous and who had access to some of the same intelligence. Thus, the Hanssen damage assessment likely required a reexamination of the Ames damage assessment, perhaps without any definitive conclusions. The Soviets or, later, the Russians could have used one set of information to confirm the other, thus having Ames and Hanssen ironically confirming each other's bona fides as useful spies.

Double agents raise a host of concerns about loyalty. Have they been turned, or are they playing a role while remaining loyal to their own service? Investigations of U.S. citizens suspected of spying bring up legal issues because of constitutional safeguards on civil liberties. Domestic phones can be tapped, but only after intelligence agents have obtained a warrant from a special federal court (the Foreign Intelligence Surveillance Act Court), which was set up by the Foreign Intelligence Surveillance Act of 1978 (FISA, pronounced "fy-za"). The FISA Court has apparently never refused a requested warrant. Agents also use other intrusive techniques, such as listening devices in the suspect's home or office; searches of home or office when the suspect is absent, including making copies of computer files; and going through garbage.

Prosecuting intelligence officers for spying was a major concern for the intelligence agencies, which feared that accused spies would threaten to reveal classified information in open court as a means of avoiding prosecution. This is known as **"graymail"** (as opposed to blackmail). To preclude this possibility, Congress in 1980 passed the Classified Intelligence Procedures Act (also known as the Graymail Law), which allows judges to review classified material in secret, so that the prosecution can proceed without fear of publicly disclosing sensitive intelligence.

In 1999, as part of a government-wide response to revelations about Chinese espionage, the FBI proposed splitting its National Security division into two separate units, one to deal with counterespionage and the other with terrorism. In 2003, the FBI created an Intelligence Division, concentrating primarily on terrorism. The 2004 intelligence legislation formally recognized the new office as the Intelligence Directorate. The FBI also proposed broadening the National Security Threat List, on which it assesses counterespionage threats, to include corporations and international criminal organizations as well as foreign governments.

In June 2005, President George W. Bush ordered a restructuring of both the Justice Department and the FBI. The position of assistant attorney general for national security has been created, overseeing counterterrorism, counterespionage, and intelligence policy. The FBI now has a National Security Service, which oversees the new Directorate of Intelligence and the Counterterrorism and Counterintelligence Division. The National Security Service is headed by an executive assistant director, who comes under the DNI for coordination of activities and budget.

In addition to the FBI, which has the primary CI responsibility in the United States, and the CIA, the Defense Investigative Service and the counterintelligence units of virtually all intelligence agencies or offices share some CI responsibility. The diffusion of the CI effort reflects the organization of the community and also highlights why coordination on CI cases has been problematic. To remedy this, Congress, in 2002, passed the Counterintelligence Enhancement Act, which called for the creation of the National Counterintelligence Executive (NCIX). The NCIX is the head of U.S. counterintelligence and is responsible for developing counterintelligence plans and policies. This includes an annual strategic CI plan, a national CI strategy, and the oversight and coordination of CI damage assessments. The NCIX directs the Office of the National Counterintelligence Executive, which had been under the office of the DCI. The intelligence law of 2004 puts the NCIX under the new DNI.

As VENONA confirms, the espionage threat during the cold war was pointed and obvious, even though some cases of Soviet espionage—such as those of Rosenberg and Hiss—still remain controversial to some people. But, as the Ames and Hanssen cases indicated, Russian espionage did not end with the cold war. Neither did U.S. activities against Russia, given the Russians arrested by dint of Ames's spying or the source who led to Hanssen. (In 2003, Russia arrested Aleksander Zaporozhsky, a former intelligence office who had settled in the United States but had been lured back to Russia. Zaporozhsky was sentenced to eighteen years for spying for the United States. Some observers believed that Russia held Zaporozhsky responsible for helping identify Hanssen.) In 1999 the Cox Committee found that China had stolen U.S. nuclear weapons designs during the 1980s, when the two states were tacit allies against the Soviet Union.

Assessing the nature and scope of the espionage threat to the United States may be more difficult in the post–cold war world than it had been before the demise of the Soviet Union, not only because the ideological conflict is over but because the sources and goals of penetrations may have changed. A 2002 report prepared for Congress listed China, France, India, Israel, Japan, and Taiwan as being among the most active collectors. The most commonly targeted types of intelligence are U.S. military capabilities, U.S. foreign policy, technological expertise, and business plans. Government officials need not be the sole targets. For certain types of intelligence, government contractors may be key. Also, just as the United States relies on liaison relationships to enhance its HUMINT, so do foreign nations. In 2001, Ana Belen Montes, a DIA analyst, was arrested for spying for Cuba. U.S. officials assume that much of the intelligence that Montes provided over seventeen years was shared by Cuba with Russia and possibly other nations. Another 2002 report, *Espionage against the United States by American Citizens, 1947–2001,* prepared by the Defense Personnel Security Research Center, noted changes in the demographics of U.S. citizens who spied against their country. Since the end of the cold war, spies have tended to be older, to have lower clearances, to be naturalized citizens instead of native-born, and to include more women. Thus, it would be naïve to believe that the need for rigorous counterintelligence and counterespionage ceased with the end of the cold war.

KEY TERMS

compartmented
counterespionage
counterintelligence
counterintelligence poly
damage assessment
double agents

graymail
lifestyle poly
mole
need to know
polygraph

FURTHER READINGS

Reliable and comprehensible discussions of counterintelligence—apart from mere spy stories—are rare.

Bearden, Milt, and James Risen. *The Main Enemy: The Inside Story of the CIA's Final Showdown with the KGB.* New York: Random House, 2003.
Benson, Robert Louis, and Michael Warner, eds. *VENONA: Soviet Espionage and the American Response, 1939–1957.* Washington, D.C.: National Security Agency and Central Intelligence Agency, 1996.
Godson, Roy S. *Dirty Tricks or Trump Cards: U.S. Covert Action and Counterintelligence.* Washington, D.C.: Brassey's, 1995.
Hitz, Frederick P. "Counterintelligence: The Broken Triad." *International Journal of Intelligence and Counterintelligence* 13 (fall 2000): 265–300.
Hood, William, James Nolan, and Samuel Halpern. "Myths Surrounding James Angleton: Lessons for American Counterintelligence." Washington, D.C.: Consortium for the Study of Intelligence, Working Group on Intelligence Reform, 1994.

Johnson, William R. *Thwarting Enemies at Home and Abroad: How to Be a Counter-intelligence Officer.* Bethesda, Md.: Stone Trail Press, 1987.

National Counterintelligence Executive. *The National Counterintelligence Strategy of the United States.* NCIX Publication No. 2005–10007, March 2005.

Perkins, David D. "Counterintelligence and Human Intelligence Operations." *American Intelligence Journal* 18 (1988).

Rafalko, Frank J. *A Counterintelligence Reader.* (Available at www.fas.org/irp/ops/ci/docs/index.html.)

Shulsky, Abram N., and Gary J. Schmitt. *Silent Warfare: Understanding the World of Intelligence.* 2d rev. ed. Washington, D.C.: Brassey's, 1983.

U.S. House Permanent Select Committee on Intelligence. *Report of Investigation: The Aldrich Ames Espionage Case.* 103d Cong., 2d sess., 1994.

———. *United States Counterintelligence and Security Concerns—1986.* 100th Cong., 1st sess., 1987.

U.S. House Select Committee on U.S. National Security and Military/Commercial Concerns with the People's Republic of China (Cox Committee). *Report.* 106th Cong., 1st sess., 1999.

Zuehlke, Arthur A. "What Is Counterintelligence?" In *Intelligence Requirements for the 1980s: Counterintelligence.* Ed. Roy S. Godson. Washington, D.C.: National Strategy Information Center, 1980.

Chapter 8

Covert Action

Covert action, along with spying, is a mainstay of popular ideas about intelligence. Like spying, covert action is fraught with myths and misconceptions. Even when understood, it remains one of the most controversial intelligence topics.

Covert action is defined in the National Security Act as "[a]n activity or activities of the United States Government to influence political, economic or military conditions abroad, where it is intended that the role of the United States Government will not be apparent or acknowledged publicly."

Some intelligence specialists have objected to the phrase "covert action," believing that the word "covert" emphasizes secrecy over policy. (The British had earlier referred to this activity as special political action—SPA.) The distinction is important, because even though these activities are secret, they are undertaken as one means to advance policy goals. This cannot be stressed enough. Proper covert actions are undertaken because policy makers have determined that they are the best way to achieve a desired end. These operations do not—or should not—proceed on the initiative of the intelligence agencies.

During the Carter administration (1977–1981), which exhibited some qualms about force as a foreign policy tool, the innocuous and somewhat comical phrase "special activity" was crafted to replace "covert action." The administration thus substituted a euphemism with a euphemism. But when the Reagan administration came into office, with different views on intelligence policy, it continued to use "special activity" in its executive orders governing intelligence.

Ultimately, what covert activities are called should not matter that much. What is significant is that in making changes in appellation the United States reveals a degree of official discomfort with the tool.

The classic rationale behind covert action is that policy makers need a **third option** (yet another euphemism) between doing nothing (the first option) in a situation in which vital interests may be threatened and sending in military force (the second option), which raises a host of difficult political issues. Not everyone would agree with this rationale, including those who would properly maintain that diplomatic activity is more than doing nothing without resorting to force.

As with counterintelligence, a pertinent question is whether covert action was a product of the cold war and whether it remains relevant today. Covert action became—under the leadership of Director of Central Intelligence (DCI) Allen Dulles during the Eisenhower administration (1953–1961)—an increasingly attractive option (see chap. 2). It had both successes and failures but was seen as a useful tool in a broad-based struggle with the Soviet Union. In the post–cold war period, situations could arise—involving proliferators, terrorists, or narcotics traffickers—in which some sort of covert action might be the preferred means of action.

THE DECISION-MAKING PROCESS

Covert action makes sense—and should be undertaken—only when tasked by duly authorized policy makers in pursuit of specific policy goals that cannot be achieved by any other means. Covert action cannot substitute or compensate for a poorly conceived policy. The planning process for covert action must begin with policy makers justifying the policy, defining clearly the national security interests and goals that are at stake, and believing that covert action is a viable means as well as the best means for achieving specified ends.

Maintaining a capability for covert action entails expenses, for the operation itself and for the infrastructure involved in mounting the action. Even though covert actions are not planned and executed overnight, a certain level of preparedness (such as having on hand equipment, transportation, false documents and other support items, and trained personnel, including foreign assets) must exist at all times. The operational support structure—which also includes prearranged meetings places, surveillance agents, letter drops, technical support—is sometimes referred to as **plumbing**. Forming and maintaining such a standby capability takes time and costs money. But the key question at this point in the decision-making process is whether the cost—both monetary and political—of carrying out a covert action is justified. Cost becomes especially important when looking at actions that may last for months or longer.

Alternatives to covert action need to be considered. If overt means of producing a similar outcome are available, they are almost certainly preferable. Using them does not preclude either covert action if overt means fail or covert action employed in conjunction with overt means, but the overt means should be tried first.

Policy makers and intelligence officials examine at least two levels of risk before approving a covert action. The first is the risk of exposure. William E. Colby, perhaps reflecting on the large-scale investigations of intelligence that dominated his tenure as DCI (1973–1976), said a director should always assume that an operation will become public knowledge at some point. A difference clearly exists between an operation that is exposed while under way or shortly after its conclusion and one that is revealed years later. Nonetheless, even a long-postponed exposure may prove to be embarrassing or politically costly.

The second risk to be weighed is failure of the operation. Failure of this nature may be costly at several levels: in human lives and as a political crisis for the nation carrying out the operation, as well as for those it may be trying to help. Decision makers must weigh the relative level of risk against the interests that are at stake. An extremely risky operation may still be worth undertaking if the stakes are high enough and no alternatives are available. In other words, the ends may justify the means, or at least the risks. For example, in the 1980s the United States was looking for ways to aid the Mujaheddin rebels in Afghanistan who were fighting Soviet invaders. One option was to arm the rebels with Stinger antiaircraft missiles, which would counter the successful Soviet use of helicopters. But policy makers were concerned that some Stingers would fall into the wrong hands or be captured by the Soviets. Ultimately, the Reagan administration decided to send the Stingers, which helped alter the course of the war. It also left Stingers in the hands of the Mujaheddin after their victory, but policy makers deemed that a smaller risk than Soviet victory in Afghanistan.

Even though intelligence analysis and operations exist only to serve policy, intelligence officers may be eager to demonstrate their covert action capabilities. Several factors may drive officers to do so: a belief that they can deliver the desired outcome, a bureaucratic imperative to prove their value, and their professional pride in doing this type of work. However, unless the operation is closely tied to agreed-upon policy goals and is supported as a viable option by the policy community, it starts off severely hampered. Covert action planners must therefore closely coordinate their plans and actions with policy offices.

Covert actions are extraordinary steps, something between the states of peace and war. That alone is enough to raise broad ethical questions, although the policy makers' willingness to maintain a covert action capability indicates some agreement among them on the propriety of its use. The specific details of an operation are likely to raise ethical issues as well. Should a democratically elected but procommunist government be subverted and overthrown (Guatemala, 1954)? Should a nation's economy be disrupted—with attendant suffering for the populace—to overthrow the government (Cuba, 1960s)? Should a group opposed to a hostile government be armed, with a view toward fomenting an insurgency (Nicaragua, 1980s)? The issues these questions raise are important not only intrinsically but also because of the risk of exposure. How do covert actions fit with the causes, standards, and morals that the United States supports?

In evaluating proposed covert actions, policy makers should examine analogous past operations. Have they been tried in this same nation or region? What were the results? Are the risk factors different? Has this type of operation been tried elsewhere? Again, with what results? Although these are commonsense questions, they run up against a governmental phenomenon: the inability to use historical examples. Decision makers are so accustomed to concentrating on near-term issues that they tend not to remember accurately past analogous situations in which they have been involved. They move from issue to issue in rapid succession, with little respite and even less reflection. Or, as Ernest R. May and Richard Neustadt pointed out in *Thinking in Time: The Uses of History for Decision Makers* (1988), they learn somewhat false lessons from the past, which are then misapplied to new circumstances.

Legislative reaction to covert actions is a bigger issue for the United States than it is for other democracies. The congressional committees that oversee the intelligence community are an integral part of the process, as providers of funding and as decision makers who need to be apprised of planned operations. However, while their support is important, it is not mandatory. The long lead times required for the operations also mean that they can be put into the budget process in advance, so that funds can be allocated for them.

Covert action does require formal approval. The president must sign an order, approving the operation, based on his finding that covert action is "necessary to support identifiable foreign policy objectives of the United States, and is important to the national security of the United States." In intelligence parlance, this document is called a **presidential finding**. Congress and the American public did not know that the president signed off on each operation until Secretary of State Henry A. Kissinger was forced to reveal as much before a congressional committee in the mid-1970s. Presidential findings are now required by law and must be in writing (except for emergencies, in which case a written record must be kept and a finding produced within forty-eight hours).

The finding is transmitted to those responsible for carrying out the operation and to the members of the House and Senate Intelligence Committees or a more limited congressional leadership group in a memo of notification (MON). Often, because of the long time lines involved, the congressional committees will already have learned about the operation via the budget process, which includes a review of the year's covert action plan. Congress may wish to be briefed on the specifics of the finding and the operation. The briefings are advisory in nature. Other than denying funding during the budget process, Congress has no basis for approving or disapproving an operation, unless specific laws or executive orders ban them—such as the acts passed by Congress in the 1980s limiting aid to the contras or the executive order banning assassination.

However, should committee members or the staffers raise serious questions, a prudent covert action briefing team reports that fact to the executive branch. This should be enough to cause the operation to be reviewed. The executive branch may still decide to go ahead, or it may make changes in the operation to respond to congressional concerns.

The covert action policy system, for all of its rules, remains fragile because of its inherent secrecy. The Iran-contra scandal underscored some of its weaknesses. A majority in Congress, opposed to support for the contras in Nicaragua, cut off funding. President Reagan, in his usual broad manner, urged his National Security Council (NSC) staff to help the contras "keep body and soul together." NSC staffer Lt. Col. Oliver L. North did this by soliciting donations from private individuals and foreign governments, alleging that DCI William J. Casey, who died just as the scandal broke, had approved his actions. North also argued that Congress's restrictions applied to Defense Department and intelligence agencies, not to the NSC staff. In a parallel activity, the NSC staff pursued clandestine efforts to improve ties to Iran and free hostages in the Middle East, despite earlier objections to this policy by the secretaries of state (George P. Shultz) and defense (Caspar W. Weinberger). Israel shipped antitank missiles to Iran at the behest of the NSC staff, with the United States replacing them in Israel's inventory. North also became involved in the Iranian initiative and suggested diverting to the contras the money that Iran had paid for the missiles.

Iran-contra pointed up several problems in the covert action process.

- Questionable delegations of authority ordered and managed covert actions (the actions of North on the NSC staff).
- Presidential findings were postdated and signed ex post facto (the finding authorizing the sale of missiles to Iran).
- Disparate operations were merged (using the Iranian money to fund the contras).
- The executive branch failed to keep Congress properly informed (disregarding the laws restricting aid to the contras and not briefing on the finding to sell missiles to Iran).

Debates on the worthiness of the respective policies involved in Iran-contra notwithstanding, NSC staff and other executive branch officials violated a host of accepted norms and rules in managing the operations.

The creation of the post of director of national intelligence (DNI) in 2004 raises new questions for the supervision of covert action. The DNI is now the president's senior intelligence adviser, which would presumably include covert action, one of the most important types of intelligence activities. Responsibility for conducting covert action remains within the Central Intelligence Agency (CIA). The law states that the new director of the CIA (DCIA) reports to the DNI, but it does not specify how extensive this reporting requirement is. The law is clear that the DNI does not have operational control over the CIA. Thus, the DNI will have to create mechanisms that give him insight into covert action capabilities and the status of ongoing operations. One can easily foresee situations in which the DNI and the DCIA will be at odds over covert action.

THE RANGE OF COVERT ACTIONS

Covert actions encompass many types of activities.

Propaganda is the old political technique of disseminating information that has been created with a specific political outcome in mind. Propaganda can be used to support individuals or groups friendly to one's own side or to undermine one's opponents. It can also be used to create false rumors of political unrest, economic shortages, or direct attacks on individuals, to name a few techniques.

Political activity is a step above propaganda, although they may be used together. Political activity enables an intelligence operation to intervene more directly in the political process of the targeted nation. As with propaganda, political activity can be used to help friends or to impede foes. For example, in the late 1940s the United States supplied scarce newsprint to centrist, anticommunist political parties in Italy and France during closely contested elections. The United States has also funneled money to political parties overseas to help during elections. Or a state can use political activity more directly against its foes, such as disrupting rallies or interfering with their publications.

The United States has tended to use economic activity against governments deemed to be hostile. Every political leadership—democratic or totalitarian—worries about the state of its economy because this has the greatest daily effect on the population: the availability of food and commodities, the stability of prices, the relative ease or difficulty with which basic needs can be met. Economic unrest often leads to political unrest. Again, other techniques may be used in conjunction with economic activity, such as propaganda to create false fears about shortages. Or the economic techniques may be more direct, such as attempts to destroy vital crops or to flood a state with counterfeit currency to destroy faith in

FIGURE 8-1   The Covert Action Ladder

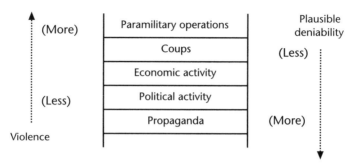

the monetary system. For years, the United States attacked Cuba's economy directly as well as indirectly via a trade embargo. Economic unrest
was also a key factor in U.S. efforts to undermine the government of Salvador Allende in Chile in the early 1970s. Economic destabilization may
be more effective against a more democratic rule, as in Chile, than against
a dictatorship, as in Cuba, which has fewer qualms about inflicting want
or privation on its people and is much less responsive to—or willing to
tolerate—popular protests.

Coups, the overthrow of a government, either directly or through
surrogates, are a further step up the covert action ladder (see Figure 8-1).
Again, a coup may be the culmination of many other techniques—propaganda, political activity, economic unrest. The United States used coups
successfully in Iran in 1953 and in Guatemala in 1954 and was involved
in undermining the Allende government in Chile, although the coup that
brought down his government was indigenous.

Paramilitary operations are the largest, most violent, and most dangerous covert actions, involving the equipping and training of large armed
groups for a direct assault on one's enemies. They do not involve the use
of a state's own military personnel in combatant units, which technically
would be an act of war. The United States was successful in this type
of operation in Afghanistan in the 1980s but failed abysmally at the Bay
of Pigs in 1961. The contra war against the Sandinistas in Nicaragua was
neither won nor lost, but the Sandinistas were defeated at the polls when
they held a free election in the midst of a deteriorating economy.

Some nations have also practiced a higher level of covert military
activity—secret participation in combat. For example, Soviet pilots flew
combat missions during the Korean War against United Nations (primarily U.S.) aircraft. This type of activity raises several issues: military action
without an act of war, possible retaliation, and the rights of combatants if
captured. The United States has largely eschewed this practice because of

such complications, preferring to allow intelligence officers to take part in paramilitary activities.

Paramilitary operations need to be distinguished from special operations forces. The most fundamental and important distinction is that special forces are uniformed military personnel conducting a variety of combat tasks not performed by traditional military arms. The United States has a Special Operations Command (SOCOM). Other such forces are the British Special Air and Special Boat Services (SAS and SBS). Paramilitary operations do not involve the use of one's own uniformed military personnel as combatants. In the war in Afghanistan (2001–), the role of paramilitary personnel appears to be closer to actual combat than was primarily the case in Nicaragua, but their main role remains training, helping supply, and offering leadership assistance to indigenous forces. The CIA's paramilitary forces in Afghanistan are part of the CIA Directorate of Operation's Special Activities Division. According to press accounts, CIA paramilitary personnel were the first U.S. forces in Afghanistan, establishing contact with members of the Northern Alliance and preparing them for the offensive against the Taliban.

The war on terrorism has focused attention on a covert activity that does not fall neatly into the customary range of actions—renditions. Renditions are the seizure of individuals wanted by the United States. These individuals are living abroad and are not in countries where the United States can use legal means to take them into custody. The operations are called renditions because the individual in question is rendered (that is, formally delivered) to U.S. custody. Renditions predate the war on terrorism, although the scale clearly has increased.

Renditions are controversial for several reasons. First, they are extraterritorial actions. In some instances, the foreign government in whose territory the rendition occurred was aware of the operation and looked the other way, allowing the rendition to proceed but preserving its own plausible deniability. In the case of terrorism, some renditions have been controversial because the United States did not retain custody of the suspects but sent them on to their home nations, most often in the Middle East. Rules about custody, civil rights, and limits on interrogation tend to be different in most of these states, with the effect that some rendered suspects have likely been subject to harsh treatment if not torture. Although the United States has sought pledges from these states as to how they would conduct interrogations, U.S. officials cannot be present at all times in these countries. Critics charge that the United States is therefore knowingly complicit in torture. Others argue that the United States cannot hold all suspects, that it is doing as much as it can to prevent torture, and that the importance of breaking up terrorist networks and gleaning information about them requires such use of foreign nations. (See chap. 13.)

In June 2005, an Italian judge named thirteen CIA officers in an indictment concerning the rendition of an Egyptian, Osama Moustafa Hassan Nasr, from Milan in 2003. Although the U.S. government made no official response, CIA officials let it be known that any rendition would have been known to the Italian government. The Italian government denied any such knowledge.

ISSUES IN COVERT ACTION

Covert action, both in concept and practice, raises a host of issues.

The most fundamental is whether such a policy option is legitimate. Like most questions of this sort, there is no correct answer. The prevailing opinions can be divided into two schools—idealists and pragmatists. Idealists argue that covert intervention by one state in the internal affairs of another violates acceptable norms of international behavior. They argue that the very concept of a third option is illegitimate. Pragmatists may accept the arguments of the idealists but contend that the self-interest of a state occasionally makes covert action necessary and legitimate. Historical practice over several centuries would tend to favor the pragmatists. Idealists would respond that the historical record does not justify covert intervention. (This debate took a curious turn with passage of the 1998 Iraq Liberation Act, in which Congress and the president agreed to spend $97 million to replace the regime of Saddam Hussein—an overt commitment to interfere in Iraq's internal affairs.)

In several instances during the nineteenth and twentieth centuries the United States intervened in other nations, primarily in the Western Hemisphere, but these activities were largely overt and usually military in nature. The United States began to use covert action in the context of the cold war. Did the nature of the Soviet threat make covert action legitimate? Did the use of this option—not only directly against the Soviet Union but also in third world nations that were often the battlegrounds of the cold war—lessen the moral differences between the United States and the Soviet Union? Again, there are broad differences of opinion. To U.S. policy makers during the administrations of Harry S. Truman (1945–1953) and Dwight D. Eisenhower (1953–1961), the Soviet threat was so large and multifaceted that the question of the legitimacy of covert action never arose. In any event, they preferred covert action to the possibility of a general war in Europe or Asia. However, some people believe that the use of the covert option blurred distinctions between the two nations that should have been important.

Assuming that, in broad terms, covert action is an acceptable option, is it circumscribed by the nature of the state against which it is being carried out? Or does this question become irrelevant if one accepts the legitimacy of covert action? For example, the United States used covert economic destabilization against Fidel Castro's Cuba and Allende's Chile. Both were communists, but Castro had seized power after a guerrilla war; Allende never commanded an electoral majority, but he had been elected according to the Chilean constitution. Castro turned Cuba into a hostile Soviet base; Allende showed only disturbing signs of friendliness to Castro and to other Soviet allies. Instead of having a second Soviet satellite in the Western Hemisphere, the United States opted to destabilize Allende in the hope of fomenting a coup against him. Should the fact that Allende had been elected according to Chilean law have been sufficient to preclude covert action by the United States? Or were U.S. national security concerns of sufficient primacy to make the covert option legitimate? This was not the first time the United States had intervened in democratic processes. For example, it gave covert assistance in a variety of forms to centrist parties in Europe in the late 1940s to preclude communist victories.

Central to the U.S. concept of covert action is **plausible deniability**—that U.S. denials of a role in the events stemming from a covert action appear plausible. The need to mask its participation stems directly from the idea that the action has to be covert. If the situation could be addressed overtly, the role of the United States would not be an issue. DCI Richard Helms (1966–1973) held that plausible deniability was an absolute requirement for a covert action but also conceded that it was becoming an outmoded concept because of the expanded requirements for oversight and notification.

Plausible deniability depends almost entirely on having the origin of the action remain covert. Once that is lost, deniability is barely plausible. Deniability may have been sustainable during the 1950s and 1960s, but this has become more difficult since the revelation that the president signs each finding to order a covert action.

The scale of the activity also matters. For example, in the aftermath of the Bay of Pigs debacle, President John F. Kennedy (1961–1963) sought counsel from his predecessor, President Eisenhower. Kennedy defended his decision not to commit air power to assist the invasion on the grounds of maintaining deniability of a U.S. role. Eisenhower scoffed, asking how—given the scale and nature of the operation—the United States could plausibly deny having taken part.

Plausible deniability also raises concerns about accountability. If one of the premises of covert action policy is the ability to deny a U.S. role, does this also allow officials to avoid responsibility for an operation that is controversial or perhaps even a failure? Or does the fact that the president must sign a finding put the responsibility on him?

The main controversy raised by propaganda activities is that of **blowback**. The CIA is precluded from undertaking any intelligence activities within the United States. However, a story could be planted in a media outlet overseas to be reported in the United States. That is blowback. This risk is probably higher today with global twenty-four-hour news agencies than it was during the early days of the cold war. Thus, inadvertently, a CIA-planted story that is false can be reported in a U.S. media outlet. In such a case, does the CIA have a responsibility to inform the U.S. media outlet of the true nature of the story? Would doing so compromise the original operation? If such notification should not be given at the time, should it be given afterward?

Not all covert actions remain covert. One of the key determinants seems to be the scale of the operation. The smaller and more discreet the operation, the easier it is to keep secret. But as operations become larger, especially paramilitary operations, the ability to keep them covert declines rapidly. Two operations undertaken during the Reagan administration— aid to the contras in Nicaragua and to the Mujaheddin in Afghanistan— illustrate the problem. Should the possibility of public disclosure affect decision makers when they are considering paramilitary operations? Or should disclosure be accepted as a cost of undertaking this type of effort, with the understanding that it is likely to be something less than covert and not plausibly deniable?

Despite the desired separation of intelligence and policy, covert action blurs the distinction in ways that analysis does not. Instead of providing intelligence to assist in the making of decisions, through covert action the intelligence community is being asked to help execute policy. Of necessity, it has a role in determining the scale and scope of an operation, about which it has the greatest knowledge. The intelligence community also has a day-to-day part to play in managing an operation.

The distinction blurs further because the intelligence community has a vested interest in the outcome of a covert action in ways that are vastly different from its interest in the outcome of a policy for which it has provided analysis. Covert action is not just an alternative means of achieving a policy end; it is also a way for the intelligence community to demonstrate its capabilities and value.

Thus, covert action makes the policy and intelligence communities closer collaborators, as the separation between them diminishes. Conversely, the intelligence community takes on additional responsibilities in the eyes of the policy community. The intelligence community bears a greater burden for a less-than-successful covert action than it does for less-than-perfect intelligence analysis.

Paramilitary operations raise numerous issues. In addition to the problem of keeping them covert and the strains they put on plausible deniability, paramilitary operations raise serious questions about the amount of time available to achieve their stated goals. Unless these operations appear to have a reasonable chance of success in a well-defined period of time, policy makers find their ensuing options limited. On the one hand, they can decide to continue the operation even if the chances of success—usually defined as some sort of military victory—appear slim. It may be that the paramilitary force is unlikely to be defeated but unlikely to win, offering the prospect of an open-ended operation. On the other hand, policy makers can decide to terminate the operation. U.S. abandonment of the Kurds in Iraq in the 1970s is a case in point. The United States had been supporting the Kurds in their struggle against Iraq to create an independent homeland. Covert aid was given to the Kurds via Iran, which also had an interest in weakening its neighbor. The Kurdish effort was inconclusive. In the mid-1970s, however, the shah decided to resolve his differences with Iraq and ordered the operation to cease. The United States complied, abruptly leaving the Kurds to fend for themselves. But when an operation such as this is shut down, extricating all of the combatants may not be possible. In such a case, what is the obligation of the power backing the operation to the combatants? Do the combatants understand the risks they have undertaken, or are they simply assets of the power backing the covert action?

Within the United States, a long-standing debate has taken place about which agency should be responsible for paramilitary operations: the CIA or the Defense Department. The CIA has traditionally run paramilitary operations because, initially, the Defense Department wanted no involvement in them. If covert action is an alternative to military operations, the Defense Department might find it difficult to keep the two options separate. International law poses another difficulty. Although no international sanction has been placed on covert action, the target may consider the use of military personnel (in or out of uniform) in such an activity to be an act of war. Finally, the involvement of the Defense Department may undercut the effort to achieve plausible deniability.

However, the Defense Department has greater expertise than the CIA in the conduct of military operations as well as a greater infrastructure to carry them out, which might save some money. Removing paramilitary operations from the CIA might spare the intelligence community some internal strains caused by having responsibility for both analysis and operations. New strains might subsequently appear in the Defense Department.

The war in Afghanistan and the war against terrorism renewed the debate. Secretary of Defense Donald H. Rumsfeld pushed for a greater role for the Special Operations Command, including recruiting and maintaining spies in enemy forces. At the same time, the CIA had increased its own paramilitary capability, both as part of DCI George J. Tenet's overall effort to enhance the Directorate of Operations and to respond to the war on terrorism. In its 2004 report, the 9/11 Commission (National Commission on Terrorist Attacks Upon the United States) recommended that the Special Operations Command take over paramilitary operations from the CIA, based on the view that the two organizations had redundant capabilities and responsibilities. The commission envisaged the CIA organizing paramilitary units, but SOCOM being responsible for final planning and execution.

A January 2004 study by the Army War College pointed out some fundamental differences in how the two groups operate, suggesting that even a collaborative effort would be difficult. For example, in joint operations, would military personnel be covered by the Geneva Convention? Would the necessary secrecy create chain of command problems and make it more difficult to communicate with or to identify friendly units? How would Congress oversee such operations? In February 2005, a study requested by President George W. Bush came out against the recommendations of the 9/11 Commission and argued that the CIA should retain its paramilitary capabilities. In June 2005, the Bush administration confirmed that the CIA's role in covert action. Still, Special Operations Command can be expected to continue to play a larger part in this area than was the case in the past, probably necessitating some clarification of duties in the future.

One concern raised by the conduct of covert actions is their possible effect on intelligence analysis, which is carried out, in part, by the same agency conducting the operation. If the CIA is conducting an operation—particularly a paramilitary operation—is it reasonable to expect the analytical part of the CIA to produce objective reports on the situation and the progress of the paramilitary operation? Or will there be a certain impetus, perhaps unstated, to be supportive of the operation? DCI Allen Dulles kept the Directorate of Intelligence—the CIA's analytical arm—ignorant of operations in Indonesia (1957–1958) and at the Bay of Pigs (1961) so as not to contaminate it with knowledge of these operations.

In seventeenth- and (to a lesser extent) eighteenth-century Europe, statesmen occasionally used assassination as a foreign policy tool. Heads of state, who were royalty, were exempt from this officially sanctioned act, but their ministers and generals were not. Soviet intelligence occasionally undertook "wet affairs," as it referred to assassinations. Israeli intelligence has allegedly killed individuals outside of Israel. The Church Committee (Senate Select Committee to Study Governmental Operations with Respect to Intelligence Activities), chaired by Frank Church, D-Idaho, was formed in 1975 to investigate allegations that the CIA had exceeded its charter. The panel found in 1976 that the United States was involved in several

Assassination: The Hitler Argument

Adolf Hitler is often cited as a good argument in favor of assassination as an occasional but highly exceptional policy option. But when would a policy maker have made the decision to have him killed? Hitler assumed power legally in 1933. Throughout the 1930s he was not the only dictator in Europe who repressed civil liberties or arrested and killed large numbers of his own population. Josef Stalin probably killed more Soviet citizens during collectivization and the great purges than the Nazis sent to death camps. Deciding to kill Hitler prior to his attacks on the Jews or the onset of World War II would have required a fair amount of foresight as to his ultimate purposes. Little about Hitler was extraordinary until he invaded Poland in 1939 and approved the "final solution" against the Jews in 1942.

Britain revealed in 1998 that its intelligence considered assassinating Hitler during the war, even as late as 1945. The British abandoned the plan not because of moral qualms or concerns about success but because they decided that Hitler was so erratic as a military commander that he was an asset for the Allies.

assassination plots in the 1960s and 1970s—the most famous being that against Fidel Castro—although none succeeded. (See box, "Assassination: The Hitler Argument.")

Since 1976 the United States has formally banned the use of assassination, either directly by the United States or through a third party. The ban has been written into three successive executive orders, the most recent signed by President Reagan in 1981, which remains in effect.

Still, the policy remains controversial. Although support for the ban was fairly widespread when instituted by President Gerald R. Ford (1974–1977), debate over the policy has been growing. Opponents continue to hold that it is morally wrong for a state to target specific individuals. But proponents have argued that assassination might be the best option in some instances and might be morally acceptable, depending on the nature of the target. Drawing up such guidelines still appears to be so difficult as to preclude a return to the previous policy. In the aftermath of the September 11, 2001, terrorist attacks, debate over the assassination ban was renewed. (See box, "The Assassination Ban: A Modern Interpretation.") The issue had changed somewhat, however, in that the United States now considered itself to be at war with terrorists, which altered the nature of the target and the legitimacy of using violent force. (See chap. 13 for a more detailed discussion of the ethical and moral issues raised by assassination.)

The Assassination Ban: A Modern Interpretation

In August 1998 the United States launched a cruise missile attack on targets in Afghanistan associated with al Qaeda leader Osama bin Laden. The United States believed that bin Laden was behind the terrorist attacks earlier that month on two U.S. embassies in East Africa.

The Clinton administration later stated that one goal of the raid was to kill bin Laden and his lieutenants. Administration officials also argued that their targeting of bin Laden did not violate the long-standing ban on assassinations. Their view was based on an opinion written by National Security Council lawyers that the United States could legally target terrorist infrastructures and that bin Laden's main infrastructure was human.

After the September 2001 attacks, bin Laden and other terrorists were seen as legitimate combatant targets, as the United States was at war against them.

ASSESSING COVERT ACTION

In addition to raising ethical and moral issues, covert action faces the difficulty of assessing its utility. When examining a covert action, what constitutes success? Is it just achieving the aims of the operation? Should human costs, if any, be factored into the equation? Is the covert action still a success if its origin has been exposed?

Some people question the degree to which covert actions produce useful outcomes. For example, critics point to the 1953 coup against Iranian premier Mohammad Mossadegh and argue that it helped lead to the Khomeini regime in 1979. Proponents argue that an operation that put in place a regime friendly to the United States for twenty-six years, in a region as volatile as the Middle East, was successful. If no covert action is likely to create permanent positive change given the volatility of politics in all nations, is there some period of time that should be used to determine the relative success of a covert action?

As with all other policies, the record of covert action is mixed, and no hard-and-fast rules have been devised for assessing them. Assistance to anticommunist parties in Western Europe in the 1940s was successful; the Bay of Pigs was a fiasco. The view here is that the Mossadegh coup was a success, for the reasons noted above. But covert action is also subject to the law of unintended consequences. Abetting the fall of Allende helped lead to the regime of Gen. Augusto Pinochet. Average Chileans were probably better off than they would have been under an evolving Marxist regime, but many people suffered repression and terror. Aid to the Muja-heddin in Afghanistan was highly successful and played an important role in the collapse of the Soviet Union. At the same time, Afghanistan remained mired in a civil war ten years after the last Soviet troops with-drew and was eventually ruled by the Taliban, who hosted the al Qaeda terrorists.

Covert action tends to be successful the more closely it is tied to spe-cific policy goals and the more carefully defined the operation is.

KEY TERMS

blowback
covert action
paramilitary operations
plausible deniability

plumbing
presidential finding
propaganda
third option

FURTHER READINGS

The works listed do not go into the details of specific operations. Instead, they focus on the major policy issues discussed in this chapter.

Barry, James A. "Covert Action Can Be Just." *Orbis* 37 (summer 1993): 375–390.

Berkowitz, Bruce D., and Allan E. Goodman. "The Logic of Covert Action." *National Interest* 51 (spring 1998): 38–46.

Chomeau, John B. "Covert Action's Proper Role in U.S. Policy." *International Journal of Intelligence and Counterintelligence* 2 (fall 1988): 407–413.

Daugherty, William J. "Approval and Review of Covert Action Programs since Rea-gan." *International Journal of Intelligence and Counterintelligence*. 17 (spring 2004): 62–80.

Gilligan, Tom. *10,000 Days with the Agency*. Boston: Intelligence Books Division, 2003.

Godson, Roy S. *Dirty Tricks or Trump Cards: U.S. Covert Action and Counterintelli-gence*. Washington, D.C.: Brassey's, 1996.

Johnson, Loch K. "Covert Action and Accountability: Decision-Making for Amer-ica's Secret Foreign Policy." *International Studies Quarterly* 33 (March 1989): 81–109.

Knott, Stephen F. *Secret and Sanctioned: Covert Operations and the American Presi-dency*. New York: Oxford University Press, 1996.

Prados, John. *Presidents' Secret Wars: CIA and Pentagon Covert Operations since World War II*. New York: William Morrow, 1986.

Reisman, W. Michael, and James E. Baker. *Regulating Covert Action: Practices, Con-texts, and Policies of Covert Coercion Abroad in International and American Law*. New Haven: Yale University Press, 1992.

Rositzke, Harry. *The CIA's Secret Operations: Espionage, Counterespionage, and Covert Action*. New York: Reader's Digest Press, 1977.

Shulsky, Abram N., and Gary J. Schmitt. *Silent Warfare: Understanding the World of Intelligence.* 2d rev. ed. Washington, D.C.: Brassey's, 1993.

Stiefler, Todd. "CIA's Leadership and Major Covert Operations: Rogue Elephants or Risk-Averse Bureaucrats?" *Intelligence and National Security* 19 (winter 2004): 632–654.

Treverton, Gregory F. *Covert Action: The Limits of Intervention in the Postwar World.* New York: Basic Books, 1987.

Chapter 9

The Role of the
Policy Maker

Most authors and experts in the area of intelligence do not consider the policy maker to be part of the intelligence process. In their opinion, once the intelligence has been given to the policy client, the intelligence process is complete. The view in this book is that policy makers play such a central role at all stages of the process that it would be a mistake to omit them. Policy makers do more than receive intelligence; they shape it. Without a constant reference to policy, intelligence is rendered meaningless. Moreover, policy makers can play a determining role at every phase of the intelligence process.

THE U.S. NATIONAL SECURITY POLICY PROCESS

Although much of this book is intended to be a generic discussion of intelligence, the main reference point is the U.S. government. Therefore, a brief discussion of how national security policy is formed in the United States is appropriate.

STRUCTURE AND INTERESTS. The five main loci of the U.S. national security policy process are

1. The president, as an individual;
2. The departments, particularly the State Department and the Defense Department, which has two major components: the civilian (the Office of the Secretary of Defense) and the military (the Joint Chiefs of Staff, or JCS, and the Joint Staff), and on certain issues, other departments may also be involved (including Justice, Commerce, Treasury, Agriculture, and, after the September 2001 attacks, the newly created Homeland Security);
3. The National Security Council (NSC) staff, which is the hub of the system;

4. The intelligence community; and
5. Congress, which controls all expenditures, makes policy in its own right, and performs oversight.

The main national security structure was remarkably stable from its inception in the National Security Act of 1947 until the intelligence law of 2004, which radically changed the top management structure of the intelligence community.

The five groups that carry out the intelligence process have varying interests. The president is a transient, mainly concerned about broad policy initiatives and, eventually, his place in history. Richard M. Nixon, who was intensely suspicious of the permanent bureaucracy, argued—correctly—that a gulf exists between the president's interests and those of the bureaucracy. Sometimes they work together; at other times they are at odds. The bureaucracy tends to be more jaded and, on occasion, to take the view that it can outlast the president, his appointees, and their preferred policies.

The principal interest of the State Department is maintaining diplomatic relations as a means of furthering U.S. policy interests. Critics of the State Department argue that Foreign Service officers sometimes forget which nation they represent, becoming advocates for the nations on which they have expertise instead of for the United States.

The Defense Department is primarily concerned with having a military capability sufficient to deter hostile nations from using force or to defeat any threats as quickly as possible. Critics of the Defense Department hold that the department overestimates its needs and threats and requires too large a margin against any potential foe. In response to the Vietnam War, the unofficial but influential rules for the use of force promulgated by Secretary of Defense Caspar W. Weinberger (1981–1987) and JCS chairman Gen. Colin L. Powell (1989–1993) set high requirements for domestic political support and force preponderance before any troops are committed.

The Department of Homeland Security (DHS) is responsible for coordinating the activities of many long-standing agencies, including the Coast Guard, Immigration and Naturalization, and the Secret Service. It has also established new components. DHS seeks to prevent new terrorist attacks in the United States and serves as a bridge between the federal government and state and local law enforcement agencies on domestic security issues.

The National Security Council, as constituted by law, consists of the president, the vice president, and the secretaries of state and defense. The chairman of the Joint Chiefs of Staff serves as the military adviser; the director of national intelligence (DNI) is subordinate to the NSC and serves as the intelligence adviser. As a corporate group, the NSC meets irregularly. The Principals Committee (called the PC) is made up of the NSC members (less the president) and is presided over by the national security adviser. The Deputies Committee (DC) meets more often. The NSC staff, which reports to the national security adviser, consists of career civil servants, military officers, and political appointees who have day-to-day responsibility for conveying the wishes of the president to the policy and intelligence communities and for coordinating among the departments and agencies. The NSC staff is primarily interested in the execution of policy as defined by the president and senior presidential appointees.

The intelligence community has no policy interests per se, although it wants to be kept informed about the course of policy to make a contribution to it.

POLICY DYNAMICS. Policy makers often refer to the "interagency process" or "the interagency." The term reflects the involvement of any and all necessary agencies and players in the process. The ultimate goal of the U.S. policy process is to arrive at a consensus that all parties can support. But consensus in the U.S. bureaucratic system means agreement down to the last detail of any paper being considered.

The process has no override mechanism, that is, no way of forcing agreement, of isolating an agency that refuses to go along. This safeguards the rights and interests of all agencies, because the agency that does not agree with the others on an issue today may not be the one that objects tomorrow. To ensure that an agency is not coerced, the interagency process emphasizes bargaining and negotiation, steering away from dictating from above or by majority rule. Bargaining has three immediate effects. First, it can require a great deal of time to arrive at positions that everyone can accept. Second, the system gives leverage to any agency that refuses to reach an agreement. In the absence of any override process, the agency that "just says 'no' " can wield enormous power. Third, the necessity of reaching agreement generates substantial pressure in favor of lowest-common-denominator decisions.

On controversial issues, the system can suffer inertia, as agencies constantly redraft papers that never achieve consensus or that one agency refuses to support, effectively bringing the system to a halt. The only way to break such logjams is for the NSC staff or someone higher, meaning the president and his senior appointees, to apply pressure. Without their intervention, the system would spin endlessly if an agency continues to hold out. Senior pressure renews the impetus to reach a conclusion or raises the prospect that officials in the holdout agency will be told to support what the president wants or to resign. But without pressure from above, holdouts suffer no penalty.

Neither the policy community nor the intelligence community is a monolith. Each has multiple players with multiple interests, which do not always coincide with one another.

THE ROLE OF THE INTELLIGENCE COMMUNITY. Policy makers accept the intelligence community as an important part of the system. But the role of intelligence varies with each administration and sometimes with each issue within an administration. The way in which an administration treats intelligence is the key determinant of the role it plays.

Everyone accepts the utility of intelligence as part of the basis upon which decisions are made. Again, translating this generality into practice is the important issue. Policy makers have many reasons to find fault with or even to ignore intelligence. They do not necessarily view intelligence in the same way as those who are producing it.

Policy makers also accept that the intelligence community can be called upon to carry out certain types of operations. Again, the willingness to use this capacity and the specific types of operations that are deemed acceptable vary with the political leadership. These elected or presidentially appointed leaders must make the final decisions on operations and are held accountable, in a political sense, if the operations fail. To be sure, intelligence officers can and do get their share of the blame, but policy makers perceive that their own costs are much greater.

WHO WANTS WHAT?

The fact that the government is not a monolithic organization helps explain why policy makers and intelligence officers have different interests. At a high macro level, everyone wants the same thing—successful national security policy—but this statement is so general that it is misleading. Success can mean different things to policy makers and intelligence officials.

The president and an administration's senior political appointees define success as the advancement of their agenda. Even though a broad continuity exists in U.S. foreign policy, each administration interprets goals individually and fosters initiatives that are uniquely its own. The success of an administration's agenda must be demonstrable in ways that are easily comprehended, because its successes are expected to have a political dividend. This is not as crass as it sounds. National security policy is created within a political system and process, the ultimate rewards of which are election and reelection to national office. Finally, policy makers expect support for their policies from the permanent bureaucracy.

The intelligence community defines its goals differently. Sherman Kent said that intelligence officers have three wishes: to know everything, to be listened to, and to influence policy for the good, as they understand it (see chap. 6). The intelligence community also wants to maintain its objectivity regarding policy. Intelligence officials do not want to become, or even to be seen as becoming, advocates for policies other than those that directly affect their activities. Only by maintaining their distance from policy can they hope to produce intelligence that is objective. But objectivity is not always easily achieved. To cite a recent example, Director of Central Intelligence (DCI) George J. Tenet (1997–2004) was intimately involved in the Israeli–Palestinian negotiations in October 1998. The Central Intelligence Agency (CIA) took responsibility for creating a security relationship between the two sides. As a result, the CIA had a vested interest in the outcome of the agreement, not because of any intelligence it had produced but because it had become a participant. In this sort of case, legitimate questions can be raised about the potential effect on subsequent analyses of the implementation of the agreement. Will analysts feel free to report that security arrangements are failing, if that is the case, knowing that their own agency is charged with implementing these same arrangements? The answer may be yes, but it is subject to serious question.

The policy maker–intelligence community relationship changes the longer the policy makers stay in office. At the outset of their relationship, policy makers tend to be more impressed and more accepting of the intelligence they receive. Even for policy makers who are returning to government service, albeit in different and usually more senior positions, this tends to be true. However, as the policy makers become more familiar with the issues for which they are responsible and with the available intelligence, they tend to have higher expectations and to become more demanding.

To some, the nature of the relationship between the DCI and the president also became a factor. Tenet enjoyed what was probably the closest relationship of any DCI to a president, usually seeing George W. Bush at least five or six days a week, and sometimes several times a day. This began upon the president's taking office in 2001, when he said he wanted daily briefings from the DCI. This was a dramatic change from the situation under Bill Clinton, when the DCI saw the president much less often. Clinton's first DCI, R. James Woolsey (1993–1995), left office in frustration over his lack of access. A great deal of the DCI's authority derived from the perception that he had access to the president when he needed it. So, for Tenet, the increased access to President Bush was a great gain. But some observers questioned whether such increased access had an effect on the DCI's objectivity. Critics cited Tenet's enthusiastic report on the likelihood of weapons of mass destruction in Iraq. However, the report by the Senate Select Committee on Intelligence said no evidence existed that the intelligence had been politicized.

The same questions are relevant for the DNI. Like the DCI before him, the DNI needs to have access to the president. In some respects this may be even more important for the DNI because, unlike the DCI, he has no large institutional base (the CIA) upon which to fall back. The DNI may have to put more effort into keeping abreast of what the intelligence community is doing and which parts of it are also communicating with the president. There is no definitive answer. Frequent contact between the DNI and the president is bound to run risks, but no DNI would be likely to choose the alternative relationship. The DNI should trust his instincts and rely on his professionalism to maintain the proper bounds on the relationship.

The intelligence community also wants to be kept informed about policy directions and preferences. Although this would seem obligatory if the intelligence community is expected to provide relevant analysis, it does not always happen. All too often, policy makers do not keep intelligence abreast, either by design or omission. Such behavior not only makes the role of intelligence more difficult but also can lead to resentment that may be played out in other ways.

Another difference between the two groups is that of outlook. As a senior intelligence officer observed, policy makers tend to be optimists. They approach problems with the belief that they can solve them. After all, this is the reason they have gone into government. Intelligence officers are skeptics. Their training teaches them to question and to doubt. Although they may see an optimistic outcome to a given situation, they also see the potential pessimistic outcomes and likely feel compelled to analyze them as potential outcomes.

A revealing indication of the potential costs of the difference in outlook emerged in 2004, when relations between the Bush administration and the CIA deteriorated seriously. Differences over the progress being made in containing the insurgency in Iraq appear to have been the main stimulus. Leaks of intelligence analyses, which some White House officials characterized as being written by "pessimists, naysayers, and hand-wringers," exacerbated the problem. At one point, President Bush said the CIA "was just guessing" about potential outcomes in Iraq, a remark that some intelligence officers found demeaning. It became customary to say that the CIA and the White House were "at war." The fact that the exchange took place in the middle of a presidential election undoubtedly added to the tension.

Several lessons are derived from this byplay. First, war or warlike situations—especially those that may be inconclusive—tend to increase the overall tension, as can be easily understood. Second, in such circumstances both parties can forget the nature of their relationship, although this is probably a greater problem for the policy makers. The combination of uncertainty and casualties, with the attendant political costs, raise the policy makers' anxiety. Third, the leadership of the intelligence community understands that it can never win this sort of struggle with policy makers and therefore will seek to avoid such confrontations. The professional ethos and training of senior intelligence officials work to preclude such an outcome. Even if their analyses prove to be correct, the costs to their relationship with senior policy officials would be so great as to result in a Pyrrhic victory. This does not mean that analysts should temper their views or to hedge what they write, but that intelligence officers are unlikely to engage in gratuitous and overt hostility to policy makers.

Finally, the policy makers' expectation of support from the permanent bureaucracy extends to the intelligence community. But they may be seeking intelligence that supports known policy preferences, thus running the risk of politicization. Politicization can also work in the other direction. The intelligence officer's desire to be listened to (Kent's second wish) may lead to analysis that is meant to please the policy makers, either consciously or unwittingly. In either case, the desire for a good working relationship can directly undermine the desired objectivity of intelligence.

THE INTELLIGENCE PROCESS: POLICY AND INTELLIGENCE

The differences between the policy and intelligence communities—and the potential for tension—appear at each stage of the intelligence process.

REQUIREMENTS. Requirements are not abstract concepts. They are the policy makers' agenda. All policy makers have certain areas on which they must concentrate as well as others on which they would like to concentrate. Some areas are of little or no interest to them but require their attention either occasionally or regularly. This mixture of preferences is important in forming the agenda and thus the requirements. For example, Secretary of State James A. Baker III was clear, upon taking office in 1989, that he was not going to spend a lot of time on the Middle East. His decision was not based on a view that the region was unimportant but that he was unlikely to achieve much in the Middle East and therefore his time would be better spent elsewhere. Senior subordinates could handle the Middle East. Iraq's invasion of Kuwait undermined his choice. Ironically, the war also helped lead to the Madrid conference—presided over by Secretary Baker—at which Israel and its Arab foes met together for the first time.

The intelligence community wants guidance on the priorities of the agenda so that its collection and reporting can be as helpful as possible. At the same time, the community tends to understand that it rarely has the luxury of ignoring a region or issue entirely, even if it is not high on the agenda—the global coverage requirement. Sooner or later, one of them is likely to blow up. That said, the intelligence community regularly makes resource choices that lead to some regions or issues receiving little attention.

The degree to which each administration formally communicates its requirements—versus relying on the intelligence community to know which issues matters—also varies. President Clinton was willing to go through a formal requirements exercise only once in eight years. Under President George W. Bush the requirements are reviewed every six months. No matter which method is used or the frequency of formal requirements, the intelligence community is held responsible for ensuring that it has collection and analytical resources on the most important issues. Policy makers also tend to expect that the intelligence community anticipates the emergence of new issues. After all, isn't this one of the main functions of intelligence? The answer is not a firm yes if you take into account the fact that surprises occur: assassinations, coups, elections, reversals of policy. Not everything can be anticipated.

The difference in the approaches of policy makers and intelligence officials to requirements is not played out entirely in formulating the requirements themselves, but in the ensuing parts of the intelligence process.

COLLECTION. Policy makers tend to be divorced from the details of collection unless they involve political sensitivities. In such cases, policy makers can have direct and dramatic effects. (*See box, "Policy Makers and Intelligence Collection."*) Their practical concerns lie, first, in the budget, as collection is one of the major intelligence costs, particularly technical intelligence. But policy makers also tend to assume, incorrectly, that everything is being covered, at least at some minimal level. Thus, when one of the low-priority issues explodes, they expect that a certain low level of collection and on-the-shelf intelligence already exists and that collection can be quickly increased. Both assumptions may be strikingly false. Collection priority decisions tend to be zero-sum games, and not all collection assets are easily fungible.

The intelligence community would rather collect more than less, although officials recognize that they cannot cover everything and hope to get policy makers to concur in the areas left uncovered. Still, collection is the bedrock of intelligence. But when policy makers place limits on collection, the intelligence community obeys, even if its preference is to collect. Like the policy makers, intelligence officials are aware of the costs of collection, but they cannot spend more on collection than the policy community is willing to allocate. The customary practice is for the policy

Policy Makers and Intelligence Collection

In several instances, policy makers have intervened in intelligence collection for political reasons.

In Cuba, at the onset of the missile crisis in 1962, Secretary of State Dean Rusk opposed sending U-2s over the island because a Chinese Nationalist U-2 had recently been shot down over China and an Air Force U-2 had accidentally violated Soviet air space in Siberia. The need for imagery of possible Soviet missile sites in Cuba was great, but Rusk had other—also legitimate—concerns about avoiding further provocation.

In Iran, several successive U.S. administrations imposed limits on intelligence collection. Basically, intelligence officers were not allowed to have contact with those in the souks (markets and bazaars) who were opposed to the shah, because the shah's regime would be offended. Instead, U.S. intelligence had to rely on the shah's secret police, Savak, which had an institutional interest in denying that any opposition existed. Thus, as the shah's regime unraveled in 1978–1979, policy makers denied U.S. intelligence the sources and contacts it needed to better analyze the situation or to influence the opposition.

Again, regarding Cuba, President Jimmy Carter unilaterally suspended U-2 flights as a gesture to improve bilateral relations. Carter came to regret his decision in 1980, when he faced the possibility that a Soviet combat brigade was in Cuba and he required better intelligence on the issue.

community to set budgetary limits on collection resources that are lower than the intelligence community would like.

Finally, the intelligence community has a greater understanding, as would be expected, of the limits of collection at any given time. Intelligence officials know that they are not collecting everything. They make decisions on a regular basis to exclude certain regions or issues. In their own budget requests, intelligence officials also determine how much of the collection to process and exploit, which is always far less than is collected. The intelligence community sees no reasons to convey these facts to the policy makers. At one level, doing so is unnecessary. An uncovered region may stay quiet, which is the bet that the intelligence managers are making. At another level, it may undermine their relationship with policy makers. Why arouse concerns about collection coverage over an issue that is not expected to be a significant priority? Their choices can lead to even worse relations should one of the regions suddenly become a concern and collection be found wanting.

ANALYSIS. Policy makers want information that enables them to make an informed decision, but they do not come to this part of the process as blank slates or wholly objective observers. Already in favor of certain policies and outcomes, they would like to see intelligence that supports their preferences. Again, this is not necessarily as crass as it sounds. Policy makers only naturally prefer intelligence that enables them to go where they want. This attitude becomes problematic only when they ignore intelligence that is compelling but contrary to their preferences.

Some policy makers also want to keep their options open for as long as possible. They may resist making important decisions. Intelligence can occasionally serve to limit options by indicating that some options are either insupportable or may have dangerous consequences. The imposition of such limitations serves as yet another area of friction.

Intelligence often deals in ambiguities and uncertainties. If a situation were known with certainty, intelligence would not be needed. *(See box, "Intelligence Uncertainties and Policy.")* Honestly reported intelligence highlights uncertainties and ambiguities, which may prove to be discomforting to policy makers for several reasons. First, if their goal is intelligence that helps them make decisions, anything that is uncertain and ambiguous is going to be less helpful or perhaps even a hindrance. Second, some policy makers cannot appreciate why the multibillion-dollar intelligence community cannot resolve issues. Many of them assume that important issues are ultimately "knowable," when in fact many are not. This attitude on the part of policy makers can serve as an impetus for intelligence analysts to reach internal agreements or to try to play down disagreements.

Policy makers may also be suspicious of intelligence that supports their rivals in the interagency policy process. They may suspect that rivals have consorted with the intelligence community to produce intelligence that undercuts their position. Finally, policy makers are free to ignore, disagree with, or even rebut intelligence and offer their own analyses. Such actions are inherent to a system that is dominated by the policy makers.

This behavior on the part of policy makers can become controversial. Although policy makers are free to disagree with or to ignore intelligence, it is not seen as legitimate for them to set up what appears to be intelligence offices of their own and separate from the intelligence community. In the period before the onset of the war in Iraq (2003–), Undersecretary of Defense Douglas Feith set up an office that he claimed was a permissible analytic cell. Critics argued that it was charged with coming up with intelligence analysis that was more supportive of preferred policies. Without admitting any fault, the office ultimately was disbanded.

The intelligence community tries to maintain its objectivity. Some policy makers raise questions that can undermine the ability of the intelligence

---

Intelligence Uncertainties and Policy

In 1987 U.S.-Soviet negotiations were drawing to a close on the Intermediate Nuclear Forces (INF) Treaty. The U.S. intelligence community had three methods for estimating the number of Soviet INF missiles that had been produced—all of which had to be accounted for and destroyed. Meanwhile, any final number given by the Soviets would be suspect.

Each of the three major intelligence agencies advocated its methodology and its number as the one that should go forward. But the senior intelligence officer responsible for the issue decided, correctly, that all three numbers had to go to President Ronald Reagan. Some agency representatives argued that this was simply pusillanimous hedging. But the intelligence officer argued that the president had to be aware of the intelligence uncertainties and the possible range of missile numbers before he signed the treaty. That was the right answer, instead of choosing, perhaps arbitrarily, among the methodologies.

---

community to fulfill Kent's wishes to be listened to and to influence policy for the good as well as to be objective. Some conflicts or disconnects can be avoided or ameliorated if the intelligence community makes an effort to convey to policy makers as early as possible the limits of intelligence analysis. The goal should be to establish realistic expectations and rules of engagement. (See box, "Setting the Right Expectations.")

COVERT ACTION. Covert action can be attractive to policy makers, because it increases available options and theoretically decreases direct political costs. Policy makers may assume that an extensive on-the-shelf operational capability exists and that the intelligence community can mount an operation on fairly short notice. The assumptions are, in effect, the operational counterpart to the assumption that all areas of the world are receiving some minimal level of collection and analytical coverage.

Policy makers want covert actions that are successful. Success is easier to define for short-term operations, but it may be elusive for those of longer duration. As a result, tension may arise between the intelligence and policy-making communities. The most senior policy makers tend to think in blocks of time no longer than four years—the tenure of a single administration. The intelligence community, as part of the permanent bureaucracy, can afford to think in longer stretches. It does not face the deadline that elections impose on an administration.

Setting the Right Expectations

During the briefings that each new administration receives, an incoming undersecretary of state was meeting with one of his senior intelligence officers on the issue of narcotics. The intelligence officer laid out in detail all the intelligence that could be known about narcotics: amounts grown, shipping routes, street prices, and so forth. "That said," the intelligence officer concluded, "there is very little you will be able to do with this intelligence."

The undersecretary asked why the briefing had ended in that manner.

"Because," the intelligence officer replied, "this is an issue where the intelligence outruns policy's ability to come up with solutions. You are likely to grow frustrated by all of this intelligence while you have no policy levers with which to react. I want to prepare you for this at the outset of our relationship so as to avoid problems later on."

The undersecretary understood.

The intelligence community harbors a certain ambivalence about covert action. A covert action gives the intelligence community an opportunity to display its capabilities in an area that is of extreme importance to policy makers. Covert action is also an area in which the intelligence community's skills are unique and are less subject to rebuttal or alternatives than is the community's analysis. However, disagreement over covert action is highly probable if policy makers request an operation that intelligence officials believe to be unlikely to succeed or inappropriate. Once the intelligence community is committed to an operation, it does not want to be left in the lurch by the policy makers. For example, in paramilitary operations, the intelligence community likely feels a greater obligation to the forces it has enlisted, trained, and armed than the policy makers do. The two communities do not view in similar ways a decision to end the operation.

POLICY MAKER BEHAVIORS. Just as certain analyst behaviors matter, so do certain policy-maker behaviors. Not every policy maker consumes intelligence in the same way. Some like to read, for example, while others prefer being briefed. Policy makers are better served if they convey their preferences early on instead of leaving them to guesswork.

Policy makers do not always appreciate the limits of what can be collected and known with certainty, the reasons behind ambiguity, and, occasionally, the propriety of intelligence. They sometimes confuse the lack of a firm estimate with pusillanimity when that may not be the case.

Given the range of issues on which they must work, senior policy makers probably are not fully conversant with every issue. The best policy makers know what they do not know and take steps to learn more. Some are less self-aware and either learn as they go along or fake it.

The most dreaded reaction to bad news is killing the messenger, referring to the practice of kings who would kill the herald who brought bad news. Messengers—including intelligence officers—are no longer killed for bringing bad news, but bureaucratic deaths do occur. An intelligence official can lose access to a policy maker or be cut out of important meetings. Both consequences befell DCI John McCone (1961–1965) when he took issue with President Lyndon B. Johnson's strategy for the Vietnam War. Policy makers have also been known to bad-mouth intelligence officers behind their backs.

Policy makers can also be a source of politicization in a variety of ways (see chap. 6): overtly—by telling intelligence officers the outcome he prefers or expects; covertly—by giving strong signals that have the same result; or inadvertently—by not understanding that his questions are being interpreted as a request for a certain outcome. Again, the repeated briefings requested by Vice President Dick Cheney in the period before the start of the war in Iraq were seen by some, mostly outside the intelligence community, as a covert pressure on the intelligence community for a certain outcome—agreement that Iraq was a threat based on its possession of weapons of mass destruction. Even though this was the analytic conclusion, an investigation by the Senate Select Committee on Intelligence that was highly critical of the analytic process found no evidence of politicization.

THE USES OF INTELLIGENCE. One of the divides between policy makers and intelligence officers is the use to which the intelligence is put. Policy makers want to take action; intelligence officers, although sympathetic and sometimes supportive, are concerned about safeguarding sources and methods and maintaining the community's ability to collect intelligence.

For example, suppose intelligence suggests that officials in a ministry in Country A have decided to arrange a clandestine sale of high-technology components to Country B, whose activities are a proliferation concern. The intelligence community has intelligence strongly indicating that the sale is going forward, although it is not clear whether Country A's leadership is fully aware of the sale. The State Department, or other executive agencies, believes that the situation is important to U.S. national interests and wants to issue a démarche to Country A to stop the sale. The intelligence community, however, argues that this will alert Country A—and perhaps Country B as well—to the fact that the United States has some good intelligence sources. At a minimum, it insists on having a hand in drafting the démarche so as to obscure its basis. This can result in a new bureaucratic tug of war, because the State Department wants the démarche to be as strong as possible to get the preferred response—cessation of the sale.

This type of situation arises so frequently that it is accepted by both sides—policy and intelligence—as one of the normal aspects of national security. The struggle is analogous to the divide between intelligence officers and law enforcement officials: Intelligence officers want to collect more intelligence, whereas law enforcement officials seek to prosecute malefactors and may need to use the intelligence to support an indictment and prosecution. On occasion, policy officials cite a piece of open-source intelligence that makes the same case that the classified intelligence does, and they then argue that it can be used as the basis of a specific course of action. However, the intelligence officers may not agree, contending that the open-source intelligence is validated only because the same information is known via classified sources. Thus, the intelligence officers may argue that even using open-source intelligence can serve to reveal classified intelligence sources and methods. In the case of imagery, at least, the greater availability of high-quality commercial imagery may obviate the entire debate.

There is no correct answer to this debate. On the one hand, the intelligence exists solely to support policy. If it cannot be used, it begins to lose its purpose. On the other hand, officials must balance the gain to be made by a specific course of action versus the gains that may be available by not revealing intelligence sources and methods. Usable intelligence is a constant general goal, but which intelligence gets used when and how is open to debate.

TENSIONS. The relationship between policy makers and the intelligence community should be symbiotic: Policy makers should rely upon the intelligence community for advice, which is a major rationale for the existence of the intelligence community. For the community to produce good advice, policy makers should keep intelligence officers informed about the major directions of policy and their specific areas of interest and priority. That said, the relationship is not one of equals. Policy and policy makers can exist and function without the intelligence community, but the opposite is not true.

The line that divides policy and intelligence—and the fact that policy makers can cross it but intelligence officers cannot—also affects the relationship. Policy makers tend to be vigilant in seeing that intelligence does not come too close to the line. However, they may ask intelligence officers for advice in choosing among policy options—or for some action—that would take intelligence over the line. If intelligence officers

decline, as they should to preserve their objectivity regardless of the outcome, policy makers may become resentful. The line also can blur at the
highest levels of the intelligence community, and the DNI may be asked
for advice that is, in reality, policy.

In the United States, partisan politics has also become a factor in the
policy–intelligence relationship. Although differences in emphasis developed from one administration to another (such as the greater emphasis on
political covert action in the Eisenhower administration), general continuity exists in intelligence policy. Moreover, until 1976, intelligence was
not seen as part of the spoils of an election victory. DCIs were not automatically replaced with each new administration, as were the heads of virtually all other agencies and departments. President Nixon (1969–1974)
tried to use the CIA for political ends in an attempt to curtail the Watergate investigations. But it was the Carter administration (1977–1981) that
ended the political separateness of the intelligence community. Jimmy
Carter, in his 1976 campaign, lumped together Vietnam, Watergate, and
the recent investigations of U.S. intelligence. When Carter won the presidency, DCI George Bush (1976–1977) offered to stay on and eschew all
partisan politics, saying that the CIA needed some continuity after the
investigations and four DCIs in as many years. President-elect Carter said
he wanted a DCI of his own choosing. This was the first time a serving
DCI had been asked to step down by a new administration. Similarly,
Ronald Reagan made "strengthening the CIA" part of his 1980 campaign
and also brought in a new DCI, William J. Casey (1981–1987). In a presidential transition within the same party, President George Bush kept on
DCI William H. Webster (1987–1991) for most of his term, but Bill Clinton replaced DCI Robert M. Gates (1991–1993) with James Woolsey.
Thus, a partisan change in the White House came to mean a change in
DCIs as well. However, in 2001, President George W. Bush retained DCI
George Tenet, who had been appointed by Clinton, despite some advice
from within Bush's own party to remove him. Tenet thus became the first
DCI since Helms to survive a party change in the presidency. However, it
is not clear that a new practice has been established.

The argument made in favor of changing DCIs (or, now, DNIs) when
a new administration takes office is that presidents must have an intelligence community leader with whom they are comfortable. But back in the
days of a nonpartisan DCI, many people in Washington, D.C., emphasized the professional nature of the DCI (even DCIs who were not career
intelligence officers) and had the sense that intelligence is in some way
different from the rest of the structure that each president inherits and
fills with his own appointees. An objective intelligence community was
not to be part of the partisan spoils of elections. The shift since 1977 has
affected the policy–intelligence relationship by tagging DCIs with a parti-

san coloration. The shift has also meant a movement away from professional intelligence officers serving as DCIs. Although professionals were not the only people tapped in the past, their selection is less likely in the future. The new intelligence legislation requires that the DNI "shall have extensive national security expertise." No further definition is provided, and the wording is purposely vague enough to allow a range of possible nominees.

Finally, external intrusions, particularly that of the electronic news media, can have an effect on the relationship. Contrary to popular belief, television news does not foster major changes in policy. It does serve as a means of communication for states and their leaders, and it competes with the intelligence community as an alternative source of information. The media do occasionally scoop the intelligence community. This is not because they know things that the intelligence community does not. Instead, the electronic media—especially the twenty-four-hour networks—put a premium on speed and have the capacity and willingness to provide updates and corrections as necessary. The intelligence community does not have the same luxury and tends to take more time in preparing its initial report. Being scooped by the media can lead policy makers to believe, mistakenly, that the media offer much the same coverage as the intelligence community—and at greater speed and less cost.

Although a number of issues are likely to create tension between policy makers and the intelligence community, conflict is not the mainstay of the policy–intelligence relationship. Close and trusting working relationships prevail between policy makers and intelligence officers at all levels. But a good working relationship is not a given, and it cannot be fully appreciated without understanding all of the potential sources of friction.

FURTHER READINGS

Despite its centrality to the intelligence process, the policy maker–intelligence relationship has not received as much attention as other parts of the process.

Betts, Richard K. "Policy Makers and Intelligence Analysts: Love, Hate, or Indifference?" *Intelligence and National Security* 3 (January 1988): 184–189.
David, Jack. *Analytic Professionalism and the Policymaking Process: Q&A on a Challenging Relationship.* Vol. 2, no. 4. Washington, D.C.: Central Intelligence Agency, Sherman Kent School for Intelligence Analysis, October 2003.
Heymann, Hans. "Intelligence/Policy Relationships." In *Intelligence: Policy and Process.* Ed. Alfred C. Maurer and others. Boulder, Colo.: Westview Press, 1985.
Hughes, Thomas L. *The Fate of Facts in a World of Men: Foreign Policy and Intelligence Making.* New York: Foreign Policy Association, 1976.
Hulnick, Arthur S. "The Intelligence Producer–Policy Consumer Linkage: A Theoretical Approach." *Intelligence and National Security* 1 (May 1986): 212–233.

Kovacs, Amos. "Using Intelligence." *Intelligence and National Security* 12 (October 1997): 145–164.

Lowenthal, Mark M. "Tribal Tongues: Intelligence Consumers and Intelligence Producers." *Washington Quarterly* 15 (winter 1992): 157–168.

Poteat, Eugene. "The Use and Abuse of Intelligence: An Intelligence Provider's Perspective." *Diplomacy and Statecraft* 11 (2000): 1–16.

Steiner, James E. "Challenging the Red Line between Intelligence and Policy." Washington, D.C.: Institute for the Study of Diplomacy, Georgetown University, 2004.

Thomas, Stafford T. "Intelligence Production and Consumption: A Framework of Analysis." In *Intelligence: Policy and Process*. Ed. Alfred C. Maurer and others. Boulder, Colo.: Westview Press, 1985.

U.S. Central Intelligence Agency, Center for the Study of Intelligence. *Intelligence and Policy: The Evolving Relationship*. Washington, D.C.: Central Intelligence Agency, June 2004.

Chapter 10

Oversight and Accountability

"Sed quis custodiet ipso custodes?" ("But who will guard the guards?"), the Roman poet and satirist Juvenal asked. The **oversight** of intelligence has always been a problem. The ability to control information is an important power in any state, whether democratic or despotic. Information that is unavailable by any other means and whose dissemination is often restricted is the mainstay of intelligence. By controlling information; by having expertise in surveillance, eavesdropping, and other operations; and by operating behind a cloak of secrecy, an intelligence apparatus has the potential to threaten heads of government. Thus, government leaders' ability to oversee intelligence effectively is vital.

In democracies, oversight tends to be a responsibility shared by the executive and legislative powers. The oversight issues are generic: budget, responsiveness to policy needs, the quality of analysis, control of operations, propriety of activities. The United States is unique in giving extensive oversight responsibilities and powers to the legislative branch. The parliaments of other nations have committees devoted to intelligence oversight, but none has the same broad oversight powers as Congress. (*See box, "A Linguistic Aside: The Two Meanings of Oversight."*)

EXECUTIVE OVERSIGHT ISSUES

The core oversight issue is whether the intelligence community is properly carrying out its functions, that is, whether the community is asking the right questions, responding to policy makers' needs, being rigorous in its analysis, and having on hand the right operational capabilities (collection and covert action). Policy makers cannot trust the intelligence community alone to answer for itself. At the same time, senior policy officials (the national security adviser, the secretaries of state and defense, the president) cannot maintain a constant vigil over the intelligence community. Outside of the intelligence community, the National Security Council

---

A Linguistic Aside: The Two Meanings of Oversight

Oversight has two definitions that are distinct, if not opposites.
- Supervision; watchful care (as in "We have oversight of that activity.")
- Failure to notice or consider (as in "We missed that. It was an oversight.")

In overseeing intelligence, Congress and the executive try to carry out the first definition and to avoid the second.

(NSC) Office of Intelligence Programs is the highest-level organization within the executive branch that provides day-to-day oversight and policy direction of intelligence. The creation of the Joint Intelligence Community Council (JICC) in the 2004 intelligence law adds a new executive oversight body. The JICC is chaired by the director of national intelligence (DNI) and its members include the secretaries of state, Treasury, defense, energy, and homeland security and the attorney general. The JICC serves the DNI as an advisory group on requirements, budgets, performance, and evaluation. Any JICC member can submit advice or an opinion contrary to that provided by the DNI to the president. Again, none of the JICC members other than the DNI has much time to devote to what are essentially intelligence management issues, thus raising questions about the likely effectiveness of the council. Meanwhile, the separate rights of JICC members to convey their views to the president means that the cabinet officers, who are already more powerful than the DNI, have additional means to challenge DNI decisions.

Since the 1953–1961 administration of Dwight D. Eisenhower (with two brief lapses), presidents have relied on the President's Foreign Intelligence Advisory Board (PFIAB) to carry out higher-level and more objective oversight than the NSC Office of Intelligence Programs does. PFIAB members are appointed by the president and usually include former senior intelligence and policy officials and individuals with relevant commercial backgrounds. (In the 1990s some people were appointed to PFIAB largely as political favors.) PFIAB can respond to problems (such as the investigation of alleged Chinese spying at Los Alamos National Laboratory) or can initiate activities (such as the Team A–Team B competitive analysis on Soviet strategic capabilities and intentions).

The PFIAB's relationship to policy makers can be subject to the same strains that are seen in the relationship between policy makers and intelligence agencies. From 2001 to 2005, PFIAB was chaired by Brent Scowcroft, who had served as national security adviser under Presidents Gerald R. Ford (1974–1977) and George Bush (1989–1993). Scowcroft spoke out against the decision to invade Iraq in 2003, which surprised some people given his previous close working relationship with George Bush. In 2005, Scowcroft was replaced by President George W. Bush, in apparent displeasure over his remarks.

The executive branch has tended to focus its oversight on issues related to espionage and covert action, although analytical issues (Team A–Team B, the September 11 terrorist attacks) are occasionally investigated. Espionage oversight is inclined to concentrate on lapses, such as the Aldrich Ames spy case or allegations of Chinese espionage. For example, in 1999 PFIAB issued a scathing report on Department of Energy security practices related to Chinese espionage. As with all other activities, executive branch organizations divide responsibility for overseeing covert action. The president is responsible for approving all covert actions, but the day-to-day responsibility for managing them resides with the director of the CIA (DCIA) and the Directorate of Operations.

One oversight issue relating to covert action centers on the operating concept of plausible deniability. In the case of large-scale paramilitary operations—such as the Bay of Pigs or the contras in Nicaragua—deniability is somewhat implausible. But many covert actions are much smaller in scale, making it possible to deny plausibly any U.S. role. Some critics of covert action argue that plausible deniability undermines accountability by giving operators an increased sense of license. Because the president will deny any connection to their activities, they operate under less constraint. The critics raise a point worth considering but overlook the professionalism of most officers.

Another oversight issue relating to covert action has to do with broad presidential findings, sometimes called **global findings**, versus narrow ones. Global findings tend to be drafted to deal with transnational issues, such as terrorism or narcotics. The broader the finding, and thus the less specificity it contains, the greater is the scope for the intelligence community to define the operations involved. Although not suggesting that the president should precisely define covert actions, a broad finding does run a greater risk of disconnecting policy preferences from operations.

Policy makers must also be concerned about the objectivity of the intelligence community when it is asked to assess or draw up a covert action. Once again, intelligence officers who feel a need to demonstrate their capabilities may not be able to assess in a cold-eyed manner the feasibility or utility of a proposed action.

Similar concerns may arise when assessing the relative success of an ongoing covert action. Have policy makers and intelligence officials agreed on the signs of success? Are these signs evident? If not, what are the accepted timelines for terminating the action? What are the plans for terminating it?

Finally, can intelligence analysts offer objective assessments of the situation in a country where their colleagues are carrying out a major covert action, particularly a paramilitary one? This issue may be of heightened concern in view of the closer partnership forged between the Directorate of Operations and Directorate of Intelligence in the mid-1990s.

The propriety of intelligence activities is also an aspect of oversight. Are the actions being conducted in accordance with law and executive orders (EOs)? All intelligence agencies have inspectors general and general counsels. In addition, the President's Intelligence Oversight Board (PIOB), a subset of PFIAB, can investigate. However, the PIOB is a reactive body, with no power to initiate probes or to subpoena. It is dependent on referrals from executive branch officials. Nonetheless, the PIOB has carried out some useful classified investigations.

The controversies that engulfed intelligence after 2001, primarily the September 11 attacks and Iraq's alleged possession of weapons of mass destruction (WMDs), led to an increased use of outside commissions to provide assessments of intelligence. In the United States, great political pressure was brought to bear on President George W. Bush to appoint a commission to investigate intelligence performance prior to September 11, after Congress's joint inquiry reported to little satisfaction on anyone's part. Similarly, after the Iraq controversy, Bush appointed a WMD commission. The prime ministers of Britain and Australia also appointed commissions to look into intelligence on Iraq. Britain's Butler Report concluded that few reliable sources were available on Iraqi WMD programs, especially human resources. Lord Butler and his colleagues found that the intelligence assessments made good use of the intelligence they did have, although much of it was inferential. As was the case in the United States, analysts did not have complete knowledge of the background of key human resources. The report also found that there was no politicization of intelligence. Australia's Flood Report made similar findings, noting the paucity of information—much of which came to Australia from the United States or Britain, and the failure to examine the political context in Iraq as well as the technical issue of WMDs—a criticism that some have made regarding U.S. intelligence. The Flood Report doubted, however, that better intelligence processes would have led to the correct conclusion about the state of Iraqi WMDs. The report also noted that there was no evidence of politicized intelligence.

A fitting conclusion to this issue, which will likely haunt the intelligence agencies in all three countries for years to come, is the report of Charles A. Duelfer, who headed the Iraq Survey Group (ISG) for the DCI. The ISG spent two years in Iraq examining the state of Iraqi WMDs after the occupation of Baghdad. Duelfer had been a senior member of the United Nations Special Commission (UNSCOM), charged with overseeing the disarmament of Iraq after the 1991 Persian Gulf War, until it was ejected by Iraqi leader Saddam Hussein in 1998. Duelfer concluded that Saddam was determined to obtain WMDs but would wait until United Nations sanctions had been lifted. But to achieve that goal, Saddam wanted to preserve the capacity to reconstitute WMDs, especially missiles and chemical weapons, as quickly as possible once the sanctions were gone. Finally, Saddam sought to create a state of strategic ambiguity, seeking to convince Iran that Iraq had WMDs as a means of deterring Iran while Iraq remained weak. If Duelfer's assessments are correct, then one could argue that the intelligence agencies were accurate in their assessment of Saddam's intentions but not the state of his inventory and that they correctly picked up the signs that he was transmitting that he had WMDs. They were not able to see through them, however.

The increased use of these commissions raises several issues. First, the commissions are, almost by definition, political in nature. A government is either trying to gain some political advantage or bowing to political pressure in creating a commission. Second, given that commissions are created by a sitting government, the issue of a commission's objectivity always arises. This is usually addressed by appointing a range of commissioners whose political views or backgrounds are diverse. But this raises a third issue. How much expertise do they bring to the subject? Intelligence, like any other profession, has its own vocabulary and its own practices, some of which are difficult for an outsider to comprehend or to learn with much facility over the course of an investigation. If too many former intelligence professionals are appointed, the commission will appear to be biased. But if most of the commissioners have little or no intelligence experience, their ability to investigate in a meaningful and perceptive manner may suffer. Finally, the political circumstances that create the commission increase the likelihood that a significant group in the body politic will be dissatisfied with the result, charging either a whitewash or a lynching.

CONGRESSIONAL OVERSIGHT

Congress approaches intelligence oversight—and all oversight issues, whether national security or domestic—from a different but equally legitimate perspective from that of the executive branch.

The concept of congressional oversight is established in the Constitution. Article I, Section 8, paragraph 18, states: "Congress shall have Power . . . To make all Laws which shall be necessary and proper for carrying into Execution the foregoing Powers, and all other Powers vested by this Constitution in the Government of the United States, or in any

Department or Officer thereof." Courts have found that the Necessary and Proper Clause includes the power to require reports from the executive on any subject that can be legislated. The essence of congressional oversight is the ability to gain access to information, usually held by the executive, which is relevant to the functioning of the government.

Apart from its constitutional mandate, a major factor driving Congress in all matters of oversight is the desire to be treated by the executive as an equal branch of government. This is not always easy to achieve, as the executive branch ultimately speaks with one voice, that of the president, while Congress has 535 members. The significant difference leads some people to question whether Congress's constitutional authority works in reality.

Moreover, in the area of national security, Congress has often given presidents a fair amount of leeway to carry out their responsibilities as commander in chief. This is not to suggest that partisan debates do not arise over national security or even intelligence issues, such as the 1960 allegations about a missile gap or the 1970s allegations about a strategic window of vulnerability (see chap. 2). To the contrary, debate has become more partisan in the post–cold war period.

Congress has several levers that it can use to carry out its oversight functions.

BUDGET. Control over the budget for the entire federal government is the most fundamental lever of congressional oversight. Article I, Section 9, paragraph 7, of the Constitution states: "No Money shall be drawn from the Treasury, but in Consequence of Appropriations made by Law; and a regular Statement and Account of the Receipts and Expenditures of all public Money shall be published from time to time."

The congressional budget process is complex and duplicative. It is composed of two major activities: **authorization** and **appropriation**. Authorization consists of approving specific programs and activities. Authorizing committees also suggest dollar amounts for the programs. The House Permanent Select Committee on Intelligence and the Senate Select Committee on Intelligence are the primary authorizers of the intelligence budget. The House and Senate Armed Services Committees authorize some defense-related intelligence programs. Appropriation consists of allocating specific dollar amounts to authorized programs. The defense subcommittees of the House and Senate Appropriations Committees perform this function for intelligence.

Technically speaking, Congress may not appropriate money for a program that it has not first authorized. If authorizing legislation does not pass before a congressional session ends, the appropriations bills contain language stating that they also serve as authorizing legislation until such

---

Congressional Humor: Authorizers versus Appropriators

The tension between those who sit on authorizing committees and those who sit on appropriations committees is pithily characterized by a joke often heard on Capitol Hill:

"Authorizers think they are gods; appropriators know they are gods."

---

legislation is passed. (President George Bush once vetoed an intelligence authorization bill because Congress had included a requirement that the president give Congress forty-eight hours' prior notice of covert actions. Congress subsequently passed a refashioned authorization bill omitting that language. The congressional staffer responsible for managing this piece of legislation was George J. Tenet, who was the staff director of the Senate Intelligence Committee and later would serve as DCI.)

Some tension usually can be felt between the authorizers and the appropriators. Authorization and appropriations bills sometimes vary widely. For example, authorizers may approve a program but find that it is not given significant funds by the appropriators. This is called **hollow budget authority**. Or appropriators may vote money for programs or activities that have not been authorized. These funds are called **appropriated but not authorized** (or "A not A"). In both cases, the appropriators are calling the tune and taking action that disregards the authorizers. (*See box, "Congressional Humor: Authorizers versus Appropriators."*)

When funds are appropriated but not authorized, the agency receives the money but may not spend it until Congress passes a bill to authorize spending. Sometimes, however, an agency submits a reprogramming request to Congress, asking permission to spend the money, and Congress can informally approve it. If Congress does not pass a new authorization bill or approve a reprogramming request, the money reverts to the Treasury at the end of the fiscal year.

After the 9/11 Commission (National Commission on Terrorist Attacks Upon the United States) issued its report, some discussion emerged about combining intelligence authorization and appropriations into one committee in each chamber. Such a change would end some of the potential budget disconnects. It also would remove intelligence budgets from the defense appropriations process. However, Congress did not act on the proposal. The Senate, in its version of the 2004 intelligence legislation, included a provision making public the budget figure for intelligence. The Senate also expected to create an appropriations subcommittee specifically for intelligence. When the unclassified budget provision was removed from the final bill, the issue of a separate Senate appropriations subcommittee for intelligence became problematic. Even if the intelligence budget figure approved by the subcommittee were kept secret, it could easily be derived by totaling up all other appropriations and subtracting that amount from the total. The remainder would be the intelligence appropriation. Thus, for the sake of secrecy, it remains more convenient to have the intelligence appropriation subsumed in the defense appropriation, which in turn makes a separate intelligence subcommittee unnecessary.

The centrality of the budget to oversight should be obvious. In reviewing the president's budget submission and crafting alternatives or variations, Congress gets to examine the size and shape of each agency, the details of each program, and the plans for spending money over the next year. No other activity offers the same degree of access or insight. Moreover, given the constitutional requirement for congressional approval of all expenditures, in no other place does Congress have as much leverage as in the budget process.

Critics of the annual budget process argue that it not only gives Congress insights and power but also subjects the executive to frequent fluctuations in funding levels, given that they can vary widely from year to year. Every executive agency dreams of having multiyear appropriations or **no year appropriations**; that is, money that does not have to be spent by the end of the fiscal year. Although some funds are allocated in these ways, Congress resists doing so on a large scale, because such a move would fundamentally undercut its power of the purse. (Appropriated funds that are not spent at the end of a fiscal year are returned to the Treasury. Each agency keeps careful watch over its spending to ensure that it spends all allocated funds by the end of the fiscal year. The Office of Management and Budget (OMB) also monitors agencies' spending rates throughout the fiscal year to ensure that they are not spending either too fast or too slowly.)

Congress has, in recent years, used supplemental appropriations bills with increasing frequency for intelligence. Basically, **supplemental appropriations** make available to agencies funds over and above the amount originally planned. In the case of an unforeseen emergency the requirement for a supplemental bill is easily understood. But when supplementals are used on a recurring basis—perhaps annually—they become problematic. Supplemental appropriations are single-year infusions of money. Although no guarantee is made for the size of any appropriation from year to year, supplementals are seen as being riskier in terms of the likelihood that they will be used again. Thus, if a crucial activity is being funded by supplemental appropriations, it may be necessary in the following year either to terminate the activity for lack of funds or to curtail some other activity in the budget (called "taking it out of hide"). Clearly, agencies would prefer to have the supplemental funds included in the base, that is, added to their regular budget, so they can plan more effectively for the ensuing years. Congress has been unwilling to do this, largely as a means of controlling growth, despite the effect that repeatedly passing supplementals has had on programs. The use of supplementals has become so regular that both Congress and executive agencies plan for them at the beginning of a budget cycle.

The budget gives Congress power over intelligence. In the 1980s, for example, Congress used the intelligence budget to restrict Reagan administration policy in Nicaragua, passing a series of amendments, sponsored by the chairman of the House Permanent Select Committee on Intelligence, Edward P. Boland, D-Mass., that denied combat-support funds for the contras. Efforts to circumvent these restrictions led to the Iran-contra scandal.

HEARINGS. Hearings are essential to the oversight process as a means of requesting information from responsible officials and obtaining alternative views from outside experts. Hearings can be open to the public or closed, depending on the subject under discussion. Given the nature of intelligence, a majority of the hearings of the two intelligence committees are closed.

Hearings are not necessarily hostile, but they are adversarial; they are not objective discussions of policy. Each administration uses hearings as a forum for advancing its specific policy choices and as opportunities to sell policy to Congress and to interested segments of the public. Congress understands this and is a skeptical recipient of information from the executive branch, regardless of party affiliation. Intelligence officials are somewhat exempt from selling policy, in that they often give Congress the intelligence community's views on an issue without supporting or attacking a given policy. They gain some protection from congressional recriminations because of the line separating policy and intelligence, unless they are perceived as having crossed that line. Again, this was a concern for some members in the case of Iraqi WMD. (Executive branch policy makers may perceive the intelligence community's congressional testimony as unsupportive or as undermining policy, even if that was not the intelligence community's intent.) However, when intelligence officials testify about intelligence policies—capabilities, budgets, programs, intelligence-related controversies—they are also in a sales mode vis-à-vis Congress.

Hearings are often followed by questions for the record (QFRs or "kew-fers") submitted to the witnesses and their agencies by members or their staffs to follow up on issues that surfaced during the hearings. Although QFRs give the executive an opportunity to make their case again or to add new supportive information, the requests are often viewed as punitive homework assignments. QFRs can also be used by Congress as a tool (or weapon) in a struggle with an agency that seems unwilling to offer information or is stubborn about certain policies.

NOMINATIONS. The ability to confirm or reject nominations is a profound political power, which resides in the Senate. Nominations for the DCI were not controversial until 1977, when President Jimmy Carter's nominee, Theodore Sorensen, withdrew his nomination after appearing before the Senate Select Committee on Intelligence and responding to a number of issues that had been discussed publicly about him. The issues included Sorensen's World War II status as a conscientious objector, which raised questions about his willingness to use covert action; and the possible misuse of classified documents in his memoirs as well as his defense of Daniel Ellsberg, who leaked to the press the classified Pentagon Papers (a Defense Department study of the Vietnam War), which raised concerns about his ability to protect intelligence sources and methods.

Since 1977 the Senate has held several other controversial DCI-nominee hearings. Robert M. Gates withdrew his first nomination in 1987 as the Iran-contra scandal unfolded. His second nomination, in 1991, featured a detailed investigation of charges that Gates had politicized intelligence to please policy makers. In 1997 Anthony Lake withdrew his nomination at the onset of what promised to be a grueling and perhaps unsuccessful series of hearings.

Critics of the nomination process—not just of intelligence positions but across the board—charge that it has become increasingly political and personal, delving into issues that are not germane to a nominee's fitness for office. Defenders of the process respond that it is a political process, that the Senate is not supposed to be a rubber stamp, and that careful scrutiny of a nominee may preclude embarrassments later on. Regardless of which view is correct, the nomination process has become so formidable that it has convinced some potential nominees to decline office.

TREATIES. Advising and consenting to an act of treaty ratification is also a power of the Senate. Unlike nominations, which require a majority vote of the senators present, treaties require a two-thirds vote of those present. Intelligence became a significant issue in treaties during the era of U.S.–Soviet arms control in the 1970s. The ability to monitor adherence to treaty provisions was and is an intelligence function. U.S. policy makers also called upon the intelligence community to give monitoring judgments on treaty provisions—that is, to adjudge the likelihood that significant cheating would be detected. The Senate Select Committee on Intelligence, created in 1976, was later given responsibility for evaluating the intelligence community's ability to monitor arms control treaties. The committee gave the Senate another lever with which to influence intelligence policy. In 1988, for example, the Senate Select Committee on Intelligence, upon evaluating the Intermediate Nuclear Forces (INF) Treaty and concerned about the upcoming Strategic Arms Reduction Treaty (START), demanded the purchase of additional imagery satellites. The Reagan administration, which had not been averse to spending money on intelligence, argued that the additional satellites were unnecessary. However, the chairman of the Senate committee, David L. Boren, D-Okla., made it clear that purchase of the satellites was a price of Senate consent to the treaties.

REPORTING REQUIREMENTS. The separation of powers between the executive branch and the legislative branch puts a premium on information. The executive tends to forward information that is supportive of its policies; Congress tends to seek fuller information to make decisions based on more than just the views that the executive volunteers. One of the ways Congress has sought to institutionalize its broad access to information is to levy reporting requirements on the executive branch. Congress often mandates that the executive report on a regular basis (often annually) on specific issues, such as human rights practices in foreign nations, the arms control impact of new weapons systems, or, during the cold war, Soviet compliance with arms control and other treaties.

Reporting requirements, which grew dramatically in the aftermath of the Vietnam War, raise several issues. Does Congress require so many reports that it cannot make effective use of them? Do the reports place an unnecessary burden on the executive branch? Would the executive branch forward the same information if there were no reporting requirements? To give some sense of the scope of activity involved, in 2002 the House Intelligence Committee said it had asked for eighty-four reports in the past year, most of which were either late or incomplete.

An important but less visible adjunct to reporting requirements is congressionally directed actions, or CDAs. CDAs are most often studies that the intelligence community is tasked to conduct by Congress, most often via the intelligence authorization act. CDAs are but one more opportunity for Congress to get the information it desires from the executive branch. As a rule, the offices responsible for producing the CDAs find them bothersome and intrusive. CDAs can be a dangerous tool in that they are cost-free for members of Congress and their staff. They have to do no more than levy the requirement. But CDAs do impose time-consuming costs on the executive agencies to which they are sent. In some years the number of CDAs has been onerous. CDAs, like other reporting requirements, also raise questions about their utility and the degree to which Congress uses them for substantive reasons.

INVESTIGATIONS AND REPORTS. One of Congress's functions is to investigate, which it may do on virtually any issue. The modern intelligence oversight system evolved from the congressional investigations of intelligence in the 1970s. Investigations tend to result in reports that summarize findings and offer recommendations for change, thus serving as effective tools in exposing shortcomings or abuses and in helping craft new policy directions. Every year the two intelligence committees report publicly on issues that have come before them. These reports may be brief because of security concerns, but they assure the rest of Congress and the public that effective oversight is being carried out, and they create policy documents that the executive must consider.

Just as the executive branch has come to rely more on outside commissions for intelligence issues, Congress has increasingly created investigations of its own. After the September 11 attacks, Congress conducted a joint inquiry, which consisted of the House and Senate Intelligence Committees. The Senate committee also undertook a long study of intelligence on Iraqi WMD. The dynamics of these investigations are different from those created in the executive. First, by definition, Congress is a partisan place, made up of a party that supports the president on most issues and one that opposes him. This can always affect an investigation. Second, Congress has some responsibility for the performance of intelligence by virtue of its control of the budget and its oversight. Thus, Congress's ability to be objective about its own role comes into question.

HOSTAGES. If the executive branch balks on some issue, Congress may seek means of forcing it to agree. One way is to take hostages—that is, to withhold action on issues that are important to the executive until the desired action is taken. This type of behavior is not unique to Congress; intelligence agencies use it as a bargaining tactic in formulating national intelligence estimates (NIEs) and other interagency products.

During the debate on the INF Treaty, the demands of the Senate Select Committee on Intelligence for new imagery satellites was one case of hostage taking. In 1993 Congress threatened to withhold action on the intelligence authorization bill until the Central Intelligence Agency (CIA) provided information on a Clinton administration Defense Department nominee, Morton A. Halperin. Halperin, who had publicly criticized U.S. covert actions in the 1970s and 1980s, eventually withdrew his nomination for the newly created post of assistant secretary of defense for democracy and peacekeeping. In 2001 the Intelligence Committees "fenced" (put a hold on) certain funds for intelligence to prod the Bush administration into nominating a new CIA inspector general. Critics argue that hostage taking is a blunt and unwieldy tool; supporters argue that it is used only when other means of reaching agreement with the executive have failed.

PRIOR NOTICE OF COVERT ACTION. One of Congress's main concerns is that it not be surprised by presidential actions, that it receive prior notice of them. Most members understand that prior notice is not the same as prior congressional approval, which is required for few executive decisions. Covert action is one of the areas where prior notice has been a contentious issue. As a rule, Congress receives advance notice of covert action in a process that has been largely institutionalized, but successive administrations have refused to make prior notice a legal requirement. A congressional demand for at least forty-eight hours' notice led to the first veto of an intelligence authorization bill, by President George Bush in 1990.

ISSUES IN CONGRESSIONAL OVERSIGHT

Oversight of intelligence raises a number of issues that are part of the "invitation to struggle," as the separation of powers has often been called.

HOW MUCH OVERSIGHT IS ENOUGH? From 1947 to 1975—the first twenty-eight years of the modern intelligence community's existence—the atmosphere of the cold war promoted fairly lax and distant congressional oversight. A remark by Sen. Leverett Saltonstall, R-Mass. (1945–1967), a member of the Senate Armed Services Committee, characterized that viewpoint: "There are things that my government does that I would rather not know about." This attitude was partly responsible for some of the abuses that investigators uncovered in the 1970s.

Working out the parameters of the intelligence oversight system has not been easy. Successive administrations, regardless of party affiliation, have tended to resist what they have seen as unwarranted intrusions.

There is no objective way to determine the proper level of oversight. On the budget, committees review each line item. They do so to make informed judgments on how to allocate funds, which is Congress's responsibility. Reviewing specific covert actions may seem intrusive, but it represents an important political step. If Congress allows the operation to proceed unquestioned, the executive branch can claim political support should problems arise later. Similarly, serious questions raised by Congress are a signal to rethink the operation, even if the ultimate decision is to go ahead as planned.

Does rigorous oversight require just detailed knowledge of intelligence programs, or does it require something more, such as information on alternative intelligence policies and programs? Congress has, on occasion, taken issue with the direction of intelligence policy and acted either to block the administration, such as the Boland amendments that prohibited

military support to the contras, or to demand changes, such as the purchase of the INF satellites.

SECRECY AND THE OVERSIGHT PROCESS. The high level of security
that intelligence requires imposes costs on congressional oversight. Members of Congress have security clearances (through TOP SECRET) by
virtue of having been elected to office. Members must have clearances to
carry out their duties. Only the executive branch can grant security clearances, but there is no basis for its granting or denying clearances to members of Congress, as this would violate the separation of powers. At the
same time, member clearances do not mean full access to the entire range
of intelligence activities. Congressional staff members who require clearances receive them from the executive branch after meeting the usual
background checks and demonstrating a need to know. Congressional
staffers are not polygraphed as a prerequisite for clearances.

Although all members are deemed to be cleared, both the House and
Senate limit the dissemination of intelligence among members who are
not on the Intelligence Committees. Although this limitation replicates
the acceptance of responsibility that all congressional committees have, in
the case of intelligence it entails additional burdens for the panels, as their
information cannot be easily shared. Thus, the Intelligence Committees
require special offices for the storage of sensitive material and must hold
many of their hearings in closed session. Both houses have also created
different levels of notification for members about intelligence activities,
depending on the sensitivity of the information. Intelligence officials may
brief only the leadership (known as the **Gang of 4**), or the leaders and the
chairmen and ranking members of the Intelligence Committees (known
as the **Gang of 8**), or some additional committee chairmen as well, or the
full Intelligence Committees.

Despite these precautions and the internal rules intended to punish
members or staff who give out information surreptitiously, Congress as an
institution has the reputation of being a fount of leaks. This image is
propagated mainly by the executive branch, which believes that it is much
more rigorous in handling classified information. In reality, most leaks of
intelligence and other national security information come from the executive, not from Congress. (In 1999 DCI George Tenet admitted before a
congressional committee that the number of leaks from executive officials
was higher than at any time in his memory.) This is not to suggest that
Congress has a perfect record on safeguarding intelligence material, but it
is far better than that of the CIA, the State or Defense Departments, or the
staff of the NSC. The reason is not superior behavior on the part of Congress so much as it is relative levers of power. Leaks occur for a variety of
reasons: to show off some special knowledge, to settle scores, or to pro-

mote or stop a policy. Other than showing off, members of Congress and their staffs have much better means than leaks to settle scores or affect policy. They control spending, which is the easiest way to create or terminate a policy or program. Even minority members and staff can use the legislative process, hearings, and the press to dissent from policies or attempt to slow them down. Officials in the executive branch do not have the same leverage and therefore resort to leaks more frequently. However, the perception of Congress as a major leaker persists.

The other issue raised by secrecy is Congress's effectiveness in acting as a surrogate for the public. The U.S. government ostensibly operates on the principle of openness: Its operations and decisions should be known to the public. (The Constitution does not mention the public's right to know, however. The Constitution safeguards freedom of speech and of the press, which are not the same as a right to information.) In the case of intelligence, the principle of openness does not apply. Some people accept the reasons for secrecy and the limitations that it imposes on public accountability. Others have concerns about the role of Congress as the public's surrogate in executive oversight. Their reasons vary, from doubts about the executive branch's willingness to be forthcoming with Congress to concerns about Congress's readiness to air disquieting information.

CONGRESS AND THE INTELLIGENCE BUDGET. A recurring issue for Congress has been whether to reveal some aspects of the intelligence budget. Article I, Section 9, paragraph 7, of the Constitution requires that accounts of all public money be published "from time to time." This phrase is vague, which allowed each successive administration to argue that its refusal to disclose the details of intelligence spending was permissible. Critics contended that this interpretation vitiated the constitutional requirement to publish some account at some point. Most advocates of publication were not asking for a detailed publication of the entire budget but wanted to know at least the total spent on intelligence annually. (See box, "Intelligence Budget Disclosure: Top or Bottom?")

The argument over publishing some part of intelligence spending appeared to have ended effectively in 1997, when DCI George Tenet revealed that overall intelligence spending for fiscal 1998 was $26.6 billion. He provided the number in response to a Freedom of Information Act suit, acting to end the suit and to limit the information that the intelligence community revealed. Tenet later refused to divulge the amount requested or appropriated for fiscal 1999, arguing that to do so would harm national security interests and intelligence sources and methods. The Senate and House disagreed on this issue in the 2004 intelligence legislation, with the House view prevailing that the budget should not be unclassified.

Intelligence Budget Disclosure: Top or Bottom?

One of the curiosities of the debate over intelligence budget disclosure was the term used for the number most at issue. The overall spending total for intelligence was alternatively described as the "top line number" or the "bottom line number." It sometimes sounded as if people on the same side—those in favor of or opposed to disclosure—were at odds with themselves.

Nonetheless, it is instructive to review the arguments that both sides raised in the debate. Proponents of disclosure cited, first and foremost, the constitutional requirement for publication. They also argued that disclosure of this one number posed no threat to national security, because it revealed nothing about spending choices within the intelligence community.

Proponents of continued secrecy tended not to cite the "time to time" language of the Constitution, which was a weak argument at best. Instead, they argued that Congress was privy to the information and was acting on behalf of the public. They also said that disclosure of the overall amount could be the beginning of demands for more detailed disclosure. Noting how little this one number revealed (and implicitly accepting their opponents' argument that its disclosure would not jeopardize security), they contended that the initial disclosure would inexorably lead to pressure for more detailed disclosures about specific agency budgets or programs and that these disclosures would have security implications.

DCI Tenet's disclosure revealed that many public estimates of the size of the intelligence budget were fairly accurate, as was the estimate that the intelligence budget is roughly one-tenth the size of the defense budget. As disclosure proponents had long argued, national security did not unravel. However, as disclosure opponents maintained, many who had advocated disclosure were dissatisfied because the figure provided so little information.

Disclosing the overall number entails political risks for U.S. intelligence. Relating spending to outputs is more difficult for intelligence than it is for virtually any other government activity. How much intelligence should $26.6 billion (or any other figure) buy? Should output be assessed by the number of reports produced? Number of covert actions undertaken? Number of spies recruited? Moreover, the overall number—which does not strike many as a small sum—leads some people to question intelligence community performance. Statements along the lines of "How could they miss that coup (or lose that spy) when they have $26.6 billion?" would ensue. Such sentiments would add little to a meaningful debate about intelligence.

Finally, just as the budget is Congress's main means of control over the intelligence community, it is also the locus of Congress's responsibility for how well intelligence performs. Congress ultimately decides which satellites are built, how many are built, and how many agents and analysts the intelligence community can afford to have on its payroll. Although this was self-evident, it did not become an issue until after the 2001 terrorist attacks. Some people observed that Congress bore some responsibility for intelligence performance because of the steep decline in resources devoted to intelligence after the fall of the Soviet Union in 1991. Budgets were cut and, according to DCI Tenet, the equivalent of twenty-three thousand positions was lost over the decade of the 1990s, affecting performance and capabilities. This apparently became a controversial issue within the joint inquiry, as some members wanted to take note of this responsibility and others refused. Ultimately, the joint inquiry's report did not address the issue.

REGULATING THE INTELLIGENCE COMMUNITY. Since the end of World War II, Congress has passed only two major pieces of intelligence legislation: the National Security Act of 1947 and the Intelligence Reform and Terrorism Prevention Act of 2004. Thus, the structure of the intelligence community was remarkably stable throughout the cold war and the immediate post–cold war period. Only as a result of the terrorist attacks and the war in Iraq was there sufficient political impetus to foster major changes. (See chap. 14.) Four presidents have issued extensive executive orders (EOs) on intelligence—Gerald R. Ford in 1976, Jimmy Carter in 1978, Ronald Reagan in 1981, and George W. Bush in 2004.

President George Washington issued the first **executive order** under his presumed authority, setting a precedent. Each president since also has done so. No specific constitutional power grants a president this authority. The authority to write EOs stems from the president's obligation, under Article II, Section 3, to "take Care that the laws be faithfully executed." EOs are legal documents but may not conflict with a law or a judicial decision. Thus, they sometimes tend to operate in areas where there are neither legislation nor judicial decisions. The major advantage of EOs is that they give presidents the flexibility to make changes in the intelligence community to meet changing needs or to reflect their own preferences about how the intelligence community should be managed or its functions limited. The major disadvantages of executive orders are that they are impermanent, subject to change by each president (or even by the same president); they are not statutes and therefore are more difficult to enforce; and they give Congress a limited role. (As a rule, the executive branch has made Congress privy to drafts of executive orders in advance of their pro-mulgation and has given Congress opportunities to comment on them.)

Despite the difficulty that Congress and the executive branch have experienced in making legislative changes, they offer the advantages of being permanent, of being statutes in law and therefore more enforceable, and of allowing Congress a major and proper role. However, legislation is more likely to raise major disputes between Congress and the executive branch and thus is more difficult to enact. Congress is also more likely to harbor several points of view on major intelligence issues than is the executive branch, where the major issues tend to be agency-parochial in nature. This divergence of views within Congress was evident during the debate on the 2004 intelligence reform bill.

Given the permanent nature of legislation, some people question whether certain regulations should not be made statutory largely because the actions they cover are embarrassing or inappropriate, such as assassi-nations. However, if legislation lists proscribed activities, does it implic-itly permit those activities that are not listed?

The parameters of congressional oversight are usually not dealt with in legislation. All congressional committees are created as part of the rules of the House and Senate. The same is true for jurisdiction and member-ship. The National Security Act does specify types of intelligence infor-mation that have to be shared with Congress, such as that relating to covert action, but the law is written as a requirement levied on the exec-utive. During the debate over the 2004 legislation some suggested com-bining the two intelligence committees into one joint committee, an old issue, for reasons of security and to reduce the time executive officials have to spend testifying, often on the same subject, before more than one committee. As has been the case in the past, congressional organization was not legislated and was left to the respective chambers.

THE ISSUE OF CO-OPTION. As eager as Congress is to be kept in-formed about all aspects of policy, a cost is incurred when it accepts infor-mation. Unless members raise questions about what they are told, they are, in effect, co-opted. Their silence betokens consent, as the maxim of English law says. They are free to dissent later on, but the administration will be quick to point out that they did not raise any questions at the time they were briefed. Having been informed before the fact tends to under-cut Congress's freedom of action after the fact.

This dynamic is not unique to intelligence, but intelligence makes it somewhat more pointed. The nature of the information, which is both secret and usually limited to certain members, makes co-option more eas-ily accomplished and has more serious consequences. It also puts additional pressure on the members of the Intelligence Committees, who are privy to the information and are acting on behalf of their entire body.

Congress has no easy way to avoid the inherent exchange of foreknowledge and consent. It is unlikely to revert to the trusting attitude expressed by Senator Saltonstall. Nor can Congress be expected to raise serious questions about every issue just to establish a record that allows it to dissent later on.

WHAT PRICE OVERSIGHT FAILURES? Even when the intelligence oversight system is working well, most members and congressional staff have difficulty running the system so as to avoid all lapses. Most members and staff involved in the process understand the difference between small lapses and large ones. Some of the larger lapses for which Congress has taken the intelligence community to task are

- Failure to inform the Senate Intelligence Committee that CIA operatives were directly involved in mining Corinto, a Nicaraguan port, during the contra war. The CIA let it appear that the contras had carried this out on their own. When the truth became known, not only did Vice Chairman Daniel Patrick Moynihan, D-N.Y., resign—though he later changed his mind—but Chairman Barry Goldwater, R-Ariz., also reprimanded DCI William J. Casey (1981–1987) in harsh and public terms.
- Failure to inform Congress on a timely basis when agents in Moscow began to disappear, which was later presumed to be the result of the espionage of CIA agent Aldrich Ames. (The assessment as to who caused the losses may change as a result of the damage assessment from the Robert Hanssen spy case.) The House Intelligence Committee issued a public report critical of the CIA, with which the CIA agreed.

Congress has at hand some levers to enforce its oversight. It can reduce the intelligence budget, delay nominations, or, in the case of a serious lapse, demand the resignation of the official involved. If the lapse is serious enough and can be traced back to the president, impeachment might be an option. In the two cases cited above, Congress did not impose any of these penalties.

But even without inflicting concrete penalties, Congress can enforce its oversight. The loss of officials' credibility before their major committees is serious in and of itself. As hackneyed as it sounds, much of Washington runs on the basis of trust and the value of one's word. Once credibility and trust are lost, as happened to Casey in the Corinto affair, they are difficult to regain.

INTERNAL DYNAMICS OF CONGRESSIONAL OVERSIGHT

Even though oversight is inherent in the entire congressional process, the way Congress organizes itself to handle intelligence oversight is somewhat peculiar.

WHY SERVE ON AN INTELLIGENCE OVERSIGHT COMMITTEE? Members of Congress take office with specific areas of interest, derived from either the nature of their district or state or their personal interests. Most members, at least early in their legislative careers, tend to focus on issues that are most likely to enhance their careers. For most members, intelligence is unlikely to fit any of these criteria. Therefore, why would members spend a portion of their limited time on intelligence?

At first blush, the disadvantages are more apparent than the advantages. Intelligence is, for most members, a distraction from their other duties and from those issues likely to be of greatest interest to their constituents. Few districts have a direct interest in intelligence. The main ones are those in the immediate Washington, D.C., area, where the major agencies are located, and those where major collection systems are manufactured. But these are a small fraction of the 435 House districts in the fifty states.

Once involved in intelligence issues, members cannot discuss much of what they are doing or what they have accomplished. Co-option is also a danger. Should something go wrong in intelligence, committee members will be asked why they did not know about it in advance. If they did know in advance, they will be asked why they did not do something about it. If they did not know, they will be asked why not. These are all difficult questions to answer.

Finally, the intelligence budget is remarkably free of pork, that is, projects to benefit a member's district or state that are earmarked for funding. Therefore, members on the committees have few opportunities to help their constituents.

With all of those disadvantages, why serve? Because some advantages accrue from membership. First, service on the Intelligence Committees allows members to perform public service within Congress, to serve on a committee where they have few, if any, direct interests. Second, their service gives members a rare opportunity to have access to a closed and often interesting body of information. Third, it gives members a role in shaping intelligence policy and, because of the relatively small size of the two committees (in the 109th Congress—2005–2007—twenty-one members on the House Intelligence Committee and fifteen on the Senate Intelligence Committee), perhaps a greater role than they would have on many of the other oversight committees. Fourth, it may offer opportunities for national press coverage on high-profile issues about which few people are conversant. Finally, because members of the two intelligence committees are selected by the majority and minority leadership of the House and Senate, being chosen is a sign of favor that can be important to a member's career. (Select committees usually have limited life spans, especially in the House. The House Intelligence Committee is called "permanent select" to denote its continued existence, even though it remains "select.")

THE ISSUE OF TERM LIMITS. Service on the House and Senate Intelligence Committees, unlike other committees, was initially limited. Congress adopted term limits for committee membership based on the view that the pre-1975 oversight system had failed, in part, because the few members involved became too cozy with the agencies they were overseeing.

The major advantage of term limits is the distance that they promote between the overseers and the overseen. Limited terms also make it possible for more members of the House and Senate to serve on the Intelligence Committees, thus adding to the knowledgeable body necessary for informed debate.

Term limits also carry disadvantages. Few members come to Congress with much knowledge of, and virtually no experience with, intelligence. Because it can be arcane and complex, requiring some time to master, members are likely to spend some portion of their tenure on the committee simply learning about intelligence. Once they have become knowledgeable and effective, they are nearing the end of their term. Term limits also make service on the Intelligence Committees less attractive, because they reduce the likelihood that a member can become chairman through seniority.

In 1996 Larry Combest, who was then chairman of the House Intelligence Committee, testified that he thought it was time to consider longer tenure on the committee, which would be to Congress's advantage. Members on the committee, however, are still limited to eight years' service. In 2004, the leaders of the Senate Intelligence Committee, Pat Roberts, R-Kan., and John D. Rockefeller IV, D-W.Va., also spoke out in favor of revising the limits, which had been dropped for the Senate panel.

BIPARTISAN OR PARTISAN COMMITTEES? The Senate and House Intelligence Committees are distinctly different in composition. Typically, the ratio of seats between the parties on committees roughly reflects the ratio of seats in each chamber as a whole. The Senate Intelligence Committee has always been exempt from this practice, with the majority party having just one more seat than the minority. Moreover, the ranking minority member is always the vice chairman of the Senate committee. The Senate leadership took these steps in 1976 to minimize the role of partisanship in intelligence. When the House Intelligence Committee was formed in 1977, the House Democratic leadership rejected the Senate model, insisting that membership on the committee be determined by the parties' ratio in the House, which reflected the will of the people as expressed in the last election.

A bipartisan committee offers opportunities for a more coherent policy, because the committee is removed—as far as is possible—from partisanship. A committee united on policy and not divided by party may also have more influence with the executive branch. In the case of the Corinto mining, Chairman Goldwater and Vice Chairman Moynihan agreed that the intelligence community was guilty of a significant and unacceptable failure. Thus, DCI Casey had no political refuge for not keeping the committee informed. Despite the continuation of this bipartisan structure on the Senate committee, the Democratic minority showed signs of restiveness in the 108th Congress (2003–2005) and the 109th Congress. A formal division of the committee's budget was made in 2004 (60 percent for the Republican majority; 40 percent for the Democratic minority). In early 2005, Democratic members sought ways to limit the powers of the committee's staff director in the areas of hiring and staff assignments. Although their goal was greater bipartisan control, the issue was discussed and decided on partisan terms.

Partisanship runs counter to the preferred myth that U.S. national security policy is bipartisan or nonpartisan. A partisan committee has the potential to be more dynamic than a bipartisan committee, where political compromise is more at a premium. In many ways, the compromise that a bipartisan committee engenders is equivalent to the lowest-common-denominator dynamic that one sees in intelligence community estimates.

In its own accidental way, Congress may have achieved the right balance, with a bipartisan intelligence committee in one chamber and a partisan committee in the other.

COMMITTEE TURF. All congressional committees guard their areas of jurisdiction jealously. For example, in 1976 when the Senate was considering the creation of an intelligence committee, the Senate Armed Services Committee resisted, seeking to preserve its jurisdiction over the DCI and the CIA. Dividing issues or agencies cleanly and clearly between or among committees is not always possible, in which cases the jurisdiction is shared and certain bills get referred to more than one committee. But jurisdiction equates to power.

There is also a more subtle aspect to congressional jurisdiction. Committees tend to become protectors of the agencies they oversee, at least when the jurisdiction or authority of these agencies is under question or attack. There is no inconsistency or hypocrisy involved in the committees serving as agencies' "best friends and severest critics." Committee members believe that they have a better and more complete understanding of the agencies they oversee. Also, if the agencies they oversee lose power, then the committees also lose power.

This dynamic, which is inherent in the committee system that dominates Congress, was in evidence during the drafting of and debate over the 2004 intelligence legislation. The Senate was initially more responsive to calls to accept the recommendations of the 9/11 Commission, but jurisdiction over the legislation went to the Senate Governmental Affairs Committee (SGAC), not the Senate Intelligence Committee. This could be rationalized in terms of jurisdiction, as the SGAC oversees government organization. However, in the past, bills of this sort had gone to the intelligence committee. Thus, the Senate leadership was not displaying much confidence in the intelligence committee for reasons that are not entirely clear. (Some believe the Senate leadership and perhaps the administration were concerned about the possible outcome as the Senate Intelligence chairman, Pat Roberts, had independently issued his own plan for intelligence reorganization that was widely seen as too radical.) In the House, the House Intelligence Committee was given jurisdiction. But, friction arose with the House Armed Service Committee, when Chairman Duncan Hunter, R-Calif., raised questions about the military's access to intelligence and the chain of command. There was a certain disingenuous aspect to this debate. Hunter made public a letter from Gen. Richard Meyers, chairman of the Joint Chiefs of Staff, stating concerns of the type that Hunter voiced, but Secretary of Defense Donald H. Rumsfeld said he had no advance knowledge of the general's action. Sen. John W. Warner, R-Va., chairman of the Senate Armed Services Committee, was supportive of Hunter but let him do most of the arguing. In the end, a DNI was created but the secretary of defense lost little if any authority over the intelligence budget or over defense intelligence agencies. As a result, the two Armed Services Committees had not lost any jurisdiction either.

How Does Congress Judge Intelligence?   An important but little-discussed issue is how Congress views and judges intelligence, as opposed to the criteria used by the executive branch. No matter how much access Congress has to intelligence, it is not a client of the intelligence community in the same way that the executive branch is, even as congressional requests for specific analytic products have increased. Congress never achieves the same level of intimacy in this area and does not have the same requirements or demands for intelligence.

The budget is one major divide. No pattern has been set as to which branch wants to spend more or less. The Reagan administration favored spending more on intelligence than Congress did and was allowed to, up to a point, after which Congress began to resist. However, the Reagan administration did not want to buy the additional imagery satellites demanded by the Senate Intelligence Committee. During the Clinton administration, it was Congress, after the Republican takeover in 1995, that was willing to spend more than was requested. Congress takes the firm view that all budget requests from the executive are just that—requests. They are nonbinding suggestions for how much money should be spent. To put it succinctly, the executive has programs, Congress has money.

The second major divide is the intimacy of the relationship that each branch has with intelligence. Executive officials may have unrealistic expectations of intelligence, but over time they have far greater familiarity with it than do the majority of members. Thus, the possibility of even larger false expectations looms in Congress. Moreover, having provided the money, members may have higher expectations of intelligence performance. At the same time, members may be more suspicious of intelligence analysis, fearing that it has been written largely to support administration policies. Members and staff rarely hear of intelligence that questions administration policies, even when such intelligence exists. Thus, the Congress–intelligence relationship is fertile ground for doubts, whether justified or not.

The relationship between Congress and the intelligence community has undergone a change in recent years. Both before and after the modern oversight system was created, the main requests Congress made of the intelligence community, other than testimony at hearings, were for briefings. Congress has had access to some intelligence products on a regular basis, but they were written for the executive branch. In the mid-1990s, Congress began to take a greater interest in the substance of intelligence analysis. Dissatisfaction among some members with an NIE about missile threats to the United States led Congress to create a commission headed by Donald Rumsfeld, which came to different conclusions about the nature of the threat.

More significant, in the period prior to the onset of the war with Iraq (2003–), members of the Senate Intelligence Committee requested that a new national intelligence estimate on Iraq's WMD programs be written, so that senators could have the benefit of reading it before they considered voting on a resolution authorizing the president to use force against Iraq. This took the intelligence relationship with Congress into a new and difficult area. Although the National Security Act states that the National

Intelligence Council "shall prepare national intelligence estimates for the Government," it is also understood that the intelligence community is part of and works for the executive branch. Meanwhile, the intelligence community finds it difficult to refuse such a request for both professional and political reasons. The resulting NIE became controversial after the war started, when surveys of Iraq did not discover the programs that were said to exist. Many senators questioned the quality of the analysis and the underlying reasons for the apparently incorrect conclusions. A criticism lodged against the intelligence community was that it had rushed the NIE, although the Senate had imposed a three-week deadline. (This particular criticism was somewhat ironic, as NIEs are usually criticized for how long they take, from several months to a year in some cases.) Although the conclusions of the NIE were not borne out, the estimate probably had little effect on the Senate as, according to press accounts, only a handful of senators read the NIE before voting. The Senate Select Committee on Intelligence investigated the intelligence community's performance on Iraqi WMD. Among its major findings were that many of the NIE's key judgments were overstated or not supported by the underlying intelligence; that the uncertainties for some judgments were not explained; that some of these judgments were then used as the basis for further judgments; that an excessive reliance was placed on foreign liaison reporting; and, most significant, that a groupthink dynamic had led to a presumption that Iraq had an ongoing WMD program. The Senate committee announced in 2005 that it would begin a review of intelligence and capabilities on Iran. The committee sought to maintain the momentum it believed it had achieved with its Iraq WMD report and also sought to get a better sense of issues and capabilities on Iran before any major changes were made in U.S. policy.

Congress likely will, in the future, make further requests for intelligence analysis crafted for its needs. This will continue to run the risks evidenced in the Iraq experience. Should these demands continue and increase, the executive branch may have to reach some sort of agreement with Congress bounding these demands.

Another major divide is partisanship. Whether it is the majority or the minority, a substantial group in Congress always opposes the administration on the basis of party affiliation as well as policy. Partisanship inevitably spills over into intelligence, often in the form of concerns that the executive branch has cooked intelligence to support policy. Dissent about intelligence policy could arise within the executive, but it would not be based on partisanship.

Thus, for a variety of reasons that are largely inherent in the U.S. system, the two branches do not view intelligence in the same way.

EXTERNAL FACTORS. The intelligence oversight system does not take place in a vacuum. Among the many factors that come into play to affect oversight, the press is a major one. The lingering effects of Watergate, including the search for scoops and major scandals, have influenced reporting on intelligence. The press, as an institution, gets more mileage out of reporting things that have gone wrong than it does from bestowing kudos for those that are going right. The fact that intelligence correctly analyzes some major event is hardly news; after all, that is its job. Moreover, in the aftermath of the 1975–1976 investigations, the intelligence community found it impossible to return to its previous state of being largely ignored by the press. The greater coverage given to intelligence and the press's emphasis on flaws and failures influence how some in Congress approach oversight.

Finally, even intelligence has partisans who appear in the guise of lobbyists. Some groups are made up of former intelligence community employees, and some advocate strong stances and spending on national security. Groups have been formed that oppose certain aspects of intelligence, usually covert action, as well as some aspects of espionage; that are concerned about U.S. policy in every region of the world; and that would prefer to see some portion of the funds devoted to intelligence spent elsewhere. Finally, there is a group made up of firms that derive large amounts of their income from the work they do for the intelligence community. All of these groups are legitimate within the U.S. political system and must be taken into account when considering how Congress oversees intelligence.

COMPETITION WITHIN THE CONGRESSIONAL AGENDA. A series of debates influencing intelligence oversight recur in every Congress, with varying degrees of strength. One is the debate between domestic and national security concerns, which is especially important when dealing with the budget. During the cold war, national security rarely suffered. In the post–cold war period, with national security concerns more difficult to define, the intelligence community had difficulty—until the terrorist attacks in 2001—maintaining level spending, let alone winning increases.

Another debate is that between civil liberties and national security. The debate is almost as old as the republic, dating back to the Alien and Sedition Acts of 1798. Other instances of civil liberties clashing with national security concerns predate the advent of the intelligence community: President Abraham Lincoln's suspension of habeas corpus during the Civil War, the arrest of antiwar dissidents during World War I, the mass arrests and detention of Japanese Americans during World War II, and acts aimed at rooting out communist subversion during the cold war. In each case, political leaders cited national emergencies to place temporary limitations on civil liberties. This debate resumed in 2001 in the aftermath of the terrorist attacks, as the Bush administration sought increased powers for surveillance, nonjudicial trials (the proposed use of military tribunals), and other types of authority.

The precedents notwithstanding, the intelligence investigations of the mid-1970s revealed several instances in which intelligence agencies violated constitutional guarantees, laws, and their own charters. The violations included surveillance of dissident groups, illegal mail openings, illegal wiretaps of U.S. citizens, and improper use of the Internal Revenue Service. Some of these actions were known by the president at the time; some were not. The revelation of these activities underscored concerns about the ability of secret agencies to act without safeguards and the need for strong executive and congressional oversight.

A third perennial congressional debate focuses on the level and range of U.S. activism abroad. From World War I through the cold war, the Democrats were largely the interventionist party; and the Republicans, the noninterventionist party. During World War II and the cold war, an interventionist consensus formed, although a Republican faction remained noninterventionist. The damage that the Vietnam War inflicted on the cold war consensus fostered a shift in the positions of the two parties. The Democrats largely became the noninterventionist party and the Republicans became the interventionist party. In the post–cold war period, a renascent noninterventionist faction grew within the Republican Party. After September 2001, wide support emerged for both military and intelligence operations abroad, although this unraveled, largely as a result of Iraq. It is not clear where this debate stands now or how it would appear should another terrorist attack take place.

Finally, the immigrant basis of the U.S. population is reflected in foreign policy debates. Every region of the world and virtually every nation are represented within the U.S. population. U.S. policies or actions around the world—real, planned, or rumored—are likely to stir reactions from some segment of the population and perhaps even different reactions. Members of Congress having ethnic ties to a region or representing constituents who do are also likely to voice opinions.

CONCLUSION

The nature of congressional oversight of intelligence changed dramatically in 1975–1976. Although Congress may go through periods of greater or lesser activism, it is unlikely to return to the laissez-faire style of oversight. Congress has become a consistent player in shaping intelligence policy.

This seems novel in the case of intelligence only because it is relatively recent. Congress has played the same activist role in all other areas of policy since adoption of the Constitution, and its role is inherent in the checks and balances system that the framers set up. The willful division of power creates a system that is a constant "invitation to struggle."

The oversight system is, of necessity, adversarial but does not have to be hostile. Any system that divides power is bound to have debates and friction. But they do not have to be played out in an antagonistic manner. When antagonism arises, it is more often the effect of personalities, issues, and partisanship than the oversight system per se.

KEY TERMS

appropriated but not authorized
appropriation
authorization
executive order
Gang of 4
Gang of 8

global finding
hollow budget authority
no year appropriations
oversight
supplemental appropriations

FURTHER READINGS

The expansion of the role of Congress as an overseer has been matched by an increasing number of books and articles on the topic. This chapter also discusses executive oversight issues, which are covered in the first entry below.

Adler, Emanuel. "Executive Command and Control in Foreign Policy: The CIA's Covert Activities." *Orbis* 23 (1959): 671–696.

Cohen, William S. "Congressional Oversight of Covert Actions." *International Journal of Intelligence and Counterintelligence* 2 (summer 1988): 155–162.

Colton, David Everett. "Speaking Truth to Power: Intelligence Oversight in an Imperfect World." *University of Pennsylvania Law Review* 137 (December 1988): 571–613.

Conner, William E. *Intelligence Oversight: The Controversy Behind the FY1991 Intelligence Authorization Act.* McLean, Va.: Consortium for the Study of Intelligence, 1993.

Currie, James. "Iran-Contra and Congressional Oversight of the CIA." *International Journal of Intelligence and Counterintelligence* 11 (summer 1998): 185–210.

Davis, Christopher M. *9/11 Commission Recommendations: Joint Committee on Atomic Energy—A Model for Congressional Oversight?* Washington, D.C.: Congressional Research Service, August 20, 2004.

Gumina, Paul. "Title VI of the Intelligence Authorization Act: Fiscal Year 1991: Effective Covert Action Reform or 'Business as Usual'?" *Hastings Constitutional Law Quarterly* (fall 1992): 149–205.

Jackson, William R. "Congressional Oversight of Intelligence: Search for a Framework." *Intelligence and National Security* 5 (July 1990): 113–147.

Johnson, Loch K. "Controlling the Quiet Option." *Foreign Policy* 39 (summer 1980): 143–153.

———. "The CIA and the Question of Accountability." *Intelligence and National Security* 12 (January 1997): 178–200.

———. "The U.S. Congress and the CIA: Monitoring the Dark Side of Government." *Legislative Studies Quarterly* 5 (November 1980): 477–499.

Latimer, Thomas K. "United States Intelligence Activities: The Role of Congress." In *Intelligence Policy and National Security*. Ed. Robert L. Pfaltzgraff Jr. and others. Hamden, Conn.: Archon Books, 1981.

Pickett, George. "Congress, the Budget, and Intelligence." In *Intelligence: Policy and Process*. Ed. Alfred C. Maurer and others. Boulder, Colo.: Westview Press, 1985.

Simmons, Robert Ruhl. "Intelligence Performance in Reagan's First Term: A Good Record or Bad?" *International Journal of Intelligence and Counterintelligence* 4 (spring 1990): 1–22.

Smist, Frank J., Jr. *Congress Oversees the United States Intelligence Community*. 2d ed. Knoxville: University of Tennessee Press, 1994.

Snider, L. Britt. *Sharing Secrets with Lawmakers: Congress as a User of Intelligence*. Washington, D.C.: Central Intelligence Agency, Center for the Study of Intelligence, 1997.

Treverton, Gregory F. "Intelligence: Welcome to the American Government." In *A Question of Balance: The President, the Congress, and Foreign Policy*. Ed. Thomas E. Mann. Washington, D.C.: Brookings Institution, 1990.

U.S. Senate Select Committee on Intelligence. *Legislative Oversight of Intelligence Activities: The U.S. Experience*. 103d Cong., 2d sess., 1994.

Chapter 11

The Legacy of the
Cold War

Although the intelligence community was not created specifically to prosecute the cold war, the community's development, forms, structures, and
practices were largely influenced by that nearly fifty-year struggle. To
understand how the intelligence community developed and its nature as
it continues to transform itself to address twenty-first-century issues, the
cold war's influence on the community needs to be examined.

THE PRIMACY OF THE SOVIET ISSUE

The Soviet issue—a series of related issues, including the Soviet Union,
Soviet satellites and third world allies, and communist parties in some
Western nations—predominated U.S. national security and foreign policy
from 1946 to 1991, when the Soviet Union ceased to exist. As a result,
the requirements for intelligence were never in doubt. Although other
issues might occasionally and temporarily supplant the Soviet issue, it
remained in the top tier of matters of interest to the policy and intelligence communities.

A great clarity and continuity also existed in the policy that intelligence was expected to support. Inspired by the career diplomat George
Kennan, the United States developed a policy of containment vis-à-vis the
Soviet Union. Kennan argued, first in his famous "long telegram" from
Moscow in February 1946 and then in his "Mr. X" article in the July 1947
issue of *Foreign Affairs,* that the Soviet Union was, by its nature, an expan-
sionist state. If the Soviet Union were contained within its own geographic limits, it would eventually be forced to deal with the inconsistencies and shortcomings of its communist system and either change or
collapse. Kennan viewed the struggle between the United States and the
Soviet Union as largely political and economic. But others responsible for
shaping policy, particularly Paul Nitze, the director of policy planning at
the State Department, who played a key role in drafting the planning

guidance document NSC-68 in early 1950, gave containment a more military dimension, as did the outbreak of the Korean War in June of that year.

THE INTELLIGENCE IMPLICATIONS OF CONTAINMENT. The containment policy included a role for intelligence analysis and operations. Analytically, the intelligence community was expected to know or be able to estimate

- Likely areas of Soviet probes or expansion;
- Imminence and strength of the probes;
- Overall Soviet strength—military, economic, and social;
- Likely Soviet allies or surrogates;
- Strength of U.S. allies or surrogates; and
- Signs of relative Soviet strength or weakness (signs of the contradictions predicted by Kennan)

This is a long list and an ironic reflection of Sherman Kent's desire to know everything.

In terms of intelligence operations, containment required

- An ability to collect intelligence on the Soviet target to enable analysts to fulfill their requirements;
- An operational ability to help blunt Soviet expansion;
- An ability to weaken the Soviet Union and its allies and surrogates;
- A counterintelligence capability to deal with Soviet espionage and possible subversion; and
- A wealth of information on Soviet military capabilities both to support the development of appropriate U.S. and North Atlantic Treaty Organization (NATO) defenses and to help target Soviet forces and facilities in the event of war.

Neither set of tasks, analytical or operational, arrived full-blown with the acceptance of the containment policy. Both sets evolved over time as the United States dealt with the Soviet problem.

THE DIFFICULTY OF THE SOVIET TARGET. The Soviet Union was a uniquely difficult target for intelligence collection and analysis. First, it was a very large nation (spread over two continents) with a remote interior, providing the Soviet leaders with a vast amount of space in which to hide capabilities they preferred to keep secret. Moreover, large portions of the Soviet Union were subject to adverse weather conditions that impeded overhead collection. Second, it was a closed and heavily policed society, which meant that large areas of the Soviet state—even in its more developed regions—were inaccessible to foreigners, even to diplomats legally posted to the Soviet Union.

Long-standing Russian traditions compounded the geographic difficulties. Russians traditionally have been suspicious of foreigners. Prior to the reign of Peter the Great (1682–1725), foreigners were often sequestered in special areas of the Russian capital, where they could be easily watched and their contact with Russians kept limited and controlled. Russians also have a tradition of obscuring the physical realities of the Russian state, which came to be known as *maskirovka,* whose roots go back to the tsars. The most famous instance of obscuring reality occurred during the reign of Catherine the Great (1762–1796). Her minister of war, Grigory Potemkin, built what appeared to be villages but, in reality, were merely facades to impress Catherine with the success of his policies. These **Potemkin villages** presaged *maskirovka.*

As the scope of the cold war spread from the Soviet Union to Europe, Asia, and then all over the world, the field within which intelligence had to be collected and analyzed and within which operations might be required expanded as well. The bilateral cold war was, in intelligence terms, a global war.

For all of these reasons, but primarily because of the size and inaccessibility of the Soviet Union, the intelligence community developed technical means to collect the required intelligence remotely. The United States continued to pursue human intelligence operations, both in the Soviet Union and against Soviet diplomats posted around the world, but the technical collection disciplines (INTs) were relied upon most. The technical INTs can be applied to post–cold war issues with some adjustments, but they cannot be replaced en masse. In effect, some aspects of the collection system are a legacy that cannot simply be scrapped or easily modified. Ironically, the relative longevity of space-borne systems—usually far beyond their estimated endurance—that has been one of their major assets now becomes something of a liability. For reasons of budget alone no one would propose scrapping functioning but older systems in favor of more modern ones.

THE EMPHASIS ON SOVIET MILITARY CAPABILITIES

The predominant question within the Soviet issue was that of the nation's military capabilities, which posed a threat to the United States and its allies.

Capabilities refer to the current forces or those being planned. The U.S. intelligence community sought information about the quantity and quality of Soviet armed forces across the board; the directions of Soviet military research and development and new capabilities the Soviets might be pursuing; the degree to which current and planned capabilities posed a threat to U.S. and allied interests; and the Soviet doctrine, that is, how the Soviets planned to employ forces in combat.

With the right collection systems, much of a potentially hostile nation state's capabilities can be known. This is particularly true of deployed conventional and strategic forces, which are difficult to conceal, as they tend to exist in identifiable garrisons and must exercise from time to time. The regularity and precision that govern each nation's military make it susceptible to intelligence collection. Forces tend to exercise in regular and predictable patterns, which also reveal how they are intended to be employed in combat. Research and development may be more difficult to track up to a point, but systems must be tested before they are deployed, again exposing them to collection.

Although the U.S. intelligence community made mistakes, such as overestimating and underestimating missile forces, overall Soviet capabilities were fairly well known in detail. Some level of comfort may even have been derived from tracking these hard objects. As one senior military intelligence officer put it, "The Soviet Union was the enemy we came to know and love." Some people dismissed the so-called **bean counting**, arguing that the military inventories were undertaken largely to justify bigger defense budgets. ("Bean counting" is a somewhat pejorative term that refers to intelligence products that tally up the number of forces, equipment, and manpower in foreign militaries. Although demanding and necessary, critics do not see these products as insightful or analytical.) The logic of this view was difficult to follow, because the intelligence community had little institutional interest in larger military forces. Within the national security sector of the budget, every dollar that went to defense was one dollar less that was available for intelligence, which was always funded at significantly lower levels than defense.

Intentions—the plans and goals of the adversary—are a more amorphous subject and pose a much more difficult collection problem. They need not be demonstrated, exercised, or exposed in advance, and they may not even be revealed by regular military exercises. Standoff or remote collection systems, which may be useful for collecting against capabilities, may reveal nothing about intentions. Signals intelligence may help reveal intentions, but this collection task may require espionage.

During the mid-1970s a **capabilities versus intentions** debate about the Soviet Union took place in the United States, largely among policy makers and influential individuals outside of government, but involving the intelligence community as well. U.S. intelligence was fairly well informed about Soviet military capabilities, but not Soviet intentions. The question was whether these intentions mattered. U.S. officials engaged in long and sometimes heated debates about whether the Soviet Union planned to conduct large-scale offensive conventional operations preemptively or at the outset of a war with NATO; whether it could carry out such operations from a standing start, that is, with forces already deployed and supplied, without bringing up telltale reserves and additional supplies, thus with little or no warning; and whether the Soviet Union thought a nuclear conflict was winnable.

Those who believed that intentions mattered argued that simply keeping track of the number of military forces was not enough to gauge the threat they posed. Only intentions made it possible to gauge the true level of threat. For example, Britain has a substantial nuclear force but is of no concern to the United States because the two nations are close allies. By taking into account Soviet intentions, the United States would have a much clearer picture of the true nature of Soviet policy, which was central to U.S. and Western security concerns. Proponents of this view believed that the Soviet threat was being underestimated because intentions were not a factor in national estimates.

Those who were less concerned about intentions argued that if one were aware of a certain level of hostility and also knew the adversary's capabilities, then knowing specific intentions was not that important. They argued that a worst case based on capabilities could serve as a planning yardstick. Finally, intentions (that is, plans) may be changed at will, making them a highly elusive target. Differences over the importance of intentions led to the Team A–Team B competitive analysis. The Team A–Team B exercise arose from concerns by members of the President's Foreign Intelligence Advisory Board (PFIAB) during the latter part of the Ford administration (1974–1977) about Central Intelligence Agency (CIA) estimates of Soviet programs. PFIAB members felt that the estimates emphasized the weapons programs and not the geopolitical strategy behind them. They convinced Director of Central Intelligence George Bush (1976– 1977) to conduct a competitive analysis, with a group of outside experts (Team B) looking at the same intelligence as the government analysts (Team A). Such a competitive exercise had promise, but the results were undercut by the fact that Team B was made up entirely of hawks, experts who were highly suspicious of Soviet motives and of intelligence community analysis. Not surprisingly, Team B's conclusions were much the same as the PFIAB concerns that prompted the study. The lack of balance in Team B diminished interest in doing this type of exercise in the future.

The track record for Soviet intentions is much less certain. The United States was never able to ascertain, for example, whether the Soviets subscribed to the nuclear doctrine of mutual assured destruction (MAD), which provided the basis for the size of U.S. strategic nuclear forces. The thinking behind MAD was that nuclear devastation was such an awesome prospect that it made nuclear forces almost unusable, the two forces holding each other in check. The United States spent many negotiating rounds of the early strategic arms control talks proselytizing the Soviets on the importance of MAD. Did the Soviets agree at last or give lip service to the idea of MAD merely as a way to get on to negotiations? Did it matter? Similarly, did the Soviets think that nuclear war was winnable? Did they plan to invade Western Europe? Soviet doctrine certainly emphasized keeping war away from the homeland, but this is true of most nations' doctrines.

Mirror imaging underlay some of the debate over Soviet intentions. Did U.S. analysts impose their own views of Soviet intentions in lieu of knowing them? Another question was the utility of **worst-case analysis**. Is it a useful analytical tool? For defense planners, the answer is yes. If they are going to commit forces to combat, they need to be able to gauge the worst level of threat they are likely to face. For other planners and analysts, the worst case may be an overestimate that is much less useful.

Finally, some people question whether the intelligence products themselves affected the intelligence process. Each year the intelligence community completed a national estimate on Soviet strategic military capabilities (NIE 11-3-8). U.S. policy makers viewed this estimate as necessary for strategic planning, including preparation of forces and budgets. But did the preparation of an annual major estimate also affect intelligence? Did it lock intelligence into set patterns, making it more difficult for the community to effect major changes or shifts in analyses? In other words, once the community had produced an NIE 11-3-8 for several years, how easy was it for analysts to propose dissenting, iconoclastic, or wholly new views? One remedy for these possible flaws was competitive analysis, tried most prominently in the Team A–Team B exercise.

Direct comparison of forces, a legitimate intelligence activity, often took place in a politicized atmosphere. Policy makers in successive administrations and Congresses tended to have preconceptions about the nature of the Soviet threat and thus viewed intelligence as being either supportive or mistaken. They engaged in long debates about quality (a U.S. advantage) versus quantity (a Soviet advantage) of weapons systems. The inconclusive nature of the debates led many to seek other means of comparison. One means was defense spending, both in direct costs and in the percentage of gross domestic product devoted to defense, which were taken as signs of intentions as well as capabilities.

THE EMPHASIS ON STATISTICAL INTELLIGENCE

Much of the intelligence that was produced (as opposed to collected) about the Soviet Union was statistical, including

- The size of Soviet and Soviet-satellite forces in terms of manpower and all levels of weaponry;
- The size of the Soviet economy and its output;
- The amount and percentage of the Soviet economy devoted to defense; and
- A variety of demographics about life in the Soviet Union.

Not all areas of inquiry were equally successful. The capabilities of the Soviet military were tracked quite well. Analysis of the Soviet economy was less successful. Ultimately, the intelligence community both overestimated the size of the Soviet economy and underestimated that portion of it devoted to defense, which probably totaled 40 percent of gross domestic product annually—a staggering level. Demographic data in the late 1980s and early 1990s pointed to a steady decline in the quality of Soviet life.

As important as the data were, the overall effort to quantify aspects of the Soviet issue had an effect of its own. Although much about this issue remained intangible, the intelligence community emphasized its ability to track various attributes in detail.

Looking back, one finds some efforts a bit comical. For example, the U.S. intelligence community devoted a great deal of time and energy—perhaps too much—to various means of comparing Soviet defense spending with that of the United States. Some analysts converted the cost of U.S. defense into rubles; others converted assessed values for the Soviet defense establishment into dollars. Each of these methodologies was artificial, and their respective proponents usually ended up preaching to the converted or to the stubbornly unbelieving regarding the Soviet threat.

What was often missing in this wealth of detailed data were the intangibles: the solidity of the Soviet state, the depth of support for it in the general population, and the degree of restiveness among the satellite populations. Few analysts questioned the stability or viability of the Soviet Union in the near term. Discussions about the possible collapse of the Soviet Union tended to be mostly hypothetical in nature as opposed to a potential policy problem.

COLLAPSE OF THE SOVIET UNION

Much of the controversy surrounding the U.S. intelligence record on the Soviet Union stems from the sudden Soviet collapse. Critics of intelligence performance argue that the demise deeply surprised the intelligence community, which had overestimated the strength of the Soviet state and thus missed the biggest story in the community's history. Some people even contended that this intelligence failure was sufficient reason for a profound reorganization of U.S. intelligence. Defenders of intelligence performance argued that the community had long reported the inner rot of the Soviet system and its weak hold on its own people and the satellite states.

The defenders of U.S. intelligence performance are, in part, correct. Intelligence provided numerous stories about the gross inefficiencies of the Soviet system, many of them anecdotal but too many to ignore. Insights into the sad realities of the Soviet system grew with the beginning of on-site inspections of Soviet intermediate nuclear forces (INF) bases in 1988. But few, if any, analysts compiled the anecdotal accounts into a prediction that the Soviet state was nearing collapse. It was weak; it might even be tottering. But no one expected that the Soviet Union would suddenly—and, most important, peacefully—pass from the scene. At least two factors were at work. First, most U.S. analysts working on the Soviet Union could not bring themselves to admit that the center of their livelihood might disappear, or that it was as weak politically as it turned out to be. Such a conclusion was inconceivable. They concentrated on the perils and pitfalls of reform but did not consider the possibility of collapse. Also, given the past brutality of Soviet (and Russian) governments, the idea of a peaceful collapse seemed impossible, leading to violent scenarios too horrific to contemplate. Second, analysts failed to factor into their calculations the role of personalities, particularly that of Mikhail S. Gorbachev, who became general secretary of the Soviet Communist Party (the most powerful position) in 1985.

The difficulty in assessing Gorbachev should not be underestimated. He came to power through the usual Politburo selection process. Like each new Soviet leader, Gorbachev promised reforms to make the admittedly inefficient state work more effectively. Eduard A. Shevardnadze, Gorbachev's foreign minister, reveals that at a certain point they both admitted that fixing the economy would require something more basic than tweaking reforms. Even while accepting this fact, Gorbachev remained committed to the basic forms of the Soviet state, not understanding that any true reform was, by definition, revolutionary. Only over time did Gorbachev come to these conclusions, and he could not accept their ultimate implications. In other words, he did not know where his reforms would lead. Should the intelligence community have known better than Gorbachev himself?

Many intelligence analysts were also slow to pick up on Gorbachev's approach to most of his foreign policy problems—arms control, Angola, even Afghanistan—which was to liquidate them as quickly as possible to be free to concentrate on more pressing domestic problems. Nor did many correctly analyze that the Soviet Union would acquiesce in the collapse of its European satellite empire. The fall occurred peacefully in 1989, as a few satellite leaders made efforts to liberalize, which led to the dissolution of the old order in all of the satellites. Czechoslovakia, maybe. But East Germany? Never. Again, the degree to which this was knowable remains uncertain. Ironically, Gorbachev succumbed to the premises of **containment** as described by George Kennan forty years earlier. Stymied abroad, Gorbachev had to face the manifold problems he had at home.

The factors that went into Gorbachev's thinking or into the sudden Soviet collapse remain unknown. Did the U.S. defense buildup under President Ronald Reagan convince Gorbachev that he needed to strike some deals with the United States or be outpaced and outspent and face even deeper economic ruin? Shevardnadze suggests that the answer is yes. Some believe that President Ronald Reagan's proposed Strategic Defense Initiative (SDI) was an important spur to arms control, not because of any near-term change that SDI might effect in the military balance but because it brought home to Soviet leaders their country's weaknesses in technology, in computers, and in wealth. One of the ways to avoid economic ruin was to strike arms control deals. (SDI was the catch-phrase for the effort promoted by President Reagan to find ways to defend against nuclear attacks. Reagan believed that such a defensive capacity, which he said the United States would share, would make all nuclear weapons obsolete.)

Whether the so-called **Reagan Doctrine**—a U.S. effort to aid anti–Soviet guerrillas—had any effect on Soviet thinking also remains unknown. The effort to aid the contras in Nicaragua became a political liability for the Reagan administration. But aid to the Mujaheddin in Afghanistan and the stalemate of that war shook the Soviet leaders. They were unable to win a war just over their border. Soviet military prowess was meaningless. Some analysts believe that a rift developed between the General Staff in Moscow and the "Afgantsy"—Soviet field commanders in the war, many of whom rallied to Boris N. Yeltsin in August 1991, when opponents of radical reform attempted to overthrow Gorbachev.

Gorbachev clearly thought that the price of empire was too high, overseas and even in Eastern Europe. What neither Western analysts nor Gorbachev himself understood was that piecemeal liquidation of these problems could not save the Soviet state.

INTELLIGENCE AND THE SOVIET PROBLEM

No U.S. intelligence estimate boldly predicted the peaceful collapse of the Soviet Union and its dissolution into several independent republics. U.S. intelligence assumed that the Soviet state would go on, perhaps ever weaker but still intact. At the same time, the community produced numerous reports about how inefficient, weak, and unsustainable (over some unknown period of time) the Soviet Union was.

Two key questions need to be answered Should intelligence have done better? Did intelligence matter for the United States in its final cold war victory?

Those who argue that intelligence should have done better do so on the grounds that the Soviet Union was the central focus of U.S. intelligence and that all of the expertise and spending over five decades should have provided greater insight into the true state of affairs. But a large gap exists between knowing that a state has fundamental weaknesses and foreseeing its collapse. To a large extent, the collapse of the Soviet Union was unprecedented. (In the past, some once-great empires, such as the Ottoman Empire, had suffered long, lingering demises. Other great empires had suffered sudden collapses, but usually in the context of war, as did the German, Austrian, and Russian empires after World War I.) Nor was there anything in Soviet behavior—which had shown its brutal side often enough—to lead analysts to expect that the nation's elite would acquiesce to its own fall from power without a struggle. An irony of history is that an attempt by the so-called power ministries of the Soviet state (the military, the defense industrial complex, the KGB—the State Security Committee) to derail Gorbachev revealed how little support the Soviet system had. (Rumors persist that Gorbachev knew about the coup or abetted it as a means of isolating his opposition.)

The debate about the performance of U.S. intelligence in the final stages of the cold war continues. Perhaps some analyst should have made the leap from the mountain of anecdotal evidence to a better picture of the true state of Soviet staying power. But much that happened from 1989 to 1991 was unknowable, both to U.S. analysts and to those taking part in the events.

How can the role of intelligence be assessed overall on the Soviet problem? In collection, U.S. intelligence performed some remarkable feats, finding sophisticated technical solutions to the problems posed by the remote and closed Soviet target. In analysis, U.S. intelligence accurately tracked Soviet military numbers and capabilities. This was important not only on a day-to-day basis but also during periods of intense confrontation, such as in Cuba in 1962, when President John F. Kennedy acted confidently because he knew a great deal about the true state of the U.S.–Soviet military balance. Discussion of Soviet intentions veered quickly to the political realm, where equally adamant hawks and doves dominated the debate, often freed from the constraints of intelligence by its unavailability. Operationally, the record is much less clear. Early efforts to foment rebellion within Soviet domains were disasters. Attempts to limit Soviet expansion were uneven. U.S. intelligence operations were successful in Western Europe, Guatemala, and Iran but were failures in Cuba and Southeast Asia. The contra war probably could have been dragged out inconclusively forever. But the intervention against Soviet forces in Afghanistan was a major and telling success. In espionage, U.S. intelligence scored large successes, such as recruiting Col. Oleg Penkovsky, and suffered a number of Soviet penetrations, some of which, notably those conducted by Aldrich Ames and Robert Hanssen, bridged the Soviet and post–Soviet Russian states.

In short, the record of intelligence in the cold war is mixed. Perhaps a better way to pose the original question might be: Would the United States have been better off or more secure without an intelligence community during the cold war?

Finally, the intelligence community in the early twenty-first century continues to be influenced by its performance in relationship to the Soviet Union. The clarity of requirements and the emphasis on remote technical collection, military capabilities, and other statistical intelligence are all cold war intelligence legacies.

KEY TERMS

bean counting
capabilities versus intentions
containment
maskirovka

Potemkin villages
Reagan Doctrine
worst-case analysis

FURTHER READINGS

As might be expected, the literature on U.S. intelligence regarding the Soviet Union is rich. The readings listed here include some older pieces that are of historical value.

Berkowitz, Bruce D., and Jeffrey T. Richelson. "The CIA Vindicated: The Soviet Collapse Was Predicted." *National Interest* 41 (fall 1995): 36–47.
Burton, Donald F. "Estimating Soviet Defense Spending." *Problems of Communism* 32 (March–April 1983): 85–93.
Firth, Noel E. *Soviet Defense Spending: A History of CIA Estimates, 1950–1990.* College Station: Texas A&M University Press, 1998.
Freedman, Lawrence. "The CIA and the Soviet Threat: The Politicization of Estimates, 1966–1977." *Intelligence and National Security* 12 (January 1997): 122–142.
———. *U.S. Intelligence and the Soviet Strategic Threat.* Boulder, Colo.: Westview Press, 1977.
Koch, Scott A., ed. *Selected Estimates on the Soviet Union, 1950–1959.* Washington, D.C.: U.S. Central Intelligence Agency, History Staff, 1993.

Lee, William T. *Understanding the Soviet Military Threat*. New York: National Strategy Information Center, 1977.

Lowenthal, Mark M. "Intelligence Epistemology: Dealing with the Unbelievable." *International Journal of Intelligence and Counterintelligence* 6 (1993): 319–325.

MacEachin, Douglas J. *CIA Assessments of the Soviet Union: The Record vs. the Charges*. Langley, Va.: Central Intelligence Agency, Center for the Study of Intelligence, 1996.

Moynihan, Daniel Patrick. *Secrecy: The American Experience*. New Haven: Yale University Press, 1998.

Pipes, Richard. "Team B: The Reality Behind the Myth." *Commentary* 82 (October 1986): 25–40.

Prados, John. *The Soviet Estimate: U.S. Intelligence and Russian Military Strength*. New York: Dial Press, 1982.

Reich, Robert C. "Re-examining the Team A–Team B Exercise." *International Journal of Intelligence and Counterintelligence* 3 (fall 1989): 387–403.

Steury, Donald P., ed. *CIA's Analysis of the Soviet Union, 1947–1991*. Washington, D.C.: U.S. Central Intelligence Agency, History Staff, 2001.

———. *Intentions and Capabilities: Estimates on Soviet Strategic Forces, 1950–1983*. Washington, D.C.: U.S. Central Intelligence Agency, History Staff, 1996.

U.S. Central Intelligence Agency, History Staff. *At Cold War's End: U.S. Intelligence on the Soviet Union and Eastern Europe, 1989–1991*. Washington, D.C.: Central Intelligence Agency, 1999.

U.S. Congress. Senate Select Committee on Intelligence. *The National Intelligence Estimate A–B Team Episode Concerning Soviet Strategic Capability and Objectives*. 95th Cong., 2d sess., 1978.

U.S. General Accounting Office. *Soviet Economy: Assessment of How Well the CIA Has Estimated the Size of the Economy*. GAO/NSIAD-91-0274. Washington, D.C., September 1991.

U.S. National Intelligence Council. *Tracking the Dragon: National Intelligence Estimates on China during the Era of Mao, 1948–1976*. Washington, D.C.: National Intelligence Council, 2004.

Chapter 12

The New Intelligence
Agenda

The end of the cold war was not the end of history, as political scientist Francis Fukuyama suggested. (Fukuyama posited that, because the struggle to advance democratic values had been the major development of the last several centuries, the collapse of the Soviet Union would bring an "end" to "history.") But the end of the cold war did remove the most central national security issue that the United States faced. In the immediate aftermath of the cold war, the role of intelligence and the issues that it should be tracking in support of U.S. policy makers did not seem entirely clear. After September 11, 2001, terrorism became the primary issue, raising a new set of questions about the intelligence agenda.

U.S. NATIONAL SECURITY POLICY AFTER THE COLD WAR

The cold war gave U.S. national security policy an easily understood point of reference. Diplomacy, defense policy, intelligence, and all else followed from the fundamental bilateral struggle with the Soviet Union. Serious debates arose in the United States over the nature of the Soviet threat, how the United States should deal with the threat overseas, defense spending levels, arms control agreements, and other major facets of the bilateral competition. But the antagonistic and hostile relationship with the Soviet Union clearly was the foremost issue in U.S. national security policy. U.S. analyses of the subtler aspects of the Soviet problem suffered significant flaws (see chap. 11). But the issues of what the intelligence community should be doing and why were rarely in doubt.

The post–cold war period offered no such clarity. The administrations of George Bush (1989–1993) and Bill Clinton (1993–2001) either failed or did not try to define U.S. national security interests in the aftermath of the cold war. The Bush administration tried the concept of new world order, which was never clearly defined and became irrelevant after Bush's defeat at the polls in 1992. The Clinton administration largely avoided such

232

grandiose concepts—despite brief forays into the concepts of preventive diplomacy, engagement, and enlargement—taking a more ad hoc approach to shaping policy. Some people suggested that the concept of national security, which had been comfortably vague to most of its practitioners, should be redefined, although few offered concrete, useful suggestions. In short, the core of U.S. national security policy remained vague after the fall of the Soviet Union in 1991. This vagueness raised several questions for U.S. intelligence that remain pertinent even after the September 2001 attacks: Has the mission of the intelligence community changed? How do policy makers and intelligence officials create and define intelligence requirements—and all that flows from them—in the absence of guiding national security concepts or policies? The terrorist attacks did not wholly answer these questions. As horrible as those attacks were, terrorism does not represent the same level of threat to the nation's existence as did the Axis in World War II or the Soviet Union. Terrorism may be the primary national security issue for years to come, but to date it has not assumed the position of overwhelming dominance that the Soviet Union did. Thus, the questions posed above remain important.

At a basic level, the answer to the question of whether the mission of the intelligence community has changed in the aftermath of the cold war is no. Its mission remains what it was: to collect and analyze information that policy makers need and to carry out covert actions as lawful authorities direct. This mission is—or should be—independent of any particular target, relationship, or crisis. It is the reason for having an intelligence community and should not be subject to the vagaries of international politics. U.S. intelligence targets and priorities have changed, but the community's mission has not.

Agenda and priorities are much more vexing matters. Director of Central Intelligence (DCI) Robert M. Gates (1991–1993) estimated that, at the height of the cold war, some 50 percent of the intelligence budget was earmarked for the Soviet Union and related issues. Everything else was secondary. That clarity of priorities is gone.

From 1991 to 2001 numerous issues jostled for top priority on the U.S. national security agenda: international economics, proliferation of weapons of mass destruction (WMD), narcotics, crime, terrorism, ecological and health issues, the post–Soviet transition in Russia, peacekeeping operations, and a variety of regional issues—the Balkans, the Middle East, central Africa, North Korea, and so on. Any one of these issues could be the most important for some period of time, but none of them maintained the dominance within the intelligence agenda that the Soviet Union once had.

The lack of a clear focus posed a severe problem for policy makers and intelligence managers. Requirements were uncertain or subject to rapid shifts. A greater diversity of talent was required. Few issues are new to the U.S. national security agenda. Economic issues, narcotics, terrorism, proliferation, and regional stability were all being addressed during the cold war. Health and ecological issues are somewhat new. All of these issues are more difficult to analyze than were the cold war political–military issues, and they are much less susceptible to bean counting.

In most cases, policy makers also found these issues more difficult to deal with than the old Soviet issues. The cold war had a certain comforting pattern of action and reaction. The United States and the Soviet Union each assumed, often correctly, that it could influence the behavior of the other through certain actions. On many of the new issues, there are no clear actions to take and sometimes no actors whom one can hope to influence. In some cases, the available intelligence outruns available or acceptable policy options. This often leads to frustration on the part of policy makers because they seek intelligence that is **actionable intelligence**, that is, intelligence with which they can do something. But this proves difficult when they do not know what they want to do.

Finally, several issues spill over into the domestic realm—economics, narcotics, crime, and terrorism—thus curtailing the activities of much of the intelligence community and creating confusion and competition between intelligence and law enforcement agencies. The problem is unique to the United States; most countries, even other democracies, have a domestic intelligence service (see chap. 15). The Central Intelligence Agency (CIA) and kindred agencies are limited in their work to foreign intelligence issues. The Federal Bureau of Investigation (FBI), however, has not been a domestic intelligence agency. Instead, it has been a law enforcement agency, responsible for capturing criminals or spies and helping bring them to a successful prosecution. The FBI began building its first dedicated intelligence unit in 2003. It obtained official status via the 2004 intelligence reform legislation as the Intelligence Directorate, which is now part of the larger FBI National Security Service. The division of responsibilities and limitations on roles has extended to the capture of individuals overseas, a practice known as rendition, because the subject is rendered up to justice. Renditions require the presence of U.S. law enforcement personnel even if the operation is primarily an intelligence operation. (This legal requirement does not extend to captured al Qaeda or Taliban members, who are considered combatants.) Thus, in responding to the post-2001 terrorist threat there was an organizational gap.

The creation of a Department of Homeland Security (DHS) in 2002 recognized the problem. DHS includes an Office of Intelligence and Analysis, which is the locus for all intelligence related to homeland security. The office receives terrorist-related intelligence from the CIA, the FBI, and other agencies and is responsible for analyzing data and making sure that important items did not slip through the foreign intelligence–domestic intelligence divide. The CIA and DHS agreed that DHS would not receive raw intelligence, meaning that at least a first-order analysis would be performed by the traditional agencies. In another break from past practice, DHS is charged with devising strategies to respond to specific homeland security threats.

The terrorism threat also fostered changes at the CIA. DCI George J. Tenet (1997–2004) decided that a distinction had to be made between the Counterterrorism Center, which was dedicated to defeating terrorists, and the effort to determine likely terrorist targets based on collected and analyzed intelligence. Thus, Tenet created the Terrorism Threat Integration Center (TTIC—pronounced "tee-tick"). As TTIC's name suggests, a major focus of its activity was to bring together disparate threads of terrorist-related intelligence. In the aftermath of the 9/11 Commission (National Commission on Terrorist Attacks Upon the United States) report, President George W. Bush agreed to create the National Counterterrorism Center (NCTC), initially by executive order. The NCTC was also provided for in the 2004 intelligence law. NCTC, which is now under the newly established director of national intelligence (DNI), replaced TTIC and is responsible for analyzing and integrating all intelligence on terrorism and counterterrorism, except for that exclusively related to domestic threats; for operational counterterrorism planning, including the assignment of operational roles; the sharing of intelligence; and acting as an intelligence bank on known or suspected terrorists, their goals, strategies, capabilities, networks, and support.

The organizational changes left a number of issues unaddressed. How is DHS to carry out its analytical functions? Simply put, the intelligence community is faced with a range of work that the United States has not conducted before, especially on itself as the analytical target. What about doctrine and process? And where is DHS to find the analysts it needs? How long will recruitment take? How will analysts be trained? Specifics about intelligence sharing, particularly between the CIA and FBI, remain unknown, although most observers agree that major improvements have been made since 2001. Finally, for NCTC, the relationship of its director to the DNI and its relationship to the CIA—particularly the Counterterrorism Center, from which it has drawn much of its staff—needs to be spelled out. The NCTC's responsibility to conduct strategic operational planning also opens many questions about the nature and scope of that activity and NCTC's relationship to the DNI because the center reports directly to the president on operational planning.

In February 2003, President George W. Bush signed a national security policy directive (NSPD-26), which created a new process for handling intelligence requirements. As would be expected, most of the burden fell to the DCI, who directs the National Intelligence Priorities Framework, in which national intelligence requirements are reviewed every six months by the National Security Council, creating a more dynamic system. The requirements are translated into resource allocation guidelines for collection and for analysis. Many observers believe this is the firmest link that has been created between requirements and resources. These responsibilities pass to the DNI, who is left free to organize his office as he sees fit.

INTELLIGENCE AND THE NEW PRIORITIES

An examination of several issues that have risen in priority in the post–cold war period reveals some of the difficulties that the intelligence community faces.

TERRORISM. The September 2001 attacks led to a greatly increased U.S. campaign against terrorism, which became the primary national security issue.

Terrorism had long been seen as a demanding issue for intelligence because of the belief that the political system would not tolerate even one terrorist attack on U.S. interests, either within the United States or overseas. The reaction to the September 2001 attacks proved this view to be false. Although many people requested reviews of intelligence, both generally and with respect to the attacks, and some called for the resignation of senior officials, the initial political costs to the intelligence community were surprisingly mild. Many would argue that only the combination of the September 11 attacks and the Iraq WMD analysis created the impetus necessary for intelligence reform legislation.

To understand the difficulties inherent in tracking and forestalling terrorism, one must recall the intelligence legacies of the cold war. Terrorist groups, unlike the Soviet Union, do not operate from large, easily identifiable infrastructures and do not rely on extensive communications networks. As more becomes known publicly about U.S. intelligence sources and methods, terrorists have made greater efforts to avoid detection. For example, al Qaeda leader Osama bin Laden reportedly gave up the use of cell phones and fax machines to avoid being located by the United States. Also, terrorist groups do not conduct large-scale repetitive exercises, as do organized military forces. Thus, the visible signature of terrorists is much smaller than is that of the Soviet Union or any nation-state. But, the intelligence community has to some extent a cold war legacy collection system developed to track a large political–military structure. (To be sure, some intelligence targets still call for these collection capabilities.)

Analysts sometimes refer to **chatter** when they describe intelligence on terrorism. "Chatter" is a difficult term to define. It refers less to precise intelligence than to patterns of intelligence: communications and movements of known or suspected terrorists. As chatter increases—more messages, even those that may not contain direct references to attacks— or as suspects suddenly drop from sight, an increased urgency is felt about the possibility of an attack. In that sense, chatter is much like indications and warning (I&W)—anything that represents a change in observed patterns is the subject of increased attention. But chatter is also imprecise and, as terrorists learn more about how the United States collects intelligence, chatter can decrease for reasons other than pending operations.

In the aftermath of the September 2001 attacks, familiar claims were made that the United States was overly reliant on technical intelligence (TECHINT) and needed more human intelligence (HUMINT). Although HUMINT can, theoretically, collect terrorist-related intelligence that TECHINT cannot, the realities of terrorism must again be examined. Terrorist groups, and certainly their leadership cells, tend to be small and well known to one another. They have tended to operate in parts of the world where the United States does not have ready access. Even if trained agents were available who knew the required language and could be provided with a plausible cover story for their presence in one of these areas, penetrating the terrorist organization would remain problematic at best. One does not simply show up in Kabul, ask for the local al Qaeda recruiting office, and then request to see the top man. (The press has made much in this regard of the activities of the American John Walker Lindh in Afghanistan. Lindh was captured fighting for the Taliban, not for al Qaeda. Recruitment into the Taliban was fairly simple. One had to be a self-professed Muslim willing to carry a gun—a far easier task than joining al Qaeda.) Finally, if HUMINT penetration were to be achieved, the new recruit would likely be asked to take part in some operation to prove his commitment to the cause. This raises important moral and ethical issues for intelligence. How far would the United States be willing to go to sustain a HUMINT penetration—putting an agent's life at risk by taking part in a terrorist operation?

Some advocacy for more HUMINT was odd in that it seemed to treat HUMINT as a numbers issue: that is, if enough agents were sent, penetrating the target would prove inevitable. Such a scenario shows a fundamental misunderstanding of how HUMINT operates and the nature of the terrorist target. HUMINT is not an en masse activity. It relies on precision.

Finally, much of U.S. HUMINT against the Soviet Union was carried out in foreign diplomatic posts outside of the Soviet Union, where Soviet officials were present and more accessible. Terrorists do not have this same overt overseas presence and thus present a smaller accessible target.

State sponsorship of, or at least acquiescence to, terrorists makes the intelligence issue more complicated. The intelligence community must collect not only against the terrorists but also against other governments and their intelligence services. At one level this is easier than is the terrorist collection itself, as it falls within more common intelligence practice. However, it also puts a further strain on intelligence resources. Liaison relationships may be questionable in such cases. For example, the government of Pakistan has been supportive of U.S. operations in Afghanistan, but the Pakistani intelligence service had been a longtime sponsor of the Taliban.

Closely related to state sponsorship is the even murkier question of relations between and among terrorist groups. For example, members of an Irish Republican Army faction were arrested after spending time with the revolutionary armed forces of Colombia (Fuerzas Armadas de Colombia, FARC). Such ties are both important and difficult to track or disrupt.

The war on terrorism adds another intelligence burden: support to military operations. This requirement encompasses both the usual military-related support and new activities. For example, the press has reported that the CIA has a Special Activities Division in the Directorate of Operations (DO) that was engaged in operations against the Taliban and al Qaeda. Although little is known publicly about the division, it would appear to occupy a niche between Special Forces and the DO's paramilitary activities in support of indigenous groups, such as the contras or the Mujaheddin. Also, some important developments have been made in imagery intelligence (IMINT) in the use of unmanned aerial vehicles and commercial imagery.

The September 2001 attacks raised new questions about intelligence–law enforcement coordination and cooperation. DHS, the NCTC, and the FBI's new National Security Service are all efforts to deal with this issue. The 2004 intelligence reform law puts a major emphasis on information sharing, which is an important aspect of all intelligence. But even information sharing is dependent, first, on information collection. For example, none of the investigations of September 11 found evidence that the one or two pieces of intelligence that might have led to the plot were somehow misdirected or not shared. Such evidence was never collected and may not have been collectible. Officials have also raised concerns about cyberattacks on the United States as part of a terrorist campaign. The main fear is that such actions could affect vital parts of the U.S. infrastructure.

The conduct of the war against terrorism raises questions about its future. U.S. officials have claimed that three-quarters of al Qaeda's senior leadership, including those who planned the 2001 attacks, were either killed or in custody. The effect on al Qaeda is unclear. Presumably, deaths and arrests led al Qaeda to rely on more clandestine means of communications, including a greater use of couriers. The ability to communicate thus has been impeded, but the ability to avoid detection and interception has been enhanced. Some have also speculated on whether the loss of senior leaders has transformed al Qaeda from an organization largely controlled by bin Ladin to one that is more like a franchise operation, with separate and largely independent cells following general direction but free to plan and operate on their own. If this is true, the al Qaeda target has become more difficult to track and to defeat.

Finally, the absence of any major attacks on the United States since 2001 (terrorist attacks took place in Madrid, Spain, in 2004 and in London, England, in 2005) raises questions as to why. Several possibilities come to mind, none of which precludes the others: Al Qaeda may be less capable. They may feel themselves deterred by the array of U.S. and others' actions. Or they simply may be in the midst of a long planning cycle. In the war on terrorism, much difficulty is found in gauging progress and having a sense of when the threat will be defeated.

PROLIFERATION. Preventing the proliferation of weapons of mass destruction has been a long-standing goal of U.S. policy, but it is now a more important issue with added dimensions. The United States has always given primary emphasis to nuclear weapons, given their lethal capability and the fact that they were central to the U.S.–Soviet relationship. But even during the cold war, the United States also worked to contain the spread of chemical and biological weapons (CBW or CW and BW).

Four major shifts have occurred in U.S. nonproliferation policy in the post–cold war era. First, policy makers and intelligence officials have given CW and BW increased attention. Concerns increased dramatically after the spate of anthrax mailings in the United States—including to members of Congress and high-profile broadcasters—shortly after the September 2001 attacks. However, no one was arrested for the mailings. Second, the collapse of the Soviet Union has added the problem of "loose nukes," a catch phrase for the weapons and associated expertise in former Soviet states that might be acquired by nations or terrorists eager to create an indigenous nuclear weapons capability. Third, the explosion of nuclear weapons by India and Pakistan in 1998 represented a setback for nonproliferation policy and raised new concerns about relations between these two nations. Fourth, the failure to find an Iraqi WMD arsenal despite intelligence estimates that it existed has probably raised the bar for the level of intelligence that will be required before the next confrontation with any potential proliferator. U.S. policy makers and foreign governments will be more skeptical in the absence of incontrovertible proof, which is always difficult to obtain.

The failure to find WMD in Iraq was a major factor in the impetus behind the 2004 intelligence legislation, which ostensibly addresses the issue of combating terrorism. Of the two issues—September 11 and Iraq WMD—the Iraq issue is far more serious in terms of the future of the intelligence community. For all of the pre–September 11 warnings about al Qaeda hostility, including the possibility of the use of aircraft, insufficient intelligence existed to act upon and disrupt the plot. Nor, in the pre-attack atmosphere, would it have been possible to implement the types of security steps in place now. The Iraq WMD issue, however, raises serious questions about analytic tradecraft, not only in WMD issues but also across the board. The Senate Intelligence Committee focused on the problem of groupthink, but more serious issues may have been at play.

- The effect of not allowing analysts better insight into the nature of HUMINT sources
- The proper way to pose alternative analytic questions that yield true alternative hypotheses instead of supporting or simply refuting the current one
- The need to rethink the prevalence of denial and deception (see chap. 6)
- The larger estimative process (see chap. 6)

Iraq WMD, like the Cuban Missile Crisis and a few other intelligence experiences, will probably be a touchstone for years to come in debates over intelligence analysis. (Iraq may also have an ironic and dangerous effect on other would-be proliferators. The lesson they may take away from Iraq's fate could be: Get a nuclear weapon. Iraq, without a weapon, was overrun with impunity, whereas North Korea, which constantly threatens that it has a nuclear weapon, is involved in rounds of fruitless negotiations.)

The role of intelligence in the WMD policy area is fairly obvious: Identify proliferation programs early enough to stop them before they are completed. Intelligence also targets the clandestine international commerce in some of the specialty items required to manufacture weapons of mass destruction. However, proliferation programs are, by their very nature, covert. Thus, the types of collection that the United States must undertake tend to come from the clandestine side of the intelligence community. The evidence of nascent programs—as well as mature programs—that U.S. intelligence might obtain may be ambiguous. Fuzzy information complicates the ability of policy makers to confront potential proliferators with confidence or to convince other nations that a problem exists. As the exposure of Pakistani A. Q. Khan's nuclear proliferation network in 2003 shows, however, doing so is not an impossible task. But it is time-consuming (the effort against Khan went on for years) and sensitive diplomatically. In the case of the Khan network, the sensitivities of Pakistan had to be taken into account, given its support for the war on terrorism. Khan's activities also confirmed the international nature of nuclear proliferation. His enterprises spanned three continents and may have been involved in more than just the Pakistan and Libyan programs. This points up another intelligence challenge: determining how vast the interconnections are between would-be proliferators and would-be providers. Although the disruption of the Khan network was a major intelligence success, parts of the program could continue to operate without Khan's guidance.

Beyond the problem of amassing convincing evidence lies the policy question: How can a would-be proliferator be stopped? The preferred means is diplomacy, but the track record in this area is unimpressive. No nation has been talked out of developing nuclear weapons by diplomacy alone. The United States has used its influence, and its leverage as the guarantor of a state's national security, to pressure a state into desisting from nuclear weapons development. Press accounts allege that the United States used this method with Taiwan in the 1980s. Some other nations— for reasons of their own—decided to abandon nuclear programs. Japan and Sweden chose not to develop programs. Argentina and Brazil agreed bilaterally to abandon their fledging efforts. The white South African government gave up its nuclear weapons and its capabilities on the eve of the black majority's advent to power. Libya's admission in 2003 that it had a range of covert WMD programs that it had formerly denied was largely a result of two factors: successful HUMINT that caught shipments going to Libya and Libya's concerns about potential U.S. actions after the invasion of Iraq. The Libya case was an intelligence and policy success but not a result of diplomacy. Many other states—Iran, Israel, and North Korea— remain unconvinced by U.S. diplomacy. Given the minimal success of moral suasion, some people have argued that the only workable solution is an active nonproliferation policy—intervening to destroy the capability, as both Israel and the 1991 Persian Gulf War allies did with Iraq. (See box, "Iraq's Nuclear Program—A Cautionary Tale.")

The Indian and Pakistani tests represented a setback for nonproliferation. The Indian test was also an intelligence setback, in that political signs were ignored and technical collection was looking elsewhere.

The loose nukes aspect of the issue adds a new and more difficult complication. The Soviet Union agreed with the goal of nuclear nonproliferation, recognizing that it could be a target of would-be proliferators. But far more daunting is the prospect of tracking unknown quantities of weapons-grade material (which even Russian and other authorities have been unable to account for with accuracy) and the international movement of experts from former Soviet states. The collapse of the post–Soviet economy and the end of the privileged status that scientists once enjoyed are incentives to would-be proliferators.

Iraq's Nuclear Program—A Cautionary Tale

During the 1980s, Iraq was one of the nations whose nuclear weapons program was closely watched by U.S. experts. The existence of a program was not in question; its status was.

On the eve of the 1991 Persian Gulf War, the considered analytical judgment, according to subsequent accounts, was that Iraq was at least five years away from a nuclear capability. After Iraq's defeat in the war, analysts learned that Iraq had been much closer to success, even though Israel had attacked and destroyed some of its facilities some years earlier.

What had gone wrong with U.S. estimates?

Iraq was and is a closed target, one of the most repressive and heavily policed states in the world. The state's nature makes collection more difficult, but that is not the answer to the question.

The answer lies in an analytical flaw, namely, mirror imaging. To manufacture the fissionable material it required, Iraq chose a method abandoned by the United States in the early days of its own nuclear program after World War II. The method works, but it is a very slow and tedious way to produce fissionable material.

For Iraq, however, it was the perfect method, not because it was slow, but because foreign analysts disregarded it. The method allowed Iraq to procure materials that were more difficult to associate with a nuclear weapons program, to mask its status. A program of this sort was also more difficult for Western analysts to spot because they largely dismissed the approach out of hand, assuming that Iraq would want—just as the United States and others had—to find the fastest way to produce fissionable material.

In the course of U.S. military action in Iraq that commenced in 2003, expected Iraqi weapons of mass destruction programs were not found. Some wondered if analysts had compensated for their earlier error by overinterpreting evidence of a possible program without considering alternative interpretations. The analysts themselves denied this assessment, and none of the postwar investigations of the intelligence community's performance found overinterpretation to have been a factor.

CW and BW proliferation require much less expertise and technical capability than nuclear proliferation does. CW and BW weapons are far less accurate than nuclear weapons, but the random terror they portend is part of their appeal to nations and terrorists. Such programs are more difficult than nuclear programs to identify and track. The anthrax scare of late 2001 underscores these points and also indicates how difficult it is to detect this type of attack in advance or to stop it once under way.

The intelligence experience of 2002–2004 in WMD is mixed. In Iraq, the analysis did not bear out. The exposure of A. Q. Khan's network points out the importance of years of determined analysis and highly successful operations to penetrate the network until enough intelligence had been established to make the case incontrovertible. The Libyan surrender also owes much to years of collection, analysis, and some highly successful operations. In short, intelligence can bring important assets to bear on WMD proliferation, but it will always be a shadowy area and one liable to analytic missteps.

NARCOTICS. Narcotics policy is a difficult area in which to work. The main goal is to prevent individuals, by a variety of means, from using drugs that the government deems addictive and harmful. Almost everyone who has ever worked on narcotics policy has said that it is a domestic issue, not a foreign policy issue. Also, given the fact that individuals use drugs for numerous reasons, preventing their use is a difficult goal to attain. For both practical and political reasons, narcotics has become, in part, a foreign policy problem, because the United States attempts to reduce the overseas production of illegal drugs and to intercept them before or just as they arrive in the country.

The intelligence community is capable of collecting and analyzing intelligence related to the illicit trade in narcotics. The plants from which certain narcotics are derived can be grown in large quantities only in certain parts of the world. Coca is produced in the Andean region of South America. Poppies, from which heroin is made, are grown predominantly in two parts of southern Asia, centering roughly on Afghanistan and Myanmar (formerly Burma). Areas where these plants are processed into narcotics are also fairly well known, as are the routes customarily used to ship the finished products to customer areas.

The real problem lies in converting this intelligence into successful policy. Efforts at crop eradication and substitution stumble on the simple economic choices facing local farmers. Narcotics crops pay more than food crops do. Processing facilities, although U.S. intelligence can locate them, tend to be small and numerous. Drugs are so profitable that small amounts, which are easily shipped, are economically attractive. Shippers can use any number of routes, which they can change in response to pressure and efforts at interdiction. Finally, narcotics activities yield money in sufficient amounts to subvert the local authorities—civil, military, and police.

All experienced policy makers point to the importance of a domestic answer. If people do not have an interest in using illegal drugs, then everything else—growth, processing, shipping, and even price—becomes irrelevant. The drugs become valueless commodities. But the elusiveness of a successful domestic response leads policy makers back to foreign policy. (Legalizing drugs might not have the same effect on production and distribution as eliminating demand, because a black market might arise to compete with government-approved providers.)

The conjunction of the narcotics trade with international crime and with terrorism adds a new dimension to the intelligence-gathering and policy-making problem. The profits from sales of narcotics, instead of being an end in themselves, now become the means to fund a different end. Also, new and more difficult demands are put on intelligence, because terrorists and criminals operate clandestinely. The United States must be able to establish intelligence about networks, contacts, relationships among individuals and groups, flows of capital, and so forth. For example, guerrilla and right-wing paramilitary groups in Colombia have used cocaine to finance their operations. Ironically, the Taliban in Afghanistan had made some progress against poppy crops (as opposed to the processed opium, much of which simply remained in storage), which has been reversed under the successor regime in Afghanistan in a classic case of competing priorities. The limitations of the Afghan government's authority in some provinces have allowed the narcotics trade to reemerge.

Finally, narcotics crosses the line established in the United States between foreign and domestic intelligence and between intelligence and law enforcement. The point at which an issue is handed from one agency to another is not always clear but is important, raising both practical and legal questions, some of which can impede prosecution.

ECONOMICS. Economics can be subdivided into several issues: U.S. economic competitiveness overseas, U.S. trading relations, **foreign economic espionage** and possible countermeasures, and the intelligence community's ability to forecast major international economic shifts that may have serious consequences for the U.S. economy.

During the late 1980s some people maintained that several of these issues (overseas competitiveness, trading relations, foreign economic espionage, **industrial espionage** undertaken by businesses, and possible countermeasures) could be addressed, in part, through a closer connection between intelligence and U.S. businesses. Few advocates of closer intelligence–business collaboration, however, had substantial answers for some of the more compelling questions that it raised (which is one reason that this approach was quickly rejected).

- If the intelligence community were to share intelligence with businesses, how would they safeguard the sources and methods used in obtaining the information? If the underlying sources and methods could not be shared, would businesses accept the intelligence?

- With whom would the intelligence be shared, or, in other words, what constitutes a "U.S. company"? In an age of multinational corporations, the concept is not easy to define.
- Given that every business sector has many competitive businesses, which ones would the community provide with intelligence? What would be the basis for selecting recipients and nonrecipients of the intelligence?
- Would providing intelligence be part of an implicit quid pro quo on the part of the government—that some action should or should not be taken by industry in exchange for access to intelligence?

The collection of foreign economic intelligence by other nations was also controversial. An aggressive collection policy was central to those proposing greater intelligence support to business. Supporters of the policy cited cases in which supposed friends of the United States, such as France, were caught engaging in such activity. Advocates saw similar activity by the United States as fighting fire with fire. Critics argued that to do so would justify the initial hostile action. They also raised some of the arguments about the limits on how such information might be used. But DCI Robert M. Gates (1991–1993) put it best when he said that no U.S. intelligence agent was "willing to die for General Motors."

Allegations of U.S. economic espionage arose in the late 1990s concerning a National Security Agency (NSA) program called **ECHELON**. In simplest terms, NSA uses the program to search through collected signals intelligence (SIGINT), using key words via a computer. Key-word searching allows more material to be processed and exploited. Some European officials claimed that ECHELON was being used to steal advanced technology secrets, which were then being passed to U.S. firms to enhance their competitiveness. Former DCI R. James Woolsey (1993–1995), in a stinging article, held that ECHELON was used to detect attempts by European firms to bribe foreign officials to make sales and to uncover the illicit transfer of dual-use technologies—technologies that have both commercial and WMD applications, such as supercomputers and some chemicals.

U.S. policy makers viewed foreign economic counterintelligence as largely noncontroversial. Most of them considered it a proper response to foreign economic intelligence, although questions were raised about the extent of the problem. Press accounts of the issue often cited the same shopworn cases, creating echo—the impression of a larger problem through repetition. But the problem may be underreported, given that many businesses do not want to admit that they have been the victims of successful foreign intelligence operations. Some people also argue that foreign economic counterintelligence, although necessary, treats the symptom but not the cause. They acknowledge that blunting attempts at economic intelligence collection may be important but contend that the issue should be addressed at a political level—perhaps by negotiations that offer nations the choice of cessation or countermeasures.

Legislation passed during the 105th Congress (1997–1999) extended the role of FBI counterintelligence in the business information area, which has been controversial. The legislation reflects a continuing expansion of FBI authority in the gray areas between foreign and domestic intelligence and between intelligence and law enforcement.

Finally, at least three serious currency-related crises have occurred since the end of the cold war. In 1995 Mexico experienced a peso melt-down, which the intelligence community apparently handled well, giving policy makers significant advance warning. In 1998 the two-year Thai economic crisis turned into a full Asian economic debacle, encompassing Indonesia, Malaysia, the Philippines, and South Korea. Little has been said about intelligence performance in this crisis. The 2000–2001 Argentine financial collapse was long evident. The likelihood that other such crises will occur in years to come underscores the importance of economic intelligence in this area, especially given the greater interrelatedness of the global financial market.

HEALTH AND ENVIRONMENT.   Health and environmental issues are relatively new to the intelligence agenda. They are sometimes treated as one issue and sometimes separately. The health issue has gained increasing prominence because of the AIDS (acquired immune deficiency syndrome) pandemic and smaller outbreaks of deadly diseases such as the ebola virus and SARS (severe acute respiratory syndrome) in East Asia. The intelligence task is largely one of tracking patterns of infection, but a large gap exists between intelligence and policy. Take AIDS as an example. The causes, means of infection, and results of AIDS are well known. Although the disease strikes people worldwide, some areas, notably eastern and central Africa, have extremely high concentrations of AIDS cases. The intelligence community's ability to track rates of infection and mortality has little effect on any useful international policy. Many of the African governments that face the highest rates of AIDS infection have chosen, for a variety of reasons, to ignore or even to deny their health crisis. The same had been true of the government of China, although it now admits the seriousness of the AIDS problem. In the case of Africa, local culture is a major factor in the spread of AIDS: toleration of polygamous relationships; low literacy rates, thus making even minimal efforts at education about prevention more difficult; and minimal use of prophylactics. Nor is it clear what these nations or the international community should be doing in the absence of any cure for the disease. Outsiders' attempts to change the cultural factors that facilitate the spread of AIDS would not only be difficult to make but also would probably be resisted as interference.

A major issue surrounding health-related crises is tracking official foreign government statements against other intelligence to determine both the extent of the health problem and the openness of the government involved. This has been a point of contention with China over SARS. For the United States, two issues are involved. One is the duty to warn, as in terrorism, that is, to alert U.S. citizens and others about potential health risks overseas. The other is an insight into the behavior of another government. Tracking an issue of this sort is a combination of covert intelligence (such as SIGINT between foreign officials) and open sources (such as reports by travelers, hospital admissions, larger than normal requests for drugs, and so on).

The environment issue is also somewhat amorphous. The basic goal—preserving a healthier global ecology—stumbles when it comes down to practicalities. As has been the case with international efforts to deal with AIDS, the nations at the center of the issue have different interests and preferences. The international community may believe that it has a vested interest in the preservation of some local ecological habitat, such as a rain forest. However, the nation whose land it is may be more interested in its own economic development than in the stewardship of a world ecological resource.

The basic intelligence tasks are identifying major threats to the environment, identifying states whose policies may be harmful to the environment, and tracking major changes in the environment. Again, a gap separates intelligence from what policy makers are supposed to do with it. Substantial intelligence community involvement in environmental policy dates back only to the late stages of the cold war.

Much of the intelligence about the health and environment issues can be carried out by means of open sources. Commercial infrared satellites can track environmental changes. The spread of disease also can be tracked overtly. Intelligence on these issues has tended to suffer from the inattention of policy makers and from the fact that overt means of collecting intelligence have been less fully developed than the clandestine means.

The anthrax attacks in the autumn of 2001 may have added a further dimension to the health issue—the ability to determine the cause of a serious outbreak of disease to differentiate between natural occurrences and terrorism. If it is believed to be terrorism, the source of the attack and the prevention of future attacks must also be undertaken. These are daunting tasks and would have to be carried out under conditions of extreme pressure in terms of time and political requirements.

PEACEKEEPING OPERATIONS. Since the end of the cold war, international peacekeeping operations have expanded dramatically. Regional outbursts of violence, most of them within the borders of one country (or former country), have required the imposition of external troops to restore and then maintain peace. The external troops have customarily been formed into multinational units. Although many of these nations have experience in allied operations—at least training operations—the participants tend to cross the boundaries of old alliances. United Nations–mandated forces in Bosnia, for example, included North Atlantic Treaty Organization (NATO) allies (Britain, France, Italy, Spain, and the United States) and their former Warsaw Pact foes (Russia, Ukraine), along with other nations. A similar array has been formed in Afghanistan. Successful military operations require strong intelligence support; multinational operations require intelligence sharing. But even in the aftermath of the cold war, some U.S. policy makers and intelligence officials are reluctant to share intelligence with former foes, nonallies, and even some allies. Responsible civil and military officials may find themselves torn between the need to keep peacekeeping partners well informed to carry out successful operations and the recognition that sources and methods may be compromised even beyond the limited peacekeeping theater of operations.

The use of peacekeeping or other internationally sanctioned operations for unilateral intelligence purposes became an issue in 1999. A former member of the United Nations Special Commission (UNSCOM)—which was responsible for monitoring Iraqi destruction of its weapons of mass destruction—alleged that the United States used a UNSCOM inspection team to plant intelligence collection devices. Some saw the U.S. action as a necessary precaution against a hostile state; others believed it violated the basis of the UNSCOM mission.

INFORMATION OPERATIONS. Still a relatively new issue on the intelligence agenda, information operations deal with the use of computer technology to wage war and also to protect the United States from similar attacks. The Persian Gulf War gave a great boost to this operational concept. Intelligence officers find that **information operations** allow them to be combatants, not just combat supporters.

The parameters of information operations have yet to be fully defined. The technology to disrupt communications and infrastructure, send false messages, and destroy vital information exists; firm operational concepts for using the technology do not. The same was true of virtually every other military technology—firearms, tanks, airplanes, and so on. Only through operations do military and intelligence officials learn the best ways to employ, and defend against, new technologies.

The widespread use of computers and the increasing dependence on them by all nations and their militaries underscore the appeal and the threat of information operations, which can weaken an opponent and lessen the chance of U.S. casualties in combat.

The doctrinal questions outnumber the accepted precepts. Should information operations be used preemptively, before hostilities begin? This would tend to preempt potential diplomatic solutions, which depend on the ability of leaders and diplomats to communicate authoritatively between capitals. One can easily envision heated debates between diplomats seeking to forestall information operations to keep lines of communications open and military officers arguing about the need to begin preparing the electronic battlefield. However, a broad and successful information operation might induce a hostile state to agree to end a crisis. It would not entail civilian casualties, as would a classic military attack. But is this the way the United States wants to behave? Would U.S. leaders feel compelled, for legal reasons, to regard an information operation as a covert action, launched with a presidential finding, instead of as a military operation? The agency largely responsible for information warfare, the National Security Agency, is both an intelligence agency and a combat support agency, so it bridges the gap. But this fact does not, in and of itself, answer the question.

Battle damage assessment (BDA), which became a major intelligence issue during the Persian Gulf War, would be difficult to perform in an information operation. Analysts in Washington (mostly at the CIA) differed with analysts in the field as to the efficacy of the air campaign in the Gulf War. How could BDA be carried out in the more opaque area of information operations? How could it be determined that an enemy's computer system had been successfully disrupted, or that the enemy had just shut it down when it recognized that an attack was under way? How could it be discovered that the enemy had backup systems? If a successful information warfare attack is a precondition for some type of overt military operation, how can it be determined that the precondition has been satisfied? How much disruption should be caused? Disrupting enemy communications is useful, but should such action preclude, for example, the ability of an enemy headquarters to signal its troops authoritatively that hostilities are to cease? Or, having disrupted the enemy's ability to communicate, how can an enemy's offer to cease hostilities, to negotiate, and so on be verified?

Tension exists between two aspects of information operations: computer network exploitation (CNE) and computer network attack (CNA). A hostile or potentially hostile computer network offers two distinct choices. One is trying to break into the network—to find out who is using it for what means, that is, who is communicating on it—and extracting useful intelligence from it, perhaps using it to manipulate those whose network it is. This is CNE. Another is to attack the network (CNA) to destroy whatever capability it represents. However, once a network has been attacked and taken down, it can no longer be exploited. Therefore someone must decide whether it is more useful to allow the network to continue as a means of gaining more intelligence, or if it is better to destroy the network.

As the United States learned in Afghanistan, there are targets in the third world for which information operations are useless and unnecessary. Under the Taliban, the electronic infrastructure of Afghanistan had been allowed to deteriorate to the point where few suitable information operations targets existed.

Turning to the defensive problem, how can it be verified that a particular state or group is responsible for an information operations attack on the United States? As with terrorism and retaliation, the source of the attack is important to find out. Moreover, if the United States were subject to such an attack, what should be the proper response? Retaliate via computers or with weapons? Again, is the response an intelligence action or a military one?

DOMINANT BATTLEFIELD AWARENESS. Supporting military forces engaged in combat operations, usually called support to military operations (SMO), is one of the highest intelligence demands. A key aspect of SMO is the concept of **dominant battlefield awareness** (DBA). At the National Defense University in June 1995, then DCI John M. Deutch (1995–1997) defined DBA as the integration of IMINT, SIGINT, and HUMINT to give "commanders real-time, or near real-time, all-weather, comprehensive, continuous surveillance and information about the battlespace in which they operate.... Dominant battlefield awareness, if achieved, will reduce—never totally eliminate—the 'fog of war,' and provide you, the military commanders, with an unprecedented combat advantage." DBA refers to the totality of information that is available to all commanders at all levels. It is not a single type of report or activity.

DBA reflects at least two trends. The first is the great strides that U.S. intelligence has made in collecting and disseminating intelligence to military commanders in the field. Commanders believe that this superiority allows them to use forces more effectively, so as to achieve ends more quickly and with fewer casualties. The second is the so-called lessons learned from the Persian Gulf War about the problems in bringing intelligence to the field and getting the right intelligence to the right military user.

Although Deutch cautioned that the "fog of war" (a term coined by nineteenth-century Prussian general and military theorist Karl von Clausewitz for the confusion and uncertainty that are inevitable in any combat) will never be eliminated, many advocates of DBA seem not to have heard him. DBA is often oversold as the ability to bring near-total intelligence to commanders. This hyperbole puts intelligence on the spot for capabilities it does not have. Unrealistically high expectations may lead commanders to place greater reliance on intelligence (which may not be forthcoming) and less on their own instincts when dealing with the fog of war, which is the ultimate skill of a combat commander. (Gen. William T. Sherman observed that Gen. Ulysses S. Grant was the superior commander because he was unconcerned about what the enemy was doing when out of sight.)

Defense Department official statements on the topic are somewhat confusing. The two key documents are *Joint Vision 2010* and *Joint Vision 2020*. Both emphasize the importance of DBA and the role of intelligence but tend to use intelligence and information technology interchangeably. However, information technology is a means to but is not the same thing as intelligence.

Another problem with DBA is that delivering on its promise could require the intelligence community to allocate a large percentage of collection assets to the task, to the detriment of other priorities elsewhere in the world. As with SMO, the question "How much is enough?" is pertinent. Finally, an essential ingredient in successful DBA is getting the right type and amount of information to the right user. An army commander's intelligence needs differ from those of an infantry squad leader or a combat pilot. Some critics are concerned that too much information is pushed down to users who have no need for it, flooding them with irrelevant intelligence simply because the means are available to do so. As a result, their jobs are made more difficult.

The military campaign in Iraq that began in 2003 illustrated both the promise and the problems involved in DBA. The vastly superior strategic and tactical intelligence of the United States and its allied forces enhanced both the general campaign plan—including the decision to make a dash for Baghdad with fairly small forces—and the ability to locate, identify, and attack in detail regular Iraqi forces. But the war also pointed out that the evolution of U.S. military doctrine (sometimes referred to as the Revolution in Military Affairs or RMA) continues to put pressure on intelligence for increasing degrees of support. Given the likelihood that the size of U.S. forces (as opposed to their mobility and lethality) will not grow much, intelligence will increasingly be seen as one of the factors that allows these relatively small forces to achieve both dominance and victory. How much support is entailed and what it means for the shape and practice of intelligence are not entirely clear. Also, it remains uncertain how the new office of a DNI will fit into the relationship between intelligence agencies—especially those such as NGA and NSA, which are national but are also designated in law as combat support agencies—and the Defense Department. The situation is especially murky because the DNI does not control any of the agencies upon which the military relies for intelligence support. The DNI could be bypassed by the Defense Department as it seeks intelligence support from national and defense agencies.

CONCLUSION

In the first decade after the end of the cold war (using as a benchmark the breaching of the Berlin Wall in 1989), the U.S. national security agenda remained largely unformed, not in terms of which issues mattered but which of them mattered the most, which would receive the highest priority over time (as opposed to immediate reactions to events), and what the United States would be willing to do to achieve its preferred ends. In the absence of clear definition, the intelligence community found it difficult to perform. Intelligence officials have a broad understanding of policy makers' preferences and immediate interests, but these do not provide the basis for making a coherent set of plans for investments, collection systems, personnel recruitment, and training. The war on terrorism offered some clarity in that it has given one issue priority over all the others, although not to the same extent as the old Soviet issue. Moreover, the terrorism issue is different from the Soviet issue in many important respects, thus emphasizing the importance of the cold war legacy for the intelligence community, as well as the need to transcend this legacy.

Many issues in the new U.S. intelligence agenda share an important hallmark: the gap between the intelligence community's ability to provide intelligence and the policy makers' ability to craft policies to address the issues and to use the intelligence. This gap may even be seen in the war against terrorism. If the disparity persists, the intelligence community and its policy clients may become disaffected. Clients want to be more than just informed; they want to act (that is, to receive opportunity analysis). And intelligence is not meant to be collected and then filed away. It is intended to assist people in making decisions or taking action. This is not to suggest that the intelligence community will suddenly disappear. But it may come to be seen as less central and necessary—a provider of information that is interesting but not as useful as it has been in the past because of the changed nature of the issues.

KEY TERMS

actionable intelligence
battle damage assessment
chatter
dominant battlefield awareness

ECHELON
foreign economic espionage
industrial espionage
information operations

FURTHER READINGS

Writings on the post–cold war intelligence agenda remain somewhat scattered across issue areas, reflecting the nature of the debate itself.

General

Colby, William. "The Changing Role of Intelligence." *World Outlook* 13 (summer 1991): 77–90.

Goodman, Allan E. "The Future of U.S. Intelligence." *Intelligence and National Security* 11 (October 1996): 645–656.

Goodman, Allan E., and Bruce D. Berkowitz. *The Need to Know.* Report of the Twentieth Century Fund Task Force on Covert Action and American Democracy. New York: Twentieth Century Fund, 1992.

Goodman, Allan E., and others. *In from the Cold.* Report of the Twentieth Century Fund Task Force on the Future of U.S. Intelligence. New York: Twentieth Century Fund, 1996.

Johnson, Loch K. *Bombs, Bugs, Drugs, and Thugs: Intelligence and America's Quest for Security.* New York: New York University Press, 2000.

Johnson, Loch K., and Kevin J. Scheid. "Spending for Spies: Intelligence Budgeting in the Aftermath of the Cold War." *Public Budgeting and Finance* 17 (winter 1997): 7–27.

U.S. National Intelligence Council. *Global Trends 2015.* Washington, D.C.: National Intelligence Council, 2000.

Economics

Fort, Randall M. *Economic Espionage: Problems and Prospects.* Washington, D.C.: Consortium for the Study of Intelligence, 1993.

Hulnick, Arthur S. "The Uneasy Relationship between Intelligence and Private Industry." *International Journal of Intelligence and Counterintelligence* 9 (spring 1996): 17–31.

Lowenthal, Mark M. "Keep James Bond Out of GM." *International Economy* (July–August 1992): 52–54.

Woolsey, R. James. "Why We Spy on Our Allies." *Wall Street Journal,* March 17, 2000, A18.

Zelikow, Philip. "American Economic Intelligence: Past Practice and Future Principles." *Intelligence and National Security* 12 (January 1997): 164–177.

Information Operations and Dominant Battlefield Awareness

Aldrich, Richard W. *The International Legal Implications of Information Warfare.* Colorado Springs, Colo.: U.S. Air Force Institute for National Security Studies, 1996.

Deutch, John M. Speech at National Defense University, Washington, D.C., June 14, 1995. (Available at www.fas.org/irp/cia/product/dci—speech—61495.html.)

Law Enforcement

Hulnick, Arthur S. "Intelligence and Law Enforcement." *International Journal of Intelligence and Counterintelligence* 10 (fall 1997): 269–286.

Snider, L. Britt, with Elizabeth Rindskopf and John Coleman. *Relating Intelligence and Law Enforcement: Problems and Prospects*. Washington, D.C.: Consortium for the Study of Intelligence, 1994.

Narcotics

Best, Richard A., Jr., and Mark M. Lowenthal. "The U.S. Intelligence Community and the Counternarcotics Effort." Washington, D.C.: Congressional Research Service, 1992.

Peacekeeping

Best, Richard A., Jr. "Peacekeeping: Intelligence Requirements." Washington, D.C.: Congressional Research Service, 1994.

Johnston, Paul. "No Cloak and Dagger Required: Intelligence Support to UN Peacekeeping." *Intelligence and National Security* 12 (October 1997): 102–112.

Pickert, Perry L. *Intelligence for Multilateral Decision and Action*. Ed. Russell G. Swenson. Washington, D.C.: Joint Military Intelligence College, 1997.

Terrorism

Cilluffo, Frank J., Ronald A. Marks, and George C. Salmoiraghi. "The Use and Limits of U.S. Intelligence." *Washington Quarterly* 25 (winter 2002): 61–74.

Grimmett, Richard F. "Terrorism: Key Recommendations of the 9/11 Commission and Recent Major Commissions and Inquiries." Washington, D.C.: Congressional Research Service, August 11, 2004.

Dominant Battlefield Awareness

Nolte, William. "Keeping Pace with the Revolution in Military Affairs," *Studies in Intelligence* 48 (2004): 1–10.

Chapter 13

Ethical and Moral Issues
in Intelligence

The phrase "ethical and moral issues in intelligence" is not as much of an oxymoron as some people consider it. Important ethical standards and moral dilemmas challenge intelligence officers and policy officials and must be dealt with. As with most discussions of ethics and morality, some of the questions have no firm or agreed-upon answers.

GENERAL MORAL QUESTIONS

The nature of intelligence operations and issues and the basis upon which they are created raise a number of broad moral questions.

SECRECY. Much intelligence work is done in secret, although the definition of intelligence set out in chapter 1 does not include secrecy as a necessary precondition. The question remains: Is secrecy necessary in intelligence? If so, how much secrecy? And at what cost?

If secrecy is necessary, what causes or drives the need? Governments have intelligence services because they seek information that others would deny them. Thus, secrecy is inherent not only in what your intelligence service is doing (collection and covert action) but also in the information that others withhold from you. You also do not want the other state to know your areas of interest. Is this second level of secrecy necessary? After all, those keeping information from you often know—or at least presume—that you want it. That is one reason for hiding it from you (although many dictatorial states attempt to control all information, understanding that it poses a threat to their regime). Or is secrecy driven primarily by your attempts to gain access to hidden information? Is it based on not allowing those who are attempting to deny you information to know that, to some degree, they have failed? How necessary is that? After all, you will act on the intelligence collected, although you will attempt to mask the reasons for your actions. Won't your opponents at least guess, based on your decisions and actions, that you have gained some access to the information they were safeguarding?

Beyond the motivations for secrecy are the costs it imposes. This does not refer to the monetary costs—for background checks, control systems for access, and so forth—which are substantial. The issue here is how operating in a secret milieu affects people. Does secrecy inherently lead to a temptation or willingness to cut corners or take steps that might be deemed unacceptable if they were not cloaked in secrecy? This is not to suggest that thousands of people are morally compromised because they work in organizations that prize secrecy. But the nature of some aspects of intelligence—primarily collection and covert action—combined with the fact that they are undertaken in secret may lower an intelligence official's inhibitions to commit questionable actions. These factors put a premium on the careful selection and training of officers and on vigorous oversight.

WAR AND PEACE. Moral philosophers and states have long presumed that the conditions of war and peace are different and allow different types of activity. The most obvious wartime activity is organized violence against the territory and citizens of other states. During peacetime, overt conflict is precluded. Does this division between acceptable peacetime and wartime norms extend to intelligence activities? Are efforts to subvert and overthrow the governments of enemy states acceptable in peacetime, as they are in wartime?

Even during periods of peace, the United States has relations with states that are hostile. The cold war between the United States and the Soviet Union may have been the epitome of such relationships: hostile at virtually all levels but never reaching the point of overt conflict between the two primary antagonists (as opposed to some of their surrogates).

A relationship such as that between the two cold war antagonists occupies a gray middle ground between peace and war. Intelligence activities—both collection and covert action—became one of the principal means by which the two countries could attack each other. Even in this unique situation, however, the United States and the Soviet Union accepted some limits. The two sides did not kill each other's nationals who were caught spying. Instead, they jailed the spies and sometimes exchanged them, as was the case with Col. Rudolf Abel, a Soviet spy imprisoned in the United States in 1957, and U-2 pilot Francis Gary Powers. (One's own national caught spying for the other side could be executed, as were Julius Rosenberg and Col. Oleg Penkovsky.) The national leadership of each side was safe from physical attacks. But did these unwritten rules create necessary boundaries, or did they serve to allow a great many other activities, including propaganda and subversion?

If a country threatens to make war or if war seems imminent, does the concept of self-defense allow states to engage preemptively in certain activities, including intelligence operations? In an age of information operations, this question is increasingly important. The George W. Bush administration in 2003 advocated a preemptive strategy as part of its rationale for the war against Iraq, but it is not clear that this will have continued support in that war's aftermath, given that the expected weapons of mass destruction (WMDs) were not found.

ENDS VERSUS MEANS. The usual answer to the question "Do the ends justify the means?" is no. But if the ends do not justify the means, what does? Policy makers face difficult choices when means and ends are in conflict. For example, during the cold war, was it proper for the United States, which advocated free elections, to interfere in Western European elections in the late 1940s to preclude communist victories? Which choice was preferable: upholding moral principles or allowing a politically unpalatable and perhaps threatening outcome? How does U.S. interference in postwar European elections compare with the subversion of the Chilean economy as a means of undermining the government of Salvador Allende?

Within the U.S. political experience, such questions represent two deeply rooted concepts: realpolitik and idealism. In the milieu of the cold war, realpolitik predominated. The moral aspect of the cold war (Western democratic ideals versus Soviet communism) made choices such as those described above easy for policy makers. Would they make the same choices in the post–cold war world in the absence of such a moral imperative?

THE NATURE OF THE OPPONENT. For nearly half a century the United States faced successive totalitarian threats: the Axis and then the Soviet Union and its satellite states. A vast gulf existed between the accepted values and behavioral norms of the United States and its allies and their opponents. Do the actions of your opponents affect the actions you may undertake? Are they a useful guide to action?

"All's fair in . . ." is one response. On the one hand, a state would be foolish to deny itself weapons or tactics that are being used by an opponent bent on the state's destruction. On the other hand, does a state not lose something important when it sinks to the level of an opponent who is amoral or immoral? John Le Carré, in his novels featuring the spy George Smiley, argued that little difference can be found between the actions of the United States and the Soviet Union during the cold war, that a certain moral equivalence existed. Was Le Carré correct, or did the moral distinctions between the two states remain strong and important, even if similarities existed in some types of intelligence operations?

NATIONAL INTEREST. The concept of national interest is not new. In the period that historians refer to as "early modern Europe," roughly the seventeenth century, all statesmen agreed that raison d'état—literally "reason of state"—guided their actions. Raison d'état implied two tenets: first, that the state embodied its own ends, and, second, that the interests of the state were guides only for actions, not resentments, emotions, or other subjective impulses. Raison d'état, as practiced in early modern Europe, also implied the use of intrigue by one state against another and the ultimate sanction: the use of force.

In the late seventeenth and eighteenth centuries, international relations were, beneath a refined veneer, brutal. One could argue that even the creation of an international body, the United Nations (UN), has done little to modify the behavior of states in the late twentieth and early twenty-first centuries. For example, witness the brutality of many parties in the dismemberment of Yugoslavia or of the Khmer Rouge in Cambodia. A direct descent follows from seventeenth-century raison d'état to twentieth-first-century national interest.

Is national interest a sufficient guide to the ethics and morality of intelligence? On the one hand, it is the only guide. If intelligence activities are not undertaken in support of the policies of the legitimate government, then they are meaningless at best or dangerous rogue operations at worst. On the other hand, legitimate governments—even those that adhere to democratic ideals and principles—can sometimes reach decisions and take actions that are morally or ethically questionable.

Thus, national interest is a difficult guideline, both indispensable and insufficient at the same time.

CHANGES IN ETHICS AND MORALS. Ethics and morals change over time. For example, slavery was accepted in Britain as late as the 1830s, in some parts of the United States as late as the 1860s, and in Brazil as late as the 1880s. Slavery reportedly continued in Sudan in the late 1990s. Less than one hundred years ago, in the 1910s, the issue of women's suffrage was still being vigorously debated in Britain and the United States; in Switzerland, the debate continued into the 1960s.

Assuming that intelligence activities are undertaken on lawful authority, should they keep abreast of changes in ethics and morality? Citizens should want to say yes. But who decides when these changes have come? How quickly do changes in ethics and morals get translated into policies and actions? For example, political intervention of the sort undertaken in Europe during the cold war is probably insupportable today (with the 1998 Iraq Liberation Act, which publicly appropriated money to foster a change in the regime in Iraq, a notable exception). But when did that change come? When the Soviet Union collapsed or earlier?

In 1975 the United States faced the prospect of seeing one of its North Atlantic Treaty Organization (NATO) allies, Portugal, elect a communist government. After a strenuous debate between the U.S. ambassador (who opposed covert intervention in the Portuguese elections) and the national security adviser (who advocated it), the United States opted not to intervene, and the Communists lost the election. The decision was based not on a new morality but on the view that the United States had more to lose by intervening and possibly being exposed than by allowing the elections to take their course. The outcome proved favorable from the U.S. perspective, as the ambassador believed it would.

A second important question prompted by changes in values is whether new standards should be imposed after the fact. For example, during the cold war the United States often supported regimes that were undemocratic and sometimes brutal, but they were anticommunist. Although some people in the United States found these relationships objectionable, many accepted their apparent necessity. In the mid-1990s, Director of Central Intelligence (DCI) John M. Deutch (1995–1997) ordered the Central Intelligence Agency (CIA) to review all of its contacts and operations to see if any involved links to human rights abuses. Many in the CIA felt that this review, and some of the actions that the CIA leadership took against some officers, was an unfair ex post facto imposition of standards. (The Constitution bars laws that are ex post facto in nature.) Was Deutch's action a necessary cleaning up of past errors or an unfair imposition of new standards on officers who had acted in good faith under old standards? In the aftermath of the September 2001 attacks, many people felt that the so-called Deutch rules had placed hobbling limits on human intelligence (HUMINT). The CIA claimed that no useful contact had been turned away because of the rules, but critics argued that their mere existence and the threat of some later punishment bred extreme caution in the Directorate of Operations. At any rate, the Deutch rules were abandoned after the terrorist attacks.

Markus Wolf ran East German intelligence operations for years, successfully penetrating many levels of the West German government, including the chancellor's office. When East Germany collapsed and was absorbed by West Germany, the German government put Wolf on trial for treason. Its rationale for doing so ran as follows: According to the constitution of West Germany, it was the one legitimate government of all Germany, and Wolf had carried out espionage against that government. (Despite its constitutional claims, West Germany had granted East Germany diplomatic recognition, and the two states had exchanged ambassadors.) Wolf argued that he had been the citizen of a separate state and therefore could not be guilty of treason. In 1993 he was convicted of espionage, but in 1995 the highest German court voided the verdict, accepting

Wolf's argument that the charge should not have been made in the first place because he had not broken the laws of the state he had served, East Germany. After receiving a suspended sentence for kidnappings carried out by agents under his authority, Wolf, in 1998, was jailed for refusing to identify an agent he had referred to in his memoirs.

A case similar to Wolf's—but with an odd twist—is that of Col. Ryszard Kuklinski, a Polish general staff officer. Kuklinski provided the United States with crucial intelligence on the Warsaw Pact during the late 1970s and early 1980s, including a December 1980 warning that the Soviets were preparing to invade Poland to end the protests of the labor movement Solidarity. The intelligence allowed the United States to use diplomatic means to forestall the Soviet invasion. Kuklinski was brought out of Poland just before martial law was declared. Kuklinski was sentenced to death in absentia. But even after the fall of the communist regime in Warsaw, many Poles were ambivalent about what Kuklinski had done. He had been motivated by his dislike of the Soviet Union and the regime it had imposed on Poland. Some Poles, however, felt that Kuklinski had spied on Poland, regardless of the Soviet issue. Even Lech Walesa, as president of Poland, refused to pardon Kuklinski. The charges were finally dropped in 1998.

ISSUES RELATED TO COLLECTION AND COVERT ACTION

Many ethical and moral issues arise from collection and covert action. As with the broad moral issues, there are many questions and little consensus on answers.

HUMINT. HUMINT collection involves the manipulation of other human beings as potential sources of information. The skills required to be a successful HUMINT collector are acquired over time with training and experience. They basically involve psychological techniques to gain trust, including empathy, flattery, and sympathy. The more direct methods of gaining cooperation include bribery, blackmail, and sex.

Two issues predominate. The first is the morality of the manipulation itself. One might argue that psychological techniques are used on someone who is already susceptible to manipulation. An unwilling subject will likely terminate the relationship. (Walk-ins are different by virtue of the fact that they volunteer their services.) Are these legitimate activities to be undertaken by a government against the citizens of another country, whether an enemy or not?

The second issue is the responsibility of the government doing the recruiting to the source.

- How far does the government's responsibility go?
- How deep an obligation, if any, does the government incur in the recruitment?
- If the HUMINT asset is compromised, how far should the recruiter go to maintain the asset's safety? Does this obligation extend to her family as well?
- What if the asset has not been productive for some time? For how long a period is the government obliged to protect the asset once the relationship ended its usefulness?
- What if the asset proves to be unproductive? Perhaps the asset has misrepresented her access and capabilities. Is there still an obligation?

One of the most compelling arguments in favor of strong and continued responsibility for recruited sources has little to do with morality and ethics. It is the more practical concern that recruitment of new sources becomes more difficult if word gets out that current or former sources are not given the support and protection they need. In other words, failing to protect a source is bad for business.

Another issue tends to be specific to certain areas, such as terrorism and narcotics, that depend heavily on HUMINT for good intelligence. To collect that intelligence, U.S. officials must develop contacts with—and usually pay money to—members of terrorist or narcotics-trafficking organizations. These people have the needed intelligence. Such a case arose in 1995, when the press reported that a CIA-paid asset was instrumental in the arrest of the terrorist known as Carlos. The asset was also a terrorist, a member of Carlos's group. (Carlos, the "Jackal," was an international terrorist during the 1970s and 1980s, usually working closely with radical Arab groups. Carlos was captured in Sudan in 1994 and was sentenced to life imprisonment in France.) Penetration of a terrorist group may require the agent to prove himself by taking part in a terrorist activity. This probably approaches a line that many would find impossible to cross. Thus, for understandable reasons, reviewing the assumptions about the efficacy of HUMINT against terrorism is necessary.

Some people find it morally objectionable that relationships are forged with those who may have engaged in activities directed against U.S. interests. Policy and intelligence officials must make a difficult choice between access to useful information that cannot be obtained through other means and the distasteful prospect of paying money to a terrorist or narcotics trafficker.

COLLECTION. Beyond the recruiting of human assets, intelligence officials use a number of techniques to collect intelligence, including the theft of material and various types of eavesdropping, which are deemed unlawful in everyday life. What legitimizes these activities as intelligence operations of the state? Within the United States, intelligence and law enforcement officials are required to have court orders for eavesdropping and other techniques, and procedures are in place to prevent intelligence collections from including information about U.S. citizens, a category that includes legally resident aliens.

The same issues arise in counterintelligence when a potential suspect has been identified. In the United States, unlike many other countries, the law requires intelligence officials to obtain a court order before performing collection activities against a possible spy.

Collection also raises the moral question of responsibility for the knowledge that has been gained. Do intelligence officials or policy makers incur any obligations by discovering some piece of intelligence? For example, during World War II, British and U.S. intelligence became aware, via signals intelligence, of the mass killing of the Jews by the Germans. The Allies did not carry out military action (bombing rail lines and camps) for two reasons. One was the belief that attacking purely military targets would end the war sooner and thus save more people in the concentration camps than would direct attacks on the camps. Another reason was concern over safeguarding the sources and methods by which the Allies had learned about the camps. What are the ethical and moral implications of the decision to desist?

In 2004, a former minister in the British government alleged that Britain and the United States had conducted espionage at the United Nations in the period prior to the 2003 Security Council vote on Iraq WMD. By international treaty the UN is supposed to be inviolate from any espionage activities, although it is widely known that many states ignored this agreement. For example, for years U.S. officials assumed that Soviet members of the UN secretariat engaged in espionage for their home country even though they were supposed to be international civil servants. In 1978, Arkady Shevchenko, a UN undersecretary, defected to the United States after having passed information to the CIA for several years. Shevchenko confirmed that the Soviet Union used the UN to gather intelligence. Separate allegations also were made that the United States had conducted intelligence collection against the International Agency for Atomic Energy (IAEA), arising from concerns over Iran's nuclear program. The IAEA, like the UN, is supposed to be inviolate from members' intelligence activities. The attraction of the UN, or other international bodies, as an intelligence collection target for any nation is obvious. Almost every nation in the world has a diplomatic presence at the UN, affording a breadth of access that is likely unavailable in many other capitals. The arrangement may be especially important for collecting against nations with whom a state does not have diplomatic relations or whose diplomatic presence worldwide is limited.

One could argue that the treaty status of the UN is no different than the sovereignty of any nation. After all, no nation permits hostile intelligence collection in its territory. This is another instance in which the raison d'etat takes precedence over treaty obligations.

COVERT ACTION. Covert actions are interventions by one state in the affairs of another. The basic ethical issue is the legitimacy of such operations. Concepts of national interest, national security, and national defense are most commonly used to support covert operations. But, taken to the extreme, every nation could be both a perpetrator and a target, creating Hobbesian anarchy. In reality, many states do not have the capability, the need, or the will to carry out covert actions against other states. But those states that do have the need and the ability believe their covert actions to be legitimate.

Covert actions also may conflict with personal goals or beliefs. Across the range of covert actions, from purely political (electoral aid, propaganda) to economic subversion and coups, innocent citizens in the targeted state can be affected and perhaps put in jeopardy. Military attacks on civilians in wartime have long been accepted as a legitimate activity, such as the large-scale bombings of cities. Are peacetime covert actions different?

Propaganda operations raise concern in the United States over blowback—the danger that a false story planted in the foreign press by U.S. intelligence might be picked up by U.S. media outlets (see chap. 8). If U.S. intelligence informs these outlets of the true nature of the story, it runs the risk of a leak, thus undoing the entire operation. How serious a concern should blowback be? Is it a major threat to the independence of the press?

What are the moral limits of operations? During the Soviet invasion of Afghanistan, some Soviet troops, dispirited by the interminable war, succumbed to the ready availability of narcotics, as had U.S. troops in Vietnam. The United States supplied arms to the anti–Soviet Mujaheddin, including sophisticated Stinger missiles. Would it have been legitimate and acceptable to take steps to increase drug use by the Soviet troops as a means of undermining their military efforts?

Paramilitary operations—the waging of war via surrogate forces, placing them somewhat beyond the norms of accepted international law—raise a number of ethical and moral issues. Are they legitimate? They raise the prospect of innocent civilians being put in jeopardy. Are there limits to paramilitary operations? For example, does the nature of the regime that is being fought matter? Are such operations legitimate against oppressive, undemocratic regimes but illegitimate against those with more acceptable forms of government? If there are differences, who determines which governments are legitimate targets and which are not?

As with HUMINT, paramilitary operations raise questions about the sponsoring power's obligations to the combatants. This is a problem particularly for operations that are unsuccessful or appear to be inconclusive. In the case of a failed operation, does the supporting power have an obligation to help extricate its surrogate combatants and move them to a safe haven? In the case of an inconclusive operation, the choices are even more difficult. The supporting state may be able to continue the paramilitary operations indefinitely, perhaps knowing that there is little chance of success, but also little prospect of defeat. Should the supporting power continue the operation despite its near-pointlessness? Or does it have a responsibility to terminate the operation? If it decides to terminate, does it have an obligation to extricate the fighters it has supported?

Even a successful operation can raise ethical and moral issues. In the aftermath of the Soviet withdrawal from Afghanistan, one faction, the Taliban, eventually took over much of the country. The Taliban imposed a strict Muslim regime on Afghanistan, much at odds with Western notions of civil liberties and the rights of women. Did the United States and its anti–Soviet partners in Afghanistan (China, Pakistan, and Saudi Arabia) bear some responsibility to attempt to moderate the rule imposed by the Taliban? Eventually, the Taliban played host to al Qaeda leader Osama bin Laden, raising further questions about the results of the earlier policy.

ASSASSINATION. Most people would, and official U.S. policy does, draw a distinction between casualties inflicted as a result of military operations and the targeted assassination of a specific individual. (See chap. 8 for further discussion of assassination and the U.S. ban on it.) At the same time and even before the 2001 terrorist attacks, the formerly broad support for the assassination ban had eroded among the general public and to some extent in the press. The change in attitude perhaps reflected some of the difficulties the United States has encountered in imposing its will since the end of the cold war.

Even if the ban were to be lifted selectively, it is difficult to imagine how useful criteria for implementing assassination could be drawn up. What level of crime or hostile activity would make someone a legitimate target? As with Britain's interest in assassinating Adolf Hitler, it is not easy to identify a potential target at the right time. Also, some possible targets are former partners. Saddam Hussein, for example, received U.S. backing in his war with Iran (1980–1988), which was then seen as the bigger problem. His behavior became problematic only after Iraq invaded Kuwait in 1990.

In the case of Osama bin Laden and other terrorist leaders, the debate over assassination became irrelevant. The United States declared itself to be at war with terrorists, making these individuals legitimate military targets.

Assassination is also a remarkably sloppy tool. Without absolute assurances about who will follow the victim into power and how the successor will behave, assassination provides no guarantee of solving the problem at hand. The political unrest in Lebanon following the assassination of former prime minister Rafik Hariri in 2005 is instructive. It is widely assumed that Hariri was killed by Syria as he opposed Syria's continued military presence in Lebanon. The result of Hariri's death was widespread protests in Lebanon and international condemnation of Syria, resulting in the beginning of the long-delayed Syrian withdrawal of military forces and intelligence officers.

The leaders that would be considered targets are not in democracies; they are in states where the mechanisms for political succession are ill defined or subject to contest. One thug could replace another. Thus the gain would be little, while the risk to international reputation would be great.

Assassination also raises the specter of reprisal. An absence of rules cuts both ways.

RENDITIONS AND TORTURE. The war on terrorism has seen an increase in renditions, the seizure of foreign nationals overseas and, in many cases, transportation to their country of origin for incarceration and interrogation (see chap. 5). Although the United States has obtained pledges from these countries about the manner in which rendered suspects are treated, allegations have been made that some of them have been tortured and that the United States is at least complicit in this torture.

Most countries have a legal sanction against torture, whether it is enforced or not. Within U.S. law, at least, torture is specifically forbidden by the Eighth Amendment to the Constitution, which bans "cruel and unusual punishment." But the war on terrorism has given rise to a debate over what constitutes torture (as opposed to harsh and even degrading treatment) and whether or not this is acceptable. The debate is also colored by the treatment of Iraqi prisoners held by the U.S. military at Abu Ghraib, where U.S. military personnel did mistreat prisoners. Several moral and ethical questions arise. First, if one were convinced that a detainee had knowledge of a proximate terrorist attack, what limits should be imposed—if any—to obtain the information he has? Does the possibility of preventing the attack and saving many lives make a harsher interrogation permissible? Second, how much transparency is desired into how these terrorist suspects are treated? The question raises an ends-and-means issue. Third, what effect does harsh treatment or torture have on the United States and the ethical purposes for which it says it is fighting terrorism?

A related issue is the ultimate fate of the senior terrorists who have been captured by the United States, including some of al Qaeda's senior planners for the 2001 attacks. Although concern is voiced about releasing them, questions arise about how long they can be held, especially without some sort of judicial proceedings. After a certain point they have no intelligence value as they have either told what they know or their information is dated. These terrorists are currently being treated as enemy combatants and therefore can be held for the duration of the conflict. But in a conflict that may have no definite end, does a time come when they have to be put on trial or released?

A FINAL LOOK AT OPERATIONAL ETHICS. Author James Barry ("Covert Action Can Be Just") has argued that criteria can be established for making morally guided decisions about intelligence operations. Barry suggests the following.

- Just cause
- Just intention
- Proper authority
- Last resort
- Probability of success
- Proportionality
- Discrimination and control

In the abstract, this is a compelling list of checkpoints for policy makers to consider before launching an operation. But policy makers do not act in the abstract. And once they have decided upon the necessity for an operation, they can find ways to rationalize each of the succeeding steps.

ANALYSIS-RELATED ISSUES

The ethical and moral issues surrounding analysis largely center on the many compromises that analysts must make as they prepare their product and deal with policy makers.

IS INTELLIGENCE TRUTH-TELLING? One of the common descriptions of intelligence is that it is the job of "telling truth to power." (This sounds fairly noble, although it is important to recall that court jesters once had the same function.) Intelligence, however, is not about truth (see chap. 1). Yet the image persists and carries with it some important ethical implications. If truth is the objective of intelligence, does that raise the stakes for analysis? Are analysts working on more than a well-informed and, they hope, successful policy? Moreover, does a goal of truth allow them greater latitude to pursue and defend their views of likely outcomes?

A problem with setting truth as a goal is that it has a relentless quality. Most individuals understand the importance of being honest most of the time (and acknowledge the occasional need to at least shade the truth). But if an analyst's goal is to tell the truth—especially to those in power who might not want to hear it—then there is no room for compromise, no possible admission of alternative views. After all, if one has the truth, those who disagree must have falsehood. Thus, an analyst cannot compromise with other analysts whose views may differ, even slightly. Moreover, what should a truth-teller do if the powerful reject his analysis, as they are free to do? Once the powerful have failed to accept the truth, is their legitimacy at stake?

These questions may seem far-fetched, but they underscore the problems raised by truth-telling. As noble as it may be as a goal, as a practical matter, truth-telling raises many problems in an already complex intelligence and policy process.

ANALYTIC PRESSURES. Assume that the role of intelligence is not to tell the truth but to provide informed analysis to policy makers to aid their decision making.

Even with this less demanding role, analysts can reach judgments that are based on deep and strongly held beliefs. They may be convinced not only of the conclusions they have reached but also of the importance of the issue for the nation. What should they do if their views are rejected, disregarded, or ignored by their policy clients?

- Accept the situation as the policy maker's prerogative and move on to the next issue?
- Attempt to raise the issue again with the policy maker, based on the possibility that the policy maker misunderstood the importance of the issue and the analysis? How often can analysts do this, either on one particular issue or as a regular practice? How does this behavior affect their credibility?
- Try to take their analysis to other policy makers, either going over the head of their original client or elsewhere in the policy process? Even if this ploy is successful, what is the cost to the analysts' relationship with the original and all other policy clients?
- Threaten to quit? Is the issue that important? Are the analysts willing to carry out the threat or risk the loss of credibility? What does quitting accomplish beyond a protest?

The multioffice or multiagency nature of intelligence analysis raises many issues of group dynamics (see chap. 6). Analyses are often the product of negotiation and compromise among several analysts with differing views. An analyst needs to consider a number of questions.

- To what extent should an analyst be willing to compromise with other analysts? Which types of trades are acceptable and which are not?
- At what point do the compromises affect the integrity of the document? If the compromises appear to have jeopardized its utility or integrity, can an analyst go back on previous compromises?
- Can an analyst warn policy makers that, in her view, the analysis has been overly compromised? In other words, at what point should an analyst feel obligated to break free of the procedural constraints of the multiagency process and venture out as a lone wolf? What types of issues merit this behavior? What is the likelihood of efficacy? What are the costs in terms of future working relationships within this process, even if one wins her point? Will there be an inevitable and irreplaceable loss of trust that makes all future interactions difficult at best?

Finally, the nature of the relationship between the intelligence officer and the policy maker is an issue. When Sherman Kent stated that the analyst wants to be believed or listened to, he was mainly referring to the quality of the analysis. However, an analyst's access also depends on the nature of the relationship itself.

- How great a concern, if any, should the relationship be for an analyst? Should she avoid stands that would alienate policy makers to keep open the best lines of communication?
- What if the analyst strongly believes that she must take a stand? Again, should the stand be tempered for the sake of the long-term relationship with policy makers?
- Alternatively, what should an analyst do in the face of pressure to produce intelligence that is perhaps more supportive of policy? Such a request may be subtle, not overt. Can, and should, the intelligence officer resist outright? How many small compromises add up to large ones that politicize the product? What if the analyst knows that the policy maker will write a memo with contrary views and will ultimately prevail? Is it still worth resisting blandishments, knowing she will lose both the argument and perhaps access to a key policy client as well?

Analysts' Options: A Cultural Difference

The two options for analysts who find they cannot compromise—fighting from within or quitting—tend to play out differently in the bureaucracies of Britain and the United States. In Britain, a strong tradition exists of quitting in protest. To cite a high-level example, Foreign Secretary Anthony Eden resigned in February 1938 when he disagreed with Neville Chamberlain's policy of appeasement toward Nazi Germany. In the United States resignation is more rare, with individuals opting instead to fight from within. Nothing definitive accounts for the difference. Several U.S. civil servants did resign, however, during the early stages of the civil war in Bosnia to protest the lack of action by the United States.

Many games are being played simultaneously: the intelligence process itself, the policy process, and the desire of the intelligence officers to have access to policy makers and to keep their funding levels safe and preferably growing. It is easy, in the abstract, to declare that the integrity of the intelligence process is primary. In the trenches, however, such a declaration is not always so obvious or so appealing.

ANALYSTS' OPTIONS. An intelligence analyst may believe that something fundamental is at stake, that neither compromise nor silence is possible. What are his options then? They boil down to two: continue the struggle from within the system or quit. (*See box, "Analysts' Options: A Cultural Difference.")* Continuing the struggle from within is appealing in that one's professional standards are preserved. But is it a realistic choice or a rationalization? Are there real prospects of continuing to fight for that viewpoint from within the bureaucratic system? For whatever reason, the viewpoint did not prevail either in the intelligence community or with policy makers. Short of capitulation, the analyst is now tagged with a certain view that has been found wanting. How influential will he be on this issue in the future? Or is the analyst, not wishing to abandon a chosen career, simply putting the best gloss on having lost? If such choices must be made, the analyst can only hope to make them over an issue of some significance. Not every issue is worth engaging at this level.

Alternatively, the analyst can quit. Honor and professional standards are preserved intact. But by quitting, the analyst abandons all hope of further influencing the process. Yes, one can attempt to influence policy from outside the government, but such attempts are rarely effective. The analyst who quits has, in effect, conceded the field to those with a different viewpoint.

OVERSIGHT-RELATED ISSUES

The demands of oversight raise ethical issues for witnesses before Congress and for the members and staff as well.

THE HELMS DILEMMA. In 1973, while testifying first before the Senate Foreign Relations Committee in executive session and then before the Senate Foreign Relations Subcommittee on Multinational Corporations in an open session, DCI Richard Helms (1966–1973) was asked if the CIA had been involved in operations to overthrow the Allende government in Chile. Helms said that the CIA had not been involved. In 1977 the Justice Department considered a charge of perjury against Helms for his false testimony. After negotiations, Helms agreed to plead guilty to a misdemeanor and was fined $2,000 and given a suspended two-year prison sentence.

Helms believed that the extreme limits that President Richard M. Nixon had put on who was allowed to know about this effort (the secretaries of state and defense were excluded) precluded his answering. Helms also believed that his testimony was accurate, in that the CIA had tried to prevent Allende's election but had not been part of the plot to overthrow him once he was in office. This fine line notwithstanding, what options did Helms have when he was asked about CIA activity in Chile?

Under the National Security Act at that time, the DCI was personally responsible for protecting the sources and methods of U.S. intelligence. (This responsibility has now passed to the director of national intelligence.) Helms found himself caught between that obligation and his obligation to testify fully and honestly before Congress. If he had stated that the CIA was involved in some way, he would have revealed operations in an open, public hearing. Alternatively, had he expressed the wish to answer that question in private, or in a closed session (although he had also not answered when in a closed session), it would have been tantamount to admitting CIA involvement. After all, if the CIA had not been involved, why not answer in public? Helms opted for a third choice: to view the question within narrow bounds, preserve secrecy, and deny CIA involvement. There may have been a fourth choice: to respond as he did in public and then visit the senators privately to discuss the realities of CIA activity in Chile. Helms apparently did not consider this choice. In 1973 oversight of CIA activity was the prerogative of a small group of members of the Senate Armed Services Committee, not those on Foreign

Relations. Thus, he also construed his oversight responsibilities within a narrow spectrum.

Did Helms make the right choice? Should he have been prosecuted for perjury under these circumstances? How responsible were the senators for asking such questions in an open session (particularly Sen. Stuart Symington, D-Mo., who knew the facts of the matter because he was also a member of the Senate Armed Services Committee, which then had oversight of the CIA)?

THE TORRICELLI CASE. In 1995 Rep. Robert G. Torricelli, D-N.J., a member of the House Permanent Select Committee on Intelligence, wrote a letter to President Bill Clinton accusing the CIA of having misled Congress about its activities in Guatemala and having had on its payroll a Guatemalan officer involved in human rights violations. Torricelli also made his letter available to the *New York Times*. He admitted having leaked the information to the press but argued that his duty as a member of Congress to preserve the integrity of government was greater than the oaths to preserve secret information that he had taken as a member of the House and the Intelligence Committee. Torricelli also argued that he had not violated committee rules, because he had received the information from a State Department officer in his personal office—that is, not within the House Intelligence Committee—and it was not clear to him that the information had been properly classified.

The chairman of the Intelligence Committee filed ethics charges against Torricelli, which were adjudicated by the House Committee on Standards of Official Conduct. The committee decided that House rules concerning the handling of classified information were vague and ordered that in the future members would have a positive obligation to ascertain the true classification of information before releasing it. The committee went on to say that, had this ambiguity been resolved at the time Torricelli released the information, he would have been guilty of violating House rules.

Torricelli believed that the information provided by the State officer, a former employee on his House staff, revealed CIA duplicity. Having written to the president, was it necessary to release the information to the *New York Times* as well? Should he first have expressed his concerns to the committee leadership or his party's leadership?

The only person in the affair who was punished was the State Department officer, Richard Nuccio, who gave the information to Torricelli. A panel appointed by DCI Deutch decided that Nuccio had provided the information without proper authorization. Nuccio lost his clearances and resigned from the State Department, eventually returning to work on

Torricelli's staff. Torricelli could have saved Nuccio by saying that he had asked Nuccio for the information. But, by doing so, Torricelli would have undercut his argument that he had been the innocent recipient.

In 1998 the Intelligence Community Whistleblower Protection Act became law, after much debate in Congress and the executive branch. The law established procedures by which intelligence community employees may report a complaint or urgent concern. They must first do so through channels in the intelligence community but are free to inform the Intelligence Committees if the community has taken no action by a specific time. Even then, the employees must inform executive branch officials that they are going to Congress and must handle their information in accordance with proper security procedures. Reflecting the Torricelli case, the whistleblower law states, "A member or employee of one of the intelligence committees who receives a complaint or information . . . does so in that member or employee's official capacity as a member or employee of that committee."

THE MEDIA

Reporters and their media outlets exist to publish stories. The First Amendment to the Constitution offers the press broad freedom: "Congress shall make no law . . . abridging the freedom . . . of the press."

The government has no way to prevent the media from reporting information that it has obtained. But freedom to publish is not the same as "the people's right to know," which is an enticing catchphrase but does not appear anywhere in the Constitution. The press's right to report also does not obligate government officials to provide information, especially classified information.

But what, if any, obligations does the press have when it obtains information with national security implications? Should press limits be self-imposed, or should the press operate on the premise of "finders keepers, losers weepers"? Just as ethics and morals change in other areas, so, too, they change in the media.

In the past the press has come upon intelligence activities and agreed not to write about them for the sake of national security. For example, reporters discovered Cuban exile training camps in Florida prior to the Bay of Pigs and also learned about the construction of the *Glomar Explorer*, built by the Hughes Corporation for the CIA to retrieve a sunken Soviet submarine.

In the post–Watergate era of investigative journalism (a wonderful redundancy, as all journalism is investigative), it is difficult to imagine that many reporters or media outlets would be willing to suspend publication or drop a story entirely. One has only to think about such scenes as U.S. television camera crews waiting onshore as the first U.S. troops landed in Somalia in 1993 to question the premise.

Still, the question remains. At what point, if any, should reporters put aside their professional and career interests for the sake of preserving the secrecy of some intelligence activity or information? What responsibilities, if any, does the press have for the results of a story it publishes?

CONCLUSION

Intelligence is not without its ethical and moral dilemmas, some of which can be excruciating. That these intelligence dilemmas exist also means that policy makers have choices to make that can have ethical and moral dimensions. Intelligence, perhaps more than any other government activity, operates on the edge of acceptable morality, occasionally dealing in techniques that would not be acceptable elsewhere in government or in private life. For most citizens, the trade-off between ethics and increased security is acceptable, provided that the intelligence community operates with rules, oversight, and accountability.

FURTHER READINGS

Barry, James A. "Covert Action Can Be Just." *Orbis* 37 (summer 1993): 375–390.
———. *The Sword of Justice: Ethics and Coercion in International Politics.* New York: Praeger, 1998.
Erskine, Tom. "'As Rays of Light to the Human Soul'? Moral Agents and Intelligence Gathering." *Intelligence and National Security* 19 (summer 2004): 359–381.
Godfrey, E. Drexel. "Ethics and Intelligence." *Foreign Affairs* 56 (April 1978): 624–642. (See also the response by Art Jacobs in the following issue.)
Helms, Richard, with William Hood. *A Look Over My Shoulder: A Life in the Central Intelligence Agency.* New York: Random House, 2003.
Herman, Michael. "Ethics and Intelligence after September 2001." *Intelligence and National Security* 19 (summer 2004): 342–358.
Lauren, Paul Gordon. "Ethics and Intelligence." In *Intelligence: Policy and Process.* Ed. Alfred C. Maurer and others. Boulder, Colo.: Westview Press, 1985.
Levinson, Sanford, ed. *Torture: A Collection.* New York: Oxford University Press, 2004.
Masters, Barrie P. "The Ethics of Intelligence Activities." National War College, National Security Affairs Forum. Washington, D.C., spring–summer 1976.
Powers, Thomas. *The Man Who Kept the Secrets: Richard Helms and the CIA.* New York: Knopf, 1979.
Sorel, Albert. *Europe under the Old Regime.* Trans. Francis H. Herrick. New York: Harper and Row, 1947.

Chapter 14

Intelligence Reform

Efforts to improve, alter, or reorganize the intelligence community are as old as the community itself. Richard A. Best Jr., in a Congressional Research Service (CRS) study prepared for the House Intelligence Committee as part of its review of intelligence community functions (*IC21: The Intelligence Community in the 21st Century*), examined nineteen major studies, reviews, and proposals, covering the period 1949 to 1996, for change in the intelligence community. For devotees and critics of the community, reform is something of a cottage industry. Like the caucus race in *Alice in Wonderland,* debates over intelligence reform seem to have neither a beginning nor an end.

"Intelligence reform" is a catchall phrase, used to connote any and all efforts to make significant changes in the intelligence community. However, in the mid-1970s, in the aftermath of the Church and Pike Committees' investigations, "reform" took on a more specific meaning. It referred to efforts to prevent the reoccurrence of abuses of authority or illegal acts that had been uncovered by the committees and the earlier "family jewels" report, written at the direction of Director of Central Intelligence (DCI) James Schlesinger (1973), describing illegal Central Intelligence Agency (CIA) activities.

The use of the word "reform" remains problematic in that it can imply that something needs fixing, as opposed to simply being improved. In this chapter, "reform" should be read in the broader, more benign sense of the word—improvement, not the correction of abuses.

THE PURPOSE OF REFORM

When one sifts through the reform proposals, a key question must be asked: What is the purpose of the reforms? Richard Best, in his CRS study, delineated three broad chronological categories of proposals.

1. To improve the efficiency of the intelligence community in the context of the cold war
2. To respond to specific intelligence failures or improprieties, including the Bay of Pigs, the "family jewels," the Iran-contra affair, and others
3. To refocus intelligence community requirements and structure in the post–cold war era

The third phase, post–cold war efforts to update the community's structure, reached a culmination with the passage of the intelligence legislation in 2004. This is not to suggest that the issue of intelligence reform is closed. It is not. The intelligence community will never reach an end state but will be subject to periodic reviews and organizational changes.

Efforts to redress glaring failures or misdeeds are easy to understand. Efforts to improve intelligence per se are more difficult to assess. Few reliable guidelines are available for measuring intelligence, which makes it difficult to determine what constitutes efficiency or how to achieve it. The problem may be bigger for analysis than it is for collection or operations. Assessing the latter two activities is more straightforward. Either the capability to collect against a target exists or it does not, and if it does, then the collection has either been accomplished or it has not. Extenuating circumstances may arise, but the evaluation process for collection is simple. Similarly, for operations, the goals are either achieved or unmet. Some operations may go on without resolution, such as U.S. support to the Nicaraguan contras, but the lack of resolution itself may be an important indicator of the likelihood of ultimate success. Analysis remains more elusive. Few efficiencies are to be had in what is essentially an intellectual process. Volumes of reports or batting averages are not useful measurements.

The terrorist attacks in 2001 brought renewed calls for intelligence reform, with some of the most persistent advocates arguing, "If not now, when?" Even so, the purposes of reform have not been entirely clear. Several different purposes, not all of which are mutually exclusive, can be discerned.

- To improve the intelligence community's ability to deal with terrorism overall
- To prevent further terrorist attacks against the United States
- To determine if the attacks occurred because of specific intelligence lapses, and, if so, who was responsible for them
- To use the attacks as an opportunity to push intelligence reform concepts, whether or not related to the attacks or the war on terrorism

However, the issue that provided the ultimate impetus for the intelligence legislation of 2004 was not the investigations into the September 11 attacks but the issue of Iraq weapons of mass destruction (WMD). The gap between prewar estimates and what was found (or not found) in Iraq since military action commenced in 2003 helped push many who had been undecided into the camp of intelligence reform. This factor also helps explain why the legislation focused on the management and oversight of analysis.

One final factor that must be taken into account is the misperception that the advent of multiple round-the-clock news media makes the intelligence community redundant. Those who hold this view believe that the community must transform itself to be more competitive.

Journalism and intelligence have some interesting similarities: the need for reliable sources, the need to make complex stories comprehensible, the tyranny of deadlines. But there are also important differences. Deadlines may be even more tyrannical for the news media—both print and broadcast, but especially the latter—than they are for the intelligence community. News broadcasts must go on the air as scheduled, regardless of the day's events. Journalists accept this operating necessity and use updates, corrections, or retractions as necessary. Whenever possible, intelligence managers and analysts seek to delay reporting (sometimes too long) until they have the story correct, or as correct as collection will allow. Also, the average noncrisis news broadcast contains a great deal of filler and repetition over a twenty-four-hour period. The intelligence community also needs to report, but not around the clock. This is a saving grace. Also, the intelligence community seeks to do more than report; value-added analysis is an essential part of what it produces. Such analysis happens much less frequently in the news media, particularly the broadcast media. When it does occur, analysis can spill over into opinion. Squabbles among the twenty-four-hour news networks about which of them has a liberal or a conservative bias underscore the problem.

Still, the misperception persists, even among some policy makers, that round-the-clock news sources upstage the work of the intelligence community. The misperception that the two are in competition may reveal a less than firm understanding of their fundamental differences, although the news media may employ concepts, technologies, and approaches that would be of use to intelligence.

ISSUES IN INTELLIGENCE REFORM

Discussions about intelligence reform tend to fall into two broad areas: structure—or reorganization—and process. Both approaches have their advocates. Ideally, the issues should be approached together. Altered structure and unaltered process can become little more than moving boxes on the bureaucratic organization chart. Changing the process without changing structure would likely end in few, if any, meaningful results, as the old structure would probably resist the new processes. The following are some of the more frequently discussed issues in intelligence reform, some of which have been mentioned in preceding chapters. Some issues have been settled by the new legislation, but they are likely to be touchstones of future debate as the new intelligence structure begins to work and remains under scrutiny.

THE ROLE OF THE DCI AND THE DNI. The most central issue in the management and functioning of the intelligence community was the gap between the responsibilities (extensive) and the authority (limited) of the DCI. Under Executive Order 12333 (1981), the DCI was "the primary adviser to the President and the NSC [National Security Council] on national foreign intelligence." The designation included "full responsibility for [the] production and dissemination of national foreign intelligence," which included the authority to task agencies beyond the CIA. These responsibilities have passed to the director of national intelligence (DNI), although it is not clear that the problem of his authorities has been resolved.

The DNI's authority remains limited and may be subject to even more stress than was the case for the DCI. Some 80 percent of intelligence agencies and their budgets remain under the direct control of the secretary of defense. Any additional power granted to the DNI can come only from the secretary of defense, which seems unlikely given the position that the Defense Department took during the formation of the new law. The argument over power is a zero-sum game. Although few, if any, secretaries of defense have believed that the DCI threatened their authority, the Defense Department was clear about preserving all of its authority during the congressional debate in 2004. Defense officials worry about two fronts: the authority of the secretary (often referred to as "Title 10 prerogatives," as spelled out in the U.S. Code) and intelligence support for military operations. The latter became the main point pushed by Defense Department supporters in the 2004 debate. In addition to the Defense Department, the DNI will likely be engaged in some level of struggle with the new director of the Central Intelligence Agency (DCIA) and perhaps the director of the National Counterterrorism Center (NCTC).

Much of the problem with the DCI's authority stemmed from the origins of the office and how the intelligence community developed. The designation DCI predates the creation of the CIA. The first DCIs ran the Central Intelligence Group (CIG), which became the CIA in the National

Security Act of 1947. President Harry S. Truman's goal in creating the CIA under the DCI was to have a central organization that could coordinate the disparate analyses coming from the State Department and the military. No one envisioned the CIA's producing finished intelligence in its own right or conducting operations. Thus, the limited authority granted to the DCI was consistent with his role as coordinator. The CIA was seen as the agency that supported this coordinative role.

As the CIA moved to fill both analytical and operational voids, the DCI's power base grew, but it also diverted his attention from his community-wide role. This is the issue that the new legislation seeks to correct, freeing the DNI from running any agency and thus allowing him to concentrate on the larger role. What remains at issue is the degree to which this larger role can be accomplished without the strong institutional base that the CIA afforded the DCI. As former acting DCI John McLaughlin (2004) noted in his testimony on the proposed legislation, the reason DCIs have relied on the CIA was that it was the only agency they could command. The DNI will not have this base on which to fall back.

The DCI's role could have been significantly enhanced if the office had been given budget execution authority over the National Foreign Intelligence Program (now the National Intelligence Program). The ability to direct the allocation and spending of money is a major source of power and control, which is why the Defense Department fought to keep this power from the DNI. But a political issue also was involved in choosing this course: It was too bureaucratic and not dramatic enough to suit those seeking major changes. Furthermore, some of the September 11 families proved an effective and difficult-to-refute lobbying force in favor of the legislation. Although some have questioned the propriety of allowing the families to dictate national security structure, they had tremendous political clout.

The Defense Department's arguments against ceding spending control to either the DCI or DNI are based on the view that such a change runs the risk of limiting intelligence support to military operations and that, without direct Defense Department control, the intelligence support may be wanting. The likelihood of this happening seems small. It is difficult to believe that any DCI or DNI would run the political risk inherent in not giving full support to the military in peacetime or in war, if for no other reason than self-protection, to avoid being blamed for military setbacks or casualties. Nothing in past practice over the nearly sixty years of the modern intelligence community's existence would suggest that any substance can be found behind this argument.

The ultimate success or failure of the new DNI position depends on how John Negroponte, who was confirmed as the first DNI in April 2005, perceives his role and how much real support he has from the president. The signals to date from President George W. Bush have been ambiguous: granting authority to the DNI, as in the case of the morning briefing, but assuring CIA that its role is not diminished. As was the case when the secretary of defense position was created in 1947, the legislation may have to be revised after a few years, once the flaws have been revealed. The DNI will be under great pressure and scrutiny from the public and from Congress to improve information sharing and the overall coherence of the intelligence community. Whether the legislation provides the levers necessary to do these jobs is not clear. The DNI will also come under tremendous political pressure should another major terrorist attack occur in the United States. Supporters of the new law argue that the creation of a DNI freed from any agency and the emphasis on information sharing will lessen the likelihood of an attack. Many intelligence officers and some outside observers fail to see any connection between the new structures and what is needed to prevent a terrorist attack, as the law seems largely to have created another layer without making any marked changes in how terrorism is addressed.

STOVEPIPES. The term "stovepipes" refers to agencies in similar or analogous lines of work (collection or analysis) that tend to compete with one another, sometimes to a wasteful and perhaps harmful extent.

The stovepipe issue is most often discussed in reference to the big three collection disciplines (INTs)—signals intelligence (SIGINT), imagery intelligence (IMINT), and human intelligence (HUMINT)—and particularly the technical INTs (especially SIGINT and IMINT). Some have proposed putting at least the technical INTs (SIGINT, IMINT, and measures and signatures intelligence or MASINT) under a single agency with the authority to decide which INTs should respond to which requirements, thus limiting some collection that may not be optimal or necessary. This solution raises questions of its own.

- Who would run such an agency? Would it matter if that person were civilian or military?
- Would this new agency be manageable?
- Given that the Defense Department currently controls all the technical INTs, would this remain true? What are the implications either way?

The main goal is some modicum of collection efficiency and improved resource management. However, the suggested solution would create a large entity, one whose inherent power might rival that of the DNI. Cooperation has been growing between the National Geospatial-Intelligence

Agency (NGA) and the National Security Agency (NSA), although still far from the point of a merger of any sort.

Some have suggested that the two HUMINT components—the CIA Directorate of Operations (DO) and the Defense Humint Service of the Defense Intelligence Agency (DIA/Humint)—be unified, also to avoid duplication. Along similar lines, some have proposed that the clandestine services (HUMINT and covert action) be a separate agency, either to improve management responsibility or to avoid contaminating analysis, or both. However, for the foreseeable future more competition is likely between the CIA and DIA/Humint and the FBI, than a merging of efforts.

In the area of collection, open-source intelligence (OSINT) is a specific reform issue. OSINT remains underutilized and has no strong organizational locus. Reformers have advanced several ideas to improve the role of OSINT, including creating an OSINT agency or office or contracting out stronger OSINT services. The common goal is to elevate OSINT to a full-standing INT that is readily available to all analysts, as opposed to the more random situation that currently exists. One of the DNI's first responsibilities is to report to Congress on the future of OSINT and the possibility of creating a separate OSINT agency. The WMD Commission (Commission on the Intelligence Capabilities of the United States Regarding Weapons of Mass Destruction) recommended creating an Open Source Directorate at CIA.

Two final collection issues that are part of the reform debate have already been discussed: the balance between HUMINT and the TECHINTs and the need for improved TPEDs (tasking, processing, exploitation, and dissemination).

Turning to analysis, the main issues highlighted in the 2004 legislation were ways to improve the oversight of intelligence at the DNI level in terms of timeliness, objectivity, and quality of analysis as well as to foster more alternative analysis. Similar issues were discussed in the 2005 WMD Commission report. Although the goals are worthy, underlying the provisions may be a changing view about the acceptable tolerances within which intelligence analysis exists. Coming up with reliable standards for assessing the quality of analysis is difficult (see chap. 6). An obvious but stark one would be "right or wrong." The problem with this standard is that most analytical issues play out over time, during which some analytical judgments are right and some are wrong. In the end, creating a balance sheet could be possible, but doing so would be secondary in importance to whether policy goals were met over that period. The intelligence community's experience with the Soviet Union is instructive. Over the forty-four years that the intelligence community spent analyzing the Soviet Union, it made numerous analytical judgments. Again, some were right and some were wrong. The wrong judgments, although problematic, never put U.S. security at risk. More important, however, is that U.S. policy, supported by intelligence, succeeded and the Soviet Union collapsed.

But September 11 and Iraq WMD, for example, reflect a starker situation. Despite multiple warnings about al Qaeda hostility and intentions, no specific intelligence warning was possible about the terrorist attacks. Many have noted that the threads of intelligence make sense only with hindsight, but a body of opinion sees September 11 as a right-or-wrong issue. The discussion may be on firmer ground with Iraq WMD. The situation on the ground did not reflect prewar estimates. Although, as DCI Tenet pointed out in his 2004 speech at Georgetown University, parts of the estimate were borne out, both over- and underestimative judgments were made, and overall the analysis was not correct. But does this argue for the acceptability or the wider utility of a right-or-wrong standard? The fear among some in the intelligence community is that little tolerance now exists for anything other than absolutely correct intelligence judgments and that the new provisions regarding analysis reflect this view. If so, then the intelligence community is doomed to fail, as it will never achieve success in a right-or-wrong system. It is also difficult, although probably necessary, to have a discussion about how right analysis can or should be. The answer is "right as often as possible." But the key to that answer is the word "possible." A level of reasonable expectations of intelligence analysis may have been lost and will be difficult to regain.

The reports of the 9/11 Commission (National Commission on Terrorist Attacks Upon the United States) and the WMD Commission also focused attention on how best to organize analysts across the community. The 9/11 Commission recommended organizing all analysts by regional or functional national intelligence centers. In the commission's concept, the centers would carry out all-source analysis and plan intelligence operations and "would be housed in whatever department or agency is best suited for them." The center concept arose during the late 1980s and early 1990s as the community put increased emphasis on transnational issues that—by definition—crossed national borders. The centers allowed analysts from various agencies to be brought together to focus on an issue, although the centers have always been dominated by the CIA. The commission's idea would do the same for other functional and, now, regional issues.

The 2004 reform law only mandated one center, the NCTC, but also stipulated that the DNI report to Congress on creating a center for nonproliferation. The creation of such a center has since been mandated. A clear expectation is presented in the legislation that other centers will be created as well. The main advantage of the centers is, in theory, the ability to get cross-cutting analysis on an issue, assuming that they are true community centers and not dominated by one agency. But centers also have disadvantages.

- To date, centers have been primarily functional in nature. Although analysts in centers do consult with their regional colleagues, this does require some effort. Centers have an occasional tendency to focus on their functional topic and to be less able to bring in the regional or national context in which these issues occur. Organizing by centers—either regional or functional—could exacerbate this tendency. Also, some of the issues handled by centers have close relationships, such as terrorism and narcotics. Sharing analyses across these boundaries can also be difficult. In other words, centers may create analytical stovepipes of their own.
- Getting resources out of or away from centers has proven difficult once they are established. Although a DNI should be able to effect changes, past performance indicates that centers do run counter to the desire for greater analytic agility.
- Centers tend to focus on the most pressing issues. In a center-based community, devoting some level of resources to those issues or regions that have lower priorities may prove even more difficult than it has been.

The WMD Commission recommended the creation of one new center, the National Counterproliferation Center (NCPC), although it would not function like the other intelligence centers. The commission also recommended the creation of mission managers to oversee both collection and analysis for the more important topics or issues. The NCPC would function as the mission manager for its issue but would not be a producer of intelligence per se. The commission's report is vague on who would decide among the mission managers when it came to resources. Presumably the DNI or someone on his staff would be designated. But it is important to understand that the two major resource decisions—collection assets and analysts—tend not to occur within similar time frames. Decisions about analysts tend to be made for longer terms, except during periods when a particular area of higher interest emerges. Decisions about collection assets tend to be more tactical as more frequent calls to adjust collection priorities may be heard. Thus, the mission manager concept will not work without an adjudicator or adjudicators who are familiar with both collection and analysis. Also, existing structures within the intelligence community are similar to the mission manager concept, albeit without authority to move resources, which the new mission managers presumably will not have either.

Closely related to the center issue is the older issue of the flexibility and agility of the analytical corps. The analytical agencies have no reserve or surge capacity. Analysis is still organized around two basic structures:

regional and topical offices. These are not mutually exclusive, but no intelligence service around the world has discovered a third organizing principle.

The problem stems, in part, from the fact that analysts have to be expert in something, which necessarily defines and limits the issues on which they can work. Creating a corps of intelligence generalists is impractical and dangerous. They will likely know a little about many issues but not much about any single issue. Successful intelligence analysis requires expertise, and long-term expertise is one of the major value-adds of the intelligence community. Thus, the problem is to maintain some level of flexibility or surge within this body of experts.

Surge is most important during crises, especially in areas that had a low priority. However, in giving a low priority to a particular issue or nation, the policy and intelligence communities have already decided not to allocate many resources to it. Short of either finding someone already on staff who has some working knowledge of the issue or dragooning others into working on it, not much can be done internally. A frequently suggested reform proposal is the creation and use of an intelligence reserve—a body of experts, either former intelligence analysts or outside experts, who can augment analytical ranks during a crisis.

Congress created such a reserve in 1996, but the intelligence community has not fully implemented it. Several issues are involved, one of which is security. Many outside experts do not have security clearances and may be unwilling to accept the restrictions they impose. Thus, they either are eliminated as sources or the intelligence community is required to find ways to tap their expertise without revealing classified information. Although the latter is not impossible, those responsible for security are likely to raise some objections. Another issue is cost. The intelligence community does not budget for such contingencies—just as the Defense Department does not budget for wartime operations during peacetime. As with the military, budget mechanisms—reallocations, supplemental appropriations—are available. The main impediment appears to be attitudes within the intelligence community.

Finally, there is the issue of redundancy in the three all-source agencies—CIA, DIA, and the State Department Bureau of Intelligence and Research. The intentional duplication stems from two fundamental operating principles of the intelligence community: the distinct intelligence needs of different senior policy makers and the concept of competitive analysis. Unless one is willing to give up either or both operating principles, one must accept the cost of the redundancy. Neither the executive branch nor Congress is likely to abandon the concepts or to accept the idea of having a single analytical agency, which has been among the more radical proposed alternatives.

INETLLIGENCE AND THE IT REVOLUTION. A major and continuing source of reform ideas stems from the ongoing information technology (IT) revolution. Some ideas concern technology; others focus on process.

The IT revolution had an interesting effect on the intelligence community. For years, its home-grown technology—that is, technology developed entirely internally or with contractors—was much more advanced than that available on the open market. However, the advent of the computer revolution allowed the open market to leapfrog over the intelligence community, through no fault of its own. The community's first reaction was to resist the externally developed technology in a classic case of the "not invented here" syndrome. Various reasons were cited, including special needs or security requirements.

The resistance phase has passed, although the intelligence community (and the rest of the government) still has problems in bringing new technologies on board quickly. Note that the word "technology" is being broadly used here, including computer technology, analytical tools and other software, and new information sources. The issue has become more difficult as the marketplace fills with many technologies and tools, all making competing claims about their capabilities. The intelligence community, like every other modern enterprise, seeks technologies that are best suited to its specific needs. A good scouting force is required that can sample as many technologies as possible and make purchasing decisions quickly. In 1995, an IT industry expert noted that computer technology was changing every eighteen months, but that the intelligence community took from two to five years to purchase a computer. Thus, at best, an analyst was getting a computer that was already six months out of date. The situation today may be better, but the rapid absorption of modern technology remains an issue.

Process is a more difficult issue. Some reform advocates suggest a looser intelligence structure, with a community of networks and more flexible organizations. Again, agility becomes a key goal.

The applicability to intelligence is uncertain. Greater flexibility in the analytical corps would be a tremendous improvement, but the intelligence community is unlikely to become completely free-form, relying on the analysts to provide its structure. Much can be said for having the ability to bring together disparate and even physically distant analysts to work on pressing issues and then to disband them or to allow new groups to form as the issues change. However, such a scenario will not eliminate the need for some bureaucratic apparatus: supervisors who can relay requirements and oversee the meeting of deadlines, reviewers of analysis, and so on. The key is to find a way to provide the necessary structure without stifling analytical fluidity. Some will bridle at what seems to be a half-hearted solution, although it may prove to be more practical in the end.

The new technologies and concepts should not be overburdened with more promise than they can deliver. The dot-com meltdown of 2001–2002 is instructive in this regard. Many prognosticators proclaimed a new economic age and the victory of virtual enterprises over bricks-and-mortar firms. However, a rapid and somewhat savage winnowing of the dot-coms occurred, while the bricks-and-mortar firms go on. The problem has been a confusion of means and ends. The IT revolution is not an end in itself, at least for intelligence. Instead, it is—or should be—a means by which the intelligence community can perform certain tasks more efficiently.

The terrorist attacks and the joint inquiry and 9/11 Commission investigations brought renewed focus on IT issues. An increased emphasis has been placed on the need to share information better. Technology is the means to this end, but it cannot make sharing happen on its own. That depends on policies that mandate sharing and penalize those who do not. Such policies have not been implemented in the past and would be difficult to enforce, but it is necessary before questioning why the technology does not work. One example of the types of policies that are needed is the concept promoted by Gen. Michael Hayden (now the principal deputy DNI), when he was the director of NSA, who urges that intelligence be "pushed out" to a waiting user as soon as possible. The intelligence can be further exploited and analyzed and then sent out to other users in more finished forms, but Hayden's basic point is that it needs to go out as soon as it is useful to someone.

Underlying the emphasis on technology may be the unstated belief that IT improvements can affect analysis. Although Americans have had a historical belief in the power of technology, no substantive cases serve as examples in which technology precluded either sharing or better analysis. Abundant stories can be told about incompatible IT systems from agency to agency, but that is not the same issue. This belief is, in some respects, the technological counterpart to the right-or-wrong analysis belief. To date, the search for improved analytical tools has not been overly successful, and for some it has taken on the aspect of a hunt for the Holy Grail. Part of the problem is that intelligence analysis remains an intellectual process, not a mechanical one. IT can be helpful in amassing data, collating it, sifting it, creating relationships among databases, and so on, but it cannot replace an insightful and experienced analyst.

The 2003 capture of Iraqi leader Saddam Hussein may be instructive. U.S. military officials and intelligence analysts assumed that Saddam had to be depending on someone for support while he was in hiding. They began by focusing attention on his innermost circle, but the search proved unavailing. So, they began to widen the group of people in whom they were interested to more relatives, tribal allies, and lower-level functionaries. More raids, more arrests, and more interrogations resulted, all of which served to expand the lists further. Eventually, they located Saddam's hideout. Although IT could have played a role—amassing names, comparing them, creating relationship maps—the key was analysis.

The other argument in favor of improved IT tools is the commonly held perception that analysts are drowning in information. No substantive studies are available to compare the amount of data available to analysts twenty years ago, when everything was in hard copy, and today. The perception may be based, in part, on confusing the means by which the intelligence is delivered, IT, and the amount that is delivered. IT has not greatly expanded the working day of the French Foreign Ministry or the Chinese army. People can still work on and produce only so much information in a given day, whether or not there is IT. Technical collectors are struggling to put out as much finished IMINT and SIGINT as they have in the past, so they are not sources of a major flood of information. IT certainly creates unnecessary redundancies of information, as the same data come in from separate sources. But this is not the same as a flood of new information. The irony is that people are looking to IT to solve the problems largely created by IT.

ADMINSTRATIVE REFORM. An important although seemingly minor issue is administrative reform. Because the intelligence community is composed of separate agencies, it has many distinct processes for security, personnel policies, training, and so on. To many, these seem wasteful and duplicative. Although significant differences exist in training a cryptanalyst, an imagery analyst, and a case officer, personnel procedures and some training are to a certain extent generic. The disparate infrastructure systems impose unnecessary costs. For example, if a terrorism analyst at DIA seeks a better job at CIA, also covering terrorism, more is involved than a simple transfer. The analyst must apply to CIA, be re-vetted for security, and resign from DIA. Managing analysts as some larger integrated corps would be an improvement. This may be a seemingly minor area where the DNI can make real progress.

OTHER REFORM CONCEPTS. Among the many other proposals for intelligence reform, a market-based intelligence community has been advocated. Proponents argue that intelligence currently exists as an essentially free benefit for policy makers, which undercuts its value to them. In part, this view may stem from the intelligence community's habit of referring to policy makers as clients or customers. Such usage represents an effort to indicate the closeness of the relationship, but it also implies a type of relationship that may not be apt. Policy makers could be more of a captive audience than they are customers. Market advocates take the term "customer" literally. They believe that if policy makers had a better understanding of the true costs of intelligence—in terms of collection, analysis, and so on—they could make more informed decisions about the specific intelligence they wanted, for which they would then be charged. Presumably, policy agencies would have intelligence expense budgets that could be spent as they saw fit. In a variant of this proposal, a mixed economy has been suggested: Policy makers would receive a certain amount of intelligence without charge but would have to supply resources if greater intelligence support was desired.

Advocates of the idea have not yet fully developed it, so considering all the questions it raises may be unfair. The underlying premise—market competition will make intelligence more efficient and more competitive—might work in some respects for issues that are currently high on the policy agenda. However, how one would handle the sudden unexpected crisis or maintain some level of expertise on less pressing issues is not clear.

The market concept also flies in the face of some generic aspects of intelligence, especially for collection. Determining the cost of collecting against specific issues is difficult, if not impossible. For example, a SIGINT or IMINT satellite over Iraq may be collecting intelligence for support to military operations or on proliferation or regional stability. Similarly, over Afghanistan, one might collect for support to military operations or on terrorism or narcotics. How does one then determine the fair cost for any one issue?

CONCLUSION

The intelligence reform debate has an inconclusive aspect, which reflects both the difficulty of the issues and choices involved and the boundless enthusiasm of reform advocates, particularly those outside the intelligence community.

Although improvements undoubtedly can be made in intelligence, determining how efficient an inherently inefficient and intellectual process can be remains elusive. A wide gulf exists between government-based reviews of the intelligence community, which largely tend to accept the status quo and thus suggest modest changes, and the more acerbic critiques offered by those wholly outside the system, many of whom are intelligence community veterans. Are these differences real, or do they reflect, to some extent, parochial prejudices? The executive branch has rarely shown enthusiasm for major reforms. At least three factors explain this. First, many, if not most, policy makers believe that their most important needs are usually met, so they are not deeply dissatisfied. Second, many proposals for reform would require greater involvement of policy makers, which they would prefer to avoid if only because they already have more than enough to do. Third, many policy makers understand some of the fragility of the intelligence community and fear the possibility of making things worse.

Furthermore, remember that intelligence is a government activity. Revolutionary proposals tend to be ignored or, at best, to be severely moderated before they are enacted.

What is certain is that the debate over intelligence reform will go on, largely on its own momentum, with heightened attention during crises or after incidents deemed to be intelligence failures.

FURTHER READINGS

Literature on intelligence reform is extensive but uneven. Many opinions and proposals are on offer, not all of which are practical, with a few hobbyhorses among them. The following readings include some of the more recent studies and some of the more thoughtful and practical works by knowledgeable observers.

Berkowitz, Bruce, and Allen Goodman. *Best Truth: Intelligence in the Information Age*. New Haven: Yale University Press, 2000.

Best, Richard A., Jr. *Proposals for Intelligence Reorganization, 1949–1996*. Washington, D.C.: Congressional Research Service, 1996. (Appendix to *IC21: The Intelligence Community in the 21st Century*; see below.)

Betts, Richard K. "Fixing Intelligence." *Foreign Affairs* 81 (January–February 2002): 43–59.

Carter, Ashton. B. "The Architecture of Government in the Face of Terrorism." *International Security* 26 (winter 2001–2002): 5–23.

Commission on the Intelligence Capabilities of the United States Regarding Weapons of Mass Destruction [WMD Commission]. *Report to the President of the United States*. Washington, D.C., March 31, 2005.

Council on Foreign Relations. *Making Intelligence Smarter: The Future of U.S. Intelligence*. New York: Council on Foreign Relations, 1996.

Eberstadt, Ferdinand. *Unification of the War and Navy Departments and Postwar Organization for National Security*. Report to James Forrestal, secretary of the Navy. Washington, D.C., 1945.

Hansen, James. "U.S. Intelligence Confronts the Future." *International Journal of Intelligence and Counterintelligence* 17 (winter 2004–2005): 674–709.

Hulnick, Arthur S. "Does the U.S. Intelligence Community Need a DNI?" *International Journal of Intelligence and Counterintelligence* 17 (winter 2004–2005): 710–730.

Johnson, Loch. "Spies." *Foreign Policy* 120 (September–October 2000): 18–26.

National Commission on Terrorist Attacks Upon the United States [9/11 Commission]. *The 9/11 Commission Report*. New York: W.W. Norton and Company, 2004.

Quinn, James L., Jr. "Staffing the Intelligence Community: The Pros and Cons of Intelligence Reserve." *International Journal of Intelligence and Counterintelligence* 13 (2000): 160–170.

Treverton, Gregory F. *Reshaping National Intelligence for an Age of Information*. New York: Cambridge University Press, 2001.

U.S. Commission on National Security/21st Century. *Road Map for National Security: Imperative for Change.* Phase III Report. Washington, D.C., 2001.

U.S. Commission on the Roles and Responsibilities of the United States Intelligence Community. *Preparing for the 21st Century: An Appraisal of U.S. Intelligence.* Washington, D.C., 1996.

U.S. House Permanent Select Committee on Intelligence. *IC21: The Intelligence Community in the 21st Century.* 104th Cong., 2d sess., 1996. (Available at www.access.gpo.gov/congress/house/intel/ic21/ic21—toc.html.)

Chapter 15

Foreign Intelligence
Services

Although this book focuses on the U.S. intelligence community, examining how intelligence in foreign countries operates is instructive, as a means both of investigating alternative intelligence choices and of benefiting from the light they shed on the U.S. intelligence community. However, a problem with sources arises. No intelligence service, even those in other democracies, has undergone the same detailed scrutiny that the U.S. intelligence community has. The reliable literature on foreign intelligence services derives mostly from the press and from some more popular, as opposed to scholarly, histories. As is often the case, the accounts tend to emphasize organization and the more sensational activities. No other intelligence service is as transparent as that of the United States.

Although virtually every nation has some type of intelligence service—if not both civilian and military, and at least the latter—the services of five nations are worthy of close examination based on their importance and breadth of activity: Britain, China, France, Israel, and Russia. As is the case with the United States, each nation's intelligence services are unique expressions of its history, needs, and preferred governmental structures.

BRITAIN

Despite their similarities and historical connections, the British and the U.S. governmental structures and civil liberties have significant differences, which are important in understanding their intelligence practices.

First, the Cabinet, which embodies Britain's executive, enjoys a supremacy beyond that of the U.S. president. The Cabinet has the right to make appointments and to take major actions (declare war, make peace, sign treaties) without conferring with Parliament, where, by definition, the Cabinet enjoys a majority in the House of Commons. Second, the division between foreign and domestic intelligence is less stark in Britain than it is in the United States. Third, Britain does not have a written bill of rights protecting specific civil liberties (although Prime Minister Tony Blair has talked about creating one). In terms of intelligence, one of the most important differences is that the British government can enforce prior restraint on the publication of articles deemed injurious to national security.

The three major intelligence components—MI5, MI6, and GCHQ—operate under statutory basis. MI5, also known as the Security Service, is a domestic intelligence service, responsible for providing security against a range of threats, including terrorism, espionage, weapons of mass destruction (WMD) proliferation, and threats to the economy and for giving support to law enforcement agencies. MI5 focuses on covertly organized threats. A major preoccupation has been combating Irish Republican Army (IRA) terrorism in Northern Ireland and Great Britain. In the 1990s, MI5 won Parliament's approval to expand its mandate to include organized crime, narcotics, immigration, and benefits fraud. The law provides authority to monitor telephones and mail (both of which require warrants from the home secretary) and to enter homes and offices of organized-crime suspects. MI5 operates under the authority of the home secretary, for whom there is no precise U.S. equivalent. (The Home Office is responsible for police, criminal justice, prisons, immigration, and other matters.) The Security Service Acts of 1989 and 1996 govern MI5. In 2004, the home secretary announced a planned 50 percent increase in MI5 with the addition of one thousand new analysts to respond to increasing concerns about terrorism. One area of emphasis is language in Arabic and South Asian languages.

MI6 is also known as the Secret Intelligence Service (SIS). Its activities are governed by the Intelligence Services Act of 1994, which also directs GCHQ. MI6 is charged with the collection (by means of human intelligence (HUMINT) and technical intelligence (TECHINT)) and production of "information relating to the activities or intentions of persons outside the British Islands." It also performs other related tasks—a legal echo of the vague Central Intelligence Agency (CIA) charter in the National Security Act. MI6 comes under the authority of the foreign secretary (equivalent to the U.S. secretary of state). Like MI5, MI6 has entered a period of growth, particularly in response to terrorism and WMD. According to British press estimates, MI6 shrank by some 25 percent during the 1990s.

GCHQ is the Government Communications Headquarters, always referred to by its initials. GCHQ is the British signals intelligence (SIGINT) agency, also operating under the foreign secretary. It is the British equivalent of the National Security Agency (NSA), with which it enjoys a close working relationship. Like NSA, GCHQ has facilities at home and overseas. The function of the Communications Electronics Security Group is reflected in its name.

The Defence Intelligence Staff (DIS), under the chief of Defence Intelligence, reports to the defence secretary. DIS controls the Defence Geographic and Imagery Agency, which, like the National Geospatial-Intelligence Agency, produces both geographic and imagery products.

Executive control of British intelligence is based on the Cabinet structure and its supporting Cabinet Office. The prime minister is responsible for all intelligence and security issues, with the support of the Ministerial Committee on the Intelligence Services, which serves an oversight and policy review function. The prime minister chairs the committee; other members are the deputy prime minister; the home, defence, and foreign secretaries; and the chancellor of the exchequer (equivalent to the U.S. secretary of the Treasury). Each Cabinet ministry has a permanent undersecretary, its senior civil servant, who has power over administrative and budget issues. The relevant permanent undersecretaries make up the Permanent Secretaries' Committee on Intelligence Services, which is chaired by the Cabinet secretary. The committee provides periodic advice on collection requirements, budgets, and other issues. A security and intelligence coordinator, who is also a career civil servant, supports the ministerial committee, assists the permanent undersecretaries in dealing with the intelligence budget, and oversees the Joint Intelligence Committee (JIC) and the Cabinet Office Intelligence and Security Secretariat. Thus, the senior managers of British intelligence have a much closer relationship to policy makers and rely on the uniquely British concept of powerful career civil servants (the permanent undersecretaries) to administer on a nonpartisan basis. The closeness of the relationship obviates some of the more formal processes developed in the United States to determine intelligence requirements and resource allocation.

A key component in British intelligence is the Joint Intelligence Committee, which is part of the Cabinet Office and has management, oversight, production, and foreign liaison functions. It serves as a link between policy makers and the intelligence components to establish and order priorities, which are then approved by the ministers. The JIC also periodically reviews agency performance in meeting established requirements. The JIC's Assessments Staff produces intelligence assessments on key issues, which are roughly equivalent to U.S. national intelligence estimates. The JIC also has a monitoring and warning role in terms of threats to British interests. The JIC is, in many respects, akin to the functions that now fall under the jurisdiction of the director of national intelligence, but the chairman of the JIC does not have the same rank or authority.

Parliament's Intelligence and Security Committee, established in 1994, oversees all three intelligence components. The committee considers the budget, administration, and policy of MI5, MI6, and GCHQ, but its oversight function is not as powerful as that exercised by U.S. congressional committees. The Intelligence and Security Committee submits an annual report to the prime minister. The report is publicly released after sensitive portions have been deleted. The government then issues a response to the report.

The close intelligence relationship between Britain and the United States is most evident in the dealings between GCHQ and NSA, but it exists elsewhere. Britain's independent imagery intelligence (IMINT) capability is restricted to airborne platforms, but it receives satellite imagery from the United States. A range of intelligence products, both collection and analytic, also is shared. British HUMINT does not completely overlap that of the United States, with Britain having some advantages in Commonwealth countries. The 2005 WMD Commission (Commission on the Intelligence Capabilities of the United States Regarding Weapons of Mass Destruction) report gives some indication of how the two HUMINT enterprises work together.

During the cold war, British intelligence suffered several Soviet espionage penetrations. The most famous was Kim Philby, who, with four other Cambridge University associates, began spying for the Soviet Union in the 1930s. Philby became MI6's CIA liaison, an invaluable position for a Soviet spy. Other Soviet spies included George Blake, an SIS officer, and Geoffrey Prime, a GCHQ employee. Most known British spies were motivated by ideological, not monetary, reasons. Allegations were made that Sir Roger Hollis, a director general of MI5, was a spy, but he was cleared after an investigation in 1974.

The British services do not conduct assassinations. However, British special forces units, the Special Air Service (SAS) and Special Boat Service (SBS), have taken part in antiterrorist activities against the IRA that some people have charged were assassinations. The most famous case occurred in March 1988, when the SAS killed three IRA members in Gibraltar. The British government claimed that the IRA members were on active service, planning a series of bomb attacks. The SAS has conducted special operations for MI6.

The British services, like those in the United States (and in Australia), came under scrutiny after the start of the Iraq war in 2003, when the expected WMD were not found. An investigation led by Lord Butler (and thus known as the Butler Report) did not find substantial flaws in how the British intelligence on Iraq was produced. However, the report noted that the intelligence sources on Iraq had grown weaker and less reliable over time and that that fact was not properly conveyed. The report also said that no evidence existed that intelligence had been politicized, which was as serious an issue in Britain as it was in the United States. In response to the concerns raised about intelligence sources, MI6 created the position of a senior quality control officer to review collected intelligence for its credibility and veracity. The new officer is known as "R," for reports officer. (The head of MI6 has traditionally been known as "C," in honor of the first head of MI6, Sir Mansfield Cumming.)

British intelligence performance has been the target of earlier investigations. In the aftermath of the Falklands War (1982), a probe by Lord Franks held that the changes in Argentina's policy regarding the Falkland Islands should have been obvious through diplomatic and open sources. However, no basis existed to conclude that the Argentine invasion could have been prevented, although the Franks report criticized the Margaret Thatcher government for not paying enough attention to the issue prior to the war.

CHINA

In the past few years, the press has written much about Chinese intelligence, stemming largely from allegations of espionage activities against the United States. Intelligence in China, as in all communist states, has a twofold purpose: internal security activities against dissidents and foreign intelligence operations. As was the case with the Soviet KGB (Komitet Gosudarstvennoi Bezopasnosti—Committee of State Security), the internal suppressive function is an important distinction between the Chinese intelligence service and those of the United States or Britain.

Chinese intelligence is run by the Ministry of State Security. As with all other security issues in China, however, the most powerful body in the state is the Central Military Commission of the Communist Party, which has much greater influence than its title would imply. (Control over the commission was a sore point between outgoing president Jiang Zhemin and his successor, Hu Jintao. Their struggle underscores the importance of the commission as a key lever of control in the Chinese government.) Three Ministry of State Security bureaus are of greatest importance in intelligence.

- Second Bureau: intelligence collection abroad
- Fourth Bureau: technology development for intelligence gathering and counterintelligence
- Sixth Bureau: counterintelligence, primarily against Chinese communities overseas

Although much controversy surrounds allegations of Chinese espionage, its existence is not in doubt. China has a well-developed HUMINT program that relies on the large overseas Chinese population. For example, Larry Wu-tai Chin was a Chinese spy who worked for the CIA for decades before being discovered in the 1980s. A more controversial, and ultimately inconclusive, case was that of Wen Ho Lee, a Los Alamos Laboratory scientist who downloaded thousands of pages of sensitive material. Chinese espionage puts special emphasis on scientific and technology targets, both civil and military. These activities were the major focus of the 1999 report of the Cox Committee (U.S. House Select Committee on U.S. National Security and Military/Commercial Concerns with the People's Republic of China), especially allegations that China had stolen an array of information about nuclear weapons and satellite-related technology. Some observers have also expressed concern about the large number of Chinese students enrolled in U.S. colleges and graduate schools, many of them in technical areas (physics, computing) that might indicate national security concerns.

In addition to HUMINT, China has an array of Earth-based SIGINT platforms and is in the process of developing an imagery satellite that it plans to launch in the next several years.

The U.S.-Chinese intelligence relationship serves as a barometer of the larger political relationship. The United States and China were hostile until President Richard M. Nixon's visit to China in 1972. That event, plus the shared fear of growing Soviet power, led to some level of intelligence cooperation. Gaining access to sites in far western China, the United States was able to recover capabilities it had lost in Iran, after the fall of the shah's government, to track Soviet missile tests. China and the United States also cooperated on the operational level, both supporting the Mujaheddin against the Soviet Union in Afghanistan in the 1980s. The collapse of the Soviet Union led to new fears on the part of China about U.S. hegemony, leading to a deterioration in relations. Chinese assertiveness prompted the prolonged captivity of a U.S. reconnaissance plane crew, which was forced to land in China after colliding with a Chinese military jet. The incident occurred after the bombing of China's embassy in Belgrade, Serbia, in May 1999—a mistake caused by the use of outdated information on that city, which did not record the embassy's new location. In January 2002 news reports alleged that the United States had planted multiple listening devices in a plane being outfitted in the United States prior to delivery to China's president. China played down the reports, bolstering the view that such intelligence incidents were largely a means of expressing official attitudes about the relationship with the United States. According to subsequent press reports, some U.S. analysts believed that the listening devices were Chinese in origin, part of an internal power struggle.

China maintains an aggressive intelligence collection effort overseas, with the United States being a primary target, especially in the areas of new military and civil technology. The possibility of tension with the United States over the future of Taiwan also puts a premium on knowledge of U.S. deployments, strategy, and tactics in the western Pacific.

China regards Taiwan as a rebellious breakaway province. The United States treats Taiwan as something like an independent state, although full, formal diplomatic relations have not been established. However, the United States does have a formal obligation to defend Taiwan.

FRANCE

The main French intelligence organization is the DGSE (Directoire Générale de la Sécurité Extérieure—General Directorate for External Security), which reports to the minister of defense. DGSE, created in 1982, is the latest in a series of French intelligence organizations.

The four major directorates largely define the DGSE mission.

- Strategic: responsible for establishing intelligence requirements with policy makers, especially the Foreign Ministry, and also conducting intelligence studies
- Intelligence: responsible for intelligence collection, particularly HUMINT, and the dissemination of this intelligence
- Technical: collects SIGINT, largely through a number of ground sites
- Operations: responsible for clandestine operations

The DST (Directoire de Surveillance Territoire—Directorate of Territorial Surveillance) is responsible for counterintelligence.

The DRM (Directoire du Renseignement Militaire—Directorate of Military Intelligence) was organized in 1992, combining a number of TECHINT entities. As its name indicates, the DRM is responsible for military intelligence and imagery analysis. France has an independent satellite imagery capability. According to some reports, DRM has branched out into political and strategic intelligence areas where DGSE has been responsible.

The DPSD (Directoire de la Protection et de la Sécurité de la Défense—Directorate for Defense Protection and Security) handles military counterintelligence and maintains, in a uniquely French function, political surveillance of the military, with a view to its political reliability. This function goes back to the French Revolution, when "representatives on mission" served as political commissars, looking over the shoulders of French commanders. It also reflects the occasional intrusion—or threatened intrusion—of the military into French political life, although this has not happened since the Algerian revolt against French rule (1954–1962).

France has independent IMINT and SIGINT capabilities, which led it to disagree with U.S. assertions about Iraqi troop movements in 1996. The Iraqi movements led the Clinton administration to send a warning to

Iraq by means of a cruise missile attack. France has also played a central role in European efforts to build an independent imagery capability.

The Operations Division of the DGSE has had much greater latitude in its activities than do the clandestine services of the United States and Britain. This includes the use of violence against certain targets. The most famous case was the sinking, in July 1985, of the *Rainbow Warrior*, a boat being used by the Greenpeace organization to protest ongoing French nuclear tests in the South Pacific. French agents planted a bomb on the *Rainbow Warrior* while it was in the harbor at Auckland, New Zealand, which resulted in the death of one person on board. France initially denied responsibility but then admitted it, leading to the resignation of the defense minister and the firing of the head of the DGSE. In 2005, the former head of DGSE, Admiral Pierre Lacoste, said that French president François Mitterand had approved sinking the boat.

France maintains a military presence in many of its colonies in western and central Africa. It is presumed that French intelligence officers have a presence there, often in advisory capacities to the local governments.

The DGSE is also active in economic espionage, including activities against U.S. firms. The targets appear to be companies that compete with major French firms, reflecting the semi-statist nature of parts of the French economy. In a response to apparent French economic espionage, in 1993, the Hughes Aircraft firm announced it would not take part in the prestigious Paris Air Show.

In the late 1990s, according to press accounts, a U.S. nonofficial cover (NOC) agent in Paris was discovered. The agent's area of concentration was economics. French press accounts in 2003 argued that one of the NOC agent's paid sources, a French government official, became a double agent at the request of the DST. As former director of central intelligence (DCI) R. James Woolsey (1993–1995) noted in an article on ECHELON, the United States had two main economic intelligence concerns: foreign bribery intended to give firms unfair economic advantages and economic counterintelligence.

As the member states of the European Union (EU) work to foster a clearer and distinct European identity and role, the issue of intelligence cooperation becomes more complex. An EU foreign policy spokesman has been designated, and nascent efforts have been made to build a European military capability that would be separate from the North Atlantic Treaty Organization (NATO). Judging from the U.S. experience, however, sharing intelligence with allies is a less straightforward proposition. Not all allies are equal. In 2004, the justice and interior ministers of European Union nations rejected an Austrian proposal to create a European Intelligence Agency that would be an analytic and monitoring center focusing only on terrorism and proliferation.

ISRAEL

Israeli intelligence proceeds from the premise that the state is, essentially, under siege. Israel has two major intelligence services: Mossad and Shin Bet. Mossad (Ha-Mossad Le-Modin Ule-Tafkidim Meyuhadim—Institute for Intelligence and Special Tasks) is responsible for HUMINT, covert action, foreign liaison, and counterterrorism, as well as for producing a series of intelligence reports. Shin Bet (Sherut ha-Bitachon ha-Klali— General Security Service) has both counterintelligence and internal security functions. A third component, Aman (Agaf ha-Modi'in—Military Intelligence), is distinct from the intelligence components of each of the services, producing a series of intelligence reports, including national estimates. The Foreign Affairs and Security Committee of the Knesset (Parliament) oversees Israeli intelligence. In 2004, the Justice Ministry and Mossad began work on a law that would define that agency's purpose, goals, and powers for the first time. The law would also make clear Mossad's subordination to the government, oversight mechanisms, the term of office for the head of Mossad, and how he is appointed.

At a basic level, the intelligence requirements of Israel are simple. It is located in the midst of states that either maintain proper diplomatic relations or remain hostile. Both kinds of neighboring states and the Israeli–occupied territories on the West Bank harbor populations that are overtly hostile to Israel and unwilling to countenance its existence. This allows a fair amount of focus but also demands a constant state of readiness. It is difficult to think of another state whose intelligence services face a similar challenge.

Given this milieu, Israeli intelligence activities have always been given a fair amount of latitude and have become both legendary and controversial. Over the years, a number of successful HUMINT penetrations into Egypt and Syria have been conducted. However, one operation against Egypt in the early 1950s was discovered, resulting in the deaths of four Israeli agents and the prolonged incarceration of several others. It became known as the Lavon affair, after the defense minister at the time, Pinhas Lavon.

A more recent controversy involved a U.S. naval intelligence analyst, Jonathan Pollard. He appears to have been a walk-in, motivated by concerns that the United States was not sharing vital intelligence with Israel. However, Pollard also accepted cash and gifts in exchange for the intelligence he provided, including intelligence reports, imagery, and information about weapons systems. In 1985 he was arrested outside the Israeli Embassy, and in 1987 he was sentenced to life imprisonment. Some people felt that the sentence was too harsh, although successive reviews of Pollard's case have upheld the initial concerns that prompted the sentence.

Israel initially attempted to pass off the case as a rogue operation but, in early 1998, admitted that Pollard had been working as a regular agent. He had also been granted Israeli citizenship. The Pollard case became a constant irritant in U.S.–Israeli relations, not only because of the ill will it engendered but also because of constant Israeli attempts to get Pollard released. Most significant, Israeli prime minister Benjamin Netanyahu raised the Pollard issue during the 1998 peace talks at Wye River, where President Bill Clinton brought the Israelis and Palestinians together. Clinton appeared to be receptive to releasing him. DCI George J. Tenet (1997–2004) reportedly threatened to resign if Pollard was pardoned and released to Israel, whereupon Clinton dropped the issue. (Pollard supporters argue that the United States traded Soviet spy Rudolf Abel for U-2 pilot Francis Gary Powers in the 1960s, thus creating a precedent. However, although the United States has proven willing to repatriate a foreign spy in exchange for a U.S. intelligence officer, it does not trade U.S. citizens convicted of espionage.) The Pollard case is a classic example of a successful penetration whose political costs may far outweigh any intelligence that was obtained.

Concerns about Israeli intelligence collection overseas continue to be problematic. In 2004, the Federal Bureau of Investigation (FBI) said that Israel had been overly aggressive in collecting information at military equipment exhibitions. The information involved appeared not to be classified but the persistence of Israelis in asking questions about certain equipment had raised concerns. The FBI also had under investigation a U.S. Defense Department official who might have passed information to Israel. New Zealand jailed and then expelled two Israelis for attempting to obtain New Zealand passports illegally. The New Zealand government accused them of being Mossad agents. They denied the allegation but admitted having committed criminal activity. Access to foreign passports is essential to all intelligence agencies, which use them to mask the identities of agents sent overseas.

In addition to its emphasis on HUMINT, Israel has developed an independent satellite imagery capability and is at the forefront of imagery cooperation between nations. Press reports cite India and Turkey as two of its partners.

Israeli intelligence has conducted a variety of covert operations abroad, including both kidnapping and assassination. The most famous kidnapping was of the Nazi official Adolf Eichmann, who was abducted in Argentina in 1960. Eichmann had been responsible for the implementation of Hitler's "final solution," the extermination of the Jews. He was brought to Israel, where he was tried and executed. In 1986 Israeli intelligence abducted Mordechai Vanunu, who had worked at Israel's secret nuclear installation at Dimona. A year after leaving Dimona, Vanunu published details about Israel's nuclear weapons program in the London *Sunday Times*. Lured from London to Rome, Vanunu was abducted and returned to Israel, where he was sentenced to eighteen years in prison.

Israeli assassinations have targeted terrorists outside of Israel or the occupied territories. Targets have included the terrorists responsible for the capture and death of Israeli athletes at the 1972 Munich Olympics, although one innocent Arab in Norway was misidentified and also killed by Israeli agents. More recently, Israel has killed a number of terrorists during the unrest in both occupied and Palestinian-controlled areas. Israel refers to these as targeted killings, or interceptions, not assassinations or military reprisals. They appear to have been carried out by either intelligence or military forces.

Like the United States and the Soviet Union, Israel has suffered a major strategic intelligence failure. In 1973 Egypt and Syria achieved strategic surprise in the opening phase of the Yom Kippur War. In a still-controversial postwar investigation, the Agranat commission primarily faulted the military leadership and Aman for the surprise. The commission found that, although many signs pointed to an impending attack, the military was overly committed to an indications and warning (I&W) concept that led them to play down what they were seeing because not all of the conceptual indicators had been observed. In other words, they had created an I&W model and refused to react to the indications they were seeing because the Arab actions did not fit the I&W concept. Thus, even with an indications and warning model, the threshold had been set too high. This experience provided a valuable lesson on the possibility of surprise. Commenting on it nine years after the war, the staff director of the Knesset committee responsible for oversight of intelligence said: "The United States [during the cold war] has to watch every part of the globe. We know who our enemies are. We only have to watch six or seven countries—and still we were surprised."

RUSSIA

More has been written about Russian intelligence than about any other except for that of the United States. Russian intelligence capabilities probably most closely parallel those of the United States, although the KGB and the CIA were not directly comparable during the cold war.

The now-defunct KGB was the last in a long line of Russian and Soviet intelligence services whose primary responsibility was to combat internal dissent. The following KGB directorates had foreign intelligence roles.

- First Chief Directorate (Foreign): responsible for all nonmilitary intelligence, foreign counterintelligence, HUMINT, foreign propaganda, and disinformation
- Eighth Chief Directorate (Communication): SIGINT, both offensive and defensive, the latter role shared with the Sixteenth Directorate (Communications Security)

One can question the KGB's effectiveness in its broader and more important internal security role. KGB leadership was involved in the abortive 1991 coup against Mikhail S. Gorbachev that led to the demise of the Soviet Union. Moreover, the KGB clearly misread—or failed to report—the depth of anticommunist discontent in both the satellite states and the Soviet Union itself.

The GRU (Glavnoye Razvedyvatelnoye Upravlnie—Main Intelligence Administration) was and remains the military intelligence organization charged with the collection of a large array of intelligence related to military issues. The GRU has HUMINT, SIGINT, and IMINT capabilities. During the cold war, the Western services viewed the GRU as an occasional rival of the KGB. (Col. Oleg Penkovsky was a GRU officer.)

As with any other HUMINT enterprise, the records of the KGB and GRU are mixed. Successful penetrations of U.S. and British services include the cases of CIA agent Aldrich Ames and FBI agent Robert Hanssen, from the former, and Philby, Blake, and Prime, from the latter. At the same time, however, Western services recruited spies in the Soviet Union and, apparently, the post–Soviet state. Oleg Penkovsky is among the best known. It should also be noted that the damage done by Ames—and perhaps Hanssen simultaneously—involved at least twelve U.S. agents. Moreover, Hanssen's arrest apparently came as a result of information supplied by a U.S. intelligence source in Russia.

Like so much else in what was the Soviet Union, the intelligence services have been forced to undergo an unplanned transition. The KGB's First Chief Directorate emerged as the SVR (Sluzhba Vneshnei Razvedki—External Intelligence Service). It is responsible for intelligence liaison, industrial espionage, and HUMINT and for the handling of Ames and Hanssen, carryover assets from the KGB period. The SVR has made much of the fact that it has reduced its overseas presence, attempting to portray itself as a more benign organization than its predecessor. Some observers believe this may be largely cosmetic. Russia is now more open and accessible than was the Soviet Union, making it easier for the SVR to have contacts with agents in Russia instead of overseas.

The KGB's counterintelligence function reemerged as the FSB (Federal'naya Sluzhba Besnopasnoti—Federal Security Service), which is responsible for internal counterintelligence, civil counterespionage, and internal security. Vladimir Putin headed the FSB from July 1998 until his elevation to the position of acting prime minister in August 1999. In 2003, Putin gave the FSB control over the border guards and FAPSI (Federalnoe Agenstvo Pravitelstvennoi Sviazi I Informatsii—Federal Agency for Government Communications and Information), which was the successor to the KGB's Eighth Chief Directorate, responsible for cryptography, SIGINT, and the Communications Troops. These functions are parallel to those of NSA, but FAPSI also controls internal electronic communications, again making comparisons imprecise. This consolidation under the FSB had led some to be concerned that the old powers of the KGB were being reconstituted.

It would have been unreasonable and impossible for Russia to scrap the old Soviet intelligence apparatus entirely and start anew. Inevitably some of the same officers would have had to be hired. The key question for Russian intelligence is part of the larger question of how far along a democracy in which laws and rights are respected by the government and its agencies has the country become. Russian historical experience offers little upon which to create such practices either in the intelligence services or the wider society. Also, Russia faces some internal problems—typified by the ongoing Chechen problem of revolt against Russian rule, which has led to terrorist attacks in Moscow and elsewhere—that create pressure against more restrained intelligence functions.

Russia's TECHINT capabilities come closest to those of the United States, although reports of deterioration in these capabilities have been persistent since the demise of the Soviet Union. Numerous press reports have noted financial constraints affecting these collection assets, in terms of both the number of satellites in orbit and problems affecting ground facilities.

In October 2001 President Putin announced that Russia would close its major SIGINT facility at Lourdes, Cuba. Located within one hundred miles of U.S. territory, the Lourdes complex reportedly could intercept telephone, microwave, and communications satellite traffic and was also reportedly used to manage Russian spy satellites. It was a major irritant in U.S.–Russian relations and an added difficult aspect of the U.S.–Cuban relationship. The closing appears to have been motivated primarily by economics. Russia paid Cuba $200 million annually for the use of the site—a sum that one Russian general said could be better used to buy "twenty communications and intelligence satellites and 100 modern radars." Two other factors that may have prompted the decision were the deterioration of the Russian spy satellite fleet, limiting the importance of Lourdes, and the steady shifting of U.S. communications from microwave to fiber-optic cable. Some Russian officials expressed the hope that the United States would reciprocate by closing some ground-based SIGINT facilities on the Russian periphery, particularly the one at Vardo, Norway. At the same time, Russia announced the closing of its base at Cam Ranh Bay, Vietnam, which had been a major U.S. base during the Vietnam War. Soviet and Russian forces used it as a base for reconnaissance aircraft and a SIGINT facility targeting China.

The Soviet intelligence apparatus conducted assassinations, or what they termed "wet affairs." The most famous was the assassination of Josef Stalin's former rival, Leon Trotsky, in Mexico City in 1940. Some analysts believed that the Soviet Union was behind the attempted assassination of Pope John Paul II in 1981, but no conclusive proof has been uncovered. It is not known if Russian policy on assassinations has changed.

Russian intelligence capability is less formidable than it was during the height of Soviet power, although it is still not a benign or powerless service. If nothing else, in former Soviet intelligence archives—and in the minds of current or former Russian intelligence officers—repose a great deal of intelligence about U.S. sources and methods. Running parallel to the "loose nukes" issue (former Soviet nuclear weapons or nuclear expertise being used in other WMD proliferation programs), concerns have been expressed about how some former Soviet intelligence officers—whose status, like that of nuclear scientists, has fallen greatly—might seek to profit from their knowledge. This intelligence issue may be even more difficult to track than loose nukes.

The Russian services have also lost important former liaison partners. The intelligence services of former Soviet satellites served, in effect, as subcontractors. The East German and Czechoslovakian services both had contacts with guerrilla and terrorist groups. The Polish service was used for industrial espionage in the West. The Bulgarian service was occasionally used for assassinations. Bulgaria also assassinated one of its own dissidents, Georgi Markov, in London in 1978. The East German state no longer exists; Poland and the Czech Republic are now part of NATO.

CONCLUSION

When assessing different intelligence services, keep in mind that most have liaison relationships with other services, thus increasing their capabilities. The degree to which these relationships complement or overlap one another is important.

As should now be evident, comparing intelligence services with one another is an inexact and somewhat pointless endeavor. Each service is—or should be—structured to address the unique intelligence requirements of its national policy makers. Although the intelligence process discussed throughout this book is somewhat generic to any particular intelligence service, the specifics of key issues—such as internal versus external security functions, the relative safety of the state, the extent and nature of international relationships and interests—shape how the intelligence service functions and what its relationship is to policy makers. Some structures also reflect each nation's distinctive national and political development. Skills and capabilities also vary from service to service. The key issue in assessing any intelligence service is the one that has pervaded this book: Does it provide timely, useful intelligence to the policy process?

FURTHER READINGS

Literature on foreign intelligence services is uneven at best. The works cited below emphasize the current status of these organizations, instead of offering historical treatments, although some of these have been cited as well. In addition, the Federation of American Scientists' Web site, www.fas.org, contains useful information on all of the services discussed in this chapter and others.

Britain
"Cats' Eyes in the Dark," *Economist,* March 19–25, 2005, 32–34.
Cradock, Percy. *Know Your Enemy: How the Joint Intelligence Committee Saw the World.* London, England: John Murray, 2002.
Falkland Islands Review. Report of a Committee of Privy Counsellors [Franks Report]. London, England: Her Majesty's Stationery Office, 1983. (Parliamentary paper Cmnd. 8787.)
Herman, Michael. "Intelligence and the Iraqi Threat: British Joint Intelligence after Butler." *RUSI Journal* (August 2004): 18–24.
Masse, Todd. "Domestic Intelligence in the United Kingdom: Applicability of the MI-5 Model to the United States." Washington, D.C.: Congressional Research Service, May 19, 2003.
National Intelligence Machinery. London, England: Stationery Office, 2000.
Review of Intelligence on Weapons of Mass Destruction: Report of a Committee Privy Counsellors [Butler Report]. London, England: Her Majesty's Stationery Office, July 14, 2004.
Security Service (MI5), www.securityservice.gov.uk (This is the official Web site of the United Kingdom's security intelligence agency.)
Smith, Michael. *New Cloak, Old Dagger: How Britain's Spies Came In from the Cold.* London, England: Gollancz, 1996.
Smith, Michael. *The Spying Game: The Secret History of British Espionage.* London, England: Politicos Publishers, 2003.
West, Nigel. "The UK's Not Quite So Secret Service." *International Journal of Intelligence and Counterintelligence* 18 (spring 2005): 23–30.
www.cabinetoffice.gov.uk (British Cabinet Office Web site)
www.five.org.uk (This unofficial site is hostile to intelligence services but has some useful information on the legal basis of the British services.)
www.gchq.gov.uk (Government Communications Headquarters Web site)
www.mi5.gov.uk (MI5 Web site)

China

Eftimiades, Nicholas. *Chinese Intelligence Operations.* Annapolis, Md.: Naval Institute Press, 1994.

U.S. House Select Committee on U.S. National Security and Military/Commercial Concerns with the People's Republic of China [Cox Committee]. 3 vols. 105th Cong., 2d sess., 1999.

France

Direction Générale de la Sécurité Extérieure, www.dgse.org (This is an unofficial but useful site, in French.)

Porch, Douglas. "French Intelligence Culture: A Historical and Political Perspective." *Intelligence and National Security* 10 (July 1995): 486–511.

Israel

Black, Ian, and Benny Morris. *Israel's Secret Wars: A History of Israel's Intelligence Services.* New York: Grove Weidenfeld, 1991.

Katz, Samuel M. *Soldier Spies: Israeli Military Intelligence.* Novato, Calif.: Presidio Press, 1992.

Raviv, Dan, and Yossi Melman. *Every Spy a Prince: The Complete History of Israel's Intelligence Community.* Boston: Houghton Mifflin, 1990.

Thomas, Gordon. *Gideon's Spies: Mossad's Secret Warriors.* New York: St. Martin's, 1999.

www.mossad.il (This is the Mossad site for new applicants.)

Russia

Albats, Yevgenia. *The State within a State: The KGB and Its Hold on Russia—Past, Present, and Future.* Trans. Catherine A. Fitzpatrick. New York: Farrar, Strauss, and Giroux, 1994.

Albini, Joseph L., and Julie Anderson. "Whatever Happened to the KGB?" *International Journal of Intelligence and Counterintelligence* 11 (spring 1998): 26–56.

Andrew, Christopher, and Oleg Gordievsky. *KGB: The Inside Story of Its Foreign Operations from Lenin to Gorbachev.* New York: HarperCollins, 1991.

Knight, Amy. *Spies without Cloaks: The KGB's Successors.* Princeton: Princeton University Press, 1996.

Waller, J. Michael. *Secret Empire: The KGB in Russia Today.* Boulder, Colo.: Westview Press, 1994.

Appendix 1

Additional Bibliographic Citations and Web Sites

This bibliography, arranged topically, contains readings that are in addition to those listed at the end of each chapter. It is not a comprehensive bibliography of intelligence literature. Instead, the works have been chosen based on their relevance to and amplification of the themes developed in the book. Some works, although older, remain highly useful.

The list of Web sites was originally compiled by John Macartney, a career intelligence officer (U.S. Air Force) and a longtime scholar and teacher of intelligence, who passed away in 2001.

REFERENCE

Lowenthal, Mark M. *The U.S. Intelligence Community: An Annotated Bibliography.* New York: Garland, 1994.

U.S. Congress. House Permanent Select Committee on Intelligence. *Compilation of Intelligence Laws and Related Laws and Executive Orders of Interest to the National Intelligence Community, as Amended through January 3, 1998.* 105th Cong., 2d sess., 1998.

Watson, Bruce W., and others, eds. *United States Intelligence: An Encyclopedia.* New York: Garland, 1990.

GENERAL WORKS

Dearth, Douglas H., and R. Thomas Goodden, eds. *Strategic Intelligence: Theory and Approach.* 2d ed. Washington, D.C.: Defense Intelligence Agency, Joint Military Intelligence Training Center, 1995.

George, Roger Z., and Robert D. Kline. *Intelligence and the National Security Strategist: Enduring Issues and Challenges.* Washington, D.C.: National Defense University Press, 2004.

Hilsman, Roger. *Strategic Intelligence and National Decisions.* Glencoe, Ill.: Greenwood, 1956.

Johnson, Loch K., and James J. Wirtz. *Strategic Intelligence: Windows on a Secret World.* Los Angeles: Roxbury Publishing Company, 2004.

Kent, Sherman. *Strategic Intelligence for American World Policy.* Princeton: Princeton University Press, 1949.

Krizan, Lisa. *Intelligence Essentials for Everyone.* Washington, D.C.: Joint Military Intelligence College, 1999.

Laqueur, Walter. *A World of Secrets.* New York: Basic Books, 1985.

HISTORIES

Andrew, Christopher. *For the President's Eyes Only.* New York: Harper Perennial Library, 1995.

Montague, Ludwell Lee. *General Walter Bedell Smith as Director of Central Intelligence: October 1950–February 1953.* University Park: Pennsylvania State University Press, 1992.

306

Ranelagh, John. *The Agency: The Rise and Decline of the CIA.* New York: Simon and Schuster, 1987.
Troy, Thomas F. *Donovan and the CIA: A History of the Establishment of the Central Intelligence Agency.* Frederick, Md.: Greenwood, 1981.

ANALYSIS—HISTORICAL

McAuliffe, Mary S., ed. *CIA Documents on the Cuban Missile Crisis 1962.* Washington, D.C.: U.S. Central Intelligence Agency, Historical Staff, 1992.
Price, Victoria S. *The DCI's Role in Producing Strategic Intelligence Estimates.* Newport: U.S. Naval War College, 1980.

COVERT ACTION—HISTORICAL

Aguilar, Luis. *Operation Zapata.* Frederick, Md.: University Publications of America, 1981.
Bissell, Richard M., with Jonathan E. Lewis and Frances T. Pudlo. *Reflections of a Cold Warrior.* New Haven: Yale University Press, 1996.
Blight, James G., and Peter Kornbluh, eds. *Politics of Illusion: The Bay of Pigs Invasion Reexamined.* Boulder, Colo.: Lynne Rienner Publishers, 1998.
Draper, Theodore. *A Very Thin Line: The Iran-Contra Affairs.* New York: Hill and Wang, 1991.
Persico, Joseph. *Casey: From the OSS to CIA.* New York: Viking, 1990.
Thomas, Ronald C., Jr. "Influences on Decisionmaking at the Bay of Pigs." *International Journal of Intelligence and Counterintelligence* 3 (winter 1989): 537–548.
U.S. Senate Select Committee to Study Governmental Operations with Respect to Intelligence Activities [Church Committee]. *Alleged Assassination Plots Involving Foreign Leaders.* 94th Cong., 1st sess., 1975.
Wyden, Peter. *The Bay of Pigs: The Untold Story.* New York: Simon and Schuster, 1979.

INTELLIGENCE WEB SITES

SEARCHABLE DATABASES

- intellit.muskingum.edu/intellsite/index.html (J. Ransom Clark, "The Literature of Intelligence: A Bibliography of Materials, with Essays, Reviews, and Comments," 2002.)

MULTIPLE SITE LINKS

- www.loyola.edu/dept/politics/intel.html (strategic intelligence)
- www.columbia.edu/cu/web/indiv/lehman/guides/intell.html (U.S. government documents, U.S. intelligence community)
- www.kimsoft.com/kim-spy.htm (intelligence and counterintelligence)

ARMED FORCES JOURNAL INTERNATIONAL

- www.afji.com.

CENTRAL INTELLIGENCE AGENCY

- www.odci.gov/csi (Center for the Study of Intelligence)
- www.foia.ucia.gov (Freedom of Information Act documents)

NATIONAL SECURITY ARCHIVE

- www.gwu.edu/~nsarchiv (declassified documents)

NEW YORK TIMES

- www.nytimes.com/library/national/index-cia.html

CONGRESSIONAL OVERSIGHT COMMITTEES

- www.senate.gov/index.htm
- intelligence.house.gov

HUMAN INTELLIGENCE

- www.fas.org/irp/wwwspy.html (Federation of American Scientists)

IMAGERY INTELLIGENCE

- www.fas.org/irp/wwwimint.html (Federation of American Scientists)
- www.fas.org/irp/imint/kh-12.htm (Federation of American Scientists)

MEASUREMENT AND SIGNATURES INTELLIGENCE

- www.fas.org/irp/program/masint—evaluation—rep.htm (Federation of American Scientists)
- www.fas.org/irp/congress/1996—rpt/ic21/ic21007.htm (Federation of American Scientists)

OPEN-SOURCE INTELLIGENCE

- www.fas.org/irp/eprint/oss980501.htm (Federation of American Scientists)
- www.fas.org/irp/wwwecon.html (Federation of American Scientists)

SIGNALS INTELLIGENCE

- www.fas.org/irp/wwwsigin.html (Federation of American Scientists)

COUNTERINTELLIGENCE

- www.ncix.gov (National Counterintelligence Executive)
- www.fbi.gov/hq/ci/cointell.htm (Federal Bureau of Investigation)
- www.dss.mil (Defense Security Service)
- www.loyola.edu/dept/politics/hula/hitzrept.html ("Abstract of Report of Investigation, The Aldrich H. Ames Case: An Assessment of CIA's Role in Identifying Ames as an Intelligence Penetration of the Agency," October 21, 1994.)

COVERT ACTION

- www.nytimes.com/library/national/cia-invismain.html (*New York Times*)

INFORMATION OPERATIONS

- www.infowar.com

CURRENT NEWS ARTICLES

- cryptome.org

INTELLIGENCE REFORM OF 1996

- www.access.gpo.gov/int/report.html (Report of the Aspin-Brown Commission: "Report of the Commission on the Roles and Capabilities of the United States Intelligence Community")

BUSINESS (COMPETITIVE) INTELLIGENCE

- www.lookoutpoint.com/index.html (Real-World Intelligence Inc.)
- www.scip.org (Society of Competitive Intelligence Professionals)
- www.stratfor.com (Stratfor)
- www.opsec.org (Operations Security Professionals Society)
- www.pcic.net (Professional Connections in the Intelligence Community)
- www.fas.org/irp/wwwecon.html (Federation of American Scientists)

FOREIGN INTELLIGENCE SERVICES

- www.csis-scrs.gc.ca (Canadian Security Intelligence Service)
- www.cse-cst.gc.ca/cse/english/home—1.html (Communications Security Establishment, Canada)
- www.asio.gov.au (Australian Security Intelligence Office)
- www.asis.gov.au (Australian Secret Intelligence Service)
- www.ona.gov.au (Office of National Assessments, Australia)
- www.defence.gov.au/dio (Defence Intelligence Organisation, Australia)

SPECIAL REPORTS

- www.carnegie.org/deadly/0697warning.htm ("The Warning-Response Problem and Missed Opportunities in Preventive Diplomacy," New York: Carnegie Commission on Preventing Deadly Conflict, 1997.)

- www.fas.org/irp/congress/1998_cr/s980731-rumsfeld.htm (U.S. Senate, "The Rumsfeld Commission Report," *Congressional Record,* daily ed., 105th Cong., 2d sess., July 31, 1998.)
- www.seas.gwu.edu/nsarchive/news/19980222.htm ("Inspector General's Survey of the Cuban Operation and Associated Documents," Central Intelligence Agency (CIA) report on the Bay of Pigs)
- www.fas.org/irp/cia/product/jeremiah.html (Comments of Adm. David Jeremiah on his investigation into actions taken by the intelligence community leading up to the Indian nuclear test of 1998)
- www.fas.org/irp/cia/product/cocaine2/index.html (CIA inspector general report: "Report of Investigation: Allegations of Connections between CIA and the Contras in Cocaine Trafficking to the United States")
- www.washingtonpost.com/wp-srv/national/longterm/drugs/front.htm ("Special Report: CIA, Contras, and Drugs: Questions Linger," *Washington Post.*)

PRIVATE ORGANIZATIONS

- www.afio.com (Association of Former Intelligence Officers)
- www.nmia.org (National Military Intelligence Association)
- www.aochq.org (Association of Old Crows)
- www.opsec.org (Operations Security Professionals Society)
- www.afcea.com (Armed Forces Communications and Electronics Association)
- www.cloakanddagger.com/dagger (Cloak and Dagger Books)
- intelligence-history.wiso.uni-erlangen.de (International Intelligence History Association)

Appendix 2

Major Intelligence Reviews or Proposals

This appendix, which lists some of the most important reviews or proposals for change in the intelligence community, is based on a 1996 Congressional Research Service report, *Proposals for Intelligence Reorganization, 1949–1996*, by Richard A. Best Jr. The synopses offer insight into the major concepts that have been put forth over the years. However, they do not capture the many proposals made by individuals.

Eberstadt Report, 1945. Laid the basic groundwork for what became the National Security Act of 1947, creating the National Security Council (NSC), a de jure director of central intelligence (DCI), and the Central Intelligence Agency (CIA). Also created a unified defense structure, as opposed to separate War and Navy Departments.

First Hoover Commission, 1949. Raised concerns about the lack of coordination among the CIA, the military, and the State Department, resulting in duplication and some biased estimates. Urged a more central role for the CIA in national intelligence.

Dulles-Jackson-Correa Report, 1949. Recommended that the DCI concentrate on community-wide issues, with a subordinate running day-to-day CIA operations.

Doolittle Report, 1954. Urged more effective espionage, counterespionage, and covert action to deal with the Soviet threat and noted the need for technical intelligence to overcome impediments to human intelligence (HUMINT) in the Soviet bloc.

Taylor Commission, 1961. Offered an assessment of the Bay of Pigs invasion that criticized all agencies involved, the planning and concept of the operation, and the plausibility of deniability. Made recommendations regarding future planning and coordination for covert action.

Kirkpatrick Report, 1961. Was an internal CIA review of the Bay of Pigs, which also criticized the operation's planners.

Schlesinger Report, 1971. Questioned the increased size and cost of the intelligence community in contrast with little apparent improvement in analysis; the cost of duplicative collection systems; and insufficient planning for future resource allocations. Recommended strengthening the role of the DCI in these areas.

Murphy Commission (Commission on the Organization of the Government for the Conduct of Foreign Policy), 1975. Raised the issue of the DCI's responsibility versus authority but did not recommend increasing the DCI's line authority to agencies beyond the CIA. Argued for the DCI to spend more time on community-wide issues, delegating CIA's management to a deputy.

Rockefeller Commission (Commission on CIA Activities within the United States), 1975. Formed in the wake of revelations about improper or illegal CIA activities (the "family jewels" report); focused largely on proposals to prevent a recurrence and to direct CIA attention solely on foreign intelligence activities.

Church Committee (Senate Select Committee to Study Governmental Operations with Respect to Intelligence Activities), 1976. Prompted by the "family jewels" revelations. Recommended legislative charters for all intelligence agencies, spelling out roles and prohibited activities. Also recommended statutory recognition of the DCI's role as principal foreign intelligence adviser, with authority to establish national intelligence requirements, the intelligence budget, and guidance for intelligence operations. Recommended that national intelligence budget be appropriated to the DCI, not to agency directors. Recommended banning assassinations.

Pike Committee (House Select Committee on Intelligence), 1976. Was House counterpart to the Church Committee. Presented recommendations not in a final approved release but as leaked to the *Village Voice* newspaper. Recommended separating the DCI from the CIA to focus on community-wide issues; a ban on assassinations in peacetime; greater congressional oversight of covert action; charter legislation for the National Security Agency; publication of the overall intelligence budget figure; and abolition of the Defense Intelligence Agency, with its functions divided between the Defense Department and CIA.

Tower Commission (*Report of the President's Special Review Board*), 1987. Formed after initial revelations about the Iran-contra affair. Recommended improvements in the structure and functioning of the NSC staff, more precise procedures for the restricted consideration of covert action, and a Joint Intelligence Committee in Congress. Raised concerns about the influence of policy makers on the intelligence process.

Boren-McCurdy, 1993. Presented recommendations of the chairmen of the Senate and House Intelligence Committees (David L. Boren, D-Okla., and Dave McCurdy, D-Okla., respectively), including creation of a director of national intelligence (DNI), with budgetary programming authority across the intelligence community; two deputy DNIs, one for analysis and estimates and one for intelligence community issues; a separate director of the CIA, subordinate to the DNI; and consolidation of analytical elements under a deputy DNI.

Aspin-Brown Commission (Commission on the Roles and Capabilities of the U.S. Intelligence Community), 1996. Studied the future of the intelligence community after the cold war. Said the intelligence community needed to function more as a true community, overcoming agency barriers. Recommended a closer tie between intelligence and policy to improve direction of roles, collection, and analysis; a second deputy DCI for the intelligence community; a fixed six-year term for the deputy DCI responsible for the CIA; realignment of the intelligence budget under discipline managers reporting to the DCI; and transfer of Defense Humint Service's clandestine recruitment role to the CIA Directorate of Operations.

IC21: The Intelligence Community in the Twenty-first Century, 1996. Study by the staff of the House Permanent Select Committee on Intelligence, contemporaneous with Aspin-Brown. Sought to create a more corporate intelligence community, with the DCI acting as a chief executive officer. Recommendations included DCI concurrence in the secretary of defense's appointments of National Foreign Intelligence Program (NFIP) defense agencies; increased DCI programmatic control over NFIP agency budgets and personnel; creation of a second deputy DCI for community management; consolidation and rationalization of certain management and infrastructure functions across the intelligence community; creation of a Technical Collection Agency to manage signals intelligence, imagery intelligence, and measurement and signatures intelligence; and creation of an intelligence community reserve.

Council on Foreign Relations Independent Task Force (Making Intelligence Smarter: The Future of U.S. Intelligence), 1996. Recommended improvements in the requirements and priorities process; less emphasis on long-term estimates on familiar topics and broad trends; greater use of open sources; increased influence of the DCI over intelligence components; and creation of an intelligence reserve.

Hart-Rudman Commission (U.S. Commission on National Security, Twenty-first Century), 2001. Recommended, in Phase II of the study, that the National Intelligence Council devote resources to the issues of homeland security and asymmetric threats; the NSC should establish a strategic planning staff, one of whose roles would be to establish national intelligence priorities; the DCI should emphasize recruitment of HUMINT sources on terrorism; and the intelligence community should place new emphasis on collection and analysis of economic and scientific and technologic security concerns and should make greater use of open-source intelligence, with budget increases for these activities.

9/11 Commission (National Commission on Terrorist Attacks Upon the United States), 2004. Some recommendations were enacted into law in 2004, primarily the supplanting of the DCI with a DNI not tied to any agency and the creation of a National Counterterrorism Center, which President George W. Bush already had under way. Also recommended that all analytic efforts be organized by topical centers and that the Defense Department be responsible for all paramilitary operations.

WMD Commission (Commission on the Intelligence Capabilities of the United States Regarding Weapons of Mass Destruction), 2005. Formed to investigate intelligence performance on Iraqi weapons of mass destruction (WMDs) and other issues. Recommended that the DNI create mission managers to be responsible for all aspects of intelligence on high-priority issues; a more integrated collection enterprise; a National Counterproliferation Center to coordinate collection and analysis for counterproliferation; an Open Source Directorate at CIA; and a new national security service within the Federal Bureau of Investigation that would include counterintelligence, counterterrorism, and intelligence activities. In June 2005, President George W. Bush accepted seventy of the seventy-four recommendations.

Author Index

Note: This index lists the names of authors from FURTHER READINGS at the end of each chapter.

Adams, Sam, 142
Adler, Emanuel, 218
Aid, Matthew M., 108
Albats, Yevgenia, 305
Albini, Joseph L., 305
Aldrich, Richard W., 253
Ambrose, Stephen E., 29
Anderson, Julie, 305
Andrew, Christopher, 305

Baker, James E., 172
Baker, John C., 107
Bamford, James, 108
Barry, James A., 172, 273
Bearden, Milt, 155
Bell, J. Dwyer, 143
Benson, Robert Louis, 108, 155
Berkowitz, Bruce D., 143, 172, 230, 253, 288
Best, Richard A., Jr., 106, 107, 254, 288
Betts, Richard K., 9, 189, 288
Black, Ian, 305
Brownell, George A., 108
Brugioni, Dino, 29, 107
Burgstaller, Eugen F., 106
Burrows, William, 106
Burton, Donald F., 230

Caldwell, George, 143
Carter, Ashton B., 288
Chomeau, John B., 172
Cilluffo, Frank J., 254
Clark, Robert M., 143
Cohen, William S., 218
Colby, William E., 29, 253
Coleman, John, 254
Colton, David Everett, 218
Conner, William E., 218
Cradock, Percy, 304
Currie, James, 218

Daugherty, William J., 172
David, Jack, 189
Davis, Christopher M., 218
Davis, Jack, 143
Day, Dwayne, 107

Deutch, John M., 254
Draper, Theodore, 29

Eberstadt, Ferdinand, 288
Eftimiades, Nicholas, 305
Elkins, Dan, 53
Erskine, Tom, 273

Firth, Noel E., 230
Forbath, Peter, 29
Ford, Harold, 143
Fort, Randall M., 253
Freedman, Lawrence, 230

Gates, Robert M., 29, 143
Gazit, Shlomo, 143
George, Roger Z., 143
Gilligan, Tom, 172
Godfrey, E. Drexel, 273
Godson, Roy, 108, 155, 172
Goodman, Allan E., 172, 253, 288
Gordievsky, Oleg, 305
Grimmett, Richard F., 254
Gumina, Paul, 218

Halpern, Samuel, 155
Hamilton, Lee, 9
Hansen, James, 288
Helms, Richard, 29, 273
Herman, Michael, 9, 273, 304
Hersh, Seymour, 29
Heuer, Richards J., 143
Heymann, Hans, 10, 189
Hilsman, Roger, 10
Hitz, Frederick P., 106, 155
Hood, William, 155, 273
Houston, Lawrence R., 29
Hughes, Thomas L, 189
Hulnick, Arthur S., 106, 189, 253, 254, 288

Immerman, Richard H., 29

Jackson, Peter, 10
Jackson, William R., 218
Jeffreys-Jones, Rhodri, 29

Johnson, Loch K., 53, 67, 143, 172, 219, 253, 288
Johnson, William R., 156
Johnston, Paul, 254

Kahn, David, 108
Karalekas, Anne, 29
Katz, Samuel M., 305
Klass, Philip, 107
Knight, Amy, 305
Knorr, Klaus, 9
Knott, Stephen F., 172
Koch, Scott A., 230
Kovacs, Amos, 190
Krizan, Liza, 67

Laqueur, Walter, 10
Latimer, Thomas K., 219
Lauren, Paul Gordon, 273
Lee, William T., 231
Levinson, Sanford, 273
Lindgren, David T., 107
Lockwood, Jonathan S., 143
Lowenthal, Mark M., 29, 53, 107, 143, 190, 231, 253, 254

MacEachin, Douglas J., 143, 231
Mann, Thomas E., 219
Marks, Ronald A., 254
Masse, Todd, 304
Masters, Barrie P., 273
Maurer, Alfred C., 10, 67, 143, 189, 190, 219, 273
McCort, Robert F., 29, 107
Melman, Yossi, 305
Mercado, Stephen C., 107
Montague, Ludwell Lee, 29
Morris, Benny, 305
Moynihan, Daniel Patrick, 29, 108, 231

Nolan, James, 155
Nolte, William, 254
Nye, Joseph S., 143

O'Connell, Kevin, 107

Peebles, Christopher, 107
Perkins, David D., 156
Persico, Joseph, 29
Pfaltzgraff, Robert L., Jr., 219
Phillips, David Atlee, 106
Pickert, Perry L., 254
Pickett, George, 219
Pipes, Richard, 143, 231
Porch, Douglas, 305
Posner, Richard, 53

Poteat, Eugene, 190
Powers, Thomas, 29, 273
Prados, John, 29, 172, 231
Price, Victoria, 143

Quinn, James L., Jr., 288

Rafalko, Frank J., 156
Ranelagh, John, 29
Raviv, Dan, 305
Reich, Robert C., 143, 231
Reisman, W. Michael, 172
Richelson, Jeffrey T., 53, 107, 230
Rieber, Steven, 143
Rindskopf, Elizabeth, 254
Risen, James, 155
Rositzke, Harry, 172
Ruffner, Kevin C., 107

Salmoiraghi, George C., 254
Scheid, Kevin J., 253
Schmitt, Gary J., 156, 173
Scott, Len, 10
Shulman, Seth, 107
Shulsky, Abram N., 10, 156, 173
Simmons, Robert Ruhl, 219
Sims, Jennifer, 10
Smist, Frank J., Jr., 219
Smith, Michael, 304
Snider, L. Britt, 219, 254
Sorel, Albert, 273
Stack, Kevin P., 143
Steiner, James E., 190
Steury, Donald P., 143, 231
Stiefler, Todd, 173

Taubman, Philip, 107
Thomas, Gordon, 305
Thomas, Stafford T., 190
Treverton, Gregory F., 173, 219, 288
Troy, Thomas F., 10, 29
Turner, Michael A., 144

Waller, J. Michael, 305
Warner, Michael, 108, 155
West, Nigel, 304
Wiebes, Cees, 108
Williamson, Ray A., 107
Wirtz, James J., 107, 108, 144
Wohlstetter, Roberta, 29, 106
Woolsey, R. James, 253
Wyden, Peter, 29

Zelikow, Philip, 253
Zuehlke, Arthur A., 156

Subject Index

Note: References to boxes, figures, and tables are indicated by "b," "f," and "t" following page numbers.

A

Abel, Rudolf, 256, 299
ABM treaty, 24
Abrams, Elliot, 137
Accountability. *See* Oversight and
  accountability
Actionable intelligence, 234
Ad hocs, 59
Administrative reform, 286
Afghanistan
  assassination and, 171b
  imagery use in, 79, 84–85
  Mujaheddin rebels, 159
  narcotics, 243
  paramilitary operations in, 163
  Soviet invasion, 172, 227, 230, 263,
    295
  Taliban, 172
  war on terrorism. *See* War on
    terrorism
Africa, 3b, 171b, 241, 246–247
Agencies. *See* Intelligence agencies
Agent acquisition cycle, 94
AIDS, 246–247
Air-breathing systems, 36–37
Air Force, 22, 36
Algeria, 89
Alien and Sedition Acts of 1798, 216
Allende, Salvador, 163, 166, 171, 270
All-source intelligence, 40, 70
al Qaeda
  avoiding detection and, 236
  communications and, 238–239
  renditions and, 234
  Taliban and, 172
  use of imagery on, 86
Alternative analysis, 132–133
Ambassadors, 41, 42
Ames, Aldrich, 26, 150–151
  damage assessment, 153
  HUMINT and, 96, 100
  oversight failure, 209
  polygraph test, 147
  Russian intelligence and, 154, 230,
    301

Analysis, 14–15, 61–62, 109–144. *See also*
  Analysts
  alternative analysis, 132–133
  analytical stovepipes, 123–124
  assessment of, 139–142
  briefings, 112–113
  competitive analysis. *See* Competitive
    analysis
  cooperative vs. competitive analysis,
    124–126
  crises vs. the norm, 113–114
  current vs. long-term intelligence,
    111–112
  dependence on data, 8
  estimates, 133–135
  ethical and moral issues, 266–270
  indications and warning, 130–131
  issues in, 124–139
  limited information for, 127–128
  metaphors, 127b
  "on the ground knowledge," 119–123
  opportunity analysis, 131
  policy makers and intelligence,
    183–184
  politicized intelligence, 136–139
  pressure from policy makers, 267–269
  production and, 54, 61–62
  redundancy of structure, 14–15
  reform, 280–281
  relationship with covert action, 16–17,
    169–170
  requirements, importance of, 110
  themes in, 110–124
  uncertainty in, 128–129
  wheat vs. chaff problem, 59–60, 71,
    102, 114, 116
Analysis-driven collection, 77
Analyst agility, 115
Analyst fungibility, 114–115
Analysts, 139–142
  altering intelligence, 137
  career tracks, 117–118
  clientism and, 119
  collection priorities and, 62, 77
  credibility of, 121

dealing with limited information, 127–128
ethics and options, 269–270
management of, 117–118
mind-sets of, 62, 118–119
mirror imaging and, 118–119
objectivity of, 116–117, 137
promotion of, 117
resignation of, 269–270
stovepipes, 116
training of, 62, 116–117
Analytical stovepipes, 123–124
Angleton, James, 151
A not A (appropriated but not authorized), 197
Anthrax, 239, 242, 247
Anti-satellite (ASAT) weapons, 89
Appropriated but not authorized (A not A), 197
Appropriation Committees, 196
Appropriations, 196–198
Argentina, 241, 246, 299
Armed Services Committees, 196
Arms control, 24, 200–201, 227
ASAT (anti-satellite) weapons, 89
Asia, 246
Aspin, Les, 60
Assassination, 169–171
    ban of, 161
    British intelligence, 293
    covert action and, 17
    ethical and moral issues, 264–265
    Hitler and, 169b
    Israeli intelligence, 299
    Russian intelligence, 303
    terrorism and, 26–27, 171b
Asset validation system, 94
Assistant Attorney General for National Security, 154
Attorney General, 36, 40
Australia, 75, 89, 133, 139, 146b, 194
Authorization, 196
Authorization bills, 196–197
Automatic change extraction, 84

B

Backscratching, 122
Baker, James, 180
Balkans task force, 124
Baseball fields, 86b
Battle damage assessment (BDA), 249
Bay of Pigs
    covert action during, 17, 166, 171
    failures in, 22, 163
    intelligence analysis of, 169
BDA (battle damage assessment), 249
Bean counting, 223, 234
Belgium, 88
Berlin Wall, 252

bin Laden, Osama, 3b, 26–27, 171b, 236, 239, 264–265
Biological weapons, 239, 242
Blair, Tony, 138, 291
Blake, George, 293
Blowback, 167, 263
Boland, Edward, 199
Bolton, John, 4
Boren, David, 201
Bosnia, 75, 248
Brandt, Willy, 101
Brazil, 88, 241, 258
Britain
    evaluation as threat, 224
    imagery and, 89
    intelligence experience, 12
    Iraq commission, 194
    politicization and, 138
    slavery and, 258
    weaknesses of intelligence analysis, 8
British intelligence
    analysts' options in, 269b
    covert action and, 157
    experience, 12
    foreign intelligence services, 290–294
    imagery and, 89
    influence on national intelligence, 19
    spying and, 146b
British Special Air Services (SAS), 164, 293
British Special Boat Services (SBS), 164, 293
Budget
    classification costs, 74–75
    collections, 69, 181–182
    covert action, 160–161
    defense budget, 42, 60
    hollow budget authority, 197
    intelligence budget, 15, 42, 205–207, 206b, 214
    oversight of, 196–199, 205–207
    post–cold war and, 69
    terrorist attacks (2001) and, 69, 216
Bulgaria, 303
Bureau of Intelligence and Research, State Department. See INR
Burma, 243
Bush, George H. W.
    failure to define national security interests, 232
    policy–intelligence relationship, 188
    politicization of, 39
    Team A–Team B competitive analysis and, 224
    veto of intelligence authorization bill and, 203
Bush, George W.
    on CIA capabilities, 169
    on commercial imagery, 85

consumer–producer relations and, 16
creation of NCTC, 235
creation of WMD Commission, 28,
    194
Executive Order on intelligence, 207
Iraq war and, 257
NSPD and, 57
PDB and, 40
policy–intelligence relationship, 188
relationship with CIA, 179
relationship with Tenet, 27, 39, 178
on requirements, 181
restructuring of DOJ, 154
restructuring of FBI, 154
Scowcroft and, 193
September 11 recommendations, 30,
    217
success of DNI and, 279
Butler, Lord, 138, 194
Butler Report, 194

C

Cabinet members, 40
Cable taps, 89
Cambodia, 258
Canada, 75, 146b
Capabilities vs. intentions, 223–224
Card, Andrew, 40
Carter, Jimmy
    campaign issues, 17, 188
    covert action, 157
    Cuba and, 182b
    Executive Order on intelligence, 207
    politicization and, 39
    SALT II treaty, 138
Casey, William, 43, 161, 188
Castro, Fidel, 22, 166, 170
CDA (Congressional Directed Actions),
    201
Cell phones, 92
Centers, 125–126
Central Intelligence Agency. See CIA
Central Intelligence Group (CIG), 136,
    277
Central Security Service. See CSS
Chamberlain, Neville, 269b
Chatter, 237
Chemical weapons, 239, 242
Cheney, Dick, 138, 186
Chernobyl, 120–121
Chernomyrolin, Viktor, 139
Chiefs of station, 41–42
Chile, 163, 166, 171–172, 270
Chin, Larry Wu-tai, 26, 147, 294–295
China
    Britain and, 88
    commercial imagery and, 89
    espionage by, 151–155, 192, 193,
        294–295
    health and, 246

intelligence capabilities, 294–296
politicized intelligence and, 137–138
spying and, 146b
U.S. reconnaissance plane incident,
    295
Church Committee, 169
CI. See Counterintelligence
CIA (Central Intelligence Agency). See
    also DCI (Director of Central
    Intelligence)
    all-source intelligence and, 135
    Ames spy scandal, 26
    centers, 125–126
    clients of, 31
    competition for resources, 125–126
    continuity of intelligence policy and,
        17
    counterintelligence and, 26, 38
    covert action and, 162
    creation of, 277
    DCIA and, 30
    DHS and, 234–235
    DI (Directorate of Intelligence). See DI
    DO (Directorate of Operations). See
        DO
    espionage, 37, 60
    FBI relationship, 26, 151
    foreign intelligence liaison, 40, 97
    headquarters, 6, 7b
    HUMINT and, 40
    imagery and, 88
    intelligence cycle, 65
    intelligence sharing and, 75
    investigations, 24, 202
    Israeli–Palestinian negotiations and,
        178
    NCTC and, 235
    Open Source Directorate and, 103
    oversight failures and, 209
    paramilitary capabilities and, 169
    paramilitary operations and, 164, 168
    PDB and, 112–113
    personnel practices, 26
    politicized intelligence, 138–139
    polygraphs, use of, 147
    president as client of, 31
    processing and exploitation imbalance,
        72
    redundancy in intelligence community
        and, 14, 283
    reform and, 274
    renditions and, 165
    Senior Analytical Service, 118
    strategic operational planning, 235
    structure of, 16–17
    VENONA intercepts and, 149, 154
CIG (Central Intelligence Group), 136,
    277
Civil liberties, 216, 272
Civil rights, 99, 259

Civil War, 12, 18, 80, 216
Classification system, 73–75, 148–149
Classified Intelligence Procedures Act, 153
Clausewitz, Karl von, 250–251
Clearance system, 148–149
Clemens, Samuel, 141
Clientism, 119
Clientitis, 119
Clinton, Bill
    assassination policy, 171b
    budget and, 214
    DCI and, 38–39, 178, 188
    hostages and, 202
    national security policy, 232–233
    PDD-35 and, 110
    Pollard issue, 298–299
    requirements and, 181
    Torricelli case and, 271
CNA (computer network attack), 249–250
CNE (computer network exploitation), 249–250
Coast Guard, 36
Codebreakers, 90
COI (Coordinator of Information), 12, 19–20
Colby, William, 159
Cold war. See also Post–cold war
    British intelligence, 293
    collapse of Soviet Union, 226–228
    containment policy, 17, 25, 220, 221, 228
    covert action, 17, 158, 165
    defense expenditures, 12
    difficulty of the Soviet target, 18, 221–222
    ends vs. means, 256–257
    espionage, 26, 154–155
    global source of intelligence and, 14, 21
    imagery, 81
    indications and warning, 130
    influence on U.S. intelligence, 13–14
    intelligence implications of containment, 221
    intelligence priorities, 56
    Korea and, 21
    legacy of, 220–231
    moral issues, 256–257
    National Security Act of 1947 and, 20
    open-source intelligence, 101
    OSINT and, 6
    primacy of the Soviet issue, 220–222, 228–230
    Soviet defense spending, 122
    Soviet military capabilities, 222–225
    Soviet strategic forces, 135
    statistical intelligence, 225–226
    technical collection costs, 69

Collection. See also Collection disciplines
    analysis-driven, 77
    budget, 69, 181–182
    capabilities in, 27
    completing priorities, 72–73
    costs of, 104
    counterintelligence, 145
    covert action and, 16–17, 263–264
    denial and deception, 77–78
    ethical and moral issues, 260–266
    of foreign economic intelligence, 244–246
    of information, 54
    intelligence and, 14
    long lead times, 69–70
    opacity of intelligence, 77
    policy and intelligence, 181–182, 182b
    processing and exploitation imbalance, 71–72
    protecting sources and methods, 73–75
    reconnaissance, post–cold war, 78–79
    reform, 280–281
    reliance on technology, 17–18
    requirements and, 59–60
    satellite limitations, 75–76
    stovepipes problem, 76–77, 97
    swarm ball, 73
    synergy, 70–71
    systems development and, 34
    themes in, 68–79
    vacuum cleaner problem, 71
Collection disciplines, 68, 76
    comparison of, 104, 105t
    human intelligence, 94–101
    imagery, 78–79, 80–89
    measurement and signatures intelligence, 93–94
    open-source intelligence, 101–104
    signals intelligence, 89–93
    strengths and weaknesses, 79–104
Colombia, 238, 244
Combest, Larry, 211
COMINT (communications intelligence), 89–92
Commerce Department, 36, 37, 85
Commercial attachés, 37
Commercial imagery, 79, 81–89, 101, 238
Committee on the Intelligence Capabilities of the United States Regarding Weapons of Mass Destruction. See WMD Commission
Communications intelligence (COMINT), 89–92
Compartmented systems, 148, 149
Competition among agencies. See Stovepipes
Competitive analysis, 14–15, 61, 124–126, 135–136, 224
Competitive intelligence exercises, 135

Computer network attack (CNA), 249–250
Computer network exploitation (CNE), 249–250
CONFIDENTIAL classification, 74b
Congress. *See also* Congressional oversight; Intelligence Committees
  covert action and, 160–161
  jurisdiction, 212–213
  leaks, 204–205
  national security policy and, 175
  polygraphs, 147, 204
  select committees, 210
  Torricelli case and, 271–272
Congressional oversight, 195–203
  bipartisan vs. partisan committees, 211–212
  budget, 196–199
  committee turf, 212–213
  competition within the congressional agenda, 216–217
  constitutional mandate for, 196, 205
  co-option, 208–209
  creation of intelligence committees, 24
  executive oversight vs., 196, 214
  extent of oversight, 203–204
  external factors, 216
  hearings, 199–200
  "hostages," 202
  intelligence budget, 205–207
  intelligence judged by Congress, 213–215
  intelligence oversight committees, 24, 210–211
  internal dynamics of, 210–217
  investigations and reports, 202
  issues in, 203–209
  limits of, 25
  nominations, 200
  price of oversight failures, 209
  prior notice of covert action, 203
  regulating the intelligence community, 207–208
  reporting requirements, 201
  role of, 18
  secrecy and, 204–205
  term limits, 211
  treaties, 200–201
"Connecting the dots," 127b
Constitution, U.S., 195–196, 205, 272
Consumer–producer relations, 15–16
Consumption. *See* Dissemination and consumption
Containment, 25, 220, 221, 228
Content analysis, 90
Contras
  analysis of, 16
  covert action and, 160, 167
  funding of, 25
  paramilitary operations and, 163

Reagan administration and, 25, 161, 199
Cooperative analysis, 124–126
Co-option, 208–209, 210
Coordinator of Information (COI), 12, 19–20
Counter Communications System, 89–90
Counterespionage, 26, 36, 38, 149–150, 151
Counterintelligence, 145–156
  Ames spy case, 26
  Attorney General for National Security and, 36
  China, 155
  CIA and, 38
  collection and, 262
  damage assessments, 152–153
  defined, 145
  external indicators and counterespionage, 149–150
  France, 155
  HUMINT and, 97
  India, 155
  internal safeguards, 146–149
  Israel, 155
  Japan, 155
  National Security Division (FBI) and, 37, 38
  problems in, 150–155
  redundancy in, 14
  responsibility for, 154
  Taiwan, 155
  types of, 145
  vetting applicants, 146
  who spies on whom, 146b
Counterintelligence Division, 154
Counterintelligence Enhancement Act, 154
Counterintelligence polygraphs, 147
Counter Surveillance Reconnaissance System (CSRS), 89
Counterterrorism, 36, 41
Counterterrorism Center, 125, 235
Counterterrorism Division, 154
Coups, 21, 163, 171, 229
Cover stories, 95–96
Covert action, 157–173
  analysis and, 16–17
  assassination, 264–265
  assessing, 171–172
  blowback and, 167, 263
  in British intelligence, 19
  budget, 160–161
  in cold war, 158, 165
  collection and, 16–17, 263–264
  Congress and, 160–161, 203
  costs of, 158
  debate over, 17
  decision-making process in, 158–162
  defined, 157

ethical and moral issues, 159–160, 260–266
HUMINT, 260–261
Iran coup and, 21
issues in, 165–170
legislative reaction to, 160
legitimacy of, 164
oversight of, 193
paramilitary operations, 17, 163–164, 167–169, 263–264
plausible deniability, 166, 167, 193
policy and intelligence, 184–185
policy makers and, 157–158, 159, 167, 184–185
in post–cold war, 158
presidential approval for, 160–161
prior notice for Congress, 203
rationale for, 157–158
risks of, 159
SIGINT and, 247
types of activities, 162–165
Cox Committee, 151, 154, 295
"Crateology," 81
Crisis mode, 113–114
Cryptographers, 90
CSRS (Counter Surveillance Reconnaissance System), 89
CSS (Central Security Service), 38
Cuba. *See also* Bay of Pigs
    Cuban missile crisis, 22, 70–71, 86b, 182b, 229
    Lourdes facility, 302
    Soviet defense spending, 122
Currency issues, 246
Current intelligence, 61, 111–112
"Cyberattacks," 238
Czechoslovakia, 228, 303

D

Damage assessment, 152–153, 249
Dangles, 96
DBA (dominant battlefield awareness), 250–252
DCI (Director of Central Intelligence). *See also* DNI (Director of National Intelligence)
    creation of COI and OSS, 19
    National Security Act and, 20–21
    nominations for, 200
    partisan politics and, 188–189
    as principal intelligence advisor to president, 30
    on proliferation of nuclear weapons, 72
    reform and, 277–279
    relationship with Congress, 43
    replacement by DNI (Director of National Intelligence), 28, 30, 38
    role of, 277–279
    stovepipes problem and, 76

DCIA (Director of Central Intelligence Agency), 40, 41–42, 162, 277
DCs (Deputies Committees), 40, 41, 176
Deception, 77–78, 94, 97–98, 240
DeConcini, Dennis, 43
Defense budget and expenditures, 12, 42, 60
Defense Department. *See* DOD
Defense Intelligence Agency. *See* DIA
Defense Investigative Service, 154
Defensive counterintelligence, 145
Democratic policies, 17, 139, 217
Denial and deception, 77–78, 240
Denied areas, 102
Denied targets, 79
Department. *See specific department name*
Deputies Committees (DCs), 40, 41, 176
Deputy Director of National Intelligence (DNI), 40, 113
Deutch, John, 43, 99, 250, 259, 271
Deutch rules, 99, 259
DHS (Department of Homeland Security), 36, 37, 43, 175, 234–235, 238
DI (Directorate of Intelligence)
    CIA, 14, 16–17, 37, 124, 193
    DO and, 194
DIA (Defense Intelligence Agency)
    all-source intelligence and, 124
    collection and, 37
    competitive analysis and, 135
    Congress and, 44
    Directorate of Intelligence (DI) and, 124
    DOD and, 31
    foreign intelligence liaison, 97
    MASINT and, 94
    MID and, 63
    politicized intelligence and, 22
    polygraphs, 147
    redundancies and, 14, 283
    secretary of defense and, 42
DIA/Humint (Defense HUMINT Service), 37, 94, 280
Directorate of Information Assurance, 37
Directorate of Operations. *See* DO
Directorate of Science and Technology (DS&T), 37
Director of Central Intelligence. *See* DCI
Director of Central Intelligence Agency. *See* DCIA
Director of National Intelligence. *See* DNI
Dissemination and consumption, 54, 62–64
    TPEDs, 61, 69, 280
Dissent channels, 135
"Distance" school, 15, 16–17
DNI (Director of National Intelligence)
    all-source intelligence, 70
    alternative analysis and, 132
    budgets and, 32–34

congressional relationships, 43, 213
covert action and, 162
creation of, 11, 28, 30
estimates and, 133–134
intelligence community relationships, 38–43
JICC and, 36
National Security Council and, 175–176
National Security Service and, 154
NCTC and, 125, 235
NGA and, 44
NIC and, 37, 63
NSA and, 44
Open Source Directorate and, 103
PDB and, 62, 113
politicization and, 137
president and, 38–43
priorities and, 57
reform and, 277–279
relationships, 38–43, 179
role of, 277–279
selection of, 189
staffing centers and, 126
stovepipes and, 76, 97
DO (Directorate of Operations)
analysis and, 16–17
counterespionage and, 38
counterintelligence and, 38
covert operations and, 193
DI and, 194
HUMINT and, 94
stovepipes and, 280
DOD (Department of Defense)
airborne systems, 36–37, 80
on DBA, 251
imagery and, 87–89
in intelligence community, 31, 32, 42, 252
Joint Vision reports, 251
in national security policy, 174, 175
NGA and, 76
NSA and, 76
paramilitary operations, 168
processing and exploitation imbalance, 71
reform and, 277–278
role of, 36
secretary of defense, 31, 32, 40, 42, 43, 277
DOE (Department of Energy), 36, 152, 193
Domestic intelligence, 6, 27, 234, 243–244
Dominant battlefield awareness (DBA), 250–252
Donovan, William, 19
Double agents, 145, 153
Downstream activities, 60–61
Drones, 37, 80, 86

Drugs. *See also* Narcotics
legalization, 244
Duelfer, Charles, 194–195
Dulles, Allen, 21, 41, 158, 169
Dulles, John Foster, 41
Duty to warn, 130

E

East Africa, 3b, 171b
East Asia, 246
East Germany, 100–101, 259–260, 303
Ebola virus, 246
ECHELON, 245, 297
Echo, 102–103, 246
Economic counterintelligence, 297
Economic espionage, 244–246, 297
Economics, 244–246
Economic unrest, 162, 166
Eden, Anthony, 269b
Egypt, 165, 298, 300
Eichmann, Adolf, 299
Eisenhower, Dwight D., 21–22, 75, 158, 165, 166
Elections involvement, 257, 259
Electronic intelligence. *See* ELINT
Electronic news media, 189
Electro-optical (EO) systems, 80
ELINT (electronic intelligence), 89–90, 93
Ellsberg, Daniel, 200
Embassies, 36, 37, 41
Encapsulation, 91
Encryption, 90
Ends vs. means, 257, 265–266
Energy Department (DOE), 36, 152, 193
Entrapment, 96
Environment and health, 246–247
EO (electro-optical) systems, 80
Espionage. *See also* HUMINT (Human Intelligence)
Ames case. *See* Ames, Aldrich
Chinese, 153–155, 192–193, 294–295
CIA and, 37, 60
in cold war, 154–155
counterespionage. *See* Counterespionage
economic espionage, 244–246, 297
Hanssen case. *See* Hanssen, Robert
oversight, 192
in post–cold war, 154–155
purpose of, 148b
Estimates, 121–122, 133–134
national intelligence estimates. *See* NIEs
predictions vs., 133
Ethical and moral issues, 255–273
analysis issues, 266–270
assassination, 264–265
changes in ethics and morals, 258–260
collection issues, 260–266

covert action issues, 159–160,
    263–264
ends vs. means, 257, 265–266
general moral questions, 255–260
Helms dilemma, 270–271
human intelligence and, 99, 237,
    260–261
media and, 272–273
national interest, 258
nature of the opponent, 257
operational ethics, 266
oversight issues, 270–272
renditions and torture, 265–266
secrecy, 255–256
Torricelli case, 271–272
war and peace, 256–257
EU (European Union), 5, 297
Executive branch
    hearings and, 199–200
    leaks, 204
    oversight, 191–195, 214
    reporting requirements for, 201
Executive orders, 207, 277
Expertise, 2–3, 283
Exploitation. *See* Processing and
    exploitation
Extraterritorial actions, 164

F

False hostages, 122
Family Jewels report, 274
FBI (Federal Bureau of Investigation). *See
    also* Hanssen, Robert
    business intelligence, 246
    CIA relationship, 26, 151, 234–235
    counterintelligence and, 38
    DHS and, 234–235
    director, 39, 40
    Hanssen spy case, 26, 147
    in intelligence community, 13, 31, 38,
        39
    Intelligence Directorate, 37
    Israel, 299
    Lee case, 151–152, 294–295
    National Security Division, 37, 38,
        153–154
    National Security Service, 36, 154
    polygraphs, use of, 147
    restructuring and, 154
FBIS (Foreign Broadcast Information
    Service), 103
Federal Bureau of Investigation. *See* FBI
Feedback, 54–55, 64
First Amendment, 272
FISA (Foreign Intelligence Surveillance
    Act of 1978), 93, 153
Flood report, 194
"Fog of war," 250–251
Footnote wars, 62, 123
Force, 256–257

Ford, Gerald R., 122, 170, 207
Foreign Broadcast Information Service
    (FBIS), 103
Foreign economic counterintelligence,
    245
Foreign economic espionage, 244–246,
    297
Foreign economic intelligence, 244–246
Foreign intelligence services, 290–303
    Britain, 290–294
    China, 294–296
    France, 296–297
    Israel, 298–300
    Russia, 300–303
Foreign Intelligence Surveillance Act of
    1978 (FISA), 93, 153
Foreign Intelligence Surveillance Court,
    153
Foreign liaison relationships, 96–97
Foreign nationals, recruiting, 94, 96,
    98–99
Foreign policy, 12. *See also specific
    presidents*
    threat-based, 13
    U.S. activism abroad, 217
Foreign Service, 37, 41, 138, 175
France, 12, 88, 146b, 162, 296–297
Freedom of Information Act, 205
Freeh, Louis, 40
French Ministry of Defense, 85
Fuchs, Klaus, 149
Fusion intelligence. *See* All-source
    intelligence

G

Gang of 4, 204
Gang of 8, 204
Gates, Robert
    on cold war, 14, 233
    on foreign economic intelligence, 245
    politicized intelligence and, 138, 200
    transnational issues and, 124
GEOINT (geospacial intelligence), 37, 80
Geosynchronous orbit, 76
Germany
    East Germany, 100–101, 259–260, 303
    imagery satellites and, 88
    Nazi Germany, 13, 19, 169b, 269b
    SIGINT and, 89
    threat-based foreign policy and, 13
    West Germany, 100–101, 259–260
Gifted analysts, 117
Global Hawk (UAV), 86, 89
Glomar Explorer, 272
Goldwater-Nichols Act of 1986, 126
"Gone native," 119
Good intelligence, 140–141
Gorbachev, Mikhail, 227–228, 229, 301
Gore, Al, 139
Goss, Porter J., 16

Government Communications
    Headquarters, 93
Grant, Ulysses S., 251
Graymail, 153
Great Britain. See Britain
Greenpeace, 297
Groupthink, 15, 28, 61, 123, 240
Guatemala, 21, 99, 159, 163, 271
Guillaume, Gunter, 100–101
Gulf War, 242b, 248–249
Guzmacan, Jacobo Arbenz, 21

H

Hale, Nathan, 94
Halperin, Morton, 202
Hanssen, Robert, 26
    damage assessment, 153, 209
    detection of, 149, 151
    HUMINT and, 100
    polygraphs and, 147
    Russian intelligence and, 230, 301
    as walk-in, 96
Hariri, Rafik, 265
Hawks and doves, 118
Hayden, Michael, 31, 42, 285
Health and environment, 246–247
Hearings, 199–200
Helms, Richard
    on DCI authority, 38
    on HUMINT sources, 98–99
    on intelligence community, 11
    on OSS, 19
    oversight issues and, 270–271
    on plausible deniability, 166
Hiss, Alger, 149, 154
Historical developments, 19–28
Hitler, Adolf, 6, 169b, 264, 299
Hollis, Roger, 293
Hollow budget authority, 197
Homeland Security Council (HSC), 30
Homeland Security Department. See DHS
Hoover, J. Edgar, 151
"Hostages," 202
House Appropriations Committee, 196
House Armed Services Committee, 44, 60
House Intelligence Committee
    committee turf and, 213
    intelligence budget and, 196, 199
    on NIEs, 135
    recommendations of, 126
    relationship with DCI, 43
    Torricelli case and, 271
Howard, Edward, 152
HSC (Homeland Security Council), 30
HSI (hyperspectral imagery), 80, 93
Hughes, Thomas, 127b
Hughes Aircraft, 297
Hughes Corporation, 272
Human intelligence. See HUMINT

Human rights, 99, 259
HUMINT (Human Intelligence). See also
    Espionage
    CIA responsibilities for, 37, 40, 42
    costs of, 97
    counterintelligence and, 151
    DBA and, 250
    deception and, 97–98
    DIA/Humint Service, 94
    ethical and moral issues, 99, 237,
        260–261
    Iraq WMD issues, 240
    reliance on technology and, 18
    security clearances and, 148–149
    stovepipes and, 76
    supporting use of, 27
HUMINT-to-HUMINT relationships,
    96–97
    reform, 279
    strengths and weaknesses, 94–101
    technical collection and, 18
    terrorism and, 97, 237, 261
Humor, 102b, 197b
Hunter, Duncan, 213
Hussein, Saddam, 27–28, 165, 195, 264
Hyperspectral imagery (HSI), 80, 93

I

IAEA (International Agency for Atomic
    Energy), 262
I&W (indications and warning), 237
Idealism, 257
IKONOS satellite, 79, 84–85
IMINT (Imagery intelligence). See also
    Satellites
    advantages of, 84
    commercial vendors, 79, 81, 84–85,
        88–89
    DBA and, 250
    NGA and, 37
    as OSINT, 101
    proliferation of, 88–89
    SIGINT and, 89
    signals intelligence vs., 91b
    stovepipes and, 76, 279
    strengths and weaknesses, 80–89
    terrorism and, 238
Immigrant population, 217
India, 73, 88, 99, 239, 299
Indications and warning, 90, 130–131, 237
Indonesia, 169, 246
Industrial espionage, 244
Information
    intelligence vs., 1–2
    leaks, 204, 271–272
    limited information in analysis,
        127–128
    maintaining secrecy of, 4–5, 6
    open information, 6

Information operations, 248–250
Information technology, 284–286
Infrared imagery (IR), 80
INF (Intermediate Nuclear Forces) Treaty,
    184b, 201, 202, 227
INR (Bureau of Intelligence and Research,
    State Dept.)
    all-source intelligence, 37, 124, 135
    in intelligence community, 31, 36
    politicized intelligence and, 137
    redundancies and, 14
    SMS and, 63
Intelligence, 1–2, 5–9, 68
    absence of, 128
    accuracy of, 140–141
    budget, 32, 42
    defined, 1–10, 9b
    development of, 11–28
    global scope of intelligence interests, 14
    historical developments, 19–28
    information vs., 1–2
    novelty of, 13
    opacity of, 77
    as organization, 9
    other government functions vs., 1
    partisan use of, 139
    policy process and, 4
    policy vs., 5b, 7
    politicized, 4, 15, 21, 117, 136–139, 178
    as process, 9
    as product, 9
    public support of, 43
    redundant analytical structure, 14–15
    statistical, 225–226
    tailored, 140
    themes in, 13–18
    truth and, 6–7
    uses of, 186–187
    value-added, 109–110, 283
    weaknesses of, 7–9
Intelligence agencies
    long-term expertise of, 2–3, 283
    purposes of, 2–5
    secrecy functions of, 4–5
    strategic surprise and, 2–3
    as support for policy process, 4
Intelligence agenda, 232–254
    dominant battlefield awareness,
        250–252
    economics, 244–246
    health and environment, 246–247
    information operations, 248–250
    intelligence and new priorities, 236–252
    narcotics, 243–244
    national security policy, post–cold war,
        232–236
    peacekeeping operations, 248
    proliferation, 239–243
    terrorism, 236–239

Intelligence Committees
    analysis and, 125
    budget and, 69
    covert action and, 160–161
    in intelligence community, 43
    oversight and, 204, 209, 210, 211
    term limits, 211
Intelligence community, 1, 11, 30–52
    alternative views of, 33–34, 34f
    communication with policy
        community, 64
    different intelligence communities,
        34–38
    effects of technology on, 18
    evaluation function, 33–34
    goals of, 176–177
    market-based, 286–287
    organizational view of, 32f
    policy interests, 176
    regulating, 207–208
    relationships, 38–48
Intelligence Community Whistleblower
    Act of 1998, 272
Intelligence Directorate (FBI), 37,
    153–154, 234
Intelligence failures, 99, 113–114
Intelligence policy, 36
Intelligence process, 54–67
    analysis and production, 61–62
    CIA view and, 65f
    collection, 59–60
    conceptualized, 65–66
    defined, 54
    dissemination and consumption,
        62–64
    feedback, 54–55, 64
    phases of, 54
    processing and exploitation, 60–61
    requirements, 55–59
Intelligence products, 9, 62–64, 109
Intelligence reform. See Reform
Intelligence Reform & Terrorism
    Prevention Act of 2004, 207
Intelligence reorganization, 28
Intentions vs. capabilities, 223–224
Interagency process, 176
Intercepts, 90
Intermediate Nuclear Forces Treaty. See
    INF Treaty
International law, 168
Internet, 101
Investigations, 24, 202
Investigative journalism, 272–273
IR (infrared imagery), 80
IRA (Irish Republican Army), 238, 291,
    293
Iran
    collection and, 182b, 262
    coup, 21, 99, 163, 171

Hezbollah and, 88
history of intelligence in, 25
Kurds and, 168
mirror imaging and, 118
missile sales to, 25
proliferation and, 241
UAVs and, 88
Iran-contra affair, 161, 199, 200
Iraq
    alternative analysis and, 132–133
    "connecting the dots" and, 127b
    executive oversight and, 195
    groupthink and, 15, 123
    hearings, 199
    HUMINT and, 98
    imagery and, 88
    information operations and, 248
    investigations, 202
    ISG (Iraq Survey Group) and, 194
    Kurds and, 168
    Kuwait and, 180
    layering and, 119
    limited intelligence and, 128
    NIEs and, 214
    nuclear program and, 242b
    politicization and, 138
    politicized intelligence and, 39
    proliferation and, 239–240
    protecting sources and, 75
    WMD, 262, 276, 281
Iraq Liberation Act of 1998, 165, 258
Iraq War, 135
Irish Republican Army (IRA), 238, 291, 293
ISG (Iraq Survey Group), 194
ISR (intelligence, surveillance, reconnaissance), 68
Israel
    assassination and, 169
    collection and, 79, 88, 101, 146b
    intelligence, 298–300
    Iran and, 161
    Israeli–Palestinian negotiations, 178
    Madrid conference and, 180
    nuclear weapons, 242b, 299–300
    strategic surprise and, 2
    terrorism and, 300
Italy, 19, 88, 162, 165
IT revolution, 284–286

J

Jaded approach, 120–121
Japan
    mirror imaging and, 8, 118
    nuclear programs and, 241
    Pearl Harbor. See Pearl Harbor
    SIGINT and, 89
    strategic surprise and, 2
JCS (Joint Chiefs of Staff), 126, 174, 213
Jeremiah, David, 72–73

JICC (Joint Intelligence Community Council), 36, 192
JMIP (Joint Military Intelligence Program), 31
John Paul II (pope), 303
Johnson, Lyndon B., 23, 38, 186
Joint Chiefs of Staff (JCS), 126, 174, 213
Joint Intelligence Community Council. See JICC
Joint Military Intelligence Program (JMIP), 31
Joint Vision 2010 (DOD), 251
Joint Vision 2020 (DOD), 251
Journalism, 96, 272–273, 276. See also Media
Justice Department, 36, 151, 152, 154, 270

K

Kampiles, 100
Kennan, George, 25, 220, 228
Kennedy, John F., 21, 22–23, 38, 166, 229
Kerry, John, 17
Key judgments (KJs), 135
Key-word search, 91, 245
KGB, 6, 300–302
Khan, A.Q., 240–241, 243
Khomeini, Ruhollah, 25, 171
Khrushchev, Nikita, 23, 70–71, 75
Kidnapping, 299
Kissinger, Henry, 160
KJs (key judgments), 135
Korea
    demilitarized zone (DMZ), 73
    history of intelligence in, 21
    North Korea, 241
    South Korea, 21, 89, 246
Korean War, 21, 163, 220
Kosovo, 103
Kuklinski, Ryszard, 260
Kurds, 168
Kuwait, 180, 264

L

Lake, Anthony, 200
LANDSAT, 79
Lavon, Pinhas, 298
Lavon affair, 298
Law enforcement, 6, 27, 234, 243–244
Leaks, 204, 271–272
Lebanon, 265
Lee, Wen Ho, 151–152, 294–295
Legal attachés, 37
Legalization of drugs, 244
Libya, 241
Lifestyle polygraphs, 147
Lincoln, Abraham, 216
Lindh, John Walker, 237
Lobbyists, 216
Logrolling, 122

Long-term intelligence, 61, 111–112
"Loose nukes," 239, 241, 303
Los Alamos National Laboratory, 151, 295
Lourdes, Cuba, 302
Lowest-common-denominator language,
    123

M

MAD (mutual assured destruction),
    224–225
Madrid conference, 180
MAGIC, 20
Malaysia, 89, 246
"Market based" intelligence community,
    286–287
Markov, Georgi, 303
MASINT (measurement and signatures
    intelligence), 76, 80, 93–94, 101,
    279
Maskirovka, 222
Mata Hari, 94
May, Ernest R., 138, 160
McCone, John, 23, 38, 186
McLaughlin, John, 278
McNamara, Robert, 22
Measurement and signatures intelligence.
    See MASINT
Media
    blowback and, 167, 263
    ethical and moral issues, 272
    freedom of the press, 272
    investigative journalism, 272
    journalism, 96, 276
    public opinion and, 43
Metaphors, 127b
Methods, protection of, 4–5, 73–75
Mexico, 89, 246
Meyers, Richard, 213
Microsatellites, 87–88
MID (Military Intelligence Digest), 63
Middle East, 180
Military information, 6
Military intelligence, 130
Military Intelligence Digest (MID), 63
Military operations
    development of intelligence and, 13
    paramilitary operations, 17, 163–164,
        167–169, 263–264
    support to (SMO), 250–252
    war on terrorism and, 238
Mirror imaging, 8, 20, 118–119, 225,
    242b
"Misses," 113–114
Missile gap, 21–22, 139
Mole, 151
Monitoring, 24
Monroe Doctrine, 12, 13
Montes, Ana, 155
Moral issues. See Ethical and moral issues
Mossadegh, Mohammad, 21, 171

Moynihan, Daniel Patrick, 212
MSI (multispectral imagery), 80, 93
Mujaheddin, 159, 167, 171, 228, 263, 295
Multispectral imagery (MSI), 80, 93
Munich Olympics, 300
Mutual assured destruction (MAD),
    224–225
Myanmar, 243

N

Nanosatellites, 88
Narcotics, 184b, 243–244, 263
NASA (National Aeronautics and Space
    Administration), 36
Nasr, Osama Moustafa Hassan, 165
National Aeronautics and Space
    Administration (NASA), 36
National Commission on Terrorist
    Attacks. See 9/11 Commission
National Counterintelligence Executive
    (NCIX), 31, 38
National Counterproliferation Center. See
    NCPC
National Counterterrorism Center. See
    NCTC
National Defense University, 250
National Foreign Intelligence Program
    (NFIP), 31
National Geospatial-Intelligence Agency.
    See NGA
National Imagery and Mapping Agency
    (NIMA). See NGA; NIMA
National intelligence, 12, 30, 40, 43
National Intelligence Council. See NIC
National Intelligence Daily, 62
National intelligence estimates. See NIEs
National intelligence officers. See NIOs
National Intelligence Priorities
    Framework (NIPF), 236
National Intelligence Program (NIP), 31,
    33
National Intelligence Security Reform Act
    of 2004, 28, 30
National interest, 258
National Reconnaissance Office. See NRO
National security
    civil liberties and, 216
    Congress and, 175
    DOD and, 174, 175
    policy development and, 174–177
    post–cold war policy and, 232–236
    president and, 174, 175
    State Department and, 174, 175
National Security Act of 1947, 20–21
    covert action defined in, 157
    DCI responsibilities and, 270, 277–278
    intelligence community structure, 175
    NIC, role of, 214–215
National Security Advisor, 176
National Security Agency. See NSA

National Security Council. *See* NSC
National Security Division (FBI), 37, 38, 153–154
National Security Policy Directive. *See* NSPD
National Security Service, 36, 238
National Security Threat List, 154
National Technical Means (NTM), 24
NATO (North Atlantic Treaty Organization)
  capabilities vs. intentions, 224
  EU separation from, 297
  imagery and, 88
  indications and warning, 130
  OSINT and, 102, 103
  peacekeeping operations and, 248
  protecting sources and, 75
Nazi Germany, 13, 19, 169b, 269b
NCIX (National Counterintelligence Executive), 31, 38, 154
NCPC (National Counterproliferation Center), 282
NCTC (National Counterterrorism Center)
  competition for resources and, 125
  creation of, 30, 281
  DNI and, 37, 39, 41, 42, 277
  relationship with CIA, 235
  as replacement for TTIC, 235
  terrorist attacks and, 238
Needs
  maintaining secrecy of, 4–5
  of policy makers, 14
Need to know, 74b, 148
Negation search, 84
Negroponte, John, 31, 41, 278–279
Netanyahu, Benjamin, 299
Neustadt, Richard, 160
New world order, 232
New Zealand, 299
NFIP (National Foreign Intelligence Program), 31
NGA (National Geospatial-Intelligence Agency)
  commercial imagery and, 85
  DBA and, 252
  DOD control of, 31, 33
  foreign intelligence liaison, 97
  Geocell and, 89
  GEOINT and, 80
  IKONOS satellite and, 84
  IMINT and, 37
  MASINT responsibility and, 94
  secretary of defense control of, 42, 76
  stovepipes and, 279–280
  war on terrorism and, 88
NIC (National Intelligence Council), 30–31, 37, 39, 40, 63, 214–215
Nicaragua, 160, 164. *See also* Contras
  Corinto, 212

NIEs (national intelligence estimates), 63–64
  alternative analysis and, 132
  as bargaining tactic, 202
  cooperation of intelligence agencies and, 123–124
  Korea and, 21
  leaks of, 135
  NIOs production of, 126
  Senate Intelligence Committee and, 214–215
Nigeria, 89
NIMA (National Imagery and Mapping Agency), 80, 84. *See also* NGA (National Geospatial-Intelligence Agency)
9/11 Commission
  committee turf and, 213
  creation of NCTC and, 235
  as election issue, 17
  intelligence budgets and, 197
  intelligence reorganization and, 28, 30, 125, 169, 281
  technology and, 285
NIOs (national intelligence officers), 37, 40, 63, 126, 133–134
NIP (National Intelligence Program), 31, 33
NIPF (National Intelligence Priorities Framework), 57, 58, 62
Nitze, Paul, 220
Nixon, Richard M., 175, 188, 270, 295
NOC (nonofficial cover), 95
Noise to signals ratio, 71, 91
Nominations, 200
Nonofficial cover, 95, 297
Nonproliferation policy, 239
Nonstate actors, 6, 78
North, Oliver, 161
North Atlantic Treaty Organization. *See* NATO
Northern Alliance, 164
North Korea, 241
Norway, 303
No year appropriations, 198
NRO (National Reconnaissance Office), 33, 36, 80, 89, 147
NSA (National Security Agency)
  Central Security Service and, 38
  DBA and, 252
  ECHELON and, 245
  foreign intelligence liaisons and, 97
  imagery and, 88
  IMINT and, 91b
  intelligence budget and, 33
  polygraphs and, 147
  processing and exploitation imbalance and, 71
  secretary of defense and, 42
  SIGINT and, 20, 37, 89, 93

stovepipes and, 279–280
VENONA and, 149
within intelligence community, 44, 76
NSC (National Security Council)
    assassination and, 171b
    as client of CIA, 31
    Deputies Committees (DCs) and, 40
    executive oversight by, 191–192
    intelligence priorities set by, 57, 58
    members of, 175–176
    policy priorities set by, 57
    Principals Committees (PCs) and, 40
    Reagan administration and, 161
    structure of, 175–176
NSPD (National Security Policy
    Directive), 57, 235
NTM (National Technical Means), 24
Nuccio, Richard, 271
Nuclear tests, 75, 297
Nuclear weapons
    China and, 146b
    India's nuclear test, 73, 99
    INF Treaty, 184b, 201, 202
    Israel, 241, 299–300
    Lee, Wen Ho and, 152
    mutual assured destruction (MAD),
        224–225
    proliferation, 73, 88, 239–243

O

Objectivity, 116, 137, 140–141, 177, 178,
    193
ODNI (Office of the Director of National
    Intelligence), 42, 113
Offensive counterintelligence, 145
Office of Intelligence and Analysis (DHS),
    36, 234
Office of Intelligence Programs (NSC), 192
Office of Management & Budget (OMB),
    198
Office of National Counterintelligence
    Executive (NCIX), 154
Office of Strategic Services (OSS), 12,
    19–20
Office of the Director of National
    Intelligence (ODNI), 42
Office of the Secretary of Defense (OSD),
    42
Official cover, 95–96
Olympics, 300
OMB (Office of Management & Budget),
    198
"On the ground knowledge," 119–123
Open information, 6
Openness vs. secrecy, 18
Open-source intelligence. See OSINT
Operational ethics, 266
Operation Iraqi Freedom, 27–28, 75
Operations and maintenance, 60
Opportunity analysis, 131

OSD (Office of the Secretary of Defense),
    42
OSINT (open-source intelligence), 76, 79,
    100, 101–104, 247, 280
OSS (Office of Strategic Services), 12, 13,
    19–20
Ostpolitik, 101
Oversight and accountability, 191–219.
    See also Congressional oversight
    definitions of, 192b
    ethical and moral issues, 270–272
    executive oversight issues, 191–195
    role of, 18

P

Pakistan, 238, 239, 240–241
P&E. See Processing and exploitation
Paramilitary operations, 17, 163–164,
    167–169, 238, 263–264
Partisan politics, 139, 188–189, 211–212,
    214
PATRIOT Act of 2001, 27
Patton, George S., 78
PCs (Principals Committees), 40, 41, 176
PDB (president's daily briefing), 40, 41,
    62, 112–113
PDD-35 (Presidential Decision Directive),
    110
Peace, 256–257
Peace Corps, 96
Peacekeeping operations, 248
Pearl Harbor, 3b, 6, 13, 20, 130
Pearl Harbor: Warning and Decision
    (Wohlstetter), 71
Pelton, Ronald, 26, 100
Penetration, 149–150
Penkovsky, Oleg, 71, 96, 98, 223, 256, 301
Pentagon Papers, 200
Persian Gulf War, 195, 242b, 248–249
PFIAB (President's Foreign Intelligence
    Advisory Board), 192, 224
Philby, Kim, 151, 293
Philippines, 246
Photo intelligence (PHOTINT). See
    IMINT (Imagery intelligence)
Photo interpreters, 86b
Pinochet, Augusto, 171
PIOB (President's Intelligence Oversight
    Board), 194
Plausible deniability, 166, 168, 193
Plumbing, 158
Poland, 169b, 260, 303
Policy, 180–189
    continuity of intelligence policy, 17
    foreign policy, 12, 13, 217
    intelligence vs., 5b, 7
    national security policy, 174–177
    relationship with intelligence, 2,
        15–16, 187–189, 286–287
    supporting the process, 4

Policy makers, 174–190
    behaviors of, 185–186
    competitive analysis and, 135–136
    covert action and, 157–158, 159, 167,
        184–185
    intelligence process and, 180–189
        analysis, 183–184
        collection, 181–182
        covert action, 184–185
        other issues, 187–189
        policy maker behaviors, 185–186
        requirements, 180–181
    intelligence process tensions, 187–189
    national security process and,
        174–177
    needs of, 14
    politicized intelligence and, 136–139
    who wants what, 177–180
Political activity, 162
Political appointees, 3
Political winners and losers, 137
Politicized intelligence
    analysis and, 136–139
    analysts and, 117
    consumer–producer relations and, 15
    Iraq WMD and, 28, 39, 178, 194
    missile gap and, 22
    policy makers and, 4
    Vietnam War and, 23
Pollard, Jonathan, 101, 298–299
Polygraphs, 146–147
Portugal, 259
Post–cold war
    budget and, 69
    collection, 78–79
    covert action, 158
    espionage, 154–155
    intelligence priorities and, 236
    national security policy, 232–236
    protecting sources, 75
    reconnaissance in, 78–79
    weapons proliferation, 289
Potemkin, Grigory, 222
"Potemkin villages," 222
Powell, Colin, 127, 175
Powers, Francis Gary, 256, 299
Predator (UAV), 86
Predictions vs. estimates, 133
President, 36, 58. See also Executive
        branch; specific presidents
    approval for covert action, 160
    as client of CIA, 31
    executive orders, 207, 277
    in national security policy, 174, 175
    reporting requirements, 201
Presidential Decision Directive 35 (PDD-
        35), 110
Presidential findings, 160, 193
President's daily briefing (PDB), 40, 41,
        62, 112–113

President's Foreign Intelligence Advisory
        Board (PFIAB), 192
President's Intelligence Oversight Board
        (PIOB), 194
Press. See Media
Prime, Geoffrey, 293
Principals Committees (PCs), 40, 41, 76
Priorities, 54, 72–73, 110–111, 236–252
Priority creep, 58
Processing and exploitation, 54–55, 60–61
    collection vs., 61
    costs of, 69
    imbalance, 71–72
    TPEDs, 61, 69, 280
Procurement, 60
Production and analysis, 61–62. See also
        Analysis
Proliferation, 72, 89, 239–243
Propaganda, 162, 263
"Proximate" school, 15, 16–17
Public's right to know, 205, 272
Putin, Vladimir, 302

R

Raison d'etat, 258
Reagan, Ronald
    budget, 214
    campaign issues, 17, 188
    covert action and, 157, 159, 167, 170
    DCI and, 138, 188
    Executive Order on intelligence, 207
    INF Treaty and, 184b
    Iran-contra affair and, 25, 161, 167
    Strategic Defense Initiative and, 228
    treaties, 138, 201
Reagan Doctrine, 228
Realpolitik, 257
"Real time" intelligence, 27, 86, 250–251
Reconnaissance. See also UAVs
        (unmanned aerial vehicles)
    collection and, 68
    denial and deception, 77–78
    in post–cold war period, 78–79
Recruiting, 94–95, 96, 98–99
Red teams, 135
Redundancy, 14–15, 283
Reform, 274–289
    administrative reform, 286
    analysis, 283
    collection, 280–281
    DCI role, 277–279
    DNI and, 277–279
    DOD and, 277–278
    human intelligence, 279
    issues in, 276–287
    IT revolution and, 284–286
    purpose of, 274–276
    stovepipes, 279–283
Renditions and torture, 164–165, 234,
        265–266

Reno, Janet, 40
Reporting requirements, 201
Republican policies, 17, 139, 217
Requirements, 33–34, 54, 55–59
  crises-driven, 113–114
  formal requirements in analysis,
    110–111
  policy and intelligence, 180–181
  reporting requirements, 201
Resolution, 80–81
Resources, 57
Right to know, 205, 272
Risk vs. take, 92
RMA (Revolution in Military Affairs), 251
Roberts, Pat, 213
Rockefeller, Nelson, 24
Roosevelt, Franklin D., 19
Rosenberg, Julius, 149, 154, 256
Rumsfeld, Donald H., 43, 87, 168, 213, 214
Rusk, Dean, 182b
Russia. See also Soviet Union
  Ames spy case, 26
  Hanssen spy case, 26
  OSINT and, 102
  protecting sources and methods and,
    75
  spying and, 146b
  strategic surprise and, 2
Russian intelligence, 12, 300–303

S

SALT I, 24
SALT II, 138
Saltonstall, Leverett, 203, 209
SAMs (surface-to-air missiles), 86
Sandinistas, 163
SARS (Severe Acute Respiratory
  Syndrome), 246
SAS (British Special Air Services), 164,
  293
Satellites, 69, 72, 75–76, 79, 81–89. See
  also IMINT (imagery intelligence)
SBS (British Special Boat Services), 164,
  293
Schlesinger, James, 274
SCIFs (sensitive compartmented
  information facilities), 149
Scottish law, 152
Scowcroft, Brent, 192–193
Scrub, 99
SDI (Strategic Defense Initiative), 228
Secrecy
  congressional oversight and, 204–205
  costs of, 256
  ethical and moral issues, 255–256
  intelligence and, 1, 43
  maintaining, 4–5
  necessity of, 255–256
  openness vs., 18
  oversight process and, 204–205

pursuit of secret information, 6
  security classifications, 74b
  security clearances, 204
Secretary of Commerce, 36, 85
Secretary of Defense (DOD), 31–32
  commercial imagery and, 85
  intelligence budget and, 277
  as intelligence client, 36
  National Security Act of 1947 and, 21
  PC (principal committee) and, 40
  processing and exploitation, 60
  relationship within intelligence
    community, 42–44
  stovepipes and, 76
  UAVs and, 87
Secretary of Energy, 36
Secretary of State, 36, 40, 41, 85, 127
Secretary's Morning Summary (SMS), 63
SECRET classification, 74b
Secret information, 6
Secret participation in combat, 164
Security classifications, 74b
Security clearances, 204
SEIB (senior executive intelligence brief),
  62–63
Senate, 200–201
Senate Appropriations Committee, 196
Senate Armed Services Committee, 44,
  212, 213, 270–271
Senate Foreign Relations Subcommittee
  on Multinational Corporations, 270
Senate Governmental Affairs Committee
  (SGAC), 213
Senate Intelligence Committee
  bipartisan/partisan committees and,
    211–212
  committee turf and, 212–213
  groupthink, 28, 123, 240
  Iraq WMD and, 39, 214
  layering, 119
  politicized intelligence, 138, 178, 186
  term limits and, 211
Senior Analytical Service, 118
Senior Executive Intelligence Brief (SEIB),
  62–63
Sensitive compartmented information
  facilities (SCIFs), 149
September 11 Terrorist Attacks, 127b,
  194, 238, 239, 276, 281. See also
  Terrorist attacks (2001)
Serbia, 103
Severe Acute Respiratory Syndrome
  (SARS), 246
SGAC (Senate Governmental Affairs
  Committee), 213
Sherman, William T., 251
Shevardnadze, Eduard, 227, 228
Shevchnenko, Arkady, 262
Shultz, George, 137, 161
Shutter control, 79, 85

SIGINT (signals intelligence)
  collection and, 89–93, 97
  DBA and, 250
  denial and deception and, 78
  IMINT vs., 91b
  key word searching and, 245
  MASINT and, 93–94
  NSA and, 37
  OSINT and, 101
  stovepipes and, 279
  strengths and weaknesses, 89–93
  terrorism and, 92
  VENONA and, 149
  World War II and, 20
Slavery, 258
Smith, Walter Bedell, 21
SMO (support to military operations),
  250–252
SMS (Secretary's Morning Summary), 63
SNIEs (special NIEs), 63
SOCOM (Special Operations Command),
  164, 168, 169
Solidarity, 260
Somalia, 273
Sorensen, Theodore, 200
Source, 95
Source protection, 74–75, 260–261
South Africa, 241
South America, 243
South Korea, 21, 89, 246
Soviet problem, 220–222, 228–230
Soviet Union. See also Cold war;
    Post–cold war; Russia
  Afghanistan, invasion of. See
    Afghanistan
  Ames spy case, 26
  arms control, 24, 200–201
  assassination and, 169
  capabilities, 75, 139, 222–225
  Chernobyl, 120–121
  Chinese intelligence and, 295
  as closed target, 18, 221–222
  collapse of, 14, 25–26, 172, 239, 281
  collection and, 77, 81
  Cuban missile crisis. See Cuba
  defense spending, 122, 226
  Guatemala coup and, 21
  Hanssen spy case, 26, 96, 149
  in Korean War, 163–164
  mirror imaging, 118
  missile gap, 21–22, 139
  proliferation and, 184b, 243–244
  requirements and, 55–56
  strategic surprise and, 2
  threat-based foreign policy and, 13
  in World War II, 3b
SPA (special political action), 157
Space Imaging Company, 84
Spain, 88
Special Activities Division, 164, 238

Special activity, 157
Special NIEs, 63
Special Operations Command. See
    SOCOM
Special operations forces, 164
Special political action (SPA), 157
Spectral analysis, 80
SPOT, 79, 85
Spread spectrum, 91
Spying, 26, 72–73. See also HUMINT
    (Human Intelligence); specific spy by
    name
  prosecution for, 153
Stalin, Josef, 140, 169b, 303
Star of David pattern, 86b
START Treaty, 201
State Department. See also Secretary of
    State
  clientitis and, 119
  Foreign Service officers and, 37, 41
  INR (Bureau of Intelligence and
    Research), 14, 31, 63, 124, 127b,
    137, 283
  national security policy, 174, 175
  politicized intelligence and, 137–138
  polygraphs, 147
Statistical intelligence, 225–226
Stinger missiles, 159, 263
Stovepipes, 76–77, 97, 123–124, 279–283
Stovepipes within stovepipes, 77
Strategic arms control agreements, 24, 201
Strategic Arms Reduction Treaty (START),
    201
Strategic Defense Initiative (SDI), 228
Strategic surprise
  avoiding, 2, 131
  intelligence agencies and, 2
  Pearl Harbor as, 3b
Strategic warning, 114
Sub-source, 95
Sudan, 258
Sun-synchronous orbit, 76
Supplemental appropriations, 198
Support to military operations (SMO),
    250–252
Surface-to-air missiles (SAMs), 86
Surge capacity, 283
Surprise attack, 130
Surrey Satellite Technology, 88, 89
Surveillance, 68
Swarm ball, 73, 76
Sweden, 120–121, 241
Switzerland, 258
Symington, Stuart, 21, 271
Syria, 265, 298, 300

T

Tactical intelligence and related activities
    (TIARA), 31
Tactical surprise, terrorist attacks as, 3b

Tailored intelligence, 140
Taiwan, 88, 241
Taliban. *See also* Afghanistan
    covert action and, 172, 264
    information operations, 250
    narcotics and, 244
    paramilitary operations and, 164
    renditions and, 234
    terrorism and, 237–238
Tasking, Processing, Exploitation, and
    Dissemination. *See* TPEDs
Team A–Team B competitive analysis, 135,
    224
TECHINTs (Technical Intelligence), 280
Technical collection, 59, 60. *See also*
    Collection
Technical Intelligence (TECHINTs), 280
Technology
    IT revolution, 284–286
    reliance on, 17–18
Telemetry intelligence. *See* TELINT
Television news, 189. *See also* Media
TELINT (telemetry intelligence), 90–92, 93
Tenet, George J.
    on commercial imagery, 85
    creation of TTIC, 125, 235
    on DNI, 40
    intelligence budget and, 197, 205–206
    intelligence sharing and, 75
    leaks and, 204
    on loss of analysts, 15, 207
    on NIPF, 58
    partisan politics and, 188
    on Pollard issue, 299
    on preventing proliferation, 72
    relationship with George W. Bush, 16,
        39, 178
    terrorist attacks and, 27, 169, 235
Term limits, 39–40, 211
Terms of reference (TOR), 133
Terrorism. *See also* War on terrorism
    analysis and, 41, 119
    assassination and, 171b
    Deutch rules and, 99, 259
    health/environment issues and, 247
    human intelligence and, 97, 236–239,
        261
    imagery and, 84–88
    indications and warning, 130–131
    Israeli intelligence, 300
    narcotics and, 244
    nature of, 56
    as new agenda, 236–239, 252
    SIGINT and, 92
    threat-based foreign policy and, 13
    threat of, 104, 233
Terrorism Threat Integration Center. *See*
    TTIC
Terrorist attacks (2001)
    assassination and, 170, 171b

    budget and, 69, 216
    collection and, 18, 99
    compared with Pearl Harbor, 3b
    covert action and, 17
    development of intelligence and,
        26–27, 110, 233
    reform and, 275
    as strategic surprise, 2
    technology, 285
    terrorism as new agenda, 236–239
Tet offensive, 23
Thailand, 89, 246
*Thinking in Time: The Uses of History for
    Decision Makers* (May & Neustadt),
    160
Third option, 157–158
Threat List, 154
TIARA (tactical intelligence and related
    activities), 31
Title 10 prerogatives, 277
TOP SECRET classification, 74b
TOP SECRET/CODEWORD classification,
    74b
TOR (terms of reference), 133
Torricelli, Robert, 271–272
Torture. *See* Renditions and torture
TPEDs (Tasking, Processing, Exploitation,
    and Dissemination), 61, 69, 280
Trade embargo, 163
Traffic analysis, 90
Transnational issues, 78–79, 124, 126,
    193
Treaties, 200–201. *See also specific treaties*
Trotsky, Leon, 303
Truman, Harry S., 21, 43, 136, 165, 278
Truth-telling, 6–7, 266–267
TTIC (Terrorism Threat Integration
    Center), 125, 235. *See also* NCTC
    (National Counterterrorism Center)
TUAVs (tactical UAVs), 87
Turkey, 88, 299
Turning agents, 145
Twain, Mark, 141
Tyranny of ad hocs, 59

U

UAVs (unmanned aerial vehicles)
    DOD and, 36–37
    imagery and, 80, 85–86
    non-U.S., 88
    use in SIGINT, 89
    war on terrorism and, 27, 238
Ukraine, 75
ULTRA, 20
Uncertainty, 128–129, 183, 184b
Undersecretary of Defense for intelligence
    (USDI), 32, 42
    relationship with defense intelligence
        agencies, 43–44
United Nations, 93, 258, 262

Unmanned aerial vehicles. *See* UAVs
UNSCOM (United Nations Special
    Commission), 194–195, 248
U.S. Ambassador to Iraq, 31
U.S.A. PATRIOT Act of 2001, 27
USDI (Undersecretary of Defense for
    intelligence), 32, 42
    relationship with Congress, 44
    relationship with NGA, 43
    relationship with NSA, 43
USS *Cole,* 3b

V

"Vacuum cleaner" problem, 71, 76
Value-added intelligence, 109–110, 283
Vanunu, Mordechai, 299
VENONA intercepts, 149, 154
Verification, 24
Vietnam War, 17, 23, 38, 175, 186, 303

W

Walesa, Lech, 260
Walker spy ring, 26, 100
Walk-ins, 96, 260, 298
War, 17, 175, 256–257. *See also specific war*
Warner, John, 213
War on terrorism, 236–239
    Afghanistan, 234, 248, 250
    bin Laden and, 264–265
    military operations and, 238
    NGA and, 88
    renditions and torture and, 265
    UAVs and, 27, 238
Warsaw Pact, 102, 130, 248, 260
Washington, George, 12, 207
Watergate, 17, 24, 188
Weapons capabilities, 91
Weapons development, 94
Weapons of mass destruction. *See* WMD
Weapons proliferation, 72, 93, 94,
    239–243
Webster, William, 40, 96, 188
Weinberger, Caspar, 161, 175
West Germany, 100–101, 259–260
Wheat vs. chaff problem, 59–60, 71, 102,
    114, 116
"Where and when" phenomenon, 84
Whistleblowers, 271–272
White, Byron, 140
"Window of vulnerability," 139
Wise, David, 152

WMD (weapons of mass destruction)
    alternative analysis and, 132–133
    analysts failures regarding, 128
    "connecting the dots" and, 127b
    ECHELON to detect, 245
    groupthink and, 15, 123
    hearings, 199
    HUMINT and, 98
    intelligence sharing and, 75
    investigations, 202
    Iraq and, 195, 242b
    layering and, 119
    MASINT, in development and
        proliferation, 94, 239–243
    NCPC and, 39
    politicization and, 138
WMD (Weapons of Mass Destruction)
    Commission
    competition for resources and, 125
    creation of, 194
    intelligence reorganization and, 28
    layering, 119
    NCPC and, 39
    politicization and, 138
    recommendations of, 103, 280–282
Wolf, Markus, 259–260
Women's suffrage, 258
Woolsey, R. James, 38–39, 43, 178, 245,
    297
World War I, 13, 80, 89, 216
World War II
    assassination and, 170b
    collection and, 262
    creation of COI and OSS and, 19–20
    denial and deception and, 78
    imagery and, 80
    intelligence oversight and, 216
    SIGINT and, 89
    strategic surprise and, 2
    threat-based foreign policy and, 13
Worst-case analysis, 225
Wye River peace talks, 299

Y

Yeltsin, Boris, 228
Yom Kippur War, 300
Yugoslavia, 124, 258

Z

Zaporozhsky, Aleksander, 154
Zimmermann Telegram, 89